THE HORSE SOLDIER

1776–1943

*The United States Cavalryman: His Uniforms, Arms,
Accoutrements, and Equipments*

VOLUME I

*The Revolution, the War of 1812,
the Early Frontier
1776–1850*

VOLUME II

*The Frontier, the Mexican War,
the Civil War, the Indian Wars
1851–1880*

VOLUME III

*The Last of the Indian Wars,
the Spanish-American War,
the Brink of the Great War
1881–1916*

VOLUME IV

*World War I, the Peacetime Army,
World War II
1917–1943*

THE HORSE SOLDIER

1776–1943

VOLUME III

*The Last of the Indian Wars, the Spanish-
American War, the Brink of the Great War*

1881–1916

The Horse Soldier
1776-1943

The United States Cavalryman: His Uniforms, Arms, Accoutrements, and Equipments

Private, Sixth Cavalry (ca. 1885), in campaign dress and with full equipment for service in the field. (See Figure 261.)

Volume III

The Last of the Indian Wars, the Spanish-American War, the Brink of the Great War

1881-1916

by Randy Steffen

illustrations by Randy Steffen

UNIVERSITY OF OKLAHOMA PRESS

NORMAN

By Randy Steffen

Horseman's Scrapbook, 3 vols. (Colorado Springs, 1959–65)

Horsemen Through Civilization, All (Colorado Springs, 1967)

United States Military Saddles, 1812–1943 (Norman, 1973)

The Horse Soldier, 1776–1943: The United States Cavalryman, His Uniforms, Arms, Accoutrements, and Equipments; Volume I, *The Revolution, the War of 1812, the Early Frontier, 1776–1850*; Volume II, *The Frontier, the Mexican War, the Civil War, the Indian Wars, 1851–1880*; Volume III, *The Last of the Indian Wars, the Spanish-American War, the Brink of the Great War, 1881–1916* (Norman, 1977, 1978)

The Company of Military Historians takes pride in sponsoring *The Horse Soldier, 1776–1943: The United States Cavalryman: His Uniforms, Arms, Accoutrements, and Equipments* as a standard reference work in military history.

George S. Pappas
President

Library of Congress Cataloging in Publication Data

Steffen, Randy, 1917–1977
    The horse soldier, 1776–1943.

    Includes index.
    CONTENTS: v. 1. The Revolution, the War of 1812, the early frontier, 1776–1850.—v. 2. The frontier, the Mexican War, the Civil War, the Indian wars, 1851–1880.—v. 3. The last of the Indian wars, the Spanish-American War, the brink of the Great War, 1881–1916.
    1. United States. Army. Cavalry—Equipment—History. 2. United States. Army. Cavalry—History. I. Title.
UE443.S83   357'.1'0973   75-26946

CONTENTS

ILLUSTRATIONS

THE HORSE SOLDIER

1776–1943

VOLUME III

The Last of the Indian Wars, the Spanish-American War, the Brink of the Great War

1881–1916

INTRODUCTION

THE MATERIAL that has been included in *The Horse Soldier* to tell the full story of the American cavalryman's uniforms, arms, and equipment has proved far too bulky to make publication of this work practical as a single volume. The narrative, reproduced specifications and regulations, and the more than 500 pages of illustrations, both color and black and white, that document the hundreds of changes, both major and subtle, would make a single volume so heavy and hard to handle that it would be difficult to use to the fullest advantage. Thus it was consideration for the serious reader and researcher that influenced the decision to publish in four volumes.

Division of the four volumes was dictated by major changes in uniforms, arms, and equipment. The eras covered in each volume are:

Volume I	1776–1850
Volume II	1851–1880
Volume III	1881–1916
Volume IV	1917–1943

Volume III is the largest of the four since it contains the myriads of complex changes that took place when the "Old Army" in its blue uniforms passed into oblivion and the modern era with its drab, earth-colored uniforms marched smartly into the beginning years of the twentieth century.

While uniforms underwent numerous changes between 1881 and 1902, the greatest changes that took place were in arms and equipment. This was true not just for cavalry, but for all branches of the Army. It was during this period that the single-shot .45-caliber carbine and rifle, still using black powder with its telltale clouds of white smoke, gave way to the bolt-action magazine Krag repeater, in a reduced caliber, using the more efficient smokeless powder.

More and better web equipment made its appearance, and horse gear was changed and improved.

The last of the fights between the Army and the Indians took place in the last decade of the nineteenth century. Perhaps it was the war with Spain that brought about most of the changes.

Volume III brings the cavalryman to the brink of his involvement in World War I, outfits him in several new patterns of drab clothing, arms him with improved side arms, a better rifle, and a saber of a brand new pattern. It seats a few squadrons of cavalry in several completely new and different types of saddles, and finally plunks the trooper back in the McClellan, where he will stay until horse cavalry is abolished.

CHAPTER ELEVEN

Final Years of the "Old Army"

1881-89

UNIFORMS

THE GENERAL PATTERN of cavalry uniforms remained the same for the entire period of the 1880's and 1890's. Some changes were made in regulations governing the wearing of the uniform, and some relatively minor changes were made in the pattern of some items of clothing—but the appearance of the trooper throughout the remainder of the century, and for the first 2 years of the new century, remained much the same.

The dress helmet did undergo a more drastic change than any other item of uniform. The last chapter of Volume II mentioned the alteration of the officer's helmet to remedy those features responsible for so many complaints.

Figure 222 shows the new helmet pattern prescribed in the *1881 Uniform Regulations*. The helmet at the left is the pattern for officers, with gilt trimmings, a gilt-chain chin strap, and buffalo-hair plume. The bands, cords, and braided flat aiguillettes were also gilt. The front and side views of the enlisted man's helmet at the right of Figure 222 show that it was identical to the officer pattern, but trimmings were brass. Bands, cords, and braided flat aiguillettes were made of worsted yellow cord.

It is important to stress once more that the shade of yellow used on all cavalry facings up to this time had been a *lemon yellow*. Not until 1887 was the color of cavalry facings changed to the deeper yellow color.

Plumes on the enlisted men's helmets were lemon-yellow horsehair, the same as they had been before, but the base of the plume was made up differently and attached to the plume socket in a slightly different manner. (See Figure 222.)

The eagle helmet plate underwent a complete change. The 1881 plate, shown in Figure 223 full size, has the motto on a scroll held in the eagle's beak and flowing across his throat in contrast to the scroll above

the eagle's head in the earlier pattern. And to designate the arm of the service there were crossed sabres under the shield for cavalry, crossed cannon for artillery, and crossed rifles for infantry. Eagles for the enlisted staff were without corps insignia. Eagles for all officers and enlisted men had the regimental number in white metal upon the shield.

Prior to the general order specifying the new helmet for 1881, only the mounted enlisted men had worn helmets for dress. Foot soldiers had worn a modified version of the 1851 dress cap, and their officers had worn the same pattern with a feather plume. The new regulations now prescribed helmets for enlisted men of all branches, although foot soldiers were still quickly identified by the spike on the top of their helmets instead of the horsehair plume of the mounted arm, as well as by the color of the facings on coat (and trousers, in the case of noncommissioned officers, who wore stripes).

The 1881 regulations also provided a new summer helmet for troops stationed in warm climates. This headgear is shown, for both officers and enlisted men, in Figure 224. The pattern shown here was the first widely issued to troops, and remained unchanged until 1889, when the shape underwent a distinct alteration.

The leather base for the officer's chin strap was made of an off-white patent leather, as was the plainer chin strap for the enlisted man's helmet. The cork bodies of the helmets were covered with white cloth, that for officers being of a much finer grade than for enlisted men.

These helmets were intended for wear with the fatigue blouse and not as a substitute for the black felt dress helmet when the dress uniform was prescribed.

Gordon Chappell, in his monograph *Summer Helmets of the U.S. Army, 1875–1910* (Cheyenne: Wyoming State Archives and Historical Department,

5

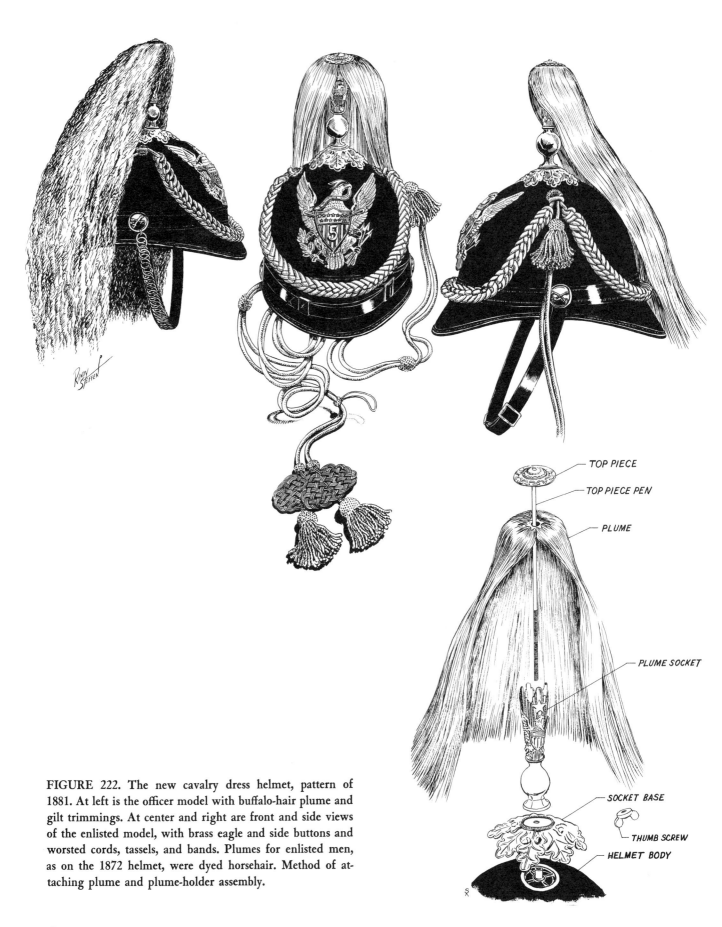

FIGURE 222. The new cavalry dress helmet, pattern of 1881. At left is the officer model with buffalo-hair plume and gilt trimmings. At center and right are front and side views of the enlisted model, with brass eagle and side buttons and worsted cords, tassels, and bands. Plumes for enlisted men, as on the 1872 helmet, were dyed horsehair. Method of attaching plume and plume-holder assembly.

TOP PIECE

TOP PIECE PEN

PLUME

PLUME SOCKET

SOCKET BASE

THUMB SCREW

HELMET BODY

1967), recounts the uneasiness with which the white cork helmet was worn in the Apache campaigns in the Southwest. The white helmet was glaringly conspicuous in the brown desert and mountains and afforded the Apaches excellent targets. Complaints and suggestions to the War Department got results, for in June, 1882,

Headquarters of the Department of Texas announced that 500 cork helmets covered with unbleached brown rather than white linen had been purchased under orders from the Secretary of War for trial. These were to be distributed to Forts Brown, Clark, Concho, Davis, Duncan, McIntosh, and Ringgold, and the Post of San Antonio, whose respective commanders were ordered to report after a period of trial the relative merits of white and tan helmets (Chappell, p. 19).

Later the same year 1,000 brown helmets were purchased for issue, and for many years both white and brown helmets continued to be issued. But the helmets were not too popular with the troopers; Quartermaster Department correspondence reveals that the men preferred most any kind of a hat to the helmet (Chappell, p. 20).

Figure 225 shows the white helmet on an officer and on an enlisted man in garrison. It also shows the pattern of the first undershirt issued to enlisted men, as well as the underdrawers issued and worn during this period. The undershirt was made of an equal mixture of wool and cotton, and was issued in 6 sizes.

While the 1872 uniform regulations made no mention of noncommissioned officers' chevrons being worn on anything but the uniform coat (dress coat), contemporary photographs clearly show that chevrons were indeed worn on the fatigue blouse. Not until 1882, in General Order No. 92, was official sanction made of this practice, when service and campaign chevrons were also authorized for wear on both overcoat and blouse.

The same general order that prescribed the issue of knit undershirts for enlisted men (G.O. No. 4, January 7, 1881) also authorized the issue of a new-pattern dark blue overshirt, piped with cord the color of the arm on lower edge of the collar and upper edge of the cuff. While the published specifications for this shirt did not mention pockets, contemporary photographs do show that piped shirts with pockets piped on the upper edges were issued and worn, as well as those without pockets.

Figure 226 shows both styles of this piped shirt.

FIGURE 223. The cavalry eagle for the 1881 helmet. Those for enlisted men were stamped from a single sheet of brass, the crossed sabres being integral with the eagle. Officer eagle plates were of a more detailed, sharper design, and the crossed sabres and shield were a separate stamping which was soldered to the eagle. Both officer and enlisted-man eagles had the number of the regiment in white metal attached to the shield. Drawn from a specimen in the author's collection. (Reproduced actual size)

Chevrons were definitely not authorized for wear on the shirt, but the shirt was authorized for wear without the blouse in the summer. Noncommissioned rank was indicated only by the width of trouser stripes when the shirt was worn without the blouse, sergeants having 1-inch-wide stripes down the outside seams and corporals, ½-inch-wide stripes. (See Uniform Color Plate V, Figure F, in Volume I of *The Horse Soldier.*)

General Order No. 4 also directed that no more gray flannel shirts be issued after the present stock on hand was exhausted.

The only significant uniform change during 1882 was specified in General Order No. 14, February 2, which announced that a change in the size of ser-

FIGURE 224. The 1881-pattern summer helmet. At top center is the enlisted man's model, plain and untrimmed except for the white enameled chin strap. The officer's model, shown in side and front views, is made of finer materials and has better workmanship. For ordinary duty, officers wore the helmet with only the removable ventilator on top as at the left. On more formal occasions the gilt spike and base were worn. Side buttons and the chain chin strap were to be worn at all times; they were generally worn looped up, unless the officer was on mounted duty.

vice-in-war chevrons was official, the aggregate width being ¾ inch, including the red cord borders, instead of ½ inch as before; in addition, this general order announced the authorization of a *campaign* stripe, identical to the service-in-war chevron except that its aggregate width was to be ½ inch instead of ¾ inch. The order limited the wearing of campaign chevrons to a single chevron for each term of enlistment, in spite of the fact that a soldier might have served in more than one campaign during that period.

A further regulation governing the wearing of service and campaign chevrons stated:

When, in addition to a war chevron, an enlisted man is entitled to a service chevron, each edge of the latter will be bound, or faced, by the former; and when, in addition to a war chevron, an enlisted man is entitled to two or more service chevrons, they will be separated by the war chevron, and the outer edge of each outside chevron will also be bound or faced by the war chevron.

General Order No. 60, June 6, 1882, further revised the above by stating, "The *service-in-war* chevron will be worn next the cuff; above this will be worn the *service* chevron or chevrons; and next above this the *campaign* chevron" (Italics added).

General Order No. 92, August 9, 1882, not only gave the enlisted man the right to wear his chevrons denoting noncommissioned rank on the sleeves of his dress coat, overcoat, and blouse, but also prescribed the wearing of service and campaign chevrons on the overcoat and blouse, all above the elbow.

A new-pattern trousers for enlisted men of all arms was prescribed in General Order No. 108, September 4, 1882. This new item differed from the old only in having a 2-inch waistband added; the 1879 pattern had none.

The dark blue piped shirts authorized in 1881 lasted only a little more than 2½ years. General Order No. 45, June 26, 1883, stipulated that "the cord, indicating

FIGURE 225. First lieutenant, left, in undress uniform with the new officer summer cork helmet (ca. 1881). The enlisted man, center, is wearing the first Army-issue undershirt. Authorized in 1881, it was knit from a mixture of wool and cotton of equal percentages and was made in 6 sizes. The sergeant major, right, wears the piped sack coat and the new enlisted man's summer helmet.

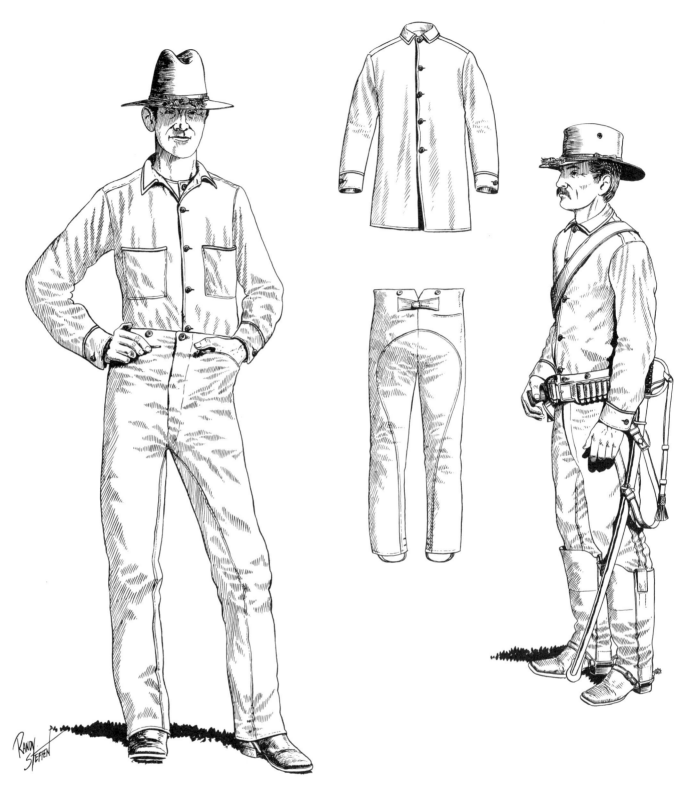

FIGURE 226. Private, left, and sergeant, U.S. Cavalry (ca. 1881), wearing the piped dark blue flannel shirts that replaced the gray shirts issued until that year. Yellow braid trims the edges of the collar, the tops of the cuffs, and the front opening plait. Both men wear the 1879-pattern trousers that are without waistband and have four buttons at the bottom of each leg, two on each side on the inside, for instep straps. The sergeant's 1-inch-wide stripes on the outside seam of his trousers signify his rank. Photographs of the period prove that shirts with and without pockets were issued in this piped pattern. The shirt at top conforms to the specifications adopted February 16, 1881.

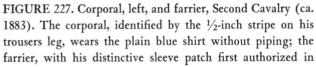

FIGURE 227. Corporal, left, and farrier, Second Cavalry (ca. 1883). The corporal, identified by the ½-inch stripe on his trousers leg, wears the plain blue shirt without piping; the farrier, with his distinctive sleeve patch first authorized in General Order No. 38, June 6, 1883, wears the new unpiped blue sack coat. The cord, indicating the arm of the service, was ordered omitted on both the blouse and overshirt in General Order No. 45, June 26, 1883.

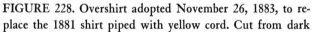

FIGURE 228. Overshirt adopted November 26, 1883, to replace the 1881 shirt piped with yellow cord. Cut from dark blue army-standard wool flannel, it was made plain with two outside pockets on the breast and was issued in 5 sizes.

the arm of the service, will hereafter be omitted on both the blouse and the dark-blue overshirt."

On November 26, 1883, a new pattern dark-blue overshirt without cord was adopted, and the pattern for this shirt, drawn from Quartermaster specifications, is shown in Figures 227 and 228.

The new *campaign* stripe authorized in 1882 and described on the preceding pages, lasted less than a year. General Order No. 38, June 6, 1883, officially abolished the campaign stripe as an authorized item of uniform. The same general order added a designating insignia for cavalry farriers—a yellow horseshoe 4 inches in diameter and worn toe uppermost in the same position on uniform coat, blouse, and overcoat as prescribed for noncommissioned-officer chevrons. This insignia for farriers is shown in Figure 227.

The same general order prescribed a change in the manner of wearing chevrons on the enlisted man's overcoat. Until the date of this order, overcoat chevrons had been worn *above* the elbow, in the same position as on the dress coat and blouse. Now regulations prescribed that the overcoat chevrons be worn *below*

the elbow with the point of the chevrons ½ inch above the cuff. Figure E on Uniform Color Plate V (in Volume I) and Figure 229 show the overcoat chevrons worn in the new position.

Figure 229 also shows details of the overcoat adopted for wear by all enlisted personnel of all branches of the Army in February, 1880—the cape being the same as that worn before by mounted troops, and the coat with the double-breasted front such as had also been worn formerly by cavalry and artillery.

It was in 1883 that cavalry companies were redesignated as troops. The word *company* was from now on reserved for the unit designation of foot regiments. From 1883 until the end of horse cavalry, the proper designation of this regimental unit was *troop*!

General Order No. 58, July 31, 1883, authorized musicians, including band members as well as field trumpeters, to wear *2 ½-inch stripes* on each trouser leg.

The same order authorized, for the very first time in recorded uniform regulations, the issue and wear-

FIGURE 229. Enlisted man's overcoat (ca. 1883) with chevrons below the elbows and with points ½ inch above cuffs, as specified in General Order No. 38, June 6, 1883. This is the pattern that had been adopted for all enlisted personnel, foot and mounted, in February, 1880. Capes for cavalrymen were lined with yellow flannel.

ing of *suspenders*. In spite of the insistence of motion picture and television producers to show cavalrymen of *all* periods wearing suspenders on the *outside* of their shirts, this was strictly against regulations until much later.

A new *cap strap* of gold on silver *cord* was prescribed for wear on the officer's forage cap by General Order No. 102, December 26, 1883. Figure 230 shows the pattern of this new cap strap. Officers were required to provide themselves with the new strap by March 1, 1884.

Leather gauntlets were authorized for wear by enlisted men of mounted regiments with the publication of General Order No. 29, April 12, 1884.

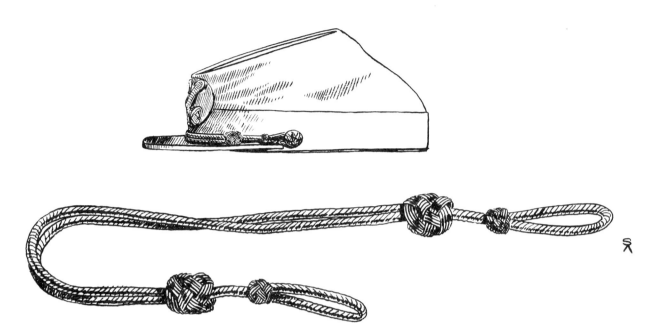

FIGURE 230. The new cord cap strap of gold on silver as prescribed for all commissioned officers below the rank of general by General Order No. 102, December 26, 1883. Offi-cers of the Army were required to provide themselves with the new cap strap on or before March 1, 1884.

Figure 231 shows the brown canvas blanket-lined overcoat adopted in 1883 for wear at northern posts. Also shown is the muskrat-fur cap adopted in 1879 to replace the unsatisfactory sealskin cap issued earlier. This coat and muskrat-fur cap is also shown on Figure G, Uniform Color Plate V, in Volume I.

General Order No. 32, April 16, 1884, prescribed the issue of a suit of canvas work clothes for fatigue duty to each enlisted man of the Army. Figure 232 shows the pattern of these garments as drawn from Quartermaster specifications and illustrations.

Figure 233 shows a cavalryman wearing the canvas hood and gloves with the 1883 blanket-lined canvas overcoat. The hood and gloves were authorized by General Order No. 32, April 16, 1884, and were for issue only to troops serving in the Departments of Dakota, the Platte, and the Columbia.

A change was made in the regulations concerning chevrons by General Order No. 107, September 12, 1884. New *gold-lace chevrons*, of the same size and pattern as the cloth chevrons, were now prescribed for wear by noncommissioned officers on the sleeves of *dress coats only*. (See Figure 234.) The new gold-lace rank devices, as well as service and service-in-war chevrons, made the dress uniform even more colorful than it had been before. The same general order changed the regulations so that service and service-in-war chevrons were authorized for wear only on the dress coat, and *not* on the *overcoat* or *blouse sleeves* as before.

Figure H on Uniform Color Plate V (in Volume I) shows the 1881-pattern helmet, and the new gold-lace chevrons and service stripes on a cavalryman's dress uniform. Figure 235 shows a chief trumpeter with the newly authorized double stripes on his trousers legs, the gold-lace chevrons and service stripes on his dress uniform, and the new leather gauntlets. The officer wears the new gold-cord cap strap on his forage cap.

An entirely new pattern for the *officer's overcoat* was prescribed by General Order No. 117, October 21, 1884. The double-breasted 1872 pattern with its removable cape was replaced by a

double-breasted ulster of dark-blue cloth, lined with dark-blue flannel, closing by means of four frog buttons of black mohair cord down the breast, and at the throat by a long mohair loop, as in standard sample, without tassel or plate, on the left side, and a black mohair frog button on the right;

FIGURE 231. Enlisted man, U.S. Cavalry (ca. 1884), with the 1883 blanket-lined brown canvas overcoat authorized for issue at northern posts. He also wears the muskrat cap with fold-down ear flaps and visor, first adopted in 1879. His gauntlets, authorized for issue in 1884, are made of goatskin, which proved unsatisfactory and was quickly replaced by calfskin.

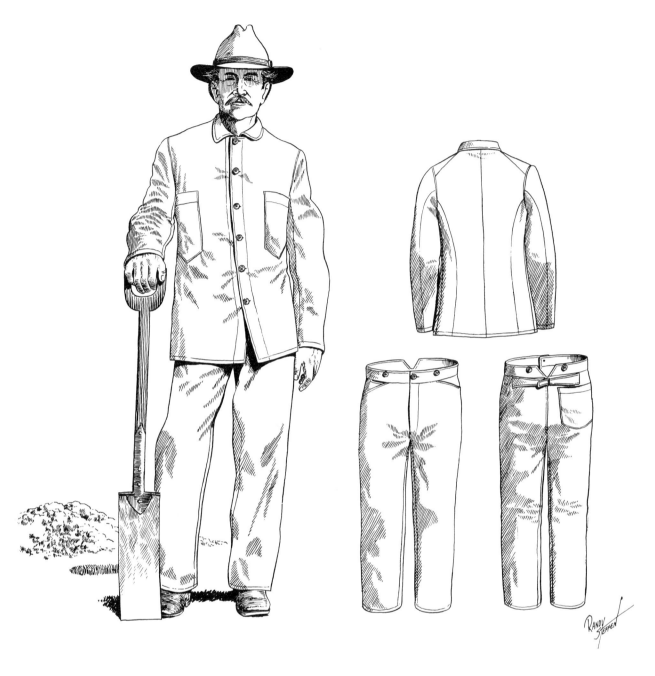

FIGURE 232. Canvas fatigue clothing for enlisted men, first adopted in 1884, consisted of a sack coat and trousers made of 6-ounce cotton duck dyed brown. According to regulations, fatigue clothing was supplied as a working dress intended to save the regular uniform.

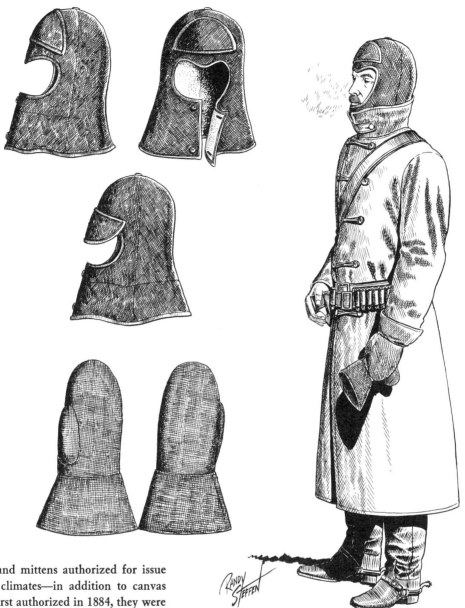

FIGURE 233. Canvas cap and mittens authorized for issue to troops stationed in cold climates—in addition to canvas fatigue coats and trousers. First authorized in 1884, they were also worn in the field during cold weather.

YELLOW FACING
CLOTH

FIGURE 234. New gold-lace chevron pattern for first sergeant, as prescribed by General Order No. 107, September 12, 1884. The new ones were made of gold-lace stripes sewn on a ground of yellow facing cloth the same size and shape as the cloth chevrons previously worn on all authorized coats. They were to be worn on the dress coat only.

FIGURE 235. Chief trumpeter, left and first lieutenant, Sixth Cavalry (ca. 1884). The musician wears the new (1881) dress helmet and gold-lace chevrons as authorized in General Order No. 107, September 12, 1884. He also wears, closest to his cuff, a service-in-war chevron. Above it are 2 additional 5-year chevrons, showing 15 years of army service, including 5 years during the Indian Wars. His trumpet is the regulation F trumpet, pattern of 1879, with the extra C crook attached. The first lieutenant wears the chasseur-pattern forage cap with the gilt cord authorized in late 1883. The combination of forage cap and dress coat with helmet cords was not unusual, according to contemporary photographs—undoubtedly it was a tolerated off-duty attire.

cord for the loops fifteen-hundredths of an inch in diameter; around each frog button on the breast a knot two and one quarter inches in diameter of black mohair cord seven-hundredths of an inch in diameter; the back slit up from the bottom from twenty to twenty-five inches, according to the height of the wearer, and closing at will by buttons, and button holes placed in a concealed flap; bottom of the skirt nine to twelve inches from the ground; a rolling collar of the same material as the coat, and broad enough when turned up to protect the ears, having a collar loop about four and a half inches long and one and a half inches wide; two horizontal side pockets on the outside, just below the hip, covered with flaps to be worn inside or out; sleeves loose without cuff or slit; back-straps to consist of two straps each about eight inches long and two inches wide, let into the side seams of back of coat; left-hand strap to have a button hole, and the right-hand strap to have two buttons about two inches apart; a hood of the same material as the coat, lined with black Italian cloth or other suitable material, made to button around the neck under the collar, and large enough to cover the head and cap, to be worn at night or in inclement weather; a vertical slit five to six inches long over the left hip, large enough to admit the sword-hilt; around each frog button on the breast a knot two and one-quarter inches in diameter of black mohair cord seven-hundredths of an inch in diameter.

The insignia of rank on the sleeves, of black flat mohair braid, one-eighth of an inch in width as follows, viz:

Colonel, five braids, single knot
Lieutenant colonel, four braids, single knot
Major, three braids, single knot
Captain, two braids, single knot
1st lieuteneant, one braid, single knot
2nd lieuteneant, without braid

Figure 236 shows the general pattern of the new ulster coat for officers, but with the slit for the sabre modified according to General Order No. 8, January 21, 1885—just months later, after it was determined that it was virtually impossible for a cavalry officer to mount his horse with just the hilt of the sabre protruding through the overcoat slit.

This same general order authorized for wear by officers

a cape of the same color and material as the coat, and reaching to the tips of the fingers when the arm is extended; a rolling collar of black velvet three inches broad, rounded at the edges and closing at the throat by a black mohair loop *a l'echelle* on the left side, without tassel or plate, and a black mohair frog button on the right. . . .

The cape was authorized for wear by all officers when not on duty with troops under arms.

General Order No. 49, April 18, 1885, provided qualification to wear the *service-in-war* chevron, or service stripe, to all enlisted men "who have served or may serve in the Army of the United States in war or such Indian campaigns approaching the magnitude of war as may from time to time be so designated by the Secretary of War." The order also specified that the chevrons to indicate service and service in war were to be worn one above the other in the order in which they were earned, ¼-inch distance to be maintained between stripes. "But one chevron will be worn for each enlistment, the 'service-in-war' chevron being worn in place of the 'service' chevron for each enlistment in which the right to wear it was earned."

The former order prohibiting the wearing of service stripes on the blouse or overcoat sleeves must not have been too clear to some in the Army, for General Order No. 49 of the 1885 series stated point-blank that *none* of the service chevrons were to be worn on the blouse or overcoat, making it clear that the order did not pertain merely to the newly authorized gold-lace chevrons, as some must have thought.

The enlisted man's overcoat underwent an official modification in 1885, one that did not affect the external appearance. General Order No. 8, January 21, 1885, directed that the *enlisted man's cape*, adjustable by means of 7 hooks and eyes located *under* the collar of the coat, might be detached and worn by enlisted men when not on duty under arms.

Apparently there were some misunderstandings concerning the wearing of insignia on helmets and caps of enlisted men, for General Order No. 104, October 3, 1885, gave detailed orders concerning insignia on headgear.

Paragraph 2759 of the uniform regulations was further clarified by adding the instructions that band musicians were to wear a lyre of white metal on the shield of their dress-helmet eagle plates, while their helmet side buttons were to bear the device of their corps or arm of the service. Thus cavalry bandsmen wore, from the date of this order, the lyre on the helmet plate instead of the regimental number, and the crossed-sabres side buttons.

Paragraph 2773 was amended to instruct trumpeters of cavalry to wear the *crossed-sabres* insignia with number of regiment and letter of company on their *forage caps.*

An important part of this same general order *abolished* the wearing of the *regimental number on the*

FIGURE 236. Commissioned officers, Tenth Cavalry (ca. 1885). The captain, left, wears the new double-breasted ulster first prescribed for officers in an 1884 general order, then slightly modified in 1885 to allow wearing the sabre outside the coat, as shown. The dress cape, right, was added to approved dress for officers in 1885, and was authorized for wear by all officers of the Army when not on duty with troops under arms.

collar of the dress coat, since this designating number was on the shield of the dress-helmet eagle plate. Another good reason for eliminating the number on the coat collar was to get rid of the inevitable stains on the yellow facings caused by polishing the white-metal letters without removing them from the collar.

General Order No. 113, October 31, 1885, prescribed a new-pattern *campaign hat* for officers and enlisted men. Color could be either black or drab for enlisted men, but officers were directed to wear black only. While either color was standard, the order directed that the color was to be uniform in each troop.

The order also directed that ordnance sergeants and soldiers attached to a cavalry regiment (or to any other corps) were to wear the shell-and-flame insignia on their forage caps. Likewise, cavalry commissary sergeants were to wear a crescent in white metal on their caps, and cavalry hospital stewards a caduceus with the points in a vertical line.

From the time the new uniform had been prescribed in 1872, the *helmet cords* had been worn so they crossed on *top* of the shoulder strap on the right shoulder. General Order No. 67, September 28, 1886, changed the manner of wearing these cords, specifying that the cords cross on the right shoulder *under* the shoulder strap.

A change in the size of officers' small coat buttons took place in the 1888 amendments to uniform regulations, as prescribed in General Order No. 6, February 8. The design remained the same, with a small

FIGURE 237. The hood prescribed for the officer's overcoat in the 1884 regulations. It was to be made of the same material as the coat, large enough to cover the head and cap, lined with black Italian cloth, and made to button around the neck, under the collar. It was to be worn at night and in inclement weather. The overcoat itself was the 1884–85 pattern.

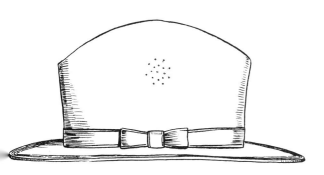

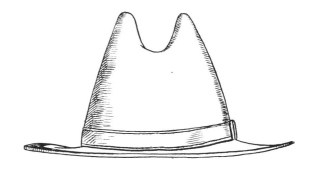

FIGURE 238. The 1885-pattern campaign hat for officers and enlisted men. This hat was authorized to be issued in either drab or black to enlisted men, but the color was to be uniform in each troop. The dimensions of the hat remained essentially the same as the 1875 pattern, but holes were punched in the sides of the crown for ventilation, and the hat bodies were made of fur felt instead of wool felt, as before. Brims were stitched with 3 rows of stitching, but were raw-edged instead of turned over. (G.O. 113, A.G.O., October 31, 1885.) Officer hats continued to be black only until 1889, when officers were allowed their choice, but from that year forward only drab hats would be issued to enlisted men.

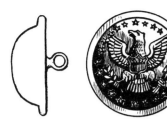

FIGURE 239. Button pattern for noncommissioned staff, 1888–1902. Large: ¾ inch; small: ⁹⁄₁₆ inch. (This pattern is identical in design to the commissioned-staff button that was regulation for more than 50 years.) Drawn from specimens in the author's collection.

letter *C* within the shield on the eagle's breast, and the size of the large coat buttons remained ⅞ inch, as they had since 1863. The small buttons now became ¹⁄₁₆ inch larger, increasing from ½ inch to ⁹⁄₁₆ inch in diameter.

Buttons for the enlisted staff were changed from the plain-border eagle design to buttons having a raised bright rim, similar to those of the general staff. Figure 239 shows the new pattern for the noncommissioned staff. Buttons for enlisted men may have undergone the same change, but I have come across no specific information relating to an increase in the size of the small enlisted-man's button. It is most likely, however, that this change was uniform for both officers and enlisted men.

In 1884 the collar of the infantry enlisted man's dress coat was changed so that instead of the facing of sky blue on the front of the collar, and the sky-blue facings on the skirt, the whole collar was made white, and the facings on the cuffs and skirts were likewise changed to white.

Not until 1888 was a similar change prescribed for enlisted men of cavalry. This change, prescribed by General Order No. 6, February 8, made the collar of the cavalry dress coat solid yellow. At the same time the belt supporters behind the side slits were also abolished. Figure 240 and Figure B on Uniform Color Plate VI (in Volume I) show the pattern of the modified dress coat. The deeper shade of yellow for facings, cord, and plume was also part of the change.

About the same time as the above change in dress coats for cavalry, the War Department also ordered distinctive pipings and facings for the noncommis-

sioned-staff corps. Trouser stripes were prescribed to be 1¼ inches wide, to set them apart from sergeants' trouser stripes.

The facings on the dress coats for these men were ordered to be piped in white, and the yellow piping that had been on the edges of the coat was replaced by white piping. Thus a staff sergeant of cavalry would wear a coat with white piping down the front and around the edges and slits of the skirt; the yellow facings on cuffs and skirts, as well as the shoulder straps and lower collar edge, would be bordered with white piping. The stripes on his trousers would be 1¼ inches wide, of yellow facing cloth.

At this same time another distinct change was made in the dress coat for all enlisted men of cavalry (and light artillery, for that matter). The design of the facing on the rear of the skirts was changed slightly—a simplification, really, of the design that had been standard since the new uniform was adopted in 1872. This new skirt-facing pattern is shown in Figure 240. By comparing it to Figure 169 in Volume II, the smooth contours of the outer edges of the new facing are quickly noticeable.

General Order No. 6 also prescribed a linen collar for wear with the enlisted man's dress coat—the first white collar to be issued to enlisted men. It is shown in Figure 241, drawn from specifications and illustrations in the Quartermaster Specifications for Clothing, Camp and Garrison Equipage. The collar was not included in the clothing allowance and had to be bought by the trooper. Figure B of Uniform Color Plate VI (in Volume I) shows the dress uniform with collar as prescribed by the new regulations.

The pattern for enlisted men's trousers was changed by General Order No. 6 as well. Figure 242 shows the new pattern and the caption explains the modifications, as contained in the Quartermaster specifications.

Under the same order, paragraphs 2724½ and 2749½ were added to the uniform regulations by direction of the Secretary of War; they directed that the uniform coats and trousers for all noncommissioned officers were to be made of finer-quality material than those for privates.

For the first time since 1851, Army regulations finally provided summer clothing for wear by troops stationed in "extreme Southern latitudes." General Order No. 80, October 17, 1888, provided that a summer suit—to consist of a sack coat, trousers, and over-

FIGURE 240. Private, Seventh Cavalry (ca. 1888), with the modified cavalry dress coat made regulation by General Order No. 6, February 8, 1888. The collar is now solid yellow, the belt support loops on the back of the coat have been omitted, and the rear skirt facing has been modified somewhat. This man wears the linen collar adopted that year for wear with the dress coat by all enlisted personnel. Compare the new design of rear skirt facing with the 1872 pattern on Figure 169 in Volume II. A deeper shade of yellow for helmet plumes and all uniform facings was adopted at the same time.

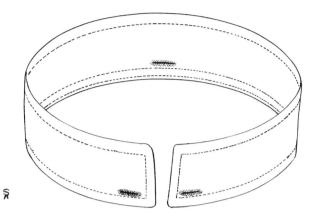

FIGURE 241. Linen collar for wear with enlisted man's dress coat, was officially approved and adopted in March, 1887, almost a year before its approval was published to the Army in the form of General Order No. 6, February 8, 1888.

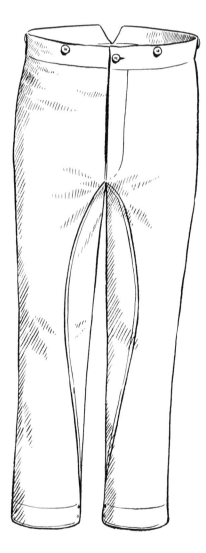

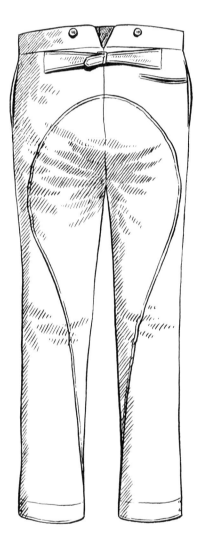

FIGURE 242. The 1888-pattern trousers for enlisted men. Made of sky-blue Kersey cloth with a waistband, side pockets, and a hip pocket on the right side, they had the usual reinforce, or saddle piece, on seat and legs. This new pattern had canvas lining on the bottom of the legs. As with previous patterns, the 1888 trousers had 4 buttons at the bottom of each leg, 2 on each side, for instep straps.

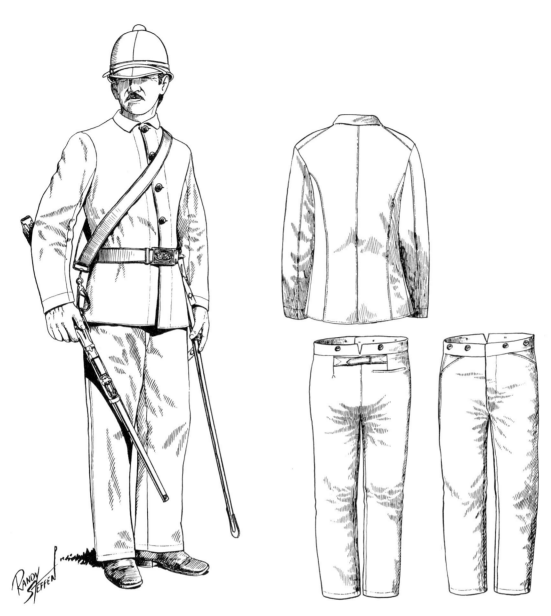

FIGURE 243. Summer sack coat and trousers for enlisted men serving in warm climates, authorized in 1888. The uniform was made of white cotton duck, bleached for noncommissioned officers, unbleached for privates.

alls, all made of cotton duck—was to be made available, but only when the necessity was certified by the department commander. Suits for noncommissioned officers were to be made of *bleached* material, while those for privates were to be made of *unbleached* material. The overalls for all ranks were to be of unbleached duck.

Figure 243 shows the pattern of coat and trousers

specified in the regulations. The Quartermaster description of the overalls was:

For Mounted Men, and also for Summer use by Noncommissioned Officers and Privates of all Arms.—To be the same as the lower or trowsers part as those for engineers.
Pattern for Engineers.— . . . The lower part to be in form of a loose pair of trowsers, with waistband; two (2) white metal buttons on front of waistband, and same kind

 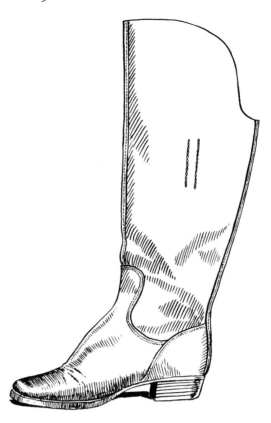 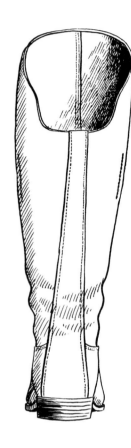

FIGURE 244. The cavalry boot pattern that replaced the earlier, shorter 2-piece-type construction that was regulation from 1872 until about 1886. The new boot afforded the cavalryman more comfort and protection than the old pattern. Now for the first time issue boots were made in 3 widths for each of the sizes in the full range from 5 to 12.

of buttons placed in proper position for use with suspenders. No covered fly. One button on center of fly opening.

Sometime around 1885 or 1886 the Quartermaster Department came up with a modified pattern for cavalry boots. The 1872 pattern had certainly been an improvement over the short, crude boot issued during the Civil War. And even the 1872 model had been further improved in 1876. Then the height of the front of the boot was about 15½ inches in the front and 14 inches in the back, according to the *Quartermaster Specifications* published in 1880.

The boot shown in Figure 244 has a height in front of about 19 inches, while the height of the back is about 14 inches. These figures varied according to the size of the boot, the specifications stating that "the length of leg to increase one-fourth (¼) inch on each size above No. 8, and decrease one-fourth (¼) inch on each size below." In like manner, "the width of leg

at top to increase one-fourth (¼) inch on each size, and letter of same, above No. 8, and decrease one-fourth (¼) inch on each size, and letter of same, below."

The modifications of this pattern of boot adopted February 20, 1889, indicate the improved cavalry boot was now being made in 8 sizes from 5 to 12, and in 3 widths for each size.

Notice that the leg of the boot is cut in two pieces, seamed up the front and back, with the back seam covered by a tapered strip of the same leather from which the leg is cut. Differing from the former 3-piece type of construction that characterized all cavalry boots issued to enlisted men, the modified pattern shown in Figure 244 is made with a separate vamp and outside counter sewed to the top—the same type of construction that is common in boot construction today.

For the first time, specific patterns for officers' boots

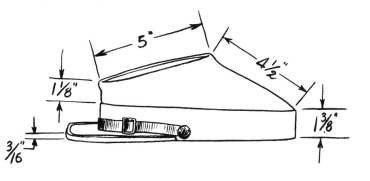

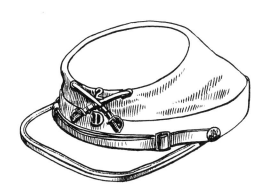

FIGURE 245. The 1889 pattern of forage cap that replaced the 1876 pattern, which was, for all practical purposes, identical to the 1872 pattern, but with better-quality material and workmanship. The band on this pattern was wider than earlier models, and the front lower. Its crown is slightly larger in diameter than before, and the back a little longer.

were prescribed in the uniform regulations. General Order No. 96, November 12, 1888, specifies: *"For all mounted officers.*—Top boots and spurs, according to patterns in the office of the Quartermaster General, to be worn on all mounted duty."

The following is an excerpt from the Annual Report of the Quartermaster General as published in the *Report of the Secretary of War* for 1889:

TOP-BOOTS FOR MOUNTED OFFICERS.

At the suggestion of General A. Baird, Inspector-General U. S. Army, concerning the adoption of a suitable top-boot for mounted officers, the Quartermaster-General directed the manufacture of samples conforming to the views of the officer referred to, and the subject having been submitted to the tactical board then in session in this city, the General Commanding the Army recommended the adoption of the sample determined upon by said board.

Standard samples have been adopted and specifications prepared and distributed to officers concerned on the 9th of January last.

The following is a copy of the specifications and of the illustration of the adopted boot:

WAR DEPARTMENT,
QUARTERMASTER-GENERAL'S OFFICE.

Specifications for top-boots for mounted officers.

The vamps and outside counters to be of calf-skin. The vamps to be lined with same leather.

The legs to be of calf-skin or enameled leather; each leg to be cut in one piece, and to be seamed at the back; the seam to be covered with a strip of same leather, neatly stitched down on each edge.

The upper part of legs to be stiffened with an inside lining of chestnut welt leather, weighing about 5 ounces to the square foot, or other suitable leather extending down about 12 inches for a No. 8 boot, and for other sizes in proportion.

The straps to be of webbing.

The out-sole to be cut from best quality sole-leather (oak-tanned, weighing from 20 to 24 pounds to the side is preferable), and the in-soles and inside counters to be cut from shoulders of same leather. The welts to be cut from best oak welt leather, weighing from 10 to 12 pounds to the side.

To conform in pattern to standard sample.

Adopted January 9, 1889, as conforming to the top-boots referred to in G. O. 96, and Circular No. 11, H. Q. A., 1888.

These boots, shown in Figure 247, were drawn from specimens in the author's collection. Their most outstanding characteristics are the extremely stiff tops and the square toes.

The pattern for the forage cap for both officers and enlisted men was slightly revised in 1889. The Quartermaster specifications indicate that it was made with a slightly larger-diameter crown than the 1876 model it replaced, and that the front was a little lower, making the length of the back longer. The band, too, was wider than on the earlier model. Generally, the quality of materials and workmanship was higher than it had been before. Figure 245 shows the dimensions of the new cap in detail.

General Sherman's attitude toward changes in the uniform, especially for officers, finally began to make sense to the junior officers commissioned after the

FIGURE 246. Top: The 1889 campaign shoe worn by cavalrymen for dismounted garrison and fatigue duty. After 1894 it was also used (with the new canvas legging for mounted troops) for some mounted duty. This higher, better-quality shoe was first adopted by the Army in the mid-1880's.

Center: Barrack shoe issued to enlisted personnel of all branches for wear off duty in the barracks. Made of brown cotton duck and calfskin, it was first issued in the mid-1880's, but was not included in the clothing allowance.

Bottom: Arctic overshoe, model of 1889, that replaced the 1876 pattern, which was much lower and closed with a single buckle. These overshoes were made of black waterproof tweed for fronts and quarters, and foxed all around the bottom with vulcanized rubber. They were termed "snow excluders" because of the gore joining the front and quarter. They were worn over cavalry boots.

1872 uniform change. Constant and seemingly foolish changes in the pattern of the undress coat, especially, became expensive and difficult to keep up with, considering the scanty pay scale for second and first lieutenants.

The 1872 undress coat was a handsome and not unpractical garment for wear in garrison and in the field. The mohair braid around the edges of the skirt and the opening at the front, the side slits, and the collar lent a dashing appearance and helped set the officer apart from the enlisted man. (See Figure C on Uniform Color Plate IV in Volume I.)

Three years later regulations specified that the undress coat for officers be changed to a plain dark blue sack coat, the same pattern as before, but without braid and without slashes at the hips. This change required wearing the sabre belt on the *outside* of the coat instead of *under* the coat, as with the 1872 pattern.

Now, with publication of the 1889 uniform regulations, officers learned that another change required them to purchase still a different pattern, although they were given an option this time—a choice of two styles. The first was similar to the 1875 pattern, but with 3 small buttons on each cuff. The second, cut to the identical pattern, could have, at the wearer's option, black mohair braid at the edges of the skirt, down the front opening, and around the bottom edge of the collar. The braid, if worn, could not be wider than ¼ inch—a skimpy distinction, indeed! Before the traditional Army blues were replaced entirely by khaki and olive-drab uniforms during the first few years of the twentieth century, there would be two more distinct changes in the undress coat for officers!

Figure 247 shows both patterns of the 1889 undress coat.

Almost as an afterthought, the Adjutant General's Office published General Order No. 89, December 17, 1889: "Officers and enlisted men will also be permitted to wear rubber ponchos and blankets, or waterproof overcoats, when necessary in the field, on fatigue and other duty, involving exposure to rainy or other inclement weather." The ironic note to this order is the paragraph printed below, dated October 5, 1889, that appeared on page 650 of the Report of the Quartermaster General and published as part of the annual *Report of the Secretary of War*.

RUBBER BLANKETS AND PONCHOS.

The present supply of these articles of equipment was

procured as far back as 1864, and quite a large number still remain in depot.

Under a former recommendation of the Quartermaster-General, embodied in Circular No. 11, H. Q. A., 1885, all the troops serving on the frontier or in active campaign have been furnished with them gratuitously, at the rate of one per annum.

In order to absorb those still on hand, and which, from year to year, become more or less damaged from age, the Quartermaster-General, on the 18th May last, recommended to the honorable the Secretary of War, that the authority to issue those blankets and ponchos gratuitously be extended to all the troops in the service.

This has been approved and embodied in the last annual price-list of clothing and equipage.

And so the dregs of the tens of thousands of rubber ponchos and rubber blankets left over from the Civil War were doled out to the troops without making them pay for these articles, which must have been next to unserviceable from such long storage.

Figure 248 shows one of the types of waterproof overcoats advertised by dealers in military equipment and uniforms of the 1880's. There is little doubt that both officers and enlisted men had worn ponchos, slickers, and waterproof overcoats all along, but this is the first time since publication of the 1872 uniform regulations that specific mention of these items had been made in official orders. I have no doubts that the quartermaster general's statement quoted above was responsible for the inclusion of this notice in General Order No. 89.

Patterns for undershirts and underdrawers seemed to change frequently. While these items did not affect the appearance of a uniformed cavalryman in any way, knowledge of the changes will round out the reader's familiarity with the subject of the American cavalryman. Figure 249 illustrates several patterns issued to troops during this period. Details for undershirts and drawers came from the published specifications of the Quartermaster Department's Clothing Bureau.

ARMS

The ten cavalry regiments continued to be armed with the .45-70 Springfield carbine, the Colt single-action revolver, and the Model 1861 light cavalry sabre throughout this period.

As you will recall, the Model 1873 Springfield carbine, although modified in a number of ways since its general issue in 1874, was replaced in 1879 or 1880

FIGURE 247. First lieutenant, left, second lieutenant, center, and captain, right, First Cavalry (ca. 1889), wearing the officer undress coat specified in the 1889 uniform regulations. The coats could be either with or without braid around the edges, at the individual's option. Both styles are shown here. Boots on the officers at the left and center are those adopted for wear by all mounted officers in 1888 and 1889. Black, with stiffened tops, their adoption, as set forth in General Order No. 96 and Circular No. 11, H.Q.A., 1888, marks the first time a specific boot pattern was made mandatory for officers of the Army.

FIGURE 248. One of the several types of privately purchased waterproof coats worn by cavalry officers even before the use of waterproof clothing for officers was officially approved via a circular from the Adjutant General's Office and published in the 1889 uniform regulations. Enlisted men had long been issued talmas and, after the Civil War, ponchos.

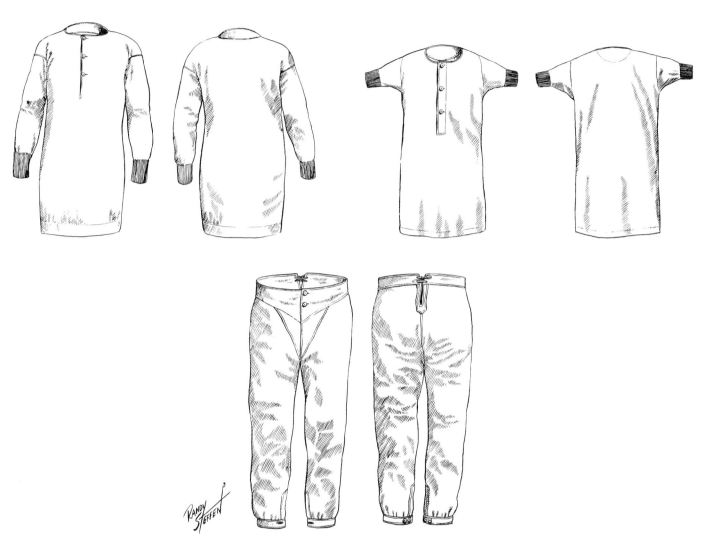

FIGURE 249. Top left: the 1891-pattern knit undershirt. Except for a more specific mixture of half wool-half cotton, this shirt differs little from the 1881 pattern. It was made and issued in 6 sizes.

Top right: The lightweight-cotton undershirt was issued for the first time in late 1890, having been approved by the quartermaster general on November 10, 1890. This garment afforded relief for troops stationed in the South and South-west, where summer heat was extreme.

Bottom: Drawers, pattern of 1888, made of unbleached canton flannel, cut and issued in 5 sizes. Except for substituting stitched bands with 2 buttons and 1 button hole on each leg for the tie strings on the 1883 pattern, there was very little difference. The next year, 1889, a ¾-inch cotton-tape loop was sewed to each hip for supporting the drawers with one of the suspender straps.

by the Model 1879 carbine, which differed from the earlier model principally in the new sight and the elimination of the stacking swivel band (the lower band of the .45-70 rifle was substituted). Other minor changes were made during this period, as well. Excellent coverage of all changes made to the Springfield carbine series is found in Kenneth M. Hammer's booklet, *The Springfield Carbine on the Western Frontier* (Bellevue, Nebraska, The Old Army Press, 3rd Edition, 1970).

It was customary throughout the period in which the .45-70 carbine was the standard cavalry arm to make all previously authorized changes each time a piece was accepted in an ordnance repair shop, so that carbines marked with the earliest model dates were found with all the improvements of the current

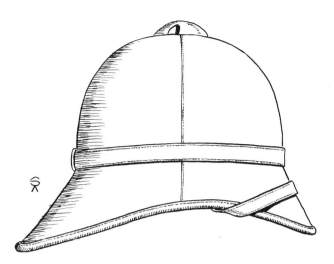 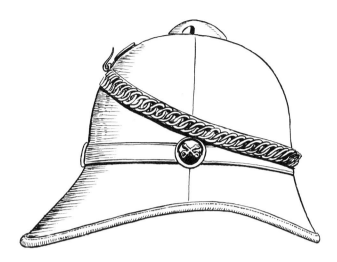

FIGURE 250. Summer-helmet pattern for enlisted men, left, and officers, right, manufactured after 1889. Both front and rear visors are larger than those on the 1880 pattern. While some officers wore the gilt spike and base for formal occasions, most wore the helmet with just side buttons and chain strap as shown above. Khaki helmets of the same pattern were also issued. Drawn from a specimen in the author's collection.

---

ordnance changes. In 1881 a new butt plate, heavier and with the form changed to provide a trap door for storage of the shell extractor and the jointed cleaning rod, was installed on all previously made carbines sent to ordnance shops for repair.

In 1884 a new-model Springfield carbine was made and issued. Designated the Model 1884, it was a little heavier than the Model 1879 and was fitted with an improved long-range sight designed by Colonel Adelbert Buffington of the Ordnance Department. The Buffington sight, shown on the carbine in Figure 251, had adjustments for windage, elevation, and drift correction. The Buffington sight was used on all Springfield carbines made after 1885.

According to Ordnance records, the first sizeable quantity of the new-model carbines was manufactured in 1886, when 5,000 Model 1884's were turned out at Springfield. Hammer's little book states that 61 Model 1884's were issued to Troop M, Seventh Cavalry, at Fort Meade, Dakota Territory, in March, 1886, for trial in the field. Other issues were made later to additional cavalry companies as the need for replacement of the older models arose.

The copper-case cartridges used in all the breech-loading Springfield carbines had been a continuous source of trouble in the fights and skirmishes with Indians since 1874. The copper, being soft, expanded in

the chamber after firing, and very often stuck so tightly that the head was pulled off by the extractor when the breech block was opened. When this happened, it was necessary to pry out the fired case with a knife, or force it out from the muzzle end with a stick or ramrod—and ramrods and sticks were too often unavailable in Indian fights.

In July, 1888, the Frankford Arsenal began production of brass-cased cartridges for the .45-70 carbines and rifles, and continued until the .30-40 Krag rifles and carbines completely replaced the .45-70 arms in the hands of the troops—about 1898, after the Spanish-American War came to a close.

HORSE EQUIPMENTS AND CAVALRY ACCOUTREMENTS

Another board of officers was convened in 1884 to further revise and improve horse equipments and cavalry accoutrements for the Army. General Order No. 73, 1885, prescribed the new and modified articles, and their descriptions, along with detailed illustrations, were published as Ordnance Memoranda No. 29 in 1891.

The McClellan saddle was retained as the standard pattern, as well as the Shoemaker bit and the 1874 curb bridle.

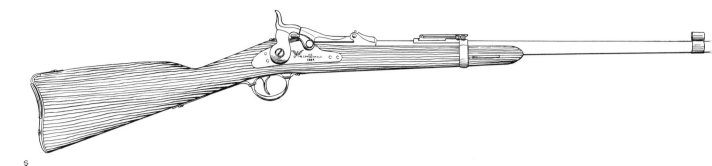

FIGURE 251. The U.S. (Springfield) carbine, Model 1884. The principal difference between this model and the earlier breech-loading Springfield carbines is the new Buffington rear sight, with windage and drift adjustment. The top of the band is grooved to fit the sight, and a clip-on front sight hood is provided. It is for this model that the weight of the bullet is increased from 405 to 500 grains—thus the correct designation for the service-carbine cartridge becomes .45-70-500. Drawn from a specimen in the National Museum Collection.

The saddle differed from the 1874 modification in that the parts of the bars directly behind the metal stirrup-leather attachment loops was made slightly thinner than they had been, and the seat, between the bars and cantle, was slightly hollowed out so as to conform more to the seat of the man, permitting him to sit farther to the rear, thereby relieving the horse's withers of a portion of the weight.

Cinch straps were riveted to the quarter-strap rings instead of the 1874-type buckled strap, and a hair cinch replaced the wide webbing girth of the older model.

The coat straps had leather "stops" riveted 10 inches from the buckles so they could not be removed from the saddle, and the stirrups were made with wider treads and larger hoods, which were riveted to the stirrup sides in a slightly different manner.

A new short carbine boot replaced the 1879 Hartman carbine socket, and saber (this is the first publication in which "saber" is spelled this way instead of the older way, "sabre") straps were issued for strapping down the saber after it was attached to the saddle by the new saber attachment.

The link strap was modified, with a slightly different snap on the end that attached to the halter ring. The watering bridle was fitted with a different pattern of snaps for attachment to the halter squares, and the reins were now sewn to the bit rings.

A new-pattern saddlebag, of the California style, replaced the 1879 bags with the belly strap, and a nosebag of slightly modified pattern and construction replaced the Model of 1874.

The issue currycomb was now made with a leather body, instead of with a japanned iron body as before, and the halter was fitted with a new type of lead-strap attachment, a combination of a ring with a square attached on a swivel. The Lyon picket pin was refined and fitted with a double swivel.

Two new patterns of side lines were issued, the Comly and the Butler-Varney. The lariat underwent a change, being made of glazed-linen plaited rope instead of twisted Italian hemp as in 1874, and the brass spurs for enlisted men had a half-concealed rowel.

A cotton-duck horse cover was added to the standard equipments for the first time, and the saddle blanket, still the same size and of the same material, was changed from a dark blue color with a yellow border to a gray color with a yellow border, still with the 6-inch-high letters *U.S.* in yellow in the center.

In August, 1884, General Order No. 95 had prescribed that saddle cloths for officers be modified by adding the number of the regiment in both flank corners. The 1885 regulations specified a saddle cloth for field officers that was somewhat larger than the 1874 pattern, and another for general and staff officers that was considerably larger than the one for line officers. This one was designed to fit *over* the saddle, and had leather-reinforced slots for the stirrup leathers to pass through. Saddle cloths for line officers were to be worn *under* the saddle, and were bound with 1½-inch-wide yellow cloth, with the number of the regiment, also in yellow cloth, 2 inches in length in each flank corner, as stated before.

A new drab-color canvas haversack with a leather

carrying strap was specified for cavalry, complete with inside pockets for the new meat can, knife, fork, and spoon, also prescribed as items of issue for the cavalryman.

The pistol holster, without the swivel attachment as modified in 1879, was made to accommodate both the Colt and the single-action Smith & Wesson revolvers. A new saber knot replaced the Model 1872 knot without the tassel, being made of narrower leather with a small tassel and a separate attachment at the top that fastened with a brass stud to the guard of the saber. The new cartridge belt had a body and cartridge loops of woven gray-colored web, with leather chape and brass bar buckle on one end, and a leather billet on the other.

The saber belt lost its saber slings, utilizing instead a single brass slide fitted with a hook. With it was issued a saber attachment, a modification of the Stuart attachment patented by J. E. B. Stuart in 1859. A new type of canteen and canteen strap allowed this piece of equipment to be snapped to a ring on the saddle.

The McKeever cartridge box was retained, but the carbine sling, made much as it had been, was narrowed to 1½ inches. The single-tongue bar buckle and sling tip remained brass, as before.

Figures 252, 253, 254, and 255 show the new equipments and accoutrements as described and illustrated in Ordnance Memorandum No. 29; they were drawn from specimens in the collections of the author and the West Point Museum.

The descriptions contained in Ordnance Memorandum No. 29 are published in their entirety below:

HORSE EQUIPMENTS.

SADDLE.

[See Figure 252-A.]

Saddle is composed of:
- 1 Tree.
- 6 Coat straps.
- 2 Girth straps with 2 safes and 2 cincha straps.
- 2 Stirrups (hooded).
- 1 Girth (hair).
- 1 Carbine boot.
- 2 Saber straps.

Saddle tree—wood.

Pommel a and *cantle b* (beech), each made of 2 pieces and framed together at top and glued; *2 side bars c* (poplar), each made of 2 pieces and glued together; they are then glued to pommel and cantle and secured with eight 2½-inch No. 12 screws. Holes are bored through side bars along junction of pommel and cantle, front and rear; side bars are grooved underneath in line with holes for fastening on rawhide cover; 1 mortise in pommel and 3 in cantle for coat straps.

Iron.—*1 pommel arc d*, with 2 holes on top and fastened to side bars with 4 rivets; *1 pommel plate e*, semicircular, fastened to the front of the pommel with 5 rivets; *1 cantle arc f*, with 3 holes on top and fastened to the side bars with 4 rivets; *1 cantle plate g*, fastened to the front of the cantle with 4 rivets.

Arcs and plates 0.1 inch thick and let in flush with the wood; rivets 1¼ inches, No. 8.

Two stirrup strap loops h, made of ¼-inch wrought iron, with the lower edges inclined from the horizontal upward and toward the front; to swing loosely in iron straps *i*, which are let in and fastened to the side bars with 3 rivets.

The tree to be smooth and well painted with white lead, and covered with rawhide to strengthen the tree; the top covering is secured in place with rawhide thongs passing through holes in front and rear of pommel and cantle and over covering.

The top and bottom covers are then sewed together with light thongs of same material.

The tree is then covered with black collar leather, 6 to 7 ounces per square foot, the seams around cantle and pommel to be reenforced with welts of leather; the seams in center of top covers to have light welts; seams on edges of side bars to be where they will not chafe the horse or rider, and to be without skirts; 4 wrought-iron saddle nails (½-inch head, japanned, 1 inch long) in side bars at points of pommel and cantle.

TRIMMING, SADDLE.

[See Figure 252-A.]

Two 1¼-inch rings *A*, held by 1⅝-inch staples driven in front ends of side bars and clinched.

Shield B with size of seat stamped on it fastened to pommel over mortise with three ¾-inch No. 2 screw pins; *6 guard plates or ovals C* in cantle and 1 in front of pommel over mortise, each fastened with two ¾-inch No. 2 screw pins; *4 foot staples D*, ¼ inch by 13/16 inch, for coat straps—2 on front of pommel, 2 containing 1¼-inch rings on rear of cantle under ovals—each fastened with two ⅞-inch No. 6 screws; *2 foot staples E*, 7/16 inch by ¾ inch, each fastened to side bars through rear girth straps with two ⅞-inch No. 6 screws for attaching saddle bag; *1 saddle-bag stud F*, fastened to rear of girth strap with a ⅜-inch No. 10 rivet, and to saddle through girth strap and cantle arc with a 1-inch No. 8 oval-head rivet. The 6 coat straps *G* are passed through mortises and foot staples, and have leather stops riveted on them 10½ inches from buckle with ⅜-inch No. 12 rivets to limit their play.

Saddle trees to be of 3 sizes, and manufactured in the following proportions:

No. 1. Length of seat, 11 inches; 15 per cent.
No. 2. Length of seat, 11½ inches; 50 per cent.
No. 3. Length of seat, 12 inches; 35 per cent.

The length of side bars to correspond with the length of

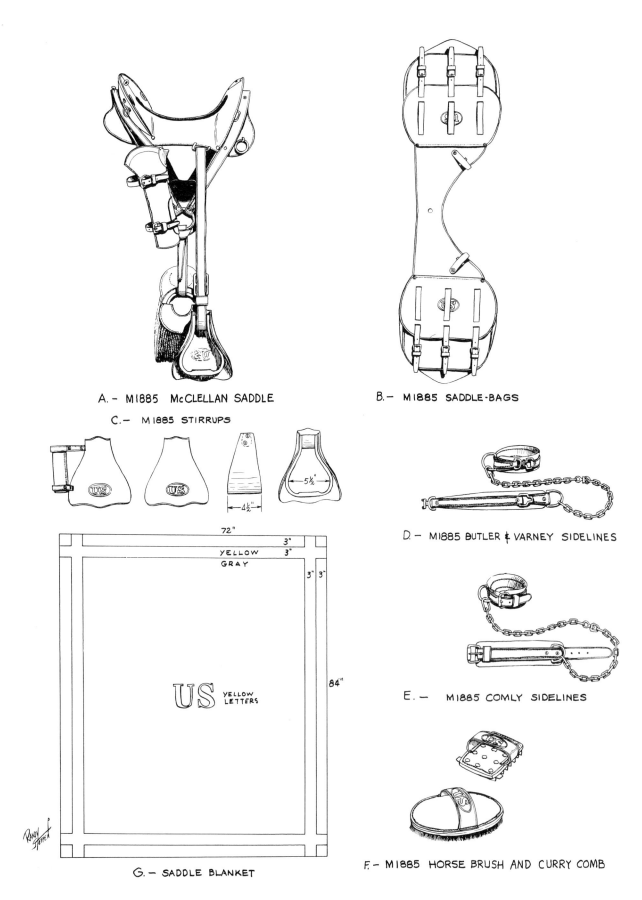

A. – M1885 McCLELLAN SADDLE

B. – M1885 SADDLE-BAGS

C. – M1885 STIRRUPS

4½"

5½"

72"
3"
YELLOW 3"
GRAY
3" 3"

US YELLOW
LETTERS

84"

D. – M1885 BUTLER & VARNEY SIDELINES

E. – M1885 COMLY SIDELINES

G. – SADDLE BLANKET

F. – M1885 HORSE BRUSH AND CURRY COMB

FIGURE 252. The 1885 horse equipments as prescribed by General Order No. 73, 1885.

36

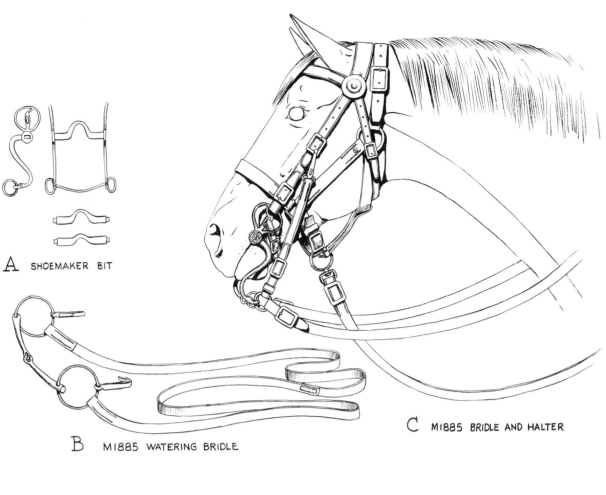

A SHOEMAKER BIT

B M1885 WATERING BRIDLE

C M1885 BRIDLE AND HALTER

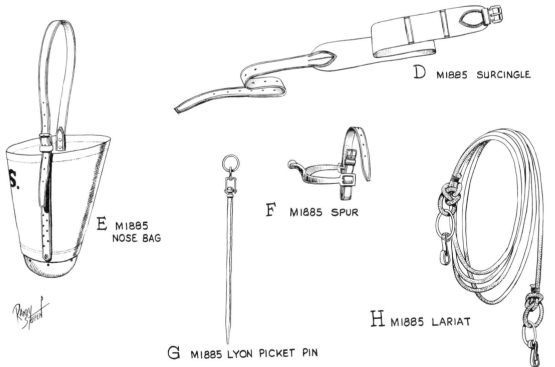

D M1885 SURCINGLE

E M1885 NOSE BAG

F M1885 SPUR

G M1885 LYON PICKET PIN

H M1885 LARIAT

FIGURE 253. The 1885 horse equipments as prescribed by General Order No. 73, 1885.

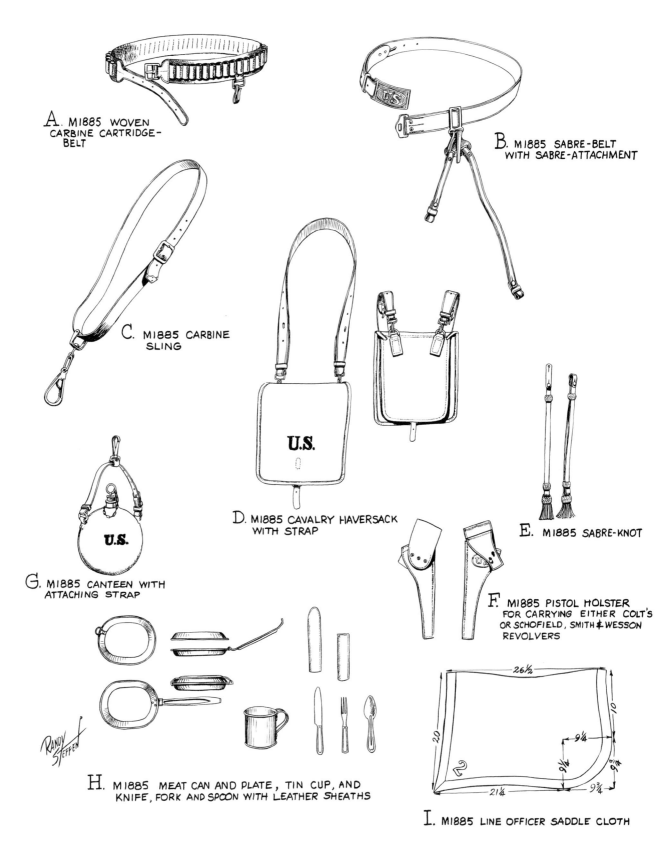

A. M1885 WOVEN CARBINE CARTRIDGE-BELT

B. M1885 SABRE-BELT WITH SABRE-ATTACHMENT

C. M1885 CARBINE SLING

D. M1885 CAVALRY HAVERSACK WITH STRAP

E. M1885 SABRE-KNOT

G. M1885 CANTEEN WITH ATTACHING STRAP

F. M1885 PISTOL HOLSTER FOR CARRYING EITHER COLT'S OR SCHOFIELD, SMITH & WESSON REVOLVERS

H. M1885 MEAT CAN AND PLATE, TIN CUP, AND KNIFE, FORK AND SPOON WITH LEATHER SHEATHS

I. M1885 LINE OFFICER SADDLE CLOTH

FIGURE 254. The 1885 cavalry accoutrements as prescribed by General Order No. 73, 1885.

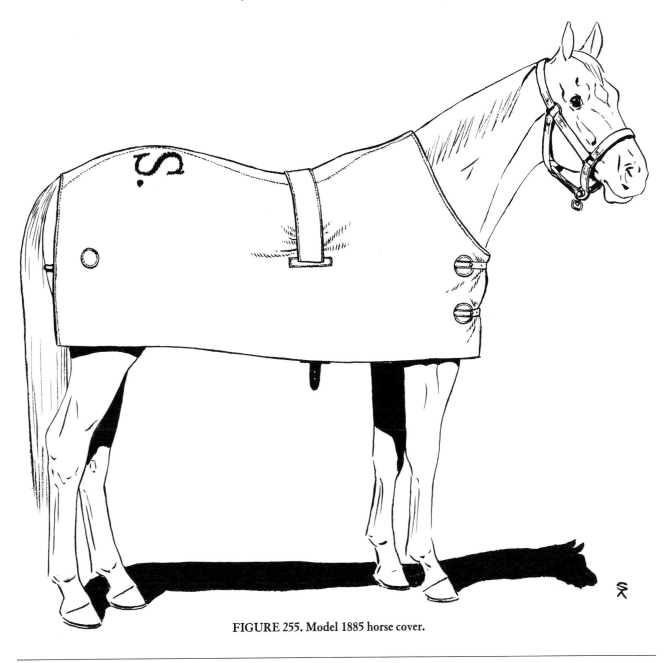

FIGURE 255. Model 1885 horse cover.

the seat; the other dimensions to be the same in all trees, as shown in the illustrations.

All metal parts used in trimming to be of brass.

GIRTH.—*Two girth straps H & H'* (harness leather) passed over pommel and cantle arcs, to which each is fastened with two 1-inch No. 8 oval-head rivets, and two ⅞-inch No. 6 screws; the ends of the front and rear straps are sewed on both sides into wrought-iron rings *I* 2½ inches in diameter; safes *J* of stout leather (of pattern in drawings) are fastened to girth straps, under rings, with ⅜-inch No. 10 rivets. *Two cincha straps K* (collar leather, 7 to 8 ounce per square foot) sewed to the rings and riveted with ⅜-inch No. 10 rivets,

1¼ inches in width for 3 feet 6 inches from ring, thence tapered to ends ½ inch wide.

COAT STRAPS *G* (collar leather, 7 to 8 ounces per square foot) with brass bar buckles and leather stops.

CINCHA *L*.—Made of hair rope, 24 strands, knotted on iron ring *V'* 4 inches in diameter; to be 7 inches wide in center when finished, and to have 2 rows woven around ring and through center to connect the strands; to have stout leather circular safes *O* under rings; the knots covered with leather *V* and sewed on safes; cinchas to be made of 3 lengths in equal proportions—16, 18, and 20 inches.

STIRRUP STRAPS *M* with iron bar buckles; 1 standing loop

Q on under side made sufficiently high to take the billet end after the strap has been passed through.

STIRRUPS *N* (*hard wood*). The sole *N'* 5½ inches wide and 4½ inches deep; the hood *φ* of thick harness leather with letters U.S. stamped on center of front, 2⅛ inches from bottom to center and riveted to stirrups by six ¾-inch No. 10 oval-head brass rivets; bottom of hood to project ¾ inch below the plane of under side of stirrup.

CARBINE BOOT *P* AND STRAPS *S & S'*. The *boot* of thick harness leather, 13⅝ inches in length and 2¼ inches interior diameter at the lower end. The opening at the upper end 5⅛ inches long by 3 inches wide, shaped so as to embrace the carbine just in front of the trigger guard and have a swell pressed in the front to allow for the projection of the rear sight. A triangular piece of leather *Z* is inserted in the front of the boot to cause it to flare so as not to catch the rear sight leaf when inserting the carbine. A curved brass plate *R* made of No. 14 sheet brass is riveted on the boot to secure this shape with three ⅜-inch No. 14 brass rivets and one ⅜-inch No. 12 brass rivet. The boot is suspended from the saddle-bag stud by a strap *T* with 2 holes near the end for adjusting the height of the boot, and riveted to the front part of the boot on the under side with a ½-inch No. 10 rivet. This strap is movable about the rivet which attaches it to the boot. The boot is fastened to the rear girth strap and girth-strap ring, off side, with two ⅞-inch straps *S* & *S'* with iron roller buckles. The upper strap is fastened to the boot on the upper and under side 3⅞ inches from the top edge with two ½-inch No. 10 rivets. The lower strap is fastened on the front with 1 rivet only.

SABER STRAPS *U*.—Have brass bar buckles, and 2 inches from the buckle a standing loop.

One strap is passed through ring in front of pommel on left side, and one through left girth strap ring, and then through rings on scabbard, and are used to secure the saber and limit its movements after it has been attached to the saddle by the saber attachment.

SADDLE BAGS.
[See Figure 252-B.]

Made of bag leather, 5 to 6 ounces per square foot; composed of *2 pouches B* with flaps *C* and *1 seat D*; gusset *G* to decrease in width 6½ inches from ends; pouches to have detachable linings (F, B, & G, Pl. V.) made of No. 9 drab duck, secured in place with 4 metallic buttons, the off side for clothing and the near side for rations, with inside pockets *P* for knife, fork, and spoon, and 3 small bags *S* for coffee and sugar and *R* for salt. The material for these bags is shown on Plate V, ready cut, with lines of folds and stitching for hems and seams marked in dotted lines thereon, making the salt bag *R* when finished 3½ inches wide and 7½ inches long, and the coffee and sugar bags *S* 5½ inches wide and 5⅞ inches long. A cord 20 inches long is run through hems of each for tying. A flap *C*, with U.S. stamped on it, to cover each pouch, and secured by 3 brass buckles and billets *E*, and to have a ⅜-inch No. 12 brass rivet in each upper corner riveted through pouch and seat. The seat of the saddle bags 17½ inches long at the rear, 18 inches at the front, and 3 inches wide in the middle; to fit smoothly over cantle arc and side bars of the saddle; to have one hole *L* for the saddle-bag stud and 2 slots *M* for foot staples; 2 key straps *K* riveted to the seat to pass through staples on saddle.

SADDLE BLANKET.
[See Figure 252-G.]

Made of pure wool, close woven, of stout yarns of a gray color, with a yellow border 3 inches wide, and 3 inches from the edge; the letters U. S., 6 inches high, of yellow color, in the center of the blanket. Dimensions, 84 inches long, 72 inches wide. Weight, 4 pounds, with 26 threads in the warp and 36 per inch in the woof. Will stand a strain of 50 pounds in the direction of the warp and 40 pounds in the direction of the woof.

SURCINGLE.
[See Figure 253-D.]

Of blue linen webbing *W*, 3½ inches wide; a 1½-inch iron roller buckle *B* with chape and standing loop on one end; 2 leather loops *C* sewed on web to take the billet; a 1½-inch billet *D* with swell sewed on the other end and reinforced with leather.

CURB BRIDLE.
[See Figure 253-C.]

Made of black bridle leather.

HEADSTALL composed of *one crown G*; the ends split 8 inches, ⅛ inch taken out of the center, forming a cheek and throat strap billet on each end.

Two cheek pieces H with brass bar buckles sewed in the upper end and billets and brass bar buckles to the lower end of each.

One throat latch K with brass bar buckles at each end.

One brow band J, 2 brass ornaments, one riveted on each side through slit in crown piece.

Reins L made of 2 pieces of leather sewed together in the center; billets *L'* and brass bar buckles on ends.

Curb bit of *Shoemaker* pattern, of good shear steel, bright finish; *2 branches B*, 4.9 inches apart at lower ends and at mouth piece, 5.3 inches at top of curve of upper part of branch, with curve at top for cheek piece billets, and slot in the branch for curb strap *N*; center of slot 1.75 inches from center of mouth piece; lower part of branch 5.1 inches long, with eye at lower end into which is welded a ring for the reins; *1 mouth piece M* 0.6 inch in diameter, securely riveted to the branches; *1 cross bar C* securely riveted to the branches near the lower end; *2 ornaments* of cast brass *D*, the letters U. S. raised thereon, riveted to the branches over ends of mouth piece. [See Figure 253-A.]

The width of arch of mouth piece is 1.9 inches for all bits.

There are three grades of severity for the bit, determined by the height of the arch of mouth piece *M*.

No. 1. Height of arch, ½ inch.
No. 2. Height of arch, 1 inch.
No. 3. Height of arch, 1½ inches.

They are manufactured and issued in the following proportions, unless otherwise called for:

No. 1. 75 per cent.
No. 2. 20 per cent.
No. 3. 5 per cent.

Curb strap N, composed of 1 safe *S*, on which is sewed a strap, the ends forming billets; 2 brass bar buckles sewed between safe and strap 2¼ inches from each end of safe.

WATERING BRIDLE.
[See Figure 253-B.]

Is composed of a bit and a pair of reins (bridle leather).

The bit consists of a steel mouth piece *A* jointed in the middle, with holes drilled in the ends, into which are welded two 2⅞-inch rings *E*; also 2 snap hooks *F* for attachment to the halter.

The reins R are in two pieces, sewed together in the center, the ends sewed into the rings of the bit.

LINK.
[See Figure 253-C.]

A *strap T* (made of collar leather 8½ to 9 ounces per square foot), with a snap hook *P* sewed in one end, and to the other a brass bar buckle and billet *Q* with sliding loop; its length will be adjusted by the billet to fit snugly the cheek piece of the bridle, being buckled in the rear rein ring of the bit and held by the snap in the upper buckle of the cheek piece.

HALTER.
[See Figure 253-C.]

Composed of 2 *cheek pieces A* (made of harness leather); one end of each cheek piece is sewed to a rectangular iron loop *B*, and the other end sewed to an iron ring *C* 1¾ inches diameter.

The crown piece D is sewed to the off cheek ring; iron bar buckle *E* and chape sewed to the near ring.

Nose band F, with ends sewed to rectangular loops *B*.

The chin strap G, with iron bar buckle *H*, 2 standing and 2 sliding loops, passing loosely through rectangular loops *B* and halter swivel rings *I*.

Throat strap J, folded on itself, making 3 thicknesses and forming at the top a loop for the throat band to pass through, and embracing in its fold at the other end a bolt which holds the ring of the halter swivel.

Throat band K passes through loop in throat strap *J* and is sewed to cheek rings. Ring of swivel *I* 1¾ inches diameter. Square *G*, 1⅛ inches wide, to which halter strap or lariat can be attached.

Halter strap L, with iron bar buckle without tongue sewed to one end and doubled on itself 6 inches.

LARIAT.
[See Figure 253-H.]

Of linen plaited rope *C*, glazed, 25 feet long (finished) and ⅜ inch diameter. At each end is an iron ring *A* 1¾ inches in diameter, with a snap hook *B*. The rope *C* is at-

tached to the rings by a bowline knot. The loose end is then tucked back through the knot and bound with copper wire.

PICKET PIN.
[See Figure 253-G.]

Of pattern known as the *Lyons* patent.

The pin X to be 15 inches long, made of ⅝-inch round iron, and the head stout enough to resist upsetting by being struck.

The swivel and ring S to be of the pattern and dimensions indicated in plate; to be painted black.

SIDE LINE.

Made of harness leather.

Two varieties of side lines are manufactured and issued, according to the conditions of service or the preference of troop commanders.

Butler & Varney, composed of 2 *leglets D* with tinned fastenings, the lay containing in one end the hook *E* of the fastening, and in the other the hasp *G*; the chape *K* containing the iron D ring *H* of the chain *M* 1⅝ inches in diameter. [See Figure 252-D.]

Comly, composed of 2 *leglets N* with 1½-inch iron roller buckles *O* in folds *P* of the lays *R* on one end, the other end forming a billet. The 1⅝-inch D ring *S* of the chain *T* is blocked in place by 2 pieces of leather and sewed between the lay and fold, and riveted with two ⅝-inch No. 10 tinned iron rivets. [See Figure 252-E.]

In both patterns of side lines the leglets are connected by a chain made of 3/16-inch iron; links ¾ inch by ⅜ inch, with swivel at middle.

The side lines are made in equal proportions, viz:

No. 1. Length of chain, 18 inches.
No. 2. Length of chain, 24 inches.
No. 3. Length of chain, 30 inches.

HORSE COVER.
[See Figure 255.]

Of No. 8 white cotton duck, the curve in the back made by straining the straight edge to a curved line; 2 *reenforces A* sewed on each front side of cover; *leather billets B* sewed to the 2 on the off side, and the chapes *C* with standing loops and iron roller buckles on the 2 on the near side.

Crupper D.—A rope covered with drab web and sewed to the inside of the cover under reenforces.

Surcingle E.—Four inches wide, of cotton duck, doubled and sewed on the outside of cover, the ends passing through slits reenforced with cotton web, to the inside of cover; a 1½-inch iron roller buckle *F* with chape and loop sewed on off side; billet *G* with a swell sewed on near side.

NOSE BAG.
[See Figure 253-E.]

Of No. 8 white cotton duck, with a flexible leather bottom *M* 6½ inches in diameter, 3½ inches deep; body hemmed on top and sewed to the bottom with 2 rows of stitching; on the off side a head strap *N* sewed to the body and riveted to the bottom; on the near side a strap *S* is fastened in the same manner, with an iron roller buckle *P* and standing loop.

Both straps are riveted to top of body and reenforced.

The sides, through straps, are perforated with ¼-inch holes, ½ inch apart; also through bottom, 1½ inches from the top, 3 inches apart. The letters U. S., 1½ inches long, stencilled on the body.

HORSE BRUSH.
[See Figure 252-F.]

Body Q oval in shape, 4½ inches by 9 inches; of stout leather, with Russia bristles; the letters U. S. stamped on leather hand strap *R*.

CURRY COMB.
[See Figure 252-F.]

Body U of 2 thicknesses of stout leather, 4¾ inches by 5 inches; sides slightly curved; 4 double rows of iron teeth *T* (one with knocker *V*, projecting ⅜ inch beyond body), each row riveted to the body by 3 iron rivets. Letters U. S. stamped on hand strap *W*.

SPURS.
[See Figure 253-F.]

Of cast brass, smooth finish, with ¾-inch bar loop on side for spur straps *F*, with steel rowels ²⁷⁄₃₂ inch diameter.

SPUR STRAPS F.
[See Figure 253-F.]

Made of collar leather, 7 to 8 ounces per square foot, with brass wire buckles and a standing loop.

CAVALRY ACCOUTREMENTS

CARBINE SLING AND SWIVEL.
[See Figure 254-C.]

Of black collar leather *Q*, 8½ to 9 ounces per square foot, with brass bar buckle *A* and tip *B*.

Swivel D of iron with D and roller; link *H* and hook *H′* of iron; guard spring of steel.

SABER BELT AND PLATE.
[See Figure 254-B.]

Of black collar leather *E*, 7 to 8 ounces per square foot, with one sliding loop; to have *1 slide G* of cast brass with loop at lower part for attaching hook of saber attachment; *1 saber hook H*, ⅛ inch wide at point, ⁷⁄₁₆ inch at butt, made of No. 14 sheet brass, bent around loop on slide; slide to be free and move on belt. *A flat brass hook* is riveted to one end of the belt to regulate its length.

A hasp K of cast brass is sewed and riveted in the other end of belt to connect with plate.

Saber belt plate F of cast brass, rectangular, 3³⁄₁₆ inches long, 2⅛ inches wide, with slot on one end to receive the belt; hook on under side.

In relief, on face of plate, the letters U. S., surrounded by an oval.

Saber belts are made of two lengths, 38 inches and 42 inches, equal quantities of each length.

SABER ATTACHMENT.
[See Figure 254-B.]

(A modification of the *Stuart* attachment.) Is made of collar leather, 7 to 8 ounces per square foot. Has a brass plate *L* with hook; slots in plate for 2 slings *M & M′* one end riveted in the slots, the other end with 2 holes with slits for 2 brass studs and 2 slide loops.

PISTOL HOLSTER.
[See Figure 254-F.]

Of black collar leather, 8½ to 9 ounces per square foot, composed of *body P, flap C, frog A,* and *bottom K,* and made so that the pistol shall fit neatly into it; to have the letters U. S., surrounded by an oval, stamped in front. *A brass button* riveted on body, the bur on the inside covered with leather and stitched in place; seam at top of body reenforced.

A circular bottom with hole punched in center, sewed in flush with bottom of holster. Flap to be sewed and riveted to the back of the body; to have 2 holes with slots for attaching to the button, permitting the use of holster for carrying either the Colt's or Schofield, Smith & Wesson revolver.

The frog for the belt is sewed and riveted to the flap and body, and is large enough to slip over the empty woven cartridge belt.

WOVEN CARTRIDGE BELT.
[See Figure 254-A.]

The belt O is of a uniform gray color. At the left-hand end is sewed a black leather chape *C*, embracing in its fold a brass bar buckle *J* and the belt. At the right-hand end a billet *N* with a leather lining. The chape and billet, where joined to the belt, to be of its full width, then abruptly narrowed down to 1½ inches and placed close to the cartridge loops *P*. On the left side of the belt a chape with brass loop and hook *R* for the saber attachment, 6½ inches from the end of the buckle chape. The belt to be manufactured in 2 sizes, and issued to troops in equal proportions, unless otherwise called for.

No. 1, with 45 loops.
No. 2, with 50 loops.

Dimensions of billet shown on plate. Lengths of the woven belts vary.

CARTRIDGE BOX.
[See Figure 213-H.]

The *McKeever* cartridge box, made of black collar leather, 8½ to 9 ounces per square foot, is made in 2 parts *B & D*, connected by a leather hinge working over a brass rod *E*, which passes through the ends of the box and is secured by a brass oval riveted on each end. A swell *F & F′* is pressed in the right-hand end of the box for carrying a screwdriver.

A brass button *G* is riveted on front *D* of box, and a billet *H* with a slitted hole on back *B* for closing box.

Two waist belt loops L riveted and sewed on back of box.

The cartridges are held in webbing loops sewed to a drab duck bellows, 10 in each section of the box. The bellows allow the cartridges to incline forward when the box is open. The letters U. S., surrounded by an oval, stamped on front of box.

SABER KNOT.
[See Figure 254-E.]

Sling M, made of light collar leather, to be soft and pliable, ends passed through *loop N* on tassel *O*; ends sewed together and hole punched and slit for button.

Tassel O of light collar leather, slit and rolled up to ¾ inch diameter; wrapped with waxed thread to the width of 11⁄16 inch from top for braiding over. The loop is then sewed on, after which it is again wrapped with waxed thread to ⅞ inch diameter.

Braiding strip of light collar leather, braided on the wrapped thread on end of the tassel.

Slide loop Q braided over with strips of light collar leather.

Button loop R, of light collar leather, punched and slit for a button.

CANTEEN.
[See Figure 254-G.]

Made of XXXX tin, circular in shape, 7¾ inches in diameter, sides oval and smooth; thickness through, 3 inches; with a triangular iron wire loop *T* soldered on each side to tin loop; mouth piece with a rim; cork capped with tin; iron wire stem riveted through cork and attached to canteen by a brass chain 3 inches long, with a ring closed on mouth piece.

Covered first with gray Petersham and afterwards with drab duck.

CANTEEN STRAP.
[See Figure 254-G.]

Of black collar leather *U*, 7 to 8 ounces per square foot, with iron roller buckle and *2 standing loops* on one end; *1 sliding loop V; snap hook W* sewed and riveted on leather loop, movable along the double strap for attachment to ring on saddle or to loop on cartridge belt.

HAVERSACK.
[See Figure 254-D.]

Of No. 9 drab duck. *The flap H* is made in 2 thicknesses, cut 14½ inches deep by 12¾ inches wide, and bound with 1-inch wide drab webbing.

A *double webbing strap A* 9 inches long by ¾ inch wide, with 2 eyelets, is sewed to the under side of flap.

The front F is cut 12 inches deep by 9⅞ inches wide; it has an outside pocket *P* for meat can and plate combined, cut 11½ inches deep by 9⅞ inches wide, rounded at bottom, with selvage top; is seamed in with the front and gusset, and felled through all.

Gusset G is cut 31½ inches long by 3½ inches wide in middle and 3⅛ inches at ends; tapers 5 inches from ends;

a brass wire buckle *B* ¾ inch wide with web chape *C* is sewed to the center.

An inside pocket J with selvage top, cut 11 inches deep by 9⅞ inches wide, sewed in with the back.

Back E cut 12 inches deep by 10¾ inches wide at top, 9⅞ inches wide through middle; *2 web chapes I* with brass D's "D" sewed on back for attaching the haversack strap.

Two inside pockets K & K', hemmed at top and sewed in with sides and across bottom, to gusset, cut 9⅜ and 8⅞ inches long by 3½ inches wide; to taper with the gusset and set in 1 inch from top, on line with inside pocket, for knife, fork, and spoon.

Mouth of haversack bound with 1-inch drab webbing, ⅜ of an inch included in the measurements for all seams.

HAVERSACK STRAP.
[See Figure 254-D.]

Of black collar leather *X*, 7 to 8 ounces per square foot, 2 inches wide in middle, tapering to 1⅛ inches at ends; *2 double brass wire hooks Y,* with rollers in fold; *2 brass hooks; 2 sliding loops.*

MEAT CAN AND PLATE.
[See Figure 254-H.]

Meat can and plate combined consists of 2 oval dishes *W & W',* made of XXXX tin, one deeper than the other, which fit together, forming a meat ration can of the following dimensions: Length, 8 inches; width, 6½ inches; depth of whole can, 1½ inches when closed.

The lower dish to be 1 inch in depth and the plate ¾ inch in depth. To the deeper dish or plate is attached a light iron handle *J*, which folds over and fastens the two parts together when closed.

TIN CUP.
[See Figure 254-H.]

Made of XXXX tin; 4 inches high, 4 inches in diameter; a tin handle, 1 inch wide at top, tapering to ⅝ inch, riveted on side.

KNIFE, FORK, AND SPOON.
[See Figure 254-H.]

Knife and fork are made of steel; handles japanned.

The spoon is made of tinned iron.

Dimensions shown on plate.

Leather sheaths, S for knife, T for fork, made of scrap leather, as shown in plate.

GUIDON STIRRUP.
[See Figure 252-C.]

(Stirrup with hood; same specifications as given for stirrup under saddle.)

Socket W of stout leather, 6 inches long, 1½ inches in diameter, inside measure, to be attached to hood by two ⅝-inch straps.

Top strap X sewed around socket, the ends reenforced, sewed, and riveted to hood.

Bottom strap X′ sewed around socket and riveted to socket and hood.

SADDLE CLOTHS.

For officers of the general staff and staff corps.

To conform in dimensions to the standard sample. To be made of dark-blue cloth, known to the trade as "*F and H Castor*," fifty-four (54) to fifty-five (55) inches wide, weighing about twenty-three (23) ounces to the lineal yard, and to be capable of standing a breaking strain of forty-four (44) pounds to the inch of warp, and fifty (50) pounds to the inch of filling; the dye to be strictly fast.

To have an inner lining of brown buckram and an outer lining of heavy black enameled cloth.

To be made in 2 halves and then neatly joined and held securely together by a strap *A* of black bridle leather one and one-quarter (1¼) inches wide, placed in the seam and stitched through the whole thickness of cloth and lining.

Each half to have a horizontal slit seven and a half (7½) inches long near the center of same; the slit on under side to be faced with a piece of bridle leather ten (10) inches long and four (4) inches wide, and rounded at the corners; stitched to the linings; the cloth edges of slit to be bound around with black enameled leather stitched through all.

The saddle cloth to be bound all around the edge with black enameled leather, to show on the outside a width of one-half (½) inch, and to be trimmed with gold lace one (1) inch wide, next the enameled leather; in each flank corner the insignia as prescribed for the forage cap, embroidered on an oval of dark-blue cloth, is sewed to the saddle cloth in the position shown on plates.

SADDLE CLOTHS FOR OFFICERS OF THE LINE.

[See Figure 254-I.]

To be of dark-blue felt, known to the trade as number "XO," of good wool stock and fast dye, seventy-two (72) inches in width, and weighing about two and one-half (2½) pounds to the linear yard. To be capable of standing a breaking strain of at least sixty (60) pounds to the square inch. To be made in 2 halves, which are neatly and securely seamed together.

The saddle cloth to be bound all around the edge with cloth, to show one and one-half (1½) inches on outside, *white for infantry, scarlet for artillery, yellow for cavalry.*

The number of the regiment in figures two (2) inches in length, made of cloth of the same color as trimmings, to be placed on each of flank corners, in the position indicated on plate.

CARBINE BOOT AND STRAPS.

[See Figure 252-A.]

The boot *P* of thick harness leather, 13⅝ inches long and 2¼ inches interior diameter at the lower end. The opening at the upper end 5⅛ inches long by 3 inches wide, shaped so as to embrace the carbine just in front of the trigger guard, and have a swell pressed in the front to allow for the projection of the rear sight. A triangular piece *Z*, of leather, is inserted in the front of the boot to cause it to flare, so as not to catch the rear sight leaf when inserting the carbine. A curved brass plate *R*, made of No. 14 sheet brass, is riveted on the boot to secure this shape with three ⅜-inch No. 14 brass rivets, and one ⅜-inch No. 12 brass rivet. The boot is suspended from the saddle-bag stud by a strap *T*, with two holes near the end for adjusting the height of the boot, and riveted to the front part of the boot on the under side with a ½-inch No. 10 rivet. This strap is movable about the rivet which attaches it to the boot. The boot is fastened to the rear girth strap and girth-strap ring, off side, with two ⅞-inch straps, *S* and *S′*, with iron roller buckles; the upper strap *S* is fastened to the boot on the upper and under side 3⅞ inches from the top edge with two ½-inch No. 10 rivets; the lower strap *S′* is fastened on the front with one rivet only.

Many officers seemed to prefer the Whitman saddle, especially for use in garrison and dress ceremonies. This saddle was procured from private contractors or military-goods dealers located in the large cities and, of course, was paid for by the individual officer out of his personal funds, as were all articles of his uniform and equipment. Figure 256 shows a first lieutenant dressed and equipped for mounted garrison duty, with the Whitman saddle and the Whitman halter-bridle.

While many officers rode the Whitman saddle for ceremony and pleasure, most preferred the issue McClellan equipments for campaign, and records indicate that it was general practice for them to draw the McClellan equipments from Quartermaster stores before setting out on a march that would last many days. It was much later that regulations prescribed this practice as being officially permissible.

Figures 257 and258 show enlisted men dressed and equipped for mounted garrison duty with the 1885 horse equipments and accoutrements prescribed for that type of duty.

As shown here, halters and halter ties were not used in garrison and at dress formations. Coat straps, now fitted with leather stops so they could not be removed from the saddle, were looped, wrapped, and buckled in the last hole, according to an article in the *Military Collector & Historian* (Vol. V, No. 3 (1953), 75–76). Colonel Harry Larter, the author and illustrator of the very accurately detailed plate that accompanied the article, "Standards of the 10th Cavalry, 1888–1890," has contributed much to the knowledge of the mounted service, both by meticulous research, as shown by his military-uniform plates and articles, and by long years of experience in the U.S. Field Artillery.

FIGURE 256. First lieutenant, Sixth Cavalry (ca. 1885), in undress uniform and equipped for garrison duty, mounted, with the Whitman saddle and Whitman combination halter-bridle, Model 1879.

Figure 259 shows a major of the Sixth Cavalry on a good private mount equipped for duty in the field. His horse equipments are the standard McClellan 85 saddle, and the other prescribed equipments contained in General Order No. 73, 1885.

Figures 260 and 261 show troopers dressed, armed, and equipped for field duty, with full saddle packs on the 1885 saddle as well as all other equipments and accoutrements specified as 1885 standards.

General Sheridan, in an effort to standardize the method of packing the saddle for the field, wrote a description which was to be adhered to by all cavalry troops. This description was published to the 10 regiments as an order, and that part relating to field packs was as follows:

. . . Armament for the trooper for field duty.—carbine (with carbine sling), cartridge belt, sabre (carried either from the belt or attached to the saddle, but always the latter when dismounting to fight on foot), pistol.

To secure uniformity, the saddle will be packed as rec-

FIGURE 257. Private, Second Cavalry (ca. 1885), in fatigue uniform and with correct equipment for garrison duty under arms. Off side.

FIGURE 258. Corporal, Second Cavalry (ca. 1885), in fatigue uniform and properly equipped for garrison duty, mounted, under arms. Near side.

FIGURE 259. Major, Sixth Cavalry (ca. 1885), in undress uniform and equipped with full pack for extended field service.

FIGURE 260. Sergeant major, Sixth Cavalry (ca. 1885), in campaign dress and equipped with full pack for field service. Near side.

FIGURE 261. Private, Sixth Cavalry (ca. 1885), in campaign dress and with full equipment for service in the field. Off side.

ommended by the cavalry equipment board of 1884, viz: Overcoat compactly rolled and strapped on pommel; blanket, with change of clothing inside, rolled in shelter-tent and strapped on cantle; nose-bag slipped over roll outside of shelter-tent, the leather bottom being pulled up snugly on the near end of roll, the strap buckled and passed over off end, the whole secured under cantle straps; side-lines to be spread out over blanket-roll and under cantle-straps, the leather ends being brought toward each other and secured; lariat rolled

around picket-pin and snapped into left rear ring, on the march to be coiled and fastened with snap to left ring, rear, the free end passing well up and under left stirrup-strap and snapped into halter-ring; canteen, with cup on strap, attached to left rear ring, pulled up snugly under blanket-roll; tin plate or meat-can, knife, fork, and spoon in off saddle-bag; curry-comb, brush, and watering bridle in near saddle-bag.

The carrying of horseshoes on riding animals to be avoided when possible. When required, however, they, the extra ammunition, and rations to be divided as to equalize the weight in each bag. When rations are not carried in the saddle-bags, the change of clothing to be so carried.

The uniform worn with the saddle packed to be the undress or field uniform.

By command of Lieutenant General Sheridan;

R. C. Drum,
Adjutant General.

Official:

MISCELLANEOUS

CAVALRY GUIDON

The Stars and Stripes swallowtailed guidon that had been adopted for cavalry in 1863 was replaced in 1885 by a pattern similar to the old dragoon-guidon pattern that had been designed for the Regiment of U.S. Dragoons in 1833.

Approved January 27, 1885, by the Secretary of War, it was prescribed as official in General Order No. 10, February 4, 1885, and was the same pattern carried by each company of the cavalry regiments until horse cavalry was abolished in 1943. The same pattern is carried today by the armor regiments. Figure 262 shows the new pattern, along with the specifications published by the Quartermaster Department.

WAR DEPARTMENT,
QUARTERMASTER GENERAL'S OFFICE.

Specifications for Cavalry Guidons.

Silk.—To be of best quality of banner silk.

Size.—To be three (3) feet five (5) inches fly from the lance and two (2) feet three (3) inches on the lance; to be cut swallow-tailed fifteen (15) inches to the fork.

Design.—Two (2) horizontal stripes, each one-half (½) the width of flag, the upper to be red and the lower white. The upper stripe to have on both sides, in the center, the number of regiment in white silk, and the lower the letter of troop in red silk. The letter and number to be block-shaped, four and three-fourths (4¾) inches high, and held in place by a border of needle-work embroidery three-sixteenths (³⁄₁₆) of an inch wide, of same color.

Lance.—To be of best quality of ash, straight grained, free from knots, and well polished. To have a nickel-plated spear-head, and at the foot a nickel-plated ferrule.

Screw-heads.—To be carefully countersunk flush with the metal, and smoothly finished.

Total length of lance nine (9) feet.

Case or cover.—To be of water-proof material, to protect the guidon when furled.

Workmanship.—To conform to standard sample on file in the Quartermaster General's Office.

CAVALRY STANDARD

In late 1883 or early 1884 the Secretary of War authorized a change in the standard for cavalry regiments. Until this time the regiments had been supplied with a banner of blue silk with the national coat of arms *painted* on its surface. But the paint did not hold up, and the War Department authorized the Quartermaster Department to start making and issuing the much more expensive *embroidered* standards to all arms.

In 1884 the manufacture of the embroidered standards began. In 1885 the quartermaster general submitted samples and specifications to the Secretary of War for a new cavalry standard to be embroidered on *yellow* silk instead of blue. Approval was given on February 4, 1886, for the new color and design, which was prescribed as official in General Order No. 31, April 13, 1887. The first issues were made subsequent to that date.

Figure 263 shows the pattern for the embroidered cavalry standard. Except for the background being yellow, it differed very little from the previous design that had been painted on a blue background.

The quartermaster general, in his report for 1889, complained about the weakening effect the painting of battle honors on standards and colors had on the silk. He announced that the General of the Army and the Secretary of War had approved his recommendation to abolish this practice and in its stead engrave the names of battles on silver rings which were to be fastened to the staffs or lances of the standards or colors.

WAR DEPARTMENT
QUARTERMASTER GENERAL'S OFFICE.

Specifications for Cavalry Standards.

Material.—To be made of a single thickness of seamless yellow banner-silk.

Dimensions.—To be four (4) feet fly, and three (3) feet on the lance.

Design.—To have the Coat of Arms of the United States as on the standard sample, and which may be described as follows:

An eagle with outstretched wings; on its breast a U. S. shield; in the right talon an olive branch with red berries and in his left ten (10) arrows bunched. A red scroll held in eagle's beak, with the motto, "E Pluribus Unum," in yellow; over the scroll a group of thirteen (13) white stars, surmounted by an arc of diverging sunrays, also in white.

Below the eagle a red scroll with the number and name of Regiment in yellow, as, for example, "3d U. S. Cavalry."

FIGURE 262. Cavalry guidon, pattern of 1885, that replaced the Stars and Stripes swallowtail that had been regulation since 1863. Now, with the same dimensions as before, the top half was red with a white regimental number, and the lower half, white with the letter of the company in red. The service guidon was made of the best-quality bunting, while the guidon used for parade and ceremony was made of the best-quality banner silk. Both had tubular waterproof fabric covers to protect them when furled. The 1885-pattern guidon was still regulation when cavalry was unhorsed early in World War II.

FIGURE 263. The new cavalry standard embroidered on yellow silk instead of blue, as before. The new pattern was approved early in 1886, but was not prescribed in a general order until April, 1887.

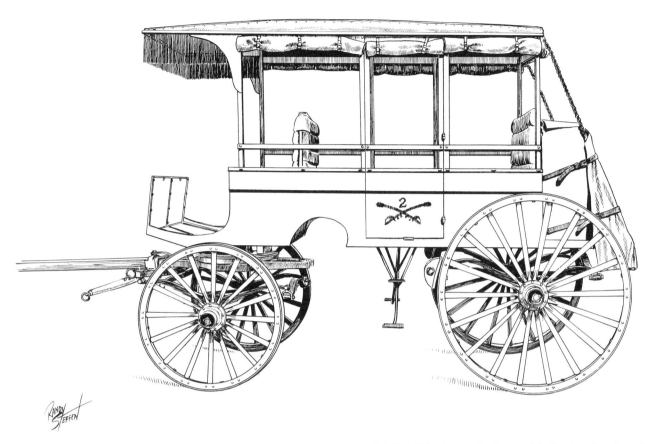

FIGURE 264. Improved Dougherty wagon, probably first used by the Army about 1885. It was listed in the "Handbook for Quartermasters" as late as 1930, although in that edition it was labeled "obsolescent," along with 7 other hand- and animal-drawn vehicles.

Embroidery.—The design, letters, and figures to be embroidered in silk, the same on both sides of the standard.

Trimming.—The standard to be trimmed on three (3) sides with U. S. silk-knotted fringe, two and one-half (2½) inches deep.

Lance.—To be of best quality of ash, straight grained, free from knots, and well polished. To have a nickel-plated spear-head, and at the foot a nickel-plated ferrule.

Screw-heads to be carefully countersunk flush with the metal and smoothly finished.

Total length of lance nine (9) feet six (6) inches.

Case or Cover.—To be of waterproof material to protect the Standard when furled.

Workmanship.—To conform in all respects to the standard sample on file in the Quartermaster General's Office.

IMPROVED DOUGHERTY WAGON

Figure 264 illustrates the improved version of the Dougherty wagon that came into use sometime in the early or mid-1880's. The bed was cut under so that a shorter turning radius was possible, and the spring suspension was generally improved to afford a more comfortable ride. The new Dougherty wagon continued to be a popular private vehicle for officers and their families. This one was drawn from a specimen in the Fort Leavenworth Post Museum.

NEW CAVALRY TACTICS (1883)

The appearance, in 1883, of a new manual of cavalry tactics brought about a number of changes for cavalry. Perhaps the most important was the redesignation of cavalry regimental units as *troops* instead of *companies*, as had been used formerly. This manual, which was written by General Phillip St. George Cooke, the father-in-law of the Confederate cavalier J. E. B. Stuart, developed from recommendations made in

53

prior years. The new double column of fours formed more compact bodies of mounted troops. In formations his manual called for the tallest men to be placed in the middle of each rank, with the rest graduated to the shortest on each flank.

MOUNTED SERVICE SCHOOL

In 1887, Congress, after much persuasion, authorized the War Department to establish a school of instruction and drill for cavalry and light artillery. This was the act of Congress approved January 29, 1887, and published in General Order No. 9, February 9, 1887.

But not until 5 years later was such a school established at Fort Riley, Kansas (March 14, 1892).

BRANDS ON PUBLIC HORSES

In the early or mid-1880's the system of branding cavalry and artillery horses was modified from that used for a decade and more. The letters *U.S.* were branded on the left shoulder, and the number of the regiment with the letter of the company above was burned on the left hip. The illustrations of the mounted cavalrymen in this chapter show the brands placed in this position.

CHAPTER TWELVE

The Little War with Spain and a New Drab Look

1890-1901

UNIFORMS

THE FIRST OFFICIAL ORDERS pertaining to the enlistment of Indians to serve as scouts for the U.S. Army were issued in 1866. At that time the Indian scouts were issued fatigue clothing only, and were required to furnish their own horses, horse equipments, and arms.

The same policy continued with respect to clothing until 1890, when the Adjutant General's Office issued Circular No. 10 on August 11. This circular prescribed for Indian scouts a dress uniform, similar to that of cavalry, only decorated with more color. In addition, specific regulations were published regarding other items of uniform and equipment, including an overcoat different from any other coat in the Army, and a distinctive guidon.

The following descriptions of Indian scout uniform and equipment items is from the published *Uniform Regulations* of the period, and were contained in all such published regulations until the change of uniform from blues to drab colors in 1902:

ENLISTED INDIAN SCOUTS.

FATIGUE HAT.

65. Of black felt, brim 3½ inches in width, crown 3½ inches high; brim to be well stiffened.

HAT CORD.

Of white worsted cord, one strand of scarlet, terminating in two tassels 1¼ inches in length, same color and material as the cord.

HAT ORNAMENT.

Two arrows crossed, to be made of nickel or some white metal, 3 inches in length, the letters U. S. S. in the upper intersection.

DARK-BLUE SHIRT.

Same as now furnished enlisted men, except that the collar is to be made deeper, to hold a neck handkerchief, as follows: Collar 2 inches wide at the back of the neck, 3½ inches in front.

OVERCOAT.

To be made of Irish frieze, or imitation of that material of some dark color, to be cut ulster shape, large and full enough to cover all accouterments; to reach within 10 inches of the ground; to be closed in front with two rows of brass buttons; to be slit well up in rear to admit of the seat in the saddle; to be provided with warm hood of same material as the coat, lined with black Italian cloth, or other suitable material, made to button around the neck, under the collar, and large enough to cover the head; to be worn at night and in inclement weather; and on each hip to have a horizontal slit covered with a flap, this for access to the revolver and ammunition. The coat to be lined throughout.

CHEVRONS AND NONCOMMISSIONED OFFICERS' STRIPES.

To be of white cloth, piped with scarlet.

TRUMPET CORD.

Of white mohair, with strand of scarlet.

GUIDON.

To be cut square, 3 feet 5 inches fly, and 2 feet 3 inches on the lance; to be made of scarlet silk, trimmed with white silk fringe 1½ inches wide; in the center and on both sides of the guidon two crossed arrows; in the upper intersection the words (in semicircle) "U. S. Scouts"; the arrows to be made of white silk, held in place by a needlework embroidery of appropriate width; letters to be embroidery, arrows 18 inches in length, letters 2 inches; in the lower intersection of the arrows there should be the letter of the troop and the name of the department to which it belongs; lance, same as prescribed for cavalry guidon, head and ferrule of nickel plate. This guidon will be used only on occasions of ceremony. There shall also be furnished to each troop a guidon similar in every respect to the foregoing, except that it shall be made of bunting and other suitable material; to be used on drills, marches, campaigns, and all other service other than occasions of ceremony. This guidon will be known as the "service guidon."

DRESS COAT.

Same as prescribed for mounted men, with facings of white, piped with scarlet.

BLOUSES.

The same as provided for enlisted men of all arms.

TROUSERS.

The same as provided for cavalry (except as prescribed above for noncommissioned officers' stripes).

HELMET.

Same as prescribed for mounted men; cords to be of white mohair with one strand of scarlet; plume to be long enough to reach 6 to 8 inches below the edge of rear visor, of white horsehair, with four strands of scarlet; ornament in front to contain crossed arrows, of white metal.

Color Plate VII shows a sergeant of Indian scouts in the prescribed dress uniform. This same uniform is also shown on Figure E of Uniform Color Plate VI (in Volume I).

Figure 265 shows the clothing and equipment described in the preceding published regulations. The special overcoat with its pointed hood is shown in color on Figure F of Uniform Color Plate VI. Its large top-opening slits that allowed the scout to draw his pistol without unbuttoning the coat are shown on Figure 265.

The only surviving specimen of the Indian scout overcoat is an unissued one, complete with pointed hood, in the collection of the Artillery and Missile Museum at Fort Sill, Oklahoma. Color of the overcoat, as shown in Figure F, Uniform Color Plate VI, is a medium gray. Both coat and detachable hood are lined with a blue material, slightly darker in shade than the sky-blue or blue-gray mixture of the uniform trousers—in spite of the specifications, which call for a lining of black cloth for the hood, at least.

Details of skirt facings and the cord on the prescribed gold-lace chevrons are shown on Figure 266.

Not many changes in uniform were adopted during this final era of the blue uniform. Changes that did occur will be treated as closely as possible in the chronological order in which they were prescribed.

Figure 267 shows the bleached muslin shirt approved for wear by enlisted men on November 13, 1890. The following specifications are from the Quartermaster Department publication covering this period:

WAR DEPARTMENT.
QUARTERMASTER GENERAL'S OFFICE.

Specifications for Muslin Shirts.

Material.—To be made of bleached muslin, fully equal to "Wamsutta, soft finish, oxx."

Style.—To be made with a single plait two and three-eighths (2⅜) inches wide, and sixteen and three-fourths (16¾) inches long, to a point, from the bottom of the neckband. Neckband to be made seven-eighths (⅞) of an inch wide at the back, and five-eighths (⅝) of an inch wide at the front when finished, and to have three button-holes well made, for studs. To be made with a yoke, two and one-fourth (2¼) inches deep at the back, four and one-half (4½) inches wide from point at side of neck to bottom, and two and three-fourths (2¾) inches wide at the end of yoke, to have two (2) button-holes, well made at the base, for studs. The opening at the back to be thirteen (13) inches long from the yoke, finished with a re-inforcing piece extending one and three-fourths (1¾) inches below the same, finished to a point, this re-inforcing piece to be one (1) inch wide at the top, and one and three-fourths (1¾) inches wide at the bottom. Wristbands to be three ply, and made in the form of a cuff, two and three-fourths (2¾) inches deep, with corners rounded, and a well made button-hole, for studs, at each side of the base of each cuff. The opening at the sleeves to be six (6) inches long above the wristband, and finished with a re-inforcing piece seven and one-fourth (7¼) inches long and one and one-fourth (1¼) inches wide next the wristband and one and one-half (1½) inches wide at the end. The opening at the sides of the shirts to be finished with gussets doubled over and securely stitched. The sleeves to be inserted with a three-fourths (¾) inch overlap-seam.

Workmanship.—All stitching to be done in the best manner with straight, sightly and perfect seams. To be equal in all respects to the standard sample.

Adopted November 13, 1890.

R. N. BATCHELDER,
Quartermaster General, U. S. A.

Figure 268 illustrates the chevrons for cavalry noncommissioned ranks and grades that were regulation in 1892. The following specifications describe their construction and dimensions:

WAR DEPARTMENT,
QUARTERMASTER GENERAL'S OFFICE.

Specifications for Cloth Chevrons and Brassards.

Cloth.—The cloth forming the groundwork for arms, arcs, and ties of chevrons to be of facing cloth (conforming to published specifications) of the same color as the facings of the uniform coat, except in the case of the Infantry overcoat chevron, when it will be of dark-blue cloth.

The cloth forming the groundwork for chevron devices to be the same as that for the uniform coat. For Pioneers and Farriers device to be cut about nine (9) by five and one-half (5½) inches; and for all other devices to be cut in shape of a quadrant of a circle having a radius of from four (4) to six (6) inches (as size of device may require), the straight sides of pieces to be neatly stitched to the under side of the upper edge of cloth of arms; the nap of the cloth to run downward when the chevron is on the sleeve.

FIGURE 265. Enlisted Indian scouts (ca. 1890) in the uniforms prescribed for them in Circular No. 10, dated August 11, 1890. The peculiar mixture of warrior splendor and military dress is shown here. The scout at left wears the special overcoat with separate hood made just for the Indian scouts. The warrior next to him wears the scout overcoat and other military garb, but retains the breech cloth, leggings, and moccasins. The center scout wears the special scout shirt with oversize collar, regulation campaign hat with Indian scout insignia, Army trousers, and cavalry boots. At right is a first sergeant of scouts in full-dress uniform, faced with white cloth piped with scarlet. The guidon is the prescribed one with white letters and arrows on a scarlet ground. Drawn from specimens in the author's collection and in the National Museum.

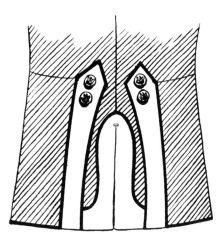

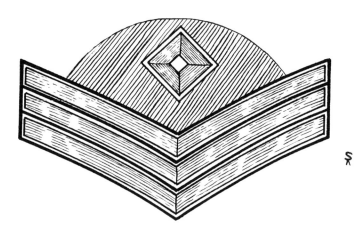

FIGURE 266. Details of skirt facings and gold-lace chevrons on the dress coat of the enlisted Indian scouts. The heavy black lines indicate scarlet piping. The fine diagonal lines indicate the dark blue uniform cloth.

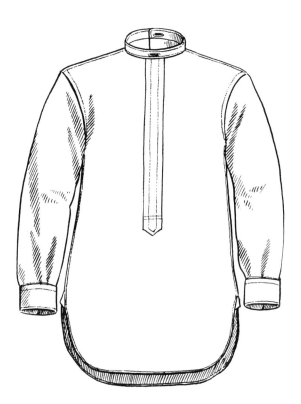

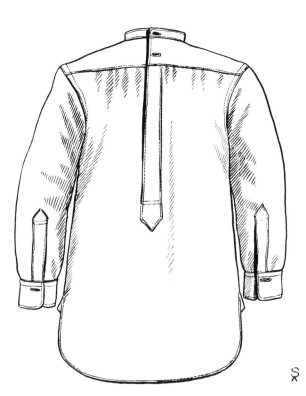

FIGURE 267. Bleached muslin shirt approved for issue to enlisted men near the end of 1890. It was to be worn under the blouse and under the dress coat. The linen collar authorized in 1888 was attached to the shirt with studs, and studs were used to fasten the cuffs.

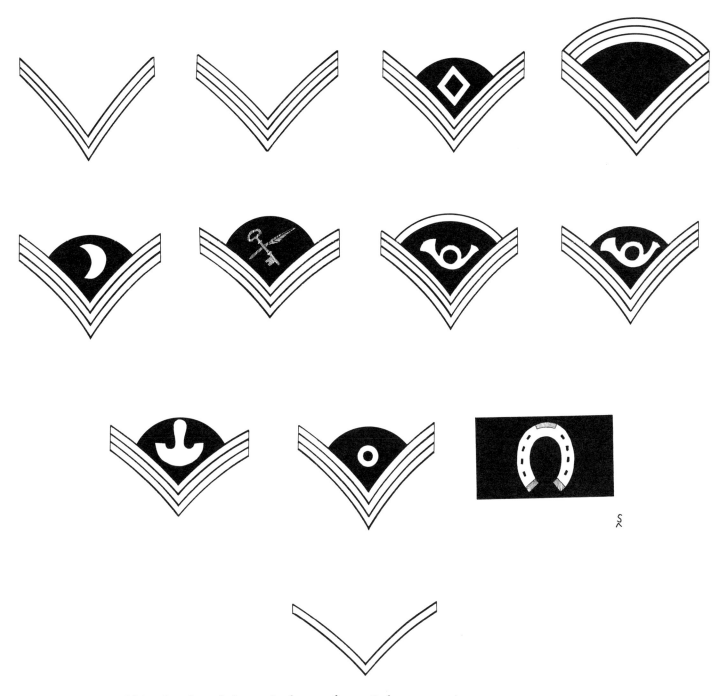

FIGURE 268. Additional ranks and changes in chevrons for noncommissioned officers of cavalry adopted March 7, 1892. Top row: corporal, sergeant, first sergeant, sergeant major. 2nd row: commissary sergeant, post quartermaster sergeant, chief trumpeter, principal musician. 3rd row: saddler sergeant, color sergeant, farrier. Bottom: lance corporal.

The cloth forming the background of devices to be of facing cloth of same color of facings of the uniform coat.

Bars and Arms.—The bars of the chevron to be outlined on the groundwork of facing cloth in rows of heavy stitching of No. 8 silk, the upper and lower edges to be finished with similar stitching.

White stitching for Engineers, Hospital Stewards, acting Hospital Stewards, Sergeants of the Signal Corps, and for overcoats for Infantry. Red stitching for Indian Scouts, and black for all others.

The arms of the chevron bars to be six (6) to seven (7) inches long, to be the arcs of a circle of about twenty-five (25) inches radius, and to meet at an angle of about ninety-six (96) degrees; distance between extreme outer ends about nine (9) inches.

Designs for Chevrons—Sergeant Major.—Three bars and an arc of three bars. The upper edge of outer bar of arc to be the arc of a circle of about seven and one-fourth (7¼) inches radius.

Quartermaster Sergeant.—Three bars and a tie of three bars. The upper bar of tie to extend horizontally from the extreme outer end of one arm of the chevron to that of the other.

Saddler Sergeant.—Three bars and a saddler's round knife, handle upward. Knife of the following dimensions: Handle one and three-fourths (1¾) inches long, three-fourths (¾) inch wide near top; five-eighths (⅝) inch near blade; blade one and one-eighth (1⅛) inches deep in center; from point to point of blade three and one-fourth (3¼) inches; center of edge one and one-fourth (1¼) inches above inner angle of chevron.

Chief Trumpeter.—Three bars and an arc of one bar, with bugle of pattern worn on cap about one and one-half (1½) inches above inner angle of chevron. The upper edge of bar of arc to be the arc of a circle of about seven and one-fourth (7¼) inches radius. Bugle to be of form, dimensions, and finish of the standard sample chevron.

Principal Musician.—Three bars and a bugle. The bugle to be the same as for Chief Trumpeter's chevrons.

Post Quartermaster Sergeant.—Three bars, and a crossed pen and key, embroidered in gold-colored silk. The key and pen to cross about two and one-half (2½) inches above the inner angle of the chevron, and to be of form, dimensions, and finish of standard sample chevron.

Commissary Sergeant.—Three bars and a crescent (points front). Distance from point to point of crescent, two (2) inches; width in center, three-fourths (¾) of one inch; center of lower edge to be about one and three-fourths (1¾) inches above inner angle of chevron.

1st Sergeant.—Three bars and an outlined lozenge, having sides about one-fourth (¼) of an inch wide. Lozenge about two and one-half (2½) inches long and two (2) inches wide, placed lengthwise about one and one-fourth (1¼) inches above inner angle of chevron.

Sergeant.—Three bars.

Regimental and Battalion Color Sergeant.—Three bars

and a sphere one-fourth (¼) of an inch wide, one and one-fourth (1¼) inches in outside diameter, and placed one and three-fourths (1¾) inches above inner angle of chevron.

Corporal.—Two bars.

Lance Corporal.—One bar.

Farrier.—A horseshoe three-fourths (¾) of an inch wide, about four and one-half (4½) inches long from outer edge of toe-piece to a line between extreme points of heels; between outer lines across center, about three and three-fourths (3¾) inches; between extreme points of heels, about two (2) inches. A toe-piece about one and three-fourths (1¾) inches long, one-half (½) inch deep, and two (2) heel-pieces about one-half (½) by three-fourths (¾) inch each, of gray facing cloth, to be stitched on. Four (4) nail-holes on each side of the shoe, at equal distances from each other, to be underlaid with blue cloth.

Workmanship.—To be in accordance with standard samples adopted this day.

Adopted March 7, 1892, in lieu of specifications of June 10, 1889, which are hereby canceled. The specifications for brassards adopted June 30, 1885, and December 27, 1889, are also canceled.

R. N. BATCHELDER,
Quartermaster General, U. S. A.

Figure 269 shows the pattern for the officer's undress coat prescribed by the 1892 regulations (See Figure G on Uniform Color Plate VI in Volume I). Again all officers were required to purchase coats as soon as their present ones wore out. This was the most ornate undress coat in the Army since 1812. But this coat was too elaborate to be practical, and in 1895 it was stripped of most of its braid to give way to a new pattern that was standard until after World War I. The slits in the sides of the skirts were like those on the 1872-pattern undress coat. The sword belt was worn *under* the coat, with the sword hook outside.

Insignia prescribed for the collar of the 1892 undress coat, in addition to the shoulder straps, was the number of the regiment in white metal on each side of the collar, as shown on Figure G, Uniform Color Plate VI (in Volume I) and on Figure 269.

The 1895 regulations prescribed shoulder straps for the undress blouse, as well as crossed gilt sabers, with the number of the regiment in the upper angle, and the letters *U.S.* in gilt metal placed on each side of the collar, as shown on Figure H of Uniform Color Plate VI and in Figure 274.

The following is from the uniform regulations published for the Army:

UNDRESS COATS FOR ALL OFFICERS.

2. For Fatigue Duty and Ordinary Wear.—A single-

FIGURE 269. Officer's undress dark blue coat, pattern of 1892, with flat-black mohair-braid trim on front, back, and sleeves. The blind button holes and frogs on the breast, the knot on the sleeve, and the decorations on the back seams are ½-inch braid; the braid on the edges of the coat, the side slits, and the collar, is 1¼ inch. In 1895 the braid was removed from the breast, sleeves, and back, but the cut of the coat and the wide braid remained the same.

breasted sack coat of dark-blue cloth or serge, with standing collar fastened with hook and eye; coat to close with a flap containing suitable concealed fastenings, the skirt to extend from one-third to two-thirds the distance from the hip joint to the bend of the knee, according to height of wearer; cut to fit the figure easily; a vertical opening at each side of hip according to pattern; shoulder straps and collar insignia to be worn. The coat to be trimmed with lustrous black mohair flat braid as follows: Edged all around the bottom, the front edges, the collar, and for six inches upward from the bottom

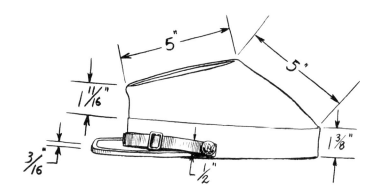

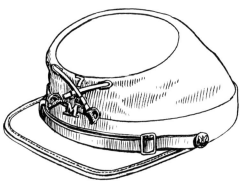

FIGURE 270. The 1892-pattern forage cap for enlisted men. Slightly modified from the cap specified in 1889, it was higher in front and slightly longer in the back. It was the same chasseur style as the pattern issued in 1872.

along both side openings to the skirt, with braid 1¼ inches wide. This coat will be worn when full dress is not required. During the warm season post commanders may authorize this coat made of white duck or flannel, to be worn with white braid, but without shoulder straps or collar insignia.

On undress duty a plain leather belt will be worn under the undress coat, the sword hook emerging through the opening of the coat on the left side. For field service, or when the pistol is carried, the belt will be worn outside the undress coat when so-directed by the commanding officer.

FOR FIELD DUTY—FOR GENERAL OFFICERS.—A blouse of dark-blue cloth or serge with four outside pockets with flaps; rolling collar, double-breasted, with two rows of buttons, grouped according to rank, same kind as those worn on dress coat. The skirt to extend from one-third to one-half the distance from the hip joint to the bend of the knee. The shoulder straps will always be worn with this coat.

FOR ALL OTHER OFFICERS.—A blouse of dark-blue cloth or serge with four outside pockets with flaps; falling collar, single-breasted, with five buttons in front, same kind as those worn on the dress coat. The skirt to extend from one-third to one-half the distance from the hip joint to the bend of the knee. The shoulder-straps will always be worn with this coat.

INSIGNIA.—For the officers' undress coats above described, will be as follows:

The letters "U. S.", gothic design (U. S. V. for volunteers), of suitable height, each followed by a period, embroidered in gold or made of gold or gilt metal, except for the Corps of Engineers, which will be embroidered in silver or made of silver, worn on each side of the collar, 1 inch from its edge and midway of its height, with distinctive insignia of suitable height, embroidered or made of metal, worn on each side of the collar about ⅝ inch from the letters "U. S.", as follows:

CAVALRY.—Two crossed sabers, 1 inch high, with number of regiment above intersection, of gold or gilt metal or embroidered in gold.

WAR DEPARTMENT,
QUARTERMASTER GENERAL'S OFFICE.

Specifications for Forage Caps.

Cloth.—To be made of wool-dyed indigo-blue cloth, fifty-four (54) inches wide, and to weigh not less than thirteen (13) ounces to the linear-yard; to contain forty-eight (48) threads to the inch in the warp, and forty-six (46) threads to the inch in the filling; to be capable of sustaining a strain of twenty-six (26) pounds to the inch in the warp and eighteen (18) pounds to the inch in the filling, and to be well sponged without refinishing before being made up into caps.

Band.—The band to be about one and three-eighths (1⅜) inches wide, strengthened by a strap of strong split leather of same width, and not less than one-sixteenth (1/16) inch in thickness all around, molded to fit the shape of the head, coated on the convex side all around with shellac or varnish, and to be sewed in between the cloth and sweat leather.

Front.—The front to rise above the surface of the visor (including the exposed portion of the band), straight and vertical, three (3) inches, the sides slightly converging from the band to the crown.

Back.—The back to be slightly convex, five (5) inches long from the band, from which it rises at an angle of forty-five (45) degrees to the crown.

Crown.—The crown to be circular and to show five (5) inches in diameter when finished; to be made upon strong "tarred board," thoroughly seasoned to prevent warping, and to be wholly covered on the inside with black enameled mus-

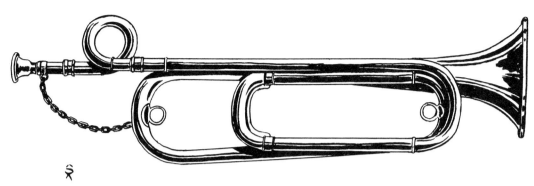

FIGURE 271. The 1892 G trumpet with detachable F crook, as issued to cavalry. This trumpet replaced the 1879 model with the much larger C crook. The rings soldered to the trumpet are for attaching the cord and tassels.

lin. The shape of the cap would thus give an incline to the crown of about one (1) inch from the rear to the front.

Visor.—To have a straight horizontal visor of patent enameled leather, black above and green underneath, about three-sixteenths (³⁄₁₆) of an inch thick, bound with fine black enameled leather, and shaped to conform to the standard sample.

Trimmings.—A small regulation button (line or staff, as may be required) on each side, immediately behind the ends of the visor, for chin-strap. The side buttons to be fire-gilt. The chin-strap to be made of good enameled leather in two (2) parts; each part about nine (9) inches long and one-half (½) inch wide, and fitted with a stout fire-gilt slide on the end of the under part, and leather keeper on the end of the upper part, through which the end, finished to a point, will project about one-half (½) an inch, to permit the strap to be adjusted at will. Sweat leather of Belgian leather, one and three-eighths (1⅜) inches wide when finished. Lining of strong black satin, fastened by its lower edge only, to the inner stiffening of the band; the upper edge gathered with strong thread over an elastic cord. Each cap to be finished with a loop of black mohair or worsted braid, one-eighth (⅛) of an inch wide, and securely fastened under the sweat leather at the back seam.

Materials, workmanship, and finish to conform to standard sample.

Adopted April 12, 1892, in lieu of specifications of March 19, 1890, which are hereby canceled.

R. N. BATCHELDER,
Quartermaster General, U. S. A.

WAR DEPARTMENT,
QUARTERMASTER GENERAL'S OFFICE.

Specifications for Trumpets and "F" Crooks.

Trumpets.—To be made of what is known as special, first-class quality trumpet brass, twenty-three (23) gauge,

strengthened at the outer edge of the bell by three-sixteenths (³⁄₁₆) of an inch solid half round brass wire; the stay of the tuning slide to be of solid half round three-sixteenths (³⁄₁₆) of an inch brass wire, fitted to the inner side of the bow, and soldered to the ferrule with hard silver solder; the back stay to be of solid wire, concave on either side, two (2) inches long, of three-sixteenths (³⁄₁₆) of an inch brass wire. To have two (2) brass rings of number nine (9) wire with one-half (½) of an inch opening, secured to three-fourths (¾) of an inch circular plates, soldered on for the trumpet cord, one at the inner portion of the top bend, and the other on the inner portion of the lower bend. The mouth ferrule to be of double thickness of tubing, about one and one-eighth (1⅛) inches long, fitting exactly the taper of the mouth-piece shank. The bell portion to be of the best hammered brass.

Each trumpet to have two (2) brass nickel-plated mouth-pieces of separate and distinct sizes; the largest size to be attached to the trumpet by a six and one-half (6½) inch nickel-plated chain.

Each trumpet to be built in the key of "G;" the slide to draw to "F," and marked and stamped with the letter "F" at the correct point to produce the key of "F." Each instrument must be made on the prototype system in order to insure a perfect equality of tone.

The trumpet, including chain and one mouth-piece, to weigh not less than seventeen and one-half (17½) ounces, the diameter of the bell to be four and three-eighths (4⅜) inches; the extreme length to be about fifteen (15) inches, not including mouth-piece; extreme width to be about four (4) inches; the entire instrument to have a thorough brass-instrument polish.

"F" Crooks.—The metal to be the same as described for the trumpet; to be about nine and one-fourth (9¼) inches long formed into a single coil, one end projecting and reinforced with a ferrule one-half (½) of an inch deep, to receive the mouth-piece; the other end properly tapered to fit the tubing of the trumpet, and adjusted thereto to produce the key of "F."

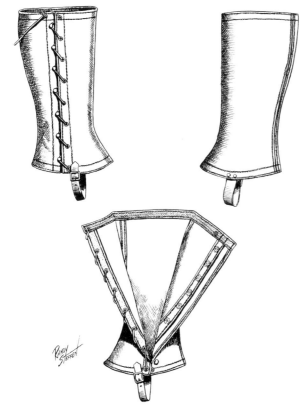

FIGURE 272. The patented leggings for mounted troops adopted February 20, 1894, by the Army. This was the first deviation from leather boots for cavalry in the Army's history. Bidders were advised that any royalties required to be paid to the patentee were to be paid by the contractor. It was the method of fastening by laces and studs (hooks) that was under patent. The leggings were made of 15-ounce brown cotton duck reinforced by strips of tanned horsehide and were manufactured in 3 sizes for issue.

All to be like and equal to the standard samples.
Adopted May 2, 1892, in lieu of specifications of February 15, 1879, which are hereby canceled.

R. N. BATCHELDER,
Quartermaster General,
U. S. Army.

WAR DEPARTMENT,
QUARTERMASTER GENERAL'S OFFICE.

Specifications for Canvas Leggins for Mounted Troops.

Material.—To be made of fifteen (15) ounce cotton duck, conforming to specifications and standard sample, and to be dyed a brown color to shade of standard sample.

Measurements.—To be made in three (3) sizes, and numbered 1, 2, and 3. Measurements as follows, which are taken when the leggin is fastened up snugly to the studs, viz:

No. 1.

Height at edge of front piece along leather stay when finished, fourteen and one-half (14½) inches.

Width at top around calf, outside measurement, fifteen and one-eighth (15⅛) inches.

Width around ankle, outside measurement, eleven and three-eighths (11⅜) inches.

Width around bottom, outside measurement, fifteen and seven-eighths (15⅞) inches.

No. 2

Height at edge of front piece along leather stay when finished, fifteen and one-half (15½) inches.

Width at top around calf, outside measurement, fifteen and one-half (15½) inches.

Width around ankle, outside measurement, eleven and three-quarter (11¾) inches.

Width around bottom, outside measurement, sixteen and one-quarter (16¼) inches.

No. 3

Height at edge of front piece along leather stay when finished, sixteen and one-half (16½) inches.

Width at top around calf, outside measurement, sixteen (16) inches.

Width around ankle, outside measurement, twelve and one-quarter (12¼) inches.

Width around bottom, outside measurement, sixteen and three-quarter (16¾) inches.

Workmanship.—Seams to be not less than one-fourth (¼) inch wide, stayed on the inside with good quality one-half (½) inch shoe-stay webbing, stitched on each edge with No. 30 cotton. Top and bottom edges to be faced with same quality material, five-eighths (⅝) inch wide, with double row of stitching of same number of cotton. The front piece to be faced on the inside along its edge with a strip of best quality tanned horse-hide, one (1) inch wide, and sizes 1 and 2 to be fitted with eight (8) one-fourth (¼) inch grommets, and size 3 with nine (9) one-fourth (¼) inch grommets, placed at equal distances. The back piece to be reinforced on the inside with a strip of best quality tanned horse-hide, one (1) inch wide, and sizes 1 and 2 to be fitted with seven (7) long brass studs, and size 3 with eight (8) long brass studs placed at equal distances and firmly clinched. The leggins to fasten with a braided cotton cord running through the grommets and around the studs. An eyelet to be placed at the bottom of back piece of the leggins where the lacing starts, and a grommet at the top to fasten the end of the cord. To have a strap at bottom, of horse-hide leather, seven and one-half (7½) inches long, fastened on the inside of leggin by one (1) row of stitching and two (2) copper rivets, and the outside by means of a buckle to be secured to the leggin with a metal strap; three (3) holes to be punched on end of strap to receive tongue of buckle.

Finish.—To conform in all respects to the sealed standard samples.

Adopted February 20, 1894.

R. N. BATCHELDER,
Quartermaster General, U. S. A.

NOTE.—It is understood that the mode of fastening the standard leggins is protected by letters patent, therefore bidders will be required to make their proposals with the understanding that payment of royalty, if any, is to be assumed by the contractor. Bids upon patterns differing from the established standard may also be made, in which case samples must accompany the proposals.

WAR DEPARTMENT,
QUARTERMASTER-GENERAL'S OFFICE.

Specifications for Forage Caps.

Cloth.—To be made of dark blue cloth, wool-dyed indigo, unless otherwise authorized by the purchasing officer; to be fifty-four (54) inches wide; to weigh not less than fourteen (14) ounces to the linear yard; to contain sixty-two (62) threads to the inch in the warp, and fifty-eight (58) threads to the inch in the filling; to be capable of sustaining a strain of not less than thirty-two (32) pounds to the inch in the warp, and twenty-eight (28) pounds to the inch in the filling; the cloth to be well sponged without refinishing, before being made up into caps.

Band.—The band to be one and one-half (1½) inches wide, formed by the material of the body of the cap, between two welts, each welt at top and bottom projecting one-eighth (⅛) inch, the bottom welt being one-eighth (⅛) inch above the base of the cap; the band to be strengthened by a strap of strong split leather, about one-sixteenth (1/16) inch thickness all around, and two and one-quarter (2¼) inches wide, sewed in between the sweat band and the body of the cap with the lining of the cap between the two.

The height of the cap to be three and one-quarter (3¼) inches all around the seam around the top without a welt and neatly stitched on each side; the diameter of the top from right to left to be six and one-half (6½) inches, and from front to back seven and five-eighths (7⅝) inches.

Visor.—To have a slanting visor of patent enameled leather, black above and green underneath, about one-eighth (⅛) inch thick, and bound with black patent leather to a depth of about three-sixteenths (3/16) inch, neatly stitched; the width of the visor from the lower edge of the cap to the inner edge of the binding at its widest part to be one and three-quarters (1¾) inches, and the entire visor to be moulded to shape.

Trimmings.—A small regulation button on each side immediately behind the ends of the visor for chin straps; the side buttons to be fire gilt; the chin strap to be made of good enameled leather in two parts, each part about ten (10) inches long and one-half (½) inch wide, fitted with a stout fire gilt slide on the end of the under part, and a leather keeper on the end of the upper part, through which the end finished to a point will project about one-half (½) inch, to permit the strap to be adjusted at will; the sweat leather to be of Belgian leather, about one and seven-eighths (1⅞) inches wide, turned on the upper edge and properly cemented; the lining of strong black satin, cut and shaped to the inner body of the

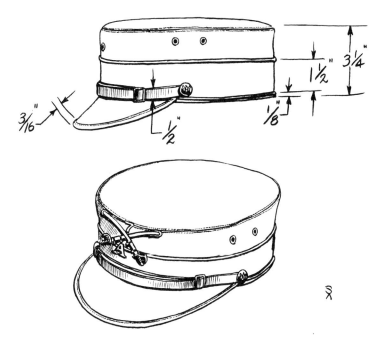

FIGURE 273. The 1895-pattern forage cap—completely different from any cap the Army had ever had. It replaced the chasseur-style forage cap that had been regulation since 1872, for both officers and enlisted men; the one shown here is for enlisted men. Drawn from a specimen in the author's collection.

cap, the crown of the lining to be made with an interlining of black muslin of good quality, there being an interlining of hair cloth of good quality, cut and shaped to the entire inner portion of the crown of the cap, extending from the top to the lower edge of the body of the cap between the band and stiffening and the body. Each cap to have four (4) black metal eyelets for ventilation, two (2) on each side, placed above the band, the center of each eyelet to be about five-eighths (⅝) inch from the upper seam of the cap and one and one-half (1½) inches apart from each other. Each cap to be finished with a loop of black Mohair or worsted braid not less than one-eighth (⅛) inch wide, and securely fastened under the sweat leather at the back of same.

The above specifications based on cap size 7⅛. Materials, workmanship, and finish to conform to standard sample.

Adopted September 5, 1895, in lieu of Specifications of April 12, 1892 (No. 324), which are hereby canceled.

GEO. H. WEEKS,
Assistant Quartermaster-General, U. S. Army,
Acting Quartermaster-General.

The 1895 uniform regulations brought about a drastic change in the style and pattern of forage caps for the entire army, officers and enlisted men alike. Figure 273 shows the new cap with its squared-off top. The pattern for officers was like that for enlisted men, but instead of the cap body being made entirely of dark blue cloth it had a band of lustrous black mohair above the visor, and a yellow silk cord as a chin strap instead of the patent-leather strap prescribed for the enlisted men's version.

Figure 274 shows this cap pattern for both the summer white undress uniform and the dark blue undress blouse for ordinary wear. (See also Figure H on Uniform Color Plate VI in Volume I.)

The officer's dark blue cap had embroidered on the front the national coat of arms in gilt thread, while the white summer version was worn without any ornament except the yellow silk-cord chin strap.

The 1897 uniform regulations provided for the wearing of certain badges on the dress-uniform coat for officers and enlisted men, as well as giving additional specifications concerning band uniforms. The following are those parts of the published regulations pertaining to the above:

62. BADGES OF MILITARY SOCIETIES.—Officers and enlisted men who, in their own right or by right of inheritance, are members of military societies of men who served in the armies and navies of the United States in the war of the Revolution, the war of 1812, the Mexican war, and the war of the rebellion, or are members of the Regular Army and Navy Union of the United States, may wear on all occasions of ceremony, when full dress is required, the distinctive badges adopted by such societies—badges to be worn on the left breast of the coat suspended by a ribbon from a bar of metal passed through their upper ends, and tops of the ribbons forming a horizontal line, the outer end of which will be from 3 to 4 inches below the top of the shoulder, according to height of wearer. Medals of honor and the several distinctive marks given for excellence in rifle practice may also be worn in the same manner by officers and enlisted men upon all occasions of ceremony. Insignia "buttons" will not be worn.

63. Bands will wear the general uniform of their regiments. Commanding officers may, upon appropriations made by the councils of administration, add such ornaments as they deem proper. Upon proper application they will be supplied by the Quartermaster's Department with mounted helmets, having cords and bands and hair plumes conforming in color to the arms of service, and lyres of white metal, aiguillettes with shoulder knots, music pouches, and white summer trousers, to be worn, upon such occasions as may be prescribed by the commanding officer.

64. Articles of band uniforms, including music pouches,

that do not form part of the annual clothing allowance, may be issued but not charged, except in case of loss or damage. The articles thus issued without charge remain the property of the United States.

These same regulations also prescribed that all mounted officers wear either white gloves or white leather gauntlets.

The 1899 uniform regulations reflected the changes made in uniform policy during the Spanish-American War in Cuba. The first deviation from the blue uniform was seen in this war, when most of the volunteer regiments were clothed with khaki cloth of varying patterns. Now, for the first time, the Regular Army units were to be issued drab-colored clothing, certainly less conspicuous and making poorer targets in combat conditions than the traditional blues.

The 1899 regulations provided a different style of dark blue serge *field service blouse* for officers, as shown in Figure A of Uniform Color Plate VII (in Volume I) and in Figure 277. The description of this new blouse is as follows, as quoted from the 1899 regulations:

FOR ALL OTHER OFFICERS.—A blouse of dark-blue cloth or serge with four outside pockets with flaps; falling collar, single-breasted, with five buttons in front, same kind as those worn on the dress coat. The skirt to extend from one-third to one-half the distance from the hip joint to the bend of the knee. The shoulder-straps will always be worn with this coat.

INSIGNIA.—For the officers' undress coats above described, will be as follows:

The letters "U. S.", gothic design (U. S. V. for volunteers), of suitable height, each followed by a period, embroidered in gold or made of gold or gilt metal, except for the Corps of Engineers, which will be embroidered in silver or made of silver, worn on each side of the collar, 1 inch from its edge and midway of its height, with distinctive insignia of suitable height, embroidered or made of metal, worn on each side of the collar about ⅝ inch from the letters "U.S.", as follows:

CAVALRY.—Two crossed sabers, 1 inch high, with number of regiment above intersection, of gold or gilt metal, or embroidered in gold.

A new field uniform for officers was also prescribed in these regulations. The officer at the right in Figure 277 wears this khaki blouse and trousers, as the Quartermaster specifications call them (the 1899 regulations call them breeches). The following is from the 1899 regulations pertaining to this new officer dress:

66

FIGURE 274. Left: the white undress uniform authorized for officers about 1895. Cut to the same pattern as the dark blue undress sack coat on the second lieutenant, right, the summer coat of white duck or flannel was trimmed with flat white braid in the same manner as the blue serge coat. The white coat was worn without shoulder straps and without ornaments of any kind, as was the white forage cap, whose sole embellishment was its yellow cord between the gilt buttons. Not until 1901 were rank insignia on shoulder loops and collar ornaments authorized on the white coat.

Right: the dark blue serge undress coat, 1895 pattern, was cut exactly like the 1892 pattern, but the half-inch flat braid loops and knots on the breast, sleeves, and seams on the back of the coat were eliminated. This same pattern of coat became the officer "dress" coat when the general uniform change took place in 1902. The forage caps are the pattern of 1895.

FIGURE 275. Medals and badges for excellence in small-arms firing, cast in white metal. They were first issued to both officers and enlisted men ca. 1895. New-pattern badges were prescribed for the Army in 1921. Drawn from specimens in the author's collection.

FIELD UNIFORMS.

4. The following-described garments, in addition to the prescribed uniform now worn, are also authorized:

(a) BLOUSE.

FOR ALL COMMISSIONED OFFICERS.—For field service a blouse of cotton drilling or khaki, light-brown color, made with a single plait 2 inches wide in the back and extending from the collar to the end of the skirt; with two outside breast pockets and two outside pockets below the waist; pockets covered by flaps, buttoned by a small regulation brass button; the breast pockets to have a plait in the middle ¾ inch wide. The coat to have standing collar, fastened by two hooks and eyes, from 1½ inches to 2 inches in width, depending on wearer; a strap on each shoulder reaching from the sleeve seam to the collar seam and buttoning at the upper point with a small brass regulation button; straps to be 1½ inches wide at sleeve and 1 inch wide at collar. Coat to be buttoned by five regulation buttons of the arm of the service. The straps to be of same material as coat and of the color of the facings of the arm.

INSIGNIA.—All officers below the grade of colonel to wear the insignia of their grade on the shoulder strap, about one-third distant from the shoulder seam to the collar; and midway between the insignia of grade and the collar will be worn, on the strap, the coat of arms of the United States, 1¼ inches high, according to design.

For all officers of the grade of colonel and above the insignia of rank only will be worn on the strap; the coat of arms to be worn on each side of the collar, in front of any other collar ornament.

All officers will wear on each side of the collar the prescribed insignia of their corps or arm of service, according to pattern.

The letters "U. S." (or "U. S. V.") will not be worn on the khaki blouse.

All insignia of grade and corps or arm of service worn on the khaki blouse will be of metal and detachable.

SHOULDER STRAPS.—The color of the shoulder straps on the khaki blouse for the several arms of the service will be as follows:

General officers and officers of the general staff, corps, and departments, dark blue.

Infantry, sky-blue.

Cavalry, yellow.

Artillery, scarlet.

(b) TROUSERS.

FOR DISMOUNTED OFFICERS.—Trousers of cotton drilling or khaki, same color as blouse, without stripes, to fit loosely above and at the knee, and follow the shape of the leg from above the calf to the top of the shoe, fastened by buttons, etc.

FOR MOUNTED SERVICE.—Breeches made of cotton drilling or khaki, same color as blouse, without stripes, to be made loose above the knee, fitting close at knee and below, extending to top of shoes and fastened with buttons; to be worn with shoes and leggings or boots.

This uniform is shown in color on Figure B of Uniform Color Plate VII (in Volume I).

During the Spanish-American War (1898) the regular cavalry regiments serving in Cuba and the Philippines wore blue shirts or blouses and sky-blue trousers with khaki leggings (often spelled "leggins" during the early years of their use) and black shoes, although some photos of that period show what appears to be khaki trousers on some troopers. The 1897 regulations contain no mention of khaki trousers.

The volunteer cavalry units sent to Cuba were issued roughly made blouses and trousers of brown or khaki material, and these earth-colored clothes no doubt influenced the change from blues to khaki in 1899.

Figure 278 shows the pattern of the new field uni-

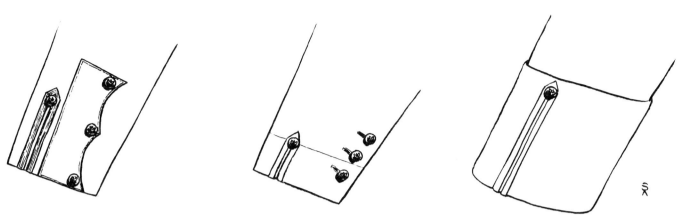

FIGURE 276. The stripes prescribed for enlisted candidates for promotion ca. 1897 "will be worn on the upper-half of each cuff and will consist of a double stripe running the length of the cuff, pointed at the upper end, and with a small button below the point of the stripe; for uniform coat [left], of gold braid; for blouse [center] and overcoat [right], of cloth of same color as facings of uniform; width of cloth or braid ¼ inch; width of space between stripes ⅛ inch." ("1897 Uniform of the U.S. Army, Regulations and Decisions.")

form prescribed for enlisted men in the 1899 uniform regulations.

There was no insignia prescribed for wear on the campaign hat for enlisted men that year. Some yellow shoulder straps were issued that attached to the khaki straps on the issue uniform, but others, of yellow cloth, were let into the shoulder seams and were a permanent part of the blouse.

The following paragraphs are from the 1899 uniform regulations, and describe the blouse, trousers, leggings, shoes, hat, and other items of clothing issued to the enlisted men for this period:

FIELD UNIFORMS.

(a) BLOUSE.

37. ALL ENLISTED MEN.—For field service, a blouse of cotton drilling or khaki, light brown color, conforming to pattern in office of the Quartermaster General. To be provided with shoulder straps, of color for the several arms of the service, as follows:

Infantry, light sky-blue.
Cavalry, yellow.
Artillery, scarlet.
Engineers, scarlet piped with white.
Post Quartermaster Sergeant, white piped with buff.
Ordnance, crimson piped with white.
Post Commissary Sergeant, white piped with cadet gray.
Electrician Sergeant, scarlet.

Signal Corps, black piped with white.
Hospital Corps, emerald green.

(b) TROUSERS.

ALL ENLISTED MEN.—For field service, trousers of cotton drilling or khaki, light-brown color, without stripes, conforming to pattern in office of Quartermaster General. Mounted troops to have a reenforce or saddle piece of the same material on seat and legs.

(c) SHOES.

ALL ENLISTED MEN.—For field service, shoes of russet leather.

CANVAS FATIGUE CLOTHING.

38. ALL ENLISTED MEN.—Of brown cotton duck, according to pattern in the office of the Quartermaster General. The suit to consist of coat and trousers. It will be worn as a working dress on extra, daily, or fatigue duty, and charged at the regulation prices.

SUSPENDERS.

39. There will be provided for issue annually to each enlisted man of the Army one pair of suspenders, according to pattern in the office of the Quartermaster General.

BOOTS AND SHOES.

40. The Quartermaster's Department manufactures the boots and shoes for the Army of the best materials and patterns possible. No particular pattern is adopted as *uniform*.

FIGURE 277. Left: major, Third Cavalry (ca. 1899). He wears the new dark blue serge field-service blouse for officers prescribed in the 1899 uniform regulations. Worn with the new blouse are the usual sky-blue trousers with the 1½-inch yellow stripe up the outer seam of each leg and the regulation 1889-pattern black boots with stiffened tops.

Right: captain, Third Cavalry, wearing the new khaki field-service blouse made of cotton drilling. The single 2-inch plait up the back and the yellow shoulder straps are distinguishing features. With it are worn the new officer-pattern field-service trousers made of khaki cotton drilling, made exactly like those of the enlisted men but of finer material—cut loose above the knee, but tight below the knee to the ankle. Without stripes, they are worn with the officer pattern of black boots. Hats are regulation drab-color campaign pattern with black-and-gold silk hat cords.

70

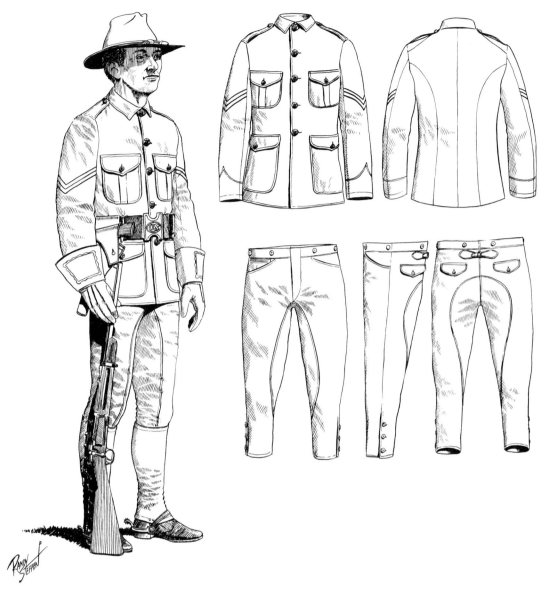

FIGURE 278. Khaki field uniform for enlisted men (ca. 1899). Developed during the Spanish-American War, this practical blouse and trousers (not yet officially termed "breeches" by the Army) were made of khaki cotton drilling and marked the Army's first real departure from traditional Army blue. Yellow shoulder straps identified the wearer as a cavalryman at a glance. The trouser legs were cut full to the knee, then followed the shape of the leg from the calf to the top of the shoe, where they fastened with 3 buttons. Canvas leggings were usually worn with this field uniform, the leather cavalry boots being reserved for wear with the blue uniforms. Two years later (1901) a directive made it mandatory to wear shoes and leggings with the khaki field dress. This corporal is armed with the recently issued .30-40 Krag magazine carbine. Drawn from specimens in the Don Heckaman collection.

BARRACK SHOES.

41. For all enlisted men, according to pattern in the office of the Quartermaster General. Uppers to be of brown cotton duck.

ARCTIC OVERSHOES.

42. ALL ENLISTED MEN.—According to pattern in the office of the Quartermaster General. They will be issued at cost price when the necessity for their issue is certified by the department commanders, at the rate of one pair during each of the first and third years of enlistment, but they do not form part of the annual money allowance of clothing of the enlisted men.

LEGGINGS.

43. ALL TROOPS.—Of brown cotton duck, according to patterns in the office of the Quartermaster General, to be worn on marches and campaigns, will be charged to the enlisted men, but do not form part of the annual money allowance for clothing.

The 1899 regulations for uniforms also reveal that white duck clothing identical to the 1888 pattern was authorized for issue to enlisted men of troops stationed in extreme southern latitudes, but each trooper had to pay for these garments himself, as they were not considered a part of the clothing allowance. (See Figure 243.)

WHITE DUCK CLOTHING.

36. Bleached cotton duck clothing, consisting of sack coat and trousers, according to pattern in the office of the Quartermaster General, is furnished for troops in extreme southern latitudes. These articles will be charged at cost prices. They do not form part of the annual money allowance.

This clothing will also be provided for all members of the hospital corps on ward duty.

The recently authorized noncommissioned rank of *lance corporal* came under new regulations this year:

A lance corporal shall wear, in addition to the uniform of a private, a chevron having one bar of lace or braid; holding a renewed appointment, he shall wear the uniform of a corporal, except the chevron shall have but one bar of lace or braid.

CHEVRONS FOR FIELD UNIFORMS (KHAKI).—As described, but of such material as may be found most suitable for service.

Even with the addition of the khaki field uniform, officers and enlisted men continued to wear sky-blue kersey trousers, with stripes for the authorized noncommissioned grades, with the full-dress uniform,

and with the dark blue blouse and 1895-pattern forage, or fatigue, cap, as it was called in the regulations for enlisted men. The following excerpts from the 1899 uniform regulations cover these and some additional items of wear not before prescribed:

TROUSERS.

33. ENLISTED MEN OF ALL ARMS EXCEPT THE CORPS OF ENGINEERS.—Light-blue kersey; to be cut and made in accordance with standard patterns in the office of the Quartermaster General. Mounted troops to have a reenforce or saddle piece, of the same material, on seat and legs.

STRIPES FOR TROUSERS.

34. Sergeants to wear a stripe 1 inch wide, corporals and lance corporals holding renewed appointments to wear a stripe ½ inch wide; and musicians to wear two stripes, each ½ inch wide, of cloth conforming to color of facing.

SHIRTS, UNDERCLOTHING, AND STOCKINGS.

35. Dark-blue flannel shirts of light or heavy quality, chambray shirts, white muslin shirts, wool knit undershirts of light or heavy quality, cotton knit undershirts and drawers, canton flannel or jean drawers, woolen and light or heavy weight cotton stockings will be provided for all enlisted men in conformity with the necessities of the service.

COLLARS.

31. ALL ENLISTED MEN.—White linen collars, according to pattern in the office of the Quartermaster General. To be worn with the uniform dress coat and blouse. The particular time when the white collar shall be worn with the blouse should be regulated by the commanding officer.

CRAVATS.

32. ALL ENLISTED MEN.—Black, according to pattern in the office of the Quartermaster General; the tie not to be worn outside the opening of the coat collar. They will be issued at cost price, at the rate of two per annum, but are not to form part of the annual money allowance of clothing.

FATIGUE AND STRAW HATS.

46. ALL ENLISTED MEN.—Of drab-colored felt, with worsted hat cords, conforming in color to arm of service, according to patterns in the office of the Quartermaster General; to be worn in the field, and in garrison only on fatigue and stable duty, at target practice, and when the rubber coat or poncho is worn; the color to be uniform for both officers and enlisted men in each troop, battery, or company. During the warm season department commanders may authorize an inexpensive straw hat, of such pattern as they may prescribe, to be worn by officers and enisted men of their commands, on fatigue and stable duty, at target practice, and when not on duty.

GLOVES.

47. ALL ENLISTED MEN.—Of white Berlin.

GAUNTLETS.

48. ALL MOUNTED MEN.—Leather gauntlets, according to pattern in Quartermaster General's Office.

SPURS.

49. ALL MOUNTED MEN.—Of yellow metal, plain surface.

OVERCOATS.

50. ALL ENLISTED MEN.—Of sky-blue cloth, double-breasted, according to pattern; the lining of the capes to conform in color to the facing on the uniform, except for infantry, in which case they will be dark blue.

The cape, according to pattern (to be adjusted by means of seven hooks beneath the collar of the coat and seven eyes upon the cape), may be detached and the coat or cape worn by enlisted men when not on duty under arms.

As seen above, black neckties, called cravats then, were issued to enlisted men, although the regulations clearly state they were not to be worn so they can be seen. These must have been worn commonly with the white muslin shirt and the dark blue blouse, and the regulations do not say anything about the cravat being visible when worn with the blouse.

The heavy winter canvas and fur clothing continued to be items of issue, as shown below:

CANVAS MITTENS AND CANVAS BLANKET-LINED CAPS.

51. Of brown cotton duck (caps lined with blanket cloth), according to pattern in the office of the Quartermaster General. They will be supplied to troops serving in extremely cold regions and to troops stationed at West Point, upon the approval of the department commander or head of the staff department or corps, as the case may be, at the rate of one pair of mittens and one cap per man per annum. The voucher will show that this issue is gratuitous and made within the above allowance. Issues in excess of such allowance will be charged to the men at regulation prices. In case of loss or destruction of any of said articles of gratuitous issue without fault or neglect on the part of the soldier to whom they have been intrusted, and so certified to by the immediate commanding officer, then the article or articles so lost or destroyed may be replaced without charge to the soldier.

FUR GAUNTLETS AND CAPS AND WOOLEN MITTENS.

52. ALL ENLISTED MEN.—According to patterns in the office of the Quartermaster General. They will be issued at cost price, at the rate of one pair of gauntlets, one cap, and two pairs of mittens per annum, when the necessity for such

issue is certified by post commanders. These articles do not form a part of the annual money allowance of clothing.

FUR CLOTHING.

53. There will be issued to troops stationed in extremely cold regions, when the necessity for such issue is certified by the department commander, overcoats made of fur or other suitable warm material, but only to men performing guard duty or field service, when exposure to weather would jeopardize life or limbs by freezing. The coats should be borne on the returns as equipage and charged to enlisted men only in case of loss or damage other than from ordinary wear and tear. If made of fur, they will, on the approach of warm weather, be turned over to the quartermaster, who will observe the directions for their preservation, as required by paragraph 1191, Army Regulations.

No khaki or drab-colored overcoat was issued before 1902, and the trooper continued to wear his sky-blue overcoat with the yellow-lined cape.

Figure 279 shows additions and changes in noncommissioned-rank chevrons and brassards as prescribed in the 1899 regulations. All the chevrons and brassards shown here were worn on all uniforms, chevrons for dress coats being made of gold-lace stripes. Chevrons and brassards for the blue blouse, the overcoat, and the new khaki field uniform were made of yellow facing cloth. Wearing of chevrons and brassards on the overshirt was not authorized by regulations until 1901.

The 1901 uniform regulations brought about a number of changes and additions concerning uniforms for officers. The first cited in the published regulations was the addition of shoulder straps to the white summer undress blouse,

to be worn with white braid and shoulder straps of the same material and color as the coat. Straps of the same pattern as provided for the field [khaki] blouse. Insignia upon collar and straps to be the same as authorized upon the field [khaki] blouse.

The new straps with their proper insignia are shown on Figure 280.

The 1901 regulations describe this insignia thus:

INSIGNIA.—All officers below the grade of colonel to wear the insignia of their grade on the shoulder strap, about one-third distant from the shoulder seam to the collar; and midway between the insignia of grade and the collar will be worn on the strap, the coat of arms of the United States, 1¼ inches high, according to design.

For all officers of the grade of colonel and above, the in-

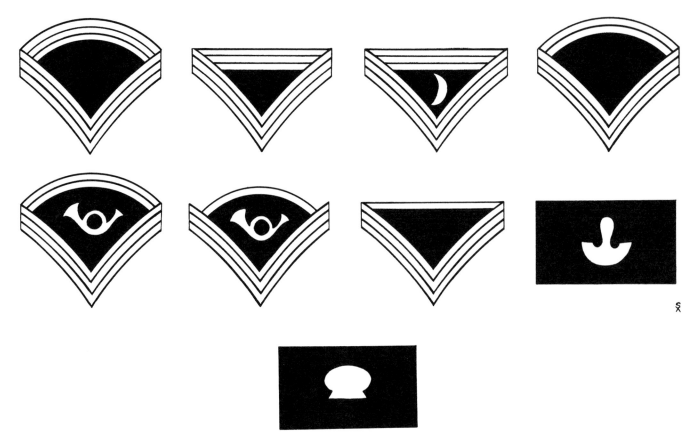

FIGURE 279. Additions and changes in noncommissioned-officer chevrons prescribed in the 1899 uniform regulations. Top row: regimental sergeant major; regimental quarter-master sergeant; regimental commissary sergeant; squadron sergeant major. Center row: chief musician; chief trumpeter; troop quartermaster sergeant; saddler. Bottom: cook.

FIGURE 280. White undress blouse and white cap (ca. 1901) for officers. The 1901 uniform regulations authorized shoulder straps for the summer blouse, with the same insignia for shoulder straps and collar as worn on the field uniform blouse. The cap was to be worn without any ornament except a yellow silk-cord chin strap of ⅛-inch silk cord.

FIGURE 280A. The sky-blue trousers (soon to be called breeches) for wear in the field with the dark blue field blouse (shown here) by officers, as prescribed in the 1901 uniform regulations. Cut like the khaki field trousers, they had the same 1½-inch yellow stripe down the outer seam of the leg as the dress trousers. This pattern would soon give way to the pegged pattern that lasted longer than the horse in the 20th century U.S. Army.

signia of rank only will be worn on the strap; the coat of arms to be worn on each side of the collar, in front of any other collar ornament.

All officers will wear on each side of the collar the prescribed insignia of their corps or arm of the service, according to pattern.

The letters "U.S." will not be worn on the khaki (or the white summer) blouse.

A new item for officers prescribed by the 1901 regulations was sky-blue breeches with a 1½-inch yellow stripe as worn on the dress and undress trousers. Termed "trousers" in the regulations, for the word *breeches* had not yet come into universal use in published uniform regulations, this new garment was described as being made "according to patterns of khaki trousers (breeches) prescribed in paragraph 5(b) of these Regulations." See Figure 280A.

Figure 281 shows the new sky-blue breeches on the officer at the left of the illustration. It also shows chevrons on the dark blue overshirt worn by the first sergeant. The 1901 regulations not only authorized both officers and enlisted men to wear the blue shirts without the blouse, but also specified that noncommissioned officers were to wear their chevrons on the sleeves, and commissioned officers "the ordinary insignia of rank on the collars of the blue shirts. . . ." (See Figures D and E, Uniform Color Plate VII, in Volume I.)

For the first time, a uniform was prescribed for veterinarians. Paragraph 28 of the 1901 Uniform Regulations states:

28. Veterinarians will wear the undress and field uniform of a second lieutenant of cavalry or artillery, according to arm of service, omitting the shoulder straps; collar and shoulder ornaments to be of white metal.

Campaign hats for officers remained black, with black and gold cords with acorn ends as before.

Paragraph 43 of the 1901 uniform regulations provided for the issue to each enlisted man annually of "one pair of suspenders or one waist belt of russet leather...."

Until the publication of the 1901 uniform regulations it had been common practice for enlisted men to crease their campaign hats in a variety of nonregulation ways. Now paragraph 50 made it known in no uncertain terms that the campaign hat was to be creased according to an accompanying illustration— and in no other way! Figure 281 shows campaign hats

on both officer and enlisted man creased according to the illustration in the regulations.

The same paragraph prescribed the wearing of the number of the regiment and the letter of the company in front. See Figure 281 and Figure E on Uniform Color Plate VII (in Volume I).

As in the past several years, the 1901 regulations stated that russet shoes and leggings would be worn with the khaki field uniform, as would leather gauntlets by cavalrymen. While it did not so specify, it is the author's opinion that the regulations implied, by omission, in this same paragraph that cavalry boots would be worn with the dress uniform, since the boot at that time was the only black footwear the trooper was issued.

Under the heading of "Band Uniforms," paragraph 67 of the 1901 uniform regulations prescribed a new uniform for drum majors. The following is the complete text of paragraph 67; Figure 282 shows the drum-major uniform for the cavalry band.

BAND UNIFORMS.

67. Bands will wear the general uniform of their regiments. Commanding officers may upon appropriations made by the councils of administration add such ornaments as they deem proper. Upon proper application they will be supplied by the Quartermaster's Department with mounted helmets, having cords and bands and hair plumes conforming in color to the arms of service, and lyres of white metal, aiguillettes with shoulder knots, music pouches, and white summer trousers, to be worn upon such occasions as may be prescribed by the department commander.

The following shall be the prescribed uniform for drum majors, viz:

FULL DRESS.

Black lynx skin shakos with plume and tassels of color of arm of service, and leather chin straps with brass scales and side buttons. The shakos for drum majors of cavalry to be of smaller dimensions than those for the other arms, according to patterns in the office of the Quartermaster General.

Dress coats according to pattern of arm of service, except that the facings and cuffs shall be of color of arms of service, ornamented with suitable braid above the cuffs, breast and skirt facings, all as per pattern in the office of the Quartermaster General.

Aiguillettes and epaulets of worsted, conforming in color to arm of service as per pattern in the office of the Quartermaster General.

Sword belt of enameled leather, of color of arm of service and regulation width.

Chevrons of gold lace, of the prescribed pattern.

Trousers of regulation patterns with stripes prescribed for sergeants of the respective arms of the service.

FIGURE 281. The 1901 uniform regulations contain the first official directive authorizing both officers and enlisted men to wear the dark blue overshirt without the blouse, but only in "extremely warm weather" when in the field on drill. This same paragraph in the regulations makes the first mention of rank insignia affixed to the blue overshirt—on the collar for officers, and on the sleeves for enlisted men. While suspenders had been an item of issue since 1883, the 1901 regulations are the first to indicate, indirectly and by in-ference only, sanction for wearing them exposed. The 1901 regulations also clearly directed that shoes and leggings were to be worn with the khaki field trousers. Depending on the weather and the commanding officer's discretion, the blue shirt or the lighter-weight khaki shirt could be worn with the khaki field trousers, not yet officially termed breeches. Here the officer wears the blue shirt with the new blue trousers, while the first sergeant wears the blue shirt with the khaki field trousers.

FIGURE 282. Drum major, Sixth Cavalry Band (ca. 1901). The uniform regulations for that year specified in detail the dress uniform for the band and, even more specifically, for the drum major. Only dismounted drum majors carried batons—drum majors of all mounted bands were to carry sabers.

The saber belt, slings, and saber knot were yellow enameled leather, and the belt plate fire gilt. At left is the back of the dress coat; at right is the drum major's undress blouse with its special yellow-lace ornamentation.

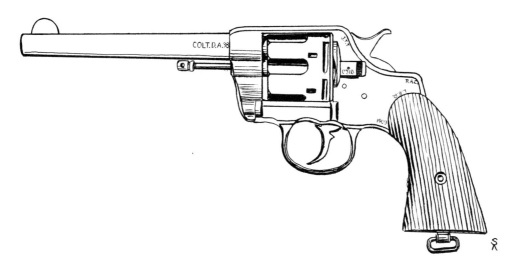

FIGURE 283. The new double-action Army revolver, Models 1892, 1894, 1895, 1896, 1901, and 1903. It was chambered for the .38-caliber long or short cartridge. This revolver was issued in large numbers and saw use in the Spanish-American and Philippine campaigns. The Army and Navy Ordnance Boards found this arm desirable because of its lighter weight, ease of loading and ejecting by means of the new swing-out cylinder, and adaptability to be used either as a single-action or double-action weapon. (James E. Serven, "Colt Firearms, 1836–1960.") But in actual warfare the .38-caliber bullet lacked stopping power against human targets, so the Army called in the .38 Colts and reissued the heavier .45 single-action Army and Model 1878 double-action Army Colts. The Models 1901 and 1903 differed from earlier models in having the butt swivel for a lanyard, as shown here. Drawn from a specimen in the author's collection.

Batons as per pattern, with silken cords and tassels, as follows: Cavalry, yellow; Artillery, scarlet; Infantry, blue and white intermixed. Only the dismounted drum majors shall carry batons. Drum majors of all mounted bands will carry swords.

UNDRESS.

The regulation blouse, cuffs and breast to be ornamented in same manner as the dress coats, with cloth chevrons of the prescribed pattern.

68. Articles of band uniforms, including shakos, epaulets, and sword belts, that do not form part of the annual clothing allowance, may be issued but not charged, except in case of loss or damage. The articles thus issued without charge remain the property of the United States.

ARMS

The first army deviation from the .45-caliber Colt single-action revolvers for issue to cavalry came in 1892, when a small quantity of Colt's "New Double Action Army Revolvers" were purchased for trial. A short time before, the Navy had adopted this double-action .38-caliber revolver as its standard firearm.

There was no difference between the so-called Army and Navy models except for the material from which the grips were made. The new revolvers issued to cavalry had walnut grips, made in two pieces, while those for the Navy were made of black hard rubber.

From 1892 to 1903, the period during which these revolvers were gradually issued to replace the larger-caliber single-action Army Colts, 68,500 were purchased by the Army. There were 6 different models of this revolver made and issued, although but minor differences existed between them. The lanyard swivel shown on the revolver in Figure 283 was added to the later models. Figure 284 shows the holster issued for this revolver. Early issues were made of black leather, later ones from russet leather.

When it was learned after the turn of the century that the .38-caliber bullet didn't have the shocking power to stop the Philippine guerrillas, the Army hastily called back the lighter double-action revolvers and reissued the .45-caliber single-action Colts from storage.

The Krag-Jorgensen system for a magazine rifle and carbine was selected by a board of officers con-

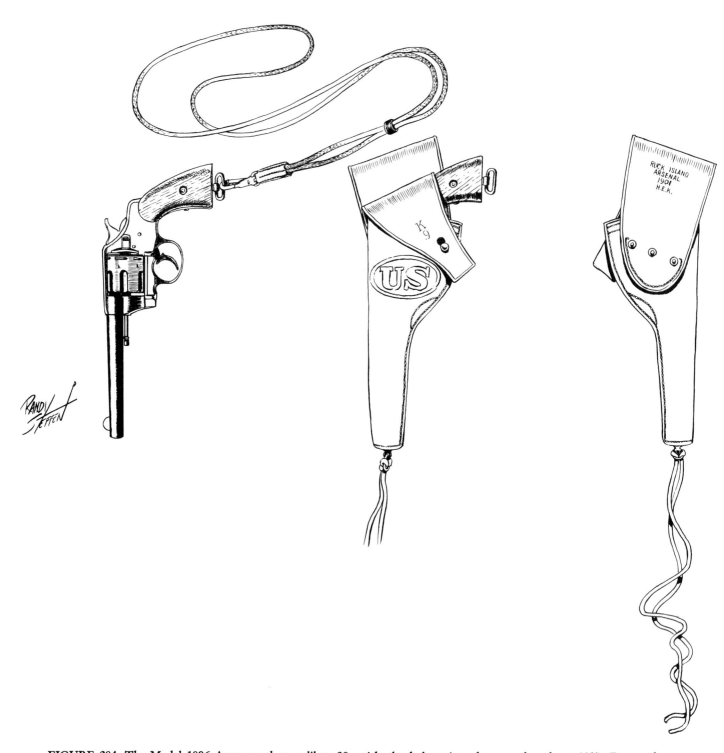

FIGURE 284. The Model 1896 Army revolver, caliber .38, with the holster issued to cavalry about 1897. Drawn from a specimen in the author's collection.

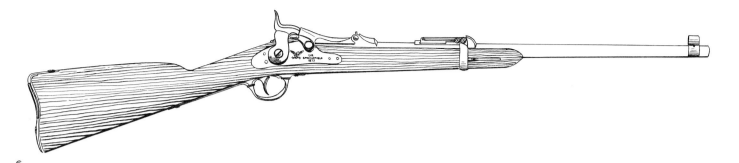

FIGURE 285. The U.S. (Springfield) carbine, Model 1890. The last of the big-bore black-powder single-shot carbines, this arm differed from the Model 1884 only in having a front sight hood secured by a pin, and the band modified by a sloping humped projection to protect the rear sight when the carbine was thrust into the short brass-throat boot. It was to be replaced shortly by the new Krag .30-caliber magazine carbine. Drawn from a specimen in the West Point Museum collection.

vened in 1890 as the most suitable one for the armed service. But not until 1894 were any of these arms produced at Springfield. After 2 years of extensive field tests, the Model 1896 carbine was made and adopted for cavalry. Figure 286 shows this new .30-caliber arm.

The 1896 Krag differed little from the earlier Model 1892. The most important changes were a recess, covered by a trap door, added to the butt stock to contain a jointed cleaning rod, and a different rear sight. Most 1892 models were changed to conform to the 1896 improvements.

The Model 1898 Krag had a bolt-handle seat that was flush with the receiver, and another new sight.

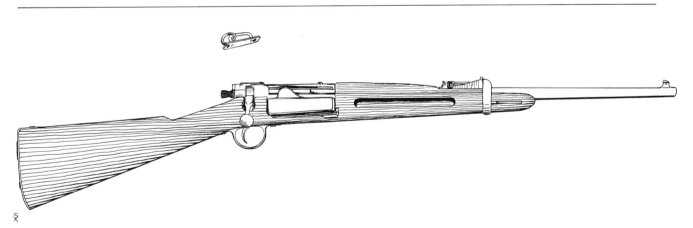

FIGURE 286. The U.S. magazine carbine, Model 1896. This Krag-Jorgensen arm of Norwegian design was the first United States service arm designed for smokeless powder, and was adopted as the result of several boards of inquiry to select a magazine rifle to replace the .45-70 single-shot Springfield adopted in 1873. An earlier-model 1892 Krag carbine was made for test, but only a few were issued for trial in the field. This arm was replaced in a few years by the Mauser-type Springfield. The carbine sling swivel plate attached to the left side of the stock is shown at the top of this drawing. Later models of the Krag carbine, differing from this Model 1896 mainly in having improved rear sights, omitted the sling swivel plate and ring, since, with the introduction and adoption of the long carbine boot, the carbine sling was no longer an article of issue. Drawn from a specimen in the author's original collection.

The hand guard was extended to project beyond the rear sight. Only 5,000 of this model were made, and not until 1899.

The final Krag carbine to be manufactured and issued was called the Model 1899. It had a different rear-sight ramp, which was protected by a rise in the hand guard. Nearly 40,000 of this model were made before production ceased in 1902. (Colonel Arcadi Gluckman, *United States Muskets, Rifles and Carbines.*)

The same sabers were used in this era as since 1872. Officers carried the Model 1872 officer's model, and enlisted men continued to be armed with the Model 1861 light cavalry saber. Saber knots for officers were the same, too, except that the 1897 uniform regulations prescribed a plaited leather or webbing saber knot for officer use in the field. Enlisted men used the lighter black leather knot recommended in 1885 by the cavalry equipment board.

HORSE EQUIPMENTS AND CAVALRY ACCOUTREMENTS

Many officers continued to purchase the Whitman saddle for their own use, both for garrison and field duty. Figure 287 shows a second lieutenant in the correct uniform for mounted garrison duty, and riding the Whitman saddle.

The headstall on his horse is the standard Model 1885, fitted with the recently adopted Model 1892 bit that replaced the larger and heavier Shoemaker bit, standard since 1874. The Model 1892 bit was also made with an additional snaffle-rein ring connected to the intersection of the bar and cheek piece for use with double reins, but many officers preferred the straight-curb model, as I have shown here and in Figure 288. The saddlecloth shown here is the one prescribed in the 1897 uniform regulations for cavalry officers, with enameled leather border and number of the regiment in enameled leather, both yellow in color for cavalry.

Figure 288 illustrates the usual field equipment used in this era with the Whitman saddle. The small valise strapped to the cantle was made especially for the peaked-cantle officer's model of the Whitman.

Figures 289 and 290 show both sides of troopers dressed and equipped for mounted garrison duty. Although canvas leggings had already been issued to some troops to replace the heavy leather cavalry boots, it was not yet mandatory for all mounted troops to wear leggings and shoes for all mounted duty. Figures 290 and 291 show troopers in field dress with boots, which at this time was permissible.

Horse equipments shown on these illustrations are the Model 1885 McClellan equipments, except for bits, which are the new Model 1892 curb bits now adopted for the cavalry service.

Halters were not used for garrison duty, and each commanding officer ordered his choice of arms for this type of mounted activity. Ten or twelve years earlier, Lieutenant General Sheridan had written an order which directed the carrying of specific arms and equipment for garrison and field duty. For service within the confines of the post and for parades and ceremony, Sheridan had limited the trooper's armament to *either* the pistol or the carbine. But since then it had become customary for some troops to parade or participate in duties, mounted, within the post armed with saber, carbine, and pistol. This was especially true when a trooper was assigned to *mounted* guard duty, as are the 2 troopers shown in Figures 289 and 290.

With the adoption of the Krag magazine carbine, the older (1885) short carbine boot was abandoned, and the new long boot adopted.

Even in 1890 the Army had been experimenting with a long boot of similar design for the Springfield carbine. Bannerman's older catalogs show clear illustrations of this boot, whose outstanding characteristic was a ring riveted at the seam close to the center of the length of the boot, to which the lower strap for attaching the carbine boot to the cantle ring was buckled. But the advent of the new bolt-action Krag curtailed the field tests of the Springfield long boot, and none were issued except a limited number for trial.

The copy of Ordnance Memorandum No. 29, covering the 1885 cavalry equipment board recommendations on cavalry equipment, now in the rare book section of the West Point Library, contains a memorandum and sketch by Captain J. Pitman, the original owner of the copy. The sketch is of the long boot for the .45-70 Springfield carbine, and is marked "rec'd May 6, 1890." Whether this note means a circular on the new boot was received then, or an actual specimen, cannot be ascertained. The sketch is accompanied by full dimensional notes. No mention is made

FIGURE 287. Second lieutenant, First Cavalry (ca. 1897), in undress uniform, and equipped for garrison duty.

of a brass throat, with which the boot illustrated in the Bannerman catalog is equipped.

The method of attachment of the Krag-carbine long boot is clearly shown in Figure 289. The top strap was buckled to the front sidebar ring on the saddle, and the long lower strap was buckled to the ring at the cantle end of the sidebar.

Service uniforms for garrison duty consisted of the new Model 1895 forage, or fatigue, cap, dark blue blouse, and sky-blue trousers, with yellow stripes for noncommissioned officers. The same blouse and trousers made up the uniform for field duty, the campaign hat being worn in place of the forage cap.

The woven Mills cartridge belt, with saber attach-

83

FIGURE 288. First lieutenant, Second Cavalry (ca. 1897), in undress uniform and with full equipment for field service.

ment riveted to the bottom on the near side, was used to hold the new .30-caliber smokeless-powder cartridges for the Krag carbine. Some belts were made with double rows of cartridge loops, others with single rows. Both were issued and used. This type of Mills belt was made in blue, gray, and tan, or khaki, color. Most Regular Army cavalry were issued the khaki-colored ones, with the other 2 colors going to militia troops.

The full field packs shown on the horses in Figures 291 and 292 conform to the regulations for this period. The overcoat is attached to the pommel, and the blanket roll inside the shelter half, with the nose bag slipped over this roll, is attached to the cantle. The saber is attached to the near side of the saddle by two saber straps, one in the brass ring at the pommel end of the bars, the other through the cinch ring. The end of the halter strap is tied in the same ring on the bars that holds the top saber strap. The rolled lariat is attached to the near cantle ring by the snap that is

FIGURE 289. Sergeant, Third Cavalry (ca. 1897), in service uniform and equipped for mounted garrison duty under arms. Off side.

used to fasten it to the halter ring when the horse is picketed, or by a small strap issued for this purpose. The canteen with its strap passed through the handle of the tin cup is attached by a snap to the near cantle ring. (See Figure 292.)

Figure 291 shows the pack from the off side. The Krag carbine is carried in the long boot, hung from pommel and cantle rings, with the muzzle under the trooper's right leg, the bolt facing away from the horse. Extra ammunition, horseshoes and nails, rations, watering bridle, and currycomb and brush are distributed in the saddlebags.

When a trooper was fighting dismounted, the saber was left attached to the saddle, but the carbine was always withdrawn from the boot and snapped to the swivel on the carbine sling when he dismounted.

The link strap, an item of issue to cavalry for many years, was permanently attached to the lower ring of the left bit cheek, or shank (see Figure 292) and was used to link together 3 horses, held by a trooper mounted on a fourth, when cavalry dismounted to fight on foot. Since 1859, at least, the method of linking horses together had been the same. With three riderless horses standing abreast and to the right of the fourth horse ridden by a trooper, the link strap of the horse farthest to the right was snapped to the halter ring of the horse standing to his left. In the same manner the link strap of that horse was snapped to the halter ring of the horse to his left, and the reins of that horse were held by the mounted trooper to his left. In this manner one man could control 4 horses even in the proximity of a fire fight.

While side lines were still issued, it was seldom that they were carried during the latter years of the 1890's. Horses were picketed at the end of the lariat, which was secured to the picket pin driven into the ground. (Col. William H. Carter, *Horses, Saddles & Bridles*, Baltimore, The Lord Baltimore Press, 1895.)

While saddles with adjustable quarter straps were not issued to cavalry until after 1904—in any quantity, that is—experimental kits for modifying the 1885 fixed quarter straps were being sent out to some cavalry troops as early as March, 1900.

The West Point Library copy of Ordnance Memorandum No. 29—the description of the 1885 cavalry equipments and accoutrements—contains another note by Captain J. Pitman that reveals his receipt of a circular concerning such a kit, along with instructions for making the modification. The handwritten copy of the list of contents and instructions was dated as having been received in March, 1900. The total weight of the materials in the kit was 2 pounds, 4½ ounces. The kit contained harness-leather straps and leather safes with rounded corners, all cut to size, along with a pair of lashing thongs with soft rawhide backs, a pair of 4¼-inch-diameter iron rings, 4 leather loops, and 10 copper rivets and burrs.

MISCELLANEOUS

DRILL REGULATIONS FOR CAVALRY

On October 3, 1891, the War Department published 3 new books of drill regulations—for cavalry, artillery, and infantry. The covers of each were of cloth colored to match the arm of the service—yellow for cavalry, red for artillery, and blue for infantry.

These works were compiled by the best minds of the service (William A. Ganoe, *The History of the United States Army*, 366–67), and the regulations for cavalry set forth rules for dividing each troop in single rank into 2, 3, or 4 platoons, depending upon the number of 4's. The squadron consisted of not more than 4 and not less than 2 troops. As a whole, the evolutions of cavalry units were simplified.

REGIMENTAL COLORS AND NATIONAL STANDARD

The cavalry regimental standard was slightly modified in pattern on March 19, 1890. In contrast to the pattern standardized in 1887, the bends of the upper and lower scrolls were changed, as was the pattern of the foliated lower scroll. The details of the eagle's plumage and talons were altered, and the word "regiment" was eliminated in the lower scroll.

Until 1895 the cavalry regiments carried only the regimental standard and company guidons in ceremonies and parades. On April 11, 1895, the quartermaster general wrote Colonel D. S. Gordon, commanding officer of the Sixth Cavalry:

Under existing regulations the Cavalry regiments of the service are furnished with yellow silken standards; they have no national colors. . . . it has occurred to the Quartermaster General that it might be found desirable to also supply the Headquarters of the Cavalry regiments with a color the same size as the "Standard" for drill purposes, and therefore a national flag of bunting with embroidered stars and name of regiment has been especially manufactured. . . .

This was approved by the Secretary of War and the Army regulations for 1895 authorized a silken cavalry national standard with dimensions of 4 feet fly and 3 feet on the lance. "Correction: National Colors, Cavalry," by Colonel Harry Larter, *Military Collector & Historian*, Vol. VI, No. 1 [1954] 2.)

CAVALRY BANDS

The 1894 army regulations increased the size of bands for the army regiments to 22, stating:

There will be allowed for each regular band 1 sergeant and 20 privates to act as musicians, in addition to the Chief Musician authorized by law; provided the total number of

FIGURE 290. Private, Eighth Cavalry (ca. 1897), in service uniform and equipped for mounted garrison duty under arms. Near side.

FIGURE 291. Corporal, Eighth Cavalry (ca. 1897), in service uniform and equipped with full pack for field service. Off side.

FIGURE 292. Chief trumpeter, Eighth Cavalry, in service uniform (ca. 1897) and with full pack for duty in the field. Near side.

PLATE 1

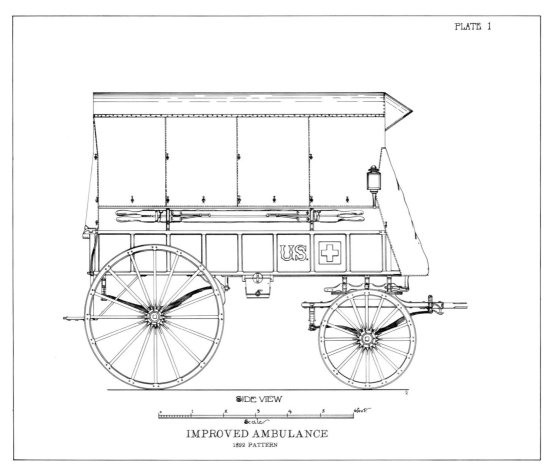

SIDE VIEW

IMPROVED AMBULANCE
1892 PATTERN

PLATE 2

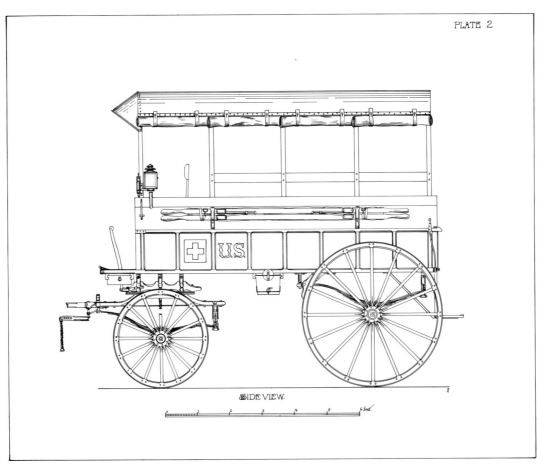

SIDE VIEW.

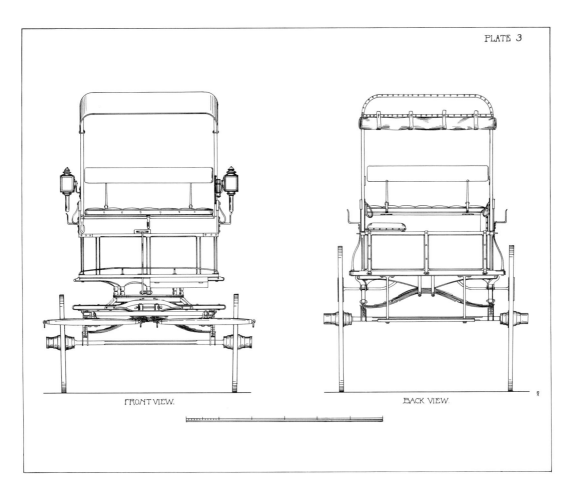

PLATE 3

FRONT VIEW.   BACK VIEW.

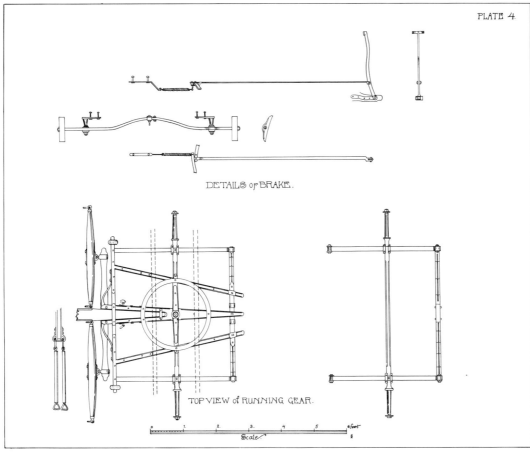

PLATE 4.

DETAILS of BRAKE.

TOP VIEW of RUNNING GEAR.

Scale

FIGURE 293. Improved ambulance, 1892 pattern.

91

FIGURE 294. The ambulance of pattern in use during the Spanish-American War and until it was slightly modified in 1909. Its distinguishing characteristics are the louvered venti-lators on each side. Drawn from a restored specimen in the National Museum.

enlisted men in a regiment, including the band, does not exceed its legal standard.

In the same year bands were authorized to include E-flat trumpets, and a pair of kettle drums was authorized for mounted-cavalry bands in lieu of snare and bass drums.

The next year, 1895, regulations allowed the addition of a chief trumpeter and a principal musician, making the allowable total for the band 24 instead of 22.

The 1897 uniform regulations prescribed helmets with hair plumes to be worn with dress uniforms for all bands. In addition, these regulations prescribed aiguillettes with shoulder knots, music pouches, and white summer trousers—to be worn as directed by the commanding officer of each regiment.

A general order dated June 24, 1899, again increased the number allowed for regimental bands to 28. The next year regulations prescribed the issue of B-flat basses and saxophones to Army bands.

AMBULANCE

Figure 293 shows 4 plates from the 1892 Quartermaster Department drawings for a new pattern of ambulance adopted for use by the Army. Many of these vehicles were attached to the cavalry regiments; some were used as private vehicles by cavalry officers for moving family and possessions from one assignment to the next.

Figure 294 shows the ambulance pattern built by Studebaker for the Army in large numbers for use in the United States, Cuba, and the Philippines during and after the Spanish-American War.

FIGURE 295. Army escort wagon used from the mid-1890's through the 1930's with very little modification.

ESCORT WAGON

Figure 295 shows the new pattern of 4-horse or 4-mule army wagon, called an "escort wagon," that became standard in the mid-1890's and was used through the 1930's with few modifications. Hundreds were used for cavalry wagon trains.

FIVE NEW CAVALRY REGIMENTS AUTHORIZED

The war in the Philippines and the nation's participation in the Boxer Rebellion in China kept our small army busy. When, in 1901, more than 30,000 militia troops whose terms of service had expired were sent home, Congress suddenly realized once more that the small Regular Army had more to do than it could possibly handle.

Accordingly, on February 2, 1901, Congress passed a bill which caused the Army to consist of 30 regiments of infantry, 1 corps of artillery, and 15 regiments of cavalry, with an appropriate staff corps.

Although the Eleventh through Fifteenth Regiments of Cavalry had their beginnings in 1901, most were not actually organized until 1902.

LAST MAJOR FIGHT WITH INDIANS

The so-called "Battle" of Wounded Knee, fought at Wounded Knee Creek in what is now the state of South Dakota, on December 29, 1890, was the last engagement of any consequence with Indians. This fight took place when revenge-thirsty troopers of the Seventh Cavalry slaughtered several hundred Sioux men, women, and children they had been sent to herd back to the Pine Ridge Reservation.

From this time on cavalry's role in guarding the frontier declined, and it became more of a police force to maintain order along the Mexican border and to aid in quelling civil disorders throughout the nation.

CHAPTER THIRTEEN

An Era of Experimentation

1902-16

SINCE THE WAR WITH SPAIN, most of the Regular Army had been concentrated in the Philippines, including a large percentage of the cavalry corps. For a change, Congress was pleased with the way the Army had been conducting itself, and particularly with the way trained and educated officers had increased the efficiency of the military operations. Because of this self-satisfied attitude, the lawmakers were more liberal than ever before with appropriations for military educational budgets.

Facilities at West Point were enlarged, and the system of garrison schools for non-West Point officers was established.

For the first time, field exercises were seriously conducted, and in September, 1902, joint maneuvers were held along the New England coast with Regular Army and militia units participating against ships of the Navy.

New cavalry-drill regulations made their appearance; the cavalry troop was formed in single rank, with divisions for platoons and squads. Squadrons of 4 troops each were commanded and drilled by majors. Most of the evolutions and specifications set forth by the new drill regulations continued in effect until horse cavalry was abandoned during World War II.

With good feeling and satisfaction so prevalent in the legislative bodies, it is easy to understand the motives that prompted the approval of legislation appropriating additional funds for a drastic change in uniforms, and an increase in activities aimed at improving arms and equipment for the military service. (Ganoe, *The History of the United States Army*.)

UNIFORMS

The *1902 Regulations for the Uniform of the United States Army* brought about a new appearance for all branches of the Army, and marked a new era. The helmets with horsehair plumes and the dress coat with the distinctive skirt facings were gone! The new dress uniforms for officers and enlisted men remained the traditional dark blue with yellow facings for cavalry and retained a much simplified plaited breast cord with flat braided ornaments for enlisted men. But more conventional caps replaced the plumed helmet, and the drab earth colors of the modern European armies had their counterparts in the khaki and olive-drab clothing of the twentieth-century American soldier.

The new uniform prescribed in the 1902 regulations saw few changes until 1907. Even then the changes were minor, and can be described and illustrated with a minimum of written text. But in order to present a complete and detailed picture of the dress that marked the cavalryman—and the rest of the Army, of course—in the third year of the new century, the complete regulations for the dress of the Army are presented here, including the official "Table of Occasions" that listed the correct articles of uniform for both officers and enlisted men for every occasion of duty.

UNIFORM OF THE UNITED STATES ARMY

GENERAL REGULATIONS.

1. The garments, head gear, foot gear, ornaments, insignia, buttons, decorations, and other articles herein specified, grouped in the manner prescribed, will constitute the uniforms of the United States Army, and will be worn on the occasions prescribed (see Table of Occasions) unless otherwise directed by proper authority.

The various articles will conform in quality, design, and color to the sealed standard patterns deposited in the War Department.

2. The proper dress will be determined by the commanding officer with due regard to prescribed regulations (see Table of Occasions), the season of the year, and the state of the weather.

Officers serving with troops will wear the prescribed uniform and will, by their appearance, set an example of neatness and strict conformity to regulations in uniform and equipment.

All officers not serving with troops shall, during the hours of duty, wear the prescribed uniform, unless authorized by the War Department to wear civilian clothing.

3. When officers or enlisted men wear civilian dress, it will not be accompanied by any mark or part of the uniform. Enlisted men, on or off duty, will not wear civilian dress without permission of their commanding officer.

4. No decoration received from a foreign government by officers or enlisted men shall be publicly shown or exposed upon the person.

5. The *medal of honor* may be worn by officers and enlisted men entitled thereto on all occasions of ceremony in full dress; the medal shall be worn pendant from the neck; the ribbon passing between the upper and lower hooks of the coat collar so that the medal proper shall hang about 1 inch below the opening of the collar. [See Figure 296.]

6. The various distinctive marks given for excellence in rifle practice may be worn on the breast by officers and enlisted men entitled to them, on all occasions of ceremony, in the manner prescribed in the next paragraph; they will precede all badges of military societies (from the wearer's right to left), and will be preceded by badges of campaigns which may be adopted by the War Department.

7. *Badges of military societies.*—Officers and enlisted men who, in their own right or by right of inheritance, are members of military societies of men who served in the armies and navies of the United States in the war of the Revolution, the war of 1812, the Mexican war, the war of the rebellion, or the Indian wars of the United States, the Spanish-American War and the incidental insurrection in the Philippines, or the China Relief Expedition, or are members of the Regular Army and Navy Union of the United States, may wear on all occasions of ceremony, when full dress is required, the distinctive badges adopted by such societies, or such other medals as may be authorized by proper authority. Officers and enlisted men who served as officers, noncommissioned officers, privates, or other enlisted men in the Regular Army, volunteer or militia forces of the United States, during the war of the rebellion, and have been honorably discharged from the service, or still remain in the same, may wear on occasions of ceremony, when full dress is required, the distinctive army badge ordered for or adopted by the army corps or division, respectively, in which they served. Badges to be worn on the left breast of the coat, suspended by a ribbon from a bar of metal passed through the upper ends and tops of the ribbons forming a horizontal line, the outer ends of which will be from 3 to 4 inches below the top of the shoulder, according to the height of the wearer.

8. Shoulder knots and shoulder straps will be worn by commissioned officers only. Shoulder straps will always be placed on the dress coat, as herein prescribed; their use on the full-dress coat is forbidden.

9. The uniform of general officers on the retired list is that prescribed for general officers of corresponding grade on the active list. If retired while serving as general officer in a corps or department, the insignia of such corps or department will be omitted. The uniform of an officer below the grade of brigadier general on the retired list is that prescribed for an officer of his rank in the corps, department, or arm of service in which he last served, except that the number of the regiment or insignia of corps or department will not be worn. A retired officer with brevet commission, either in the regular or volunteer service of the Army of the United States, may wear the uniform of his highest brevet grade, and a retired officer who has held a commission, not brevet, in the volunteer service, may wear the uniform of his highest grade in that service, except that the number of the regiment or insignia of corps or department will not be worn. Retired officers may, at their option, wear the pattern of uniform which was prescribed at the date of their retirement, or as prescribed herein, but the two uniforms will not be mixed.

10. In case of inclement weather when capes, waterproofs, or overcoats are worn, shoulder knots will take the place of epaulets for general officers.

11. When a particular coat or vestment is required by the church to which a chaplain belongs he may wear such coat or vestment while conducting services.

12. In foreign countries, on occasions of reviews, public balls, entertainments given by military or naval authorities, or messes, or by civil officials, during official visits of ceremony, and at social functions partaking of an official character, officers will appear in uniform suitable for the occasion.

13. The saber will be habitually worn hooked up when dismounted, guard to the rear; when worn with the overcoat, the belt will be inside and the saber outside of the overcoat. The proper saber knot will always be worn with the saber.

14. Enlisted men will not be permitted to wear any articles of uniform which are not furnished by the Quartermaster's Department.

15. The service uniforms are made of wool or cotton. The woolen uniform is prescribed for wear in the United States proper, including Alaska, and will be furnished in heavy weight for winter wear and light weight for summer. The cotton uniform is prescribed for tropical use only, except as authorized in paragraph 108, at emplacements.

16. It is not permitted to combine outer garments of wool with others of cotton in the service uniform of officers or enlisted men.

The material of the service uniform, the overcoat, and the service hat, will be made water repellent, as nearly as practicable.

DESCRIPTION OF GARMENTS AND OTHER ARTICLES OF UNIFORM FOR OFFICERS OF THE ARMY.

FULL-DRESS COAT.

[See Figure 296 and Figure G on Uniform Color Plate VII in Volume I.]

17. *For all officers, except chaplains.*—A double-breasted frock coat of dark-blue cloth, with standing collar; the skirt to extend from one-half to three-quarters the distance from the point of the hip to the bend of the knee; the lining to be black, with pockets on the inside of skirt, and the coat to conform, in material and cut, to the sealed pattern in the office of the Quartermaster General.

For general officers the collar will be made of blue-black velvet; the sleeve will have a cuff of blue-black velvet 4 inches wide. For other officers the collar will be made of the same material as the coat, and the cuffs will simply be a continuation of the material of the sleeves.

Shoulder ornaments.—For general officers, epaulets (see paragraph 37).

For all other officers, shoulder knots of gold-wire cord, as hereafter described under "Shoulder knots" (par. 38). [See Figure 297.] To be securely fastened to the coat, and to be made detachable for all officers.

Collar ornament.—The ornamentation of the collar for the *General* will be such as he may prescribe; for the *Lieutenant General*, such as he may prescribe, after consultation with the General.

For other general officers the collar will be ornamented with a band of oak leaves embroidered in gold, and extending all the way around.

For all other officers the ornament will consist of two bands of ½ inch gold-wire lace, two vellums, passing all around the collar and parallel with its edge, the upper edge of the upper band being ¼ inch from the edge of the collar, the lower edge of the lower band resting on the collar seam. The upper band to be brought down parallel to the front edge of the collar and distant ¼ inch therefrom, and to be joined to the lower band. The two bands of gold-wire lace to be on a ground of silk or cloth of the color of the facings of the corps, department, or arm of the service, with an interval of not less than ¼ inch nor more than ¾ inch between the bands.

Sleeve ornament.—The ornamentation of the sleeve for the *General* will be such as he may prescribe; for the *Lieutenant General*, such as he may prescribe, after consultation with the General.

For *other general officers* the velvet cuff of the sleeve will be ornamented with a band of oak leaves embroidered in gold, passing around the cuff; the top of the band of oak leaves to be 1 inch below the upper edge of the velvet cuff; to be surmounted by two stars for a major general and one star for a brigadier general, embroidered in silver, each star to have one point up and placed above the velvet cuff.

For general officers of the staff departments, except the General Staff Corps, the proper insignia will be placed 1 inch above the velvet cuff, and the stars, as before, 1 inch above the insignia.

For *all other officers* the sleeve will be ornamented with a band of ½ inch gold-wire lace, two vellums, passing around the cuff 2½ inches from the end of the sleeve: to be surmounted by the insignia of rank, indicated by flat gold-wire lace ⅛ inch in width (see Insignia, par. 56). The insignia of the corps, department, or arm of service, in gold or silver metal or embroidery (see Insignia, par. 56), will be placed in the center of the open space under the lace insignia. [See Figure 296 and Figure G on Uniform Color Plate VII in Volume I.]

Buttons.—Two regulation gilt buttons will be placed at the back of the waist, and one regulation gilt button near the end of each skirt, making four buttons on the back of the coat, for all officers.

Three small regulation gilt buttons will be placed on the cuff at sleeve, for general officers only.

For officers of the various grades regulation gilt buttons will be placed on the breast of the coat as follows:

General.—Two rows, twelve in each row, placed by fours, the distance between rows being from 8 to 10 inches at the top and from 4 to 5 inches at the bottom; rows and groups to be symmetrically disposed.

Lieutenant General.—The same as for the General, except that there will be ten buttons in each row, the upper and lower groups by threes and the middle groups by fours.

Major general.—The same as for the General, except that there will be nine buttons in each row, placed by threes.

Brigadier general.—The same as for the General, except that there will be eight buttons in each row, placed in pairs.

Colonel, lieutenant colonel, and major.—The same as for the General, except that there will be nine buttons in each row, buttons at equal intervals. [See Figure 296.]

Captain, first lieutenant, second lieutenant, and additional second lieutenant.—The same as for a colonel, except that there will be seven buttons in each row. [See Figure 296.]

For the Chief of Engineers.—The same as that of general officers with the following exceptions:

Piping: A piping of scarlet velvet ⅛ inch wide, to be placed along the upper and outer edges of the lapels, continuing down the edges of the skirt to the bottom, and from top of back flaps in middle of back to bottom of skirt.

Skirt facings: To be of scarlet velvet with one row of ½ inch gold two-line vellum thread lace placed upon white braid, showing 3⁄32 inch of braid on each side, ¼ inch from the outer edge of the scarlet velvet, following the vertical and horizontal lines, with a regulation gilt button placed in the lower corner of the scarlet velvet just inside the gold lace.

For all other officers of the Corps of Engineers.—The same as for other officers with the following exceptions:

Piping: A piping of scarlet cloth ⅛ inch wide, to be placed around the base of neck, the edge of collar lace along top, and down the front edge of lapel, stopping at the bottom, and from top of back flap in the middle of the back to the bottom of skirt.

Skirt facings: To be of scarlet cloth with one row of ½ inch gold-wire two-vellum lace placed upon white braid, showing 3⁄32 inch of braid on each side, ¼ inch from the outer edge of the scarlet cloth, following the vertical and horizontal lines, with a regulation gilt button placed in the lower corner of the scarlet cloth just inside the gold lace.

For chaplains.—A black frock coat, without ornamenta-

FIGURE 296. Major, chaplain, and first lieutenant, Fifth Cavalry (ca. 1906), in the 1902 pattern of dress uniforms. The major wears the uniform prescribed for mounted-full-dress occasions, while chaplain and lieutenant are dressed for a dismounted-full-dress event. The major wears the new (1904) pattern of Medal of Honor pendant at the throat and, from left to right, the Spanish-American Medal and the In-dian Wars Medal on his breast. The lieutenant wears the Philippine Campaign Medal on his coat—all according to explicit regulations governing the wearing of medals and badges. The chaplain's full-dress coat is cut on the same pattern as those of line officers, but has but one row of black cloth-covered buttons and is without ornamentation of any kind. He wears the prescribed black chaplain's hat.

tion, with standing collar, one row of nine black silk buttons on the breast. Of same length as for other officers. [See Figure 296.]

DRESS COAT.

18. *For general officers.*—A sack coat of dark-blue cloth or serge; three small regulation gilt buttons will be placed on the cuff at sleeve; high rolling collar; double-breasted, with two rows of regulation gilt buttons grouped according to rank, as on the full-dress coat; the skirt to extend one-third the distance from the point of the hip to the bend of the knee. A slit extending from 2 inches above to 2 inches below the hip, so as to permit of hooking up of saber. A shoulder strap, as hereafter described (par. 39), will be placed on each

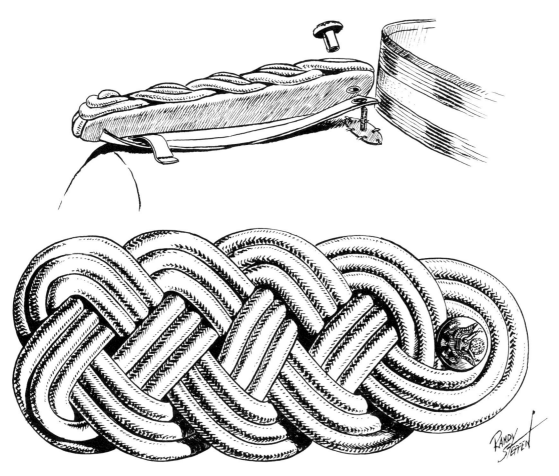

FIGURE 297. Shoulder knot for officers, pattern of 1902, made of gold-bullion cord. It was attached to the coat as shown. Reproduced actual size.

shoulder, adjacent to the seam, and collar ornaments (see Insignia, par. 56) on the collar. Inside pockets.

For all other officers.—A single-breasted sack coat of dark-blue cloth or serge, with standing collar fastened with two hooks and eyes; coat to close with flap containing suitable concealed fastenings; slit not exceeding 3 inches for hooking up saber; the skirt to extend from one-third to two-thirds the distance from the point of the hip to the bend of the knee, according to the height of the wearer, cut to fit the figure easily; a vertical opening at each side of the hip, according to pattern. The coat to be trimmed with lustrous flat black mohair braid 1¼ inches wide, as follows; Edged all around the bottom, the front edges, the collar, and for 6 inches upward from the bottom along both side openings of the skirt. [See Figure 298 and Figure G on Uniform Color Plate VII in Volume I.]

Shoulder straps, as hereafter described (par. 39), and collar ornaments (see Insignia, par. 56) will be worn with this garment.

SERVICE COAT.

19. *For all officers.*—A single-breasted sack coat of olive-drab woolen material or khaki-colored cotton material, made with two outside breast choked-bellows pockets and two outside pockets of same pattern below the waist; pockets to be without plaits and covered by flaps, rounded at edges, buttoned by a small regulation button. The coat to have falling collar, from 1 to 1¼ inches in width, depending on the wearer. On each shoulder a loop of the same material as the coat let in at shoulder seam and reaching from the sleeve seam to the edge of the collar, and buttoning at the upper end with a small regulation button; loops to be 2 inches wide at the shoulder end and 1 inch wide at the collar end. The coat to fit closely at the waist and loosely at the chest, at least 5 inches in excess of the chest measurement; buttoned down the front with five regulation buttons. The skirt to extend one-third the distance from the point of the hip to the bend of the knee. Sleeves to be without cuffs. All buttons for this coat to be of

dull-finish bronze metal. [This coat is shown on the veterinarian in Figure 299, without the rank insignia as specified for officers in the next paragraph.]

Collar ornaments (see Insignia, par. 56) will be worn with this garment [branch insignia and national coat of arms, as on enlisted man's collar in Figure 302]. The insignia of rank, as prescribed in paragraph 56, will be placed on the shoulder loop, near the sleeve seam. Chaplains will wear a plain Latin cross of dull-finish bronze metal in lieu of the insignia of rank.

Officers of the General Staff Corps, except the Chief of Staff, will wear a band of black braid ½ inch wide on the sleeve of the service coat, the lower edge of the braid 3 inches from the end of the sleeve.

WHITE COAT.

20. *For all officers.*—A single-breasted sack coat of white material, with standing collar fastened with two hooks and eyes, white metal; coat to close with a flap containing suitable concealed fastenings. The skirt to extend from one-third to two-thirds the distance from the point of the hip to the bend of the knee, according to the height of the wearer: cut to fit the figure easily; a vertical opening at each side of the hip, according to pattern. The coat to be trimmed with white flat braid 1¼ inches wide, as follows: Edged all around the bottom, the front edges, the collar, and for 6 inches upward from the bottom along both side openings of the skirt. White shoulder loops of the same material as the coat, let in at shoulder seam, and of the pattern prescribed for the service coat. [See Figure 322.]

Insignia on the collar to be the same as prescribed for the dress coat; insignia of rank to be placed on the shoulder loop, as prescribed for the service coat.

OVERCOAT.
[See Figure 299.]

21. *For all officers.*—A double-breasted ulster of olive-drab woolen material according to sealed pattern in the office of the Quartermaster General, suitably lined and closing by means of five large buttons 45 lines diameter; a standing rolling collar, the "stand" to be not less than ¾ nor more than 1¾ inches, and the turn down (falling) part not less than 4 nor more than 5 inches in width. Collar in front to be closed by two hooks and eyes; a flap of same material as the coat 5 inches in length and 2 inches in width, provided with one button-hole at each end, made detachable, so as to close the falling part of the collar when worn closed.

A pocket on each side placed vertically, lower end of pocket 2 inches below the hip bone extending from 8 to 10 inches upward. Over the pockets a flap of same length, rounded at edges and closed by a small button at middle of flaps. Slits of pockets to be cut through linings, thus permitting the slings to come through left pocket hole for hooking up of saber. The back to be slit up from the bottom 20 to 25 inches and closed by small buttons under concealed flap, the latter buttoning from right to left.

Coat to extend down the legs from 8 to 10 inches below the knee, according to the height of the wearer. Sleeves loose, without cuffs or slit. Back straps placed at waist line, let in at the side seams, and to button together by two large buttons.

A hood of same material as coat, lined with suitable material of same color; made to button around the neck under the collar by means of five small buttons. Hood to be large enough to cover the head and cap. When in garrison the hood will ordinarily be worn only at night or in inclement weather. Under arms, only when prescribed by the commanding officer.

All buttons to be of horn conforming in color to the material of the coat.

The front corners of the skirt to be provided with buttons or hooks so that said corners may be turned back when it is necessary to facilitate marching.

Insignia on sleeve.—Sleeve insignia of rank as prescribed (see Insignia, par. 56); in addition thereto, the insignia of corps, department, or arm of service, of dull-finish bronze metal, will be placed in the middle of the lower loop 1½ inches above the end of the sleeve.

For general officers the insignia will consist of a band of lustrous black mohair braid, 1¼ inches wide, placed with its lower edge 2½ inches above end of sleeve; surmounted by the proper number of stars, 1 inch in diameter, of dull-finish bronze metal, placed ¼ inch above the braid; the stars to be surmounted by a band of lustrous black mohair braid ½ inch wide, ¼ inch above the stars.

Overcoats for chaplains to be without insignia of rank.

Officers of the General Staff Corps, except general officers, will wear a band of black mohair braid ⅞ inch wide on the sleeve, the lower edge of braid to be 2½ inches above the end of the sleeve, the lower ends of the prescribed insignia of rank to rest upon the upper edge of this band.

CAPES.
[See Figure 299.]

22. *For all officers.*—To be of dark-blue cloth without braid binding, reaching at least to the tips of the fingers with the arm dropped at the side and not below the knee; with a rolling collar of black velvet 3 inches broad, and closing at the throat with a long loop. It may be worn by all officers when not on duty with troops under arms. To be lined as follows:

For general officers and officers of the Staff Corps and departments.—Dark blue.

For officers of infantry.—Light blue.

For officers of artillery.—Scarlet.

For officers of cavalry.—Yellow.

FULL-DRESS TROUSERS.

23. *For general officers.*—Of dark-blue cloth, with two stripes of gold-wire lace ½ inch wide with ¼ inch interval between them, mounted upon light-weight velvet of color of cuffs and collar of coat and placed along the outside seam of the trousers. In the case of the Chief of Engineers the interval between the two stripes shall be scarlet velvet.

For officers holding permanent appointments in the Staff

FIGURE 298. Chaplain, second lieutenant, and first lieutenant, Fourth Cavalry (ca. 1905). The chaplain and the second lieutenant are wearing the mounted-dress uniform prescribed for officers in the 1902 and 1905 regulations. The first lieu-

tenant wears the prescribed dress uniform for dismounted. The dress coat is the same pattern as the previous undress coat for officers.

FIGURE 299. Left: Veterinarian's service uniform (ca. 1905), like that of a second lieutenant of cavalry, but with a winged horse hoof under the crossed sabers on the collar and without the letters "U.S." The year 1901 was the first time that uniforms for veterinarians had been mentioned in uniform regulations.

Center: Officer's overcoat, made of fine olive-drab woolen material (ca. 1905). The two braids forming the sleeve knot indicate this officer is a captain. In 1905 bronze crossed sabers were placed under the lower loop of the sleeve knot. He wears the olive-drab service cap and drab leather gloves. The enlisted man's overcoat was cut on the same pattern, but with cuffs and regulation bronze buttons instead of horn buttons.

Right: Officer's cape (ca. 1905) with falling black velvet collar, but without braid around the lower edge as on former patterns. This cape was for wear with dress or full-dress uniform when not on duty with troops under arms.

Corps and departments, except Engineers.—Of dark-blue cloth, with one stripe of gold-wire lace ⅞ inch wide along each outside seam.

For officers of cavalry, artillery, and infantry.—Of sky-blue cloth, with stripes 1½ inches wide, welted at the edges; the color of the stripes to be that of the facings of the respective corps or arms, except that for officers of infantry the stripes shall be white.

For all officers of the Corps of Engineers.—Of dark-blue cloth, with stripes of scarlet cloth 1½ inches in width, with a piping of white cloth ⅛ inch in width.

For chaplains.—Of plain black or blue-black cloth, without stripe, welt, or cord.

DRESS TROUSERS.

24. *For general officers, officers holding permanent appointments in the Staff Corps and departments, except Engineers.*—Of dark-blue cloth without stripe, welt, or cord, except that for the Chief of Artillery the trousers shall be of light-blue cloth with the addition of a stripe of scarlet cloth 1½ inches wide.

For all other officers.—The same as for full dress.

WHITE TROUSERS.

25. *For all officers.*—Of plain white material to match the white coat, without stripe, welt, or cord.

SERVICE TROUSERS.

26. *For all officers.*—Of olive-drab woolen or khaki-colored cotton material, to match the coat, without stripe, welt, or cord.

DRESS BREECHES.
[See Figures 296 and 298.]

27. *For all officers.*—Of same material and with same stripes as dress trousers, cut in the prescribed pattern and fastened from the knee down with dark bone buttons of appropriate size or with laces.

SERVICE BREECHES.

28. *For all officers.*—Of olive-drab woolen or khaki-colored cotton material, to match the service coat, without stripe, welt, or cord. To be made loose about the seat and above the knees; to fit closely below the knee, extending to the tops of the shoes, and to be fastened with tapes or laces or buttons. [See veterinarian in Figure 299.] To have a reenforce or saddle piece of the same material on the seat and legs for officers required to be mounted.

CHAPEAU.

29. *For general officers, for full dress, dismounted.*—According to pattern in the office of the Quartermaster General; to be worn with the front peak turned slightly to the left, showing the gilt ornaments upon the right side.

FULL-DRESS CAP.

30. *For general officers, mounted.*—A full-dress cap, to be of the same pattern and material as the full-dress cap for other officers, except that it will have a blue-black velvet band between the two lower welts 1¾ inches wide and midway thereon an embroidered design of oak leaves in gold 1 inch wide surrounding the cap; and on the visor an ornament of oak leaves embroidered in gold on the upper surface, as described below.

For all other officers, except chaplains.—To be of dark-blue cloth, with three cloth welts; total depth, 3½ inches; diameter across the top, 8¾ inches for a cap of size 7, the top to be ⅛ inch larger or smaller for every size above or below above-named size. The sides to be made in four pieces; to be 1½ inches between upper welts and stiffened with haircloth and wire around crown. Between the two lower welts a band 1¾ inches in width to be arranged as follows: Gold lace, ½ inch wide; background, ¾ inch wide; gold lace, ½ inch wide. The background between the bands of gold lace will be as follows: Of silk, the color being that of the facings of the corps, department, or arm of service (see par. 54). Visor to be of black patent leather, 1¾ inches deep at the center and of green color underneath; to droop at an angle of 45 degrees; to be ornamented with oak leaves embroidered in gold on the upper surface, for all officers above the rank of captain. Cap to be provided with flat gold cap strap, ⅜ inch wide, to be held at the sides by two small regulation gilt buttons. The cap badge shall be the coat of arms of the United States, embroidered in gold, as per pattern, and so placed that the tip of the eagle wings shall be ¾ inch below the top welt of the cap. All the details to be in accordance with sealed pattern in the office of the Quartermaster General. [See Figure 296 and Figure G on Uniform Color Plate VII in Volume I.]

DRESS CAP.
[See Figure 298.]

31. To be the same as the full-dress cap, except that instead of the gold lace and colored background, the space between the lower welts shall be covered as follows: For general officers, by a band of blue-black velvet; for all other officers, by a band of lustrous black mohair braid. The visor ornament of gold oak leaves is also excepted.

CHAPLAIN'S HAT.
[See Figures 296 and 298.]

32. Chaplains will wear with the full-dress and dress uniform a black hat, similar in shape to the service hat; to be ornamented with a cord of gold bullion and black silk intermixed, according to sealed pattern in the office of the Quartermaster General.

SERVICE CAP (OLIVE DRAB).
[See officer in overcoat in Figure 299.]

33. *For all officers.*—Of olive-drab serge, conforming to sealed pattern in the office of the Quartermaster General; to be made with three welts: Total depth, 3½ inches; diameter across the top, 8¾ inches for a cap of size 7; the top to be ⅛ inch larger or smaller for every size above or below size above named. The sides or bell to be made in four pieces,

seams equidistant; to be 1½ inches between welt joining top pieces to bell and top welt of band.

To have a band of lustrous mohair braid of olive-drab color 1¾ inches wide between the two lower welts.

To have a visor of black enameled leather, lined on underside with dark-green embossed leather, securely cemented to body of visor with the best rubber cement. The visor to be bound with black enameled leather to a depth of about 3/16 inch, upper edge of binding to be neatly turned in and stitched; the width of visor at its widest part to be 1⅝ inches, to be molded to shape at an angle of 45 degrees.

Trimmings: Chin strap to be made of best enameled black leather in two parts, with the necessary keepers of the same material; to be held in place by two small regulation buttons of dull-finish bronze. Lining to be of best quality olive-drab cotton and worsted serge, cut and shaped to the inner body of the cap, crown to be joined at the seam of the crownpiece of the cap, stitched therewith and to the band to hold lining securely in place. No stiffening of any kind to be used in crown or bell of cap. The inside band to be of a strong flexible material protected by a sweat leather of best quality, leather properly sewed in, turned on upper edge, and securely cemented.

Each cap to have four enameled-metal eyelets, as near color of serge as possible; to be placed above the band, two on each side of cap, the center of each eyelet to be halfway between upper welt of band and crown seam and 1¼ inches apart.

The cap badge shall be the coat of arms of the United States, of dull-finish bronze metal, detachable.

To be worn with the olive-drab service uniform as prescribed.

SERVICE CAP (COTTON KHAKI).
[See Figure 319.]

34. *For all officers.*—Of cotton khaki, U. S. Army standard. To conform in pattern to the service cap of olive-drab serge. Tops to be detachable and without bands. Each cap to be provided with two covers. Cap badge, visor, and strap to be same as specified for olive-drab service caps. To be worn with the cotton-khaki service uniform as prescribed.

WHITE CAP.

35. *For all officers.*—Of white linen or cotton duck, with removable top, conforming to the pattern of the service cap; the band between the two lower welts to be of white braid; the visor, cap strap, and buttons to be as prescribed for the dress cap. Cap badge not to be worn with this cap.

SERVICE HAT.
[See Figure 299.]

36. Of felt, of color of the service uniform, as nearly as practicable, according to sealed pattern in the office of the Quartermaster General. To be ornamented with a double cord ¼ inch in diameter, as follows: For *general officers* to be of gold bullion; for *all other officers*, of gold bullion and black silk intermixed.

EPAULETS.

37. *For general officers.*—Of gold, with solid crescent, according to sealed pattern in the office of the Quartermaster General. The only device will be the coat of arms of the United States embroidered in gold, placed in the center of the crescent.

SHOULDER KNOTS.
[See Figure 297.]

38. *For all officers except chaplains.*—Of gold-wire cord ¼ inch in diameter, formed of three cords in four plaits and rounded top, finished with small gilt regulation button; about 5½ inches long, extending from the seam of the sleeve to the seam of the collar; slightly stiffened with a flexible backing, which is to be covered with cloth of the color of the coat; to be made detachable.

SHOULDER STRAPS.

39. *General.*—Dark-blue cloth, 1⅜ inches wide and 4 inches long, bordered with an embroidery of gold ¼ inch wide; two silver embroidered stars of five rays each and gold embroidered "Arms of the United States" between them.

Lieutenant General.—Dark-blue cloth, 1⅜ inches wide and 4 inches long, bordered with an embroidery of gold ¼ inch wide; three silver-embroidered stars of five rays each, one star on the center of the strap and one at each end, equidistant between the center and outer edge of the strap, the center star to be the largest.

Major general.—The same as for a Lieutenant General, except that there will be two stars instead of three; the center of each star to be 1 inch from the outer edge of the gold embroidery on the ends of the strap; both stars of the same size.

Brigadier general.—The same as for a major general, except that there will be one star at the center of the strap instead of two stars.

The strap for the Chief of Artillery will be of scarlet cloth.

Colonel.—The same as for a brigadier general, omitting the star, with a silver-embroidered spread eagle on the center of the strap, 2 inches between the tips of the wings, having in the right talon an olive branch and in the left a bundle of arrows; an escutcheon on the breast as represented in the "Arms of the United States." Color of the cloth of the straps to be as stated under "Colors of Facings" (par. 54).

Lieutenant colonel.—The same as for a colonel, according to corps, department, or arm of service, omitting the eagle, with a silver-embroidered leaf at each end, each leaf extending ⅞ inch from the end of the strap.

Major.—The same as for a lieutenant colonel, with a gold-embroidered leaf at each end instead of the silver leaf; each leaf extending ⅞ inch from the end of the strap.

Captain.—The same as for a major, omitting the leaves; at each end two silver embroidered bars of the same width as the border, placed parallel to the ends of the strap; the distance between them and the border equal to the width of the border.

First lieutenant.—The same as for a captain; at each end one silver-embroidered bar of the same width as the border, placed parallel to the ends of the strap, at a distance from the border equal to the width of the border.

Second lieutenant or additional second lieutenant.—The same as for a first lieutenant, omitting the bars.

Chaplain.—The same as for a second lieutenant, with a plain Latin cross of silver in the center; cloth of strap to be dark blue.

AIGUILLETTES.

40. *For officers of the General Staff Corps, except the Chief of Staff, for the Adjutant General of the Army, officers of The Military Secretary's Department, officers of the Inspector General's Department, aids-de-camp to general officers, regimental adjutants, and adjutants of artillery districts.*—Of gold-wire cord, according to sealed pattern in the office of the Quartermaster General.

SASHES.

41. *For general officers.*—Buff silk ribbon 3 to 4 inches wide, or buff silk net, or buff silk and gold thread or webbing with silk bullion fringe edges; general officers above the grade of brigadier general will wear the sash across the body from the right shoulder to the left side, and not extended around the waist.

For brigadier generals.—The sash to be as prescribed. It shall be made up and fastened with a flat catch, knot arranged ready for adjustment. Sash to be worn only in one thickness around the waist so as to fit snugly over the belt, fastened with a metal clasp, and to be tied in a double bow; tassels pendant midway between the hip and knee.

The color of the sash for the Chief of Artillery will be scarlet instead of buff.

CRAVATS.

42. *For all officers, except chaplains.*—Of black silk, the tie not to be worn outside the opening of the collar.

For chaplains.—A white or black tie.

GLOVES.

43. Of drab-colored leather, according to sealed pattern in the office of the Quartermaster General. White gloves of plain white cotton, wool, or leather.

SABERS.
[See Figures 296 and 298.]

44. *For all officers, except chaplains.*—According to sealed pattern in the office of the Chief of Ordnance; the guard to be of German silver and the scabbard of steel. Officers who have provided themselves with the German silver scabbard formerly prescribed will be permitted to continue its use as long as it presents a creditable appearance.

SABER KNOTS.
[See Figures 296 and 298.]

45. *For general officers.*—Heavy gold cord with acorn ends, according to sealed pattern in the office of the Quartermaster General.

For all other officers, except chaplains.—Strap and acorn to be of gold bullion and black silk interwoven.

The gold-lace saber knots will be worn on full-dress and dress occasions. On other occasions officers will wear a saber knot of plaited russet leather, according to pattern in the office of the Quartermaster General.

FULL-DRESS SABER BELTS.

46. *For all officers, except chaplains.*—A waist belt not less than 1½ inches nor more than 2 inches wide, with detachable slings, to be worn outside of the full-dress coat. To be made of the following materials and facings:

For general officers, except brigadier generals.—Of red Russia leather, with three stripes of gold embroidery, having detachable embroidered Russia-leather slings, as per sealed pattern in the office of the Quartermaster General.

For brigadier generals.—A black webbing belt, according to sealed pattern in the office of the Quartermaster General, with detachable Russia-leather slings, same as the slings for other general officers. The belt to be fastened with a flat, smooth brass buckle, and to be worn on the outside of the coat under the sash.

For all field officers.—One broad stripe of gold lace on black-enameled leather, according to sealed pattern in the office of the Quartermaster General.

For all officers holding permanent appointments in the Staff Corps and departments, except Engineers, below the rank of field officer.—Four stripes of gold lace interwoven with black silk on black-enameled leather, according to sealed pattern in the office of the Quartermaster General.

For officers of cavalry, artillery, and infantry below the rank of field officer.—Four stripes of gold-wire lace interwoven with silk of the color of arm of service, according to sealed pattern in the office of the Quartermaster General. [See Figure 296 and Figure G on Uniform Color Plate VII in Volume I.]

For officers of Engineers.—Same as for officers of artillery.

FULL-DRESS BELT PLATE.

47. *For all officers, except chaplains.*—Gilt, rectangular, 2 inches wide, with bright raised rim, according to sealed pattern in the office of the Quartermaster General; a silver wreath of laurel encircling the "Arms of the United States;" stars also of silver; eagle, shield, scroll, edge of the cloud and rays, bright. The motto "E pluribus unum," upon the scroll.

DRESS AND SERVICE BELT.
[See Figure 319 and veterinarian in Figure 299.]

48. *For all officers, except chaplains.*—Of stuffed russet leather or pigskin, with detachable slings of the same material, provided with a buckle of dull-finish bronze, according to sealed pattern in the office of the Chief of Ordnance. To be worn under the dress coat and overcoat, and outside the service coat.

In the field the use of a belt made with cross belts over the shoulders, and adapted to carry saber and pistol, according

FIGURE 300. Regulation Army buttons, pattern of 1902, for officers and enlisted men. They were made in both gilt and dull bronze, except the large overcoat button at the top, which was made in dull bronze only for enlisted men's overcoats. Reproduced actual size.

to sealed pattern in the office of the Chief of Ordnance, is authorized. [See Figure 319.]

A belt of black webbing with detachable slings of stuffed russet leather or pigskin, may be worn under the dress coat. Full-dress slings will be worn with the full-dress uniform and the russet-leather or pigskin slings with all other uniforms.

SHOULDER BELTS.

49. *For the Chief Signal Officer.*—For full dress, a shoulder belt of red Russia leather having three stripes of gold embroidery, with field-glass case attached.

For all other officers of the Signal Corps.—For full dress, a shoulder belt corresponding to their waist belt, with field-glass case attached.

All as per sealed patterns in the office of the Quartermaster General.

BOOTS.

50. *For all mounted officers.*—To be of stuffed russet leather or of polished black, black enamel, or patent leather, according to sealed pattern in the office of the Quartermaster General. The spur rest to be 1¾ inches above bottom of heel.

SHOES.

51. *For all officers.*—High shoes of stuffed russet leather or of polished black, black enamel, or patent leather.

SPURS.

52. *For all mounted officers.*—Of white metal, without chains, according to sealed pattern in the office of the Chief of Ordnance. The projecting stud to be of only sufficient length to prevent the strap slipping; to have a half concealed rowel, showing on the upper side only; buckle to be plain; to be worn with black straps with full-dress and dress uniform, and with russet-leather straps with the leggings and russet-leather boots.

LEGGINGS.

53. *For all officers.*—Stuffed russet-leather leggings of the pattern known as the "strap puttee." Mounted officers may substitute stuffed russet-leather boots. In the field a canvas legging, as furnished by the Quartermaster's Department, may be worn.

COLORS OF FACINGS.

54. *For general officers and officers holding permanent appointments in the Staff Corps and departments, except as herein mentioned.*—Dark blue.

For officers of Engineers.—Scarlet, piped with white.

For officers of the Signal Corps.—Orange, piped with white.

For officers of the Ordnance Department.—Black, piped with scarlet.

For officers of the Medical Corps.—Maroon.

For officers of the Quartermaster's Department.—Buff.

For officers of cavalry.—Yellow.

For officers of artillery.—Scarlet.

For officers of infantry.—Light blue.

BUTTONS.
[See Figure 300.]

55. *For all officers, except Engineers.*—Circular, slightly convex, of gold or gilt metal, or of dull-finish bronze metal, as prescribed; device, coat of arms of the United States. To be of two sizes, (1) the "regulation button," exterior diameter, 36 lines, about ⅞ inch; (2) the "small regulation button," exterior diameter, 25 lines, about 9/16 inch.

For officers of Engineers.—Circular, slightly convex, of gold or gilt metal, or of dull-finish bronze metal, as prescribed, of same sizes as for other officers; device, an eagle holding in his beak a scroll with the word "Essayons," a bastion with embrasures in the distance surrounded by water, with a rising sun.

INSIGNIA.

56. To conform to sealed patterns in the office of the Quartermaster General.

(*a*) The letters "U. S.", gothic design, each followed by a period, will be worn by all officers on the collar of the dress, service, and white coats, placed at a distance of 1 inch from each end of the collar, a suitable space to be left between the letters. To be followed by the letter "V" to designate United States Volunteers. On the dress and white coats the letters will be of gold or gilt metal, except that for officers of the Corps of Engineers they will be of silver metal. On the service coat they will be of dull-finish bronze metal for all officers.

(*b*) *Insignia of corps, department, or arm of service.* To be placed on the sleeves of the full-dress coat and overcoat, as prescribed in paragraphs 17 and 21 [See Figures 296 and 299]; and on the collar of the dress, service, and white coats, at a distance of ⅝ inch from the letters "U.S." [See Figures 298, 319, and 322]; to be of metal or embroidery for the full-dress coat, and of metal as hereinafter prescribed for the dress and the white coats, and of dull-finish bronze metal for the service coat and overcoat.

The Chief of Staff.—Such device as he may prescribe.

The General Staff Corps.—The coat of arms of the United States of gold and enamel superimposed upon a silver star. This device will not be worn by general officers of the General Staff Corps on the sleeves of the full-dress coat and overcoat. Until the change in the collar ornaments from the coat of arms of the United States to the letters "U. S." takes effect, the device herein prescribed for the General Staff Corps will, when worn as a collar ornament, be in lieu of the coat of arms and the device of the corps, department, or arm of service, to which the officer permanently belongs.

The Adjutant General and The Military Secretary's Department.—A shield of gold or gilt metal.

Inspector General's Department.—Gold or gilt sword and fasces, crossed and wreathed.

Judge-Advocate General's Department.—Sword and pen in gold or gilt metal, crossed and wreathed.

Quartermaster's Department.—Sword and key crossed on a wheel, surmounted by a spread eagle; of gold or gilt metal, platinum, and enamel.

Subsistence Department.—A silver crescent, ½ inch between cusps, cusps to the rear.

Pay Department.—A diamond, with diagonals ¾ inch and 1 inch in length, in gold or gilt metal, placed with shorter diagonal vertical.

Medical Department.—A caduceus, of gold or gilt metal.

Corps of Engineers.—A silver turretted castle.

Ordnance Department.—Shell and flame, of gold or gilt metal.

Signal Corps.—Two crossed signal flags and a burning torch, in gold and silver.

Chief of Bureau of Insular Affairs.—A bunch of seven arrows, with wings on sides, 1 inch in height, in gold or gilt metal.

Professors and Associate Professors of the United States Military Academy.—Shield and helmet surmounted by a scroll, in gold or gilt metal.

Cavalry.—Two crossed sabers, 1 inch high, with number of regiment above intersection; of gold or gilt metal. [See Figures 298, 319, and 322.]

Artillery.—Two crossed cannons, design to be 1 inch high, of gold or gilt metal, with oval at intersection having a scarlet center.

The red oval in the insignia for officers of coast artillery to exhibit an oblong projectile in gilt outline; for officers of field artillery, a gilt wheel in outline.

Infantry.—Two crossed rifles, design to be 1 inch high, with number of regiment above intersection; of gold or gilt metal.

Aids-de-camp.—A device, 1⅓ inches high, consisting of a shield of the United States, of properly colored enamel, ¾ inch high and ¾ inch wide at time, surmounted by a gold or gilt eagle, with wings displayed. On the blue field of the shield a star or stars, according to rank of the general on whose staff the officer is serving.

This device is to be worn on the collar of the dress coat and on the sleeves of the full-dress coat and overcoat in lieu of corps or arm of service device.

Regimental staff officers.—Regimental adjutants, quartermasters, commissaries, adjutants of artillery districts, and squadron and battalion adjutants will wear in the lower angles of their insignia the devices (of gold or gilt metal) of the respective departments to which their duties correspond. The battalion adjutant and quartermaster of engineer battalions will wear the same devices above the center turret.

Chaplains.—The same as for regimental staff officers, except that the pendant design shall be a Latin cross of gold or gilt metal.

(*c*) *Insignia of rank.*

General and Lieutenant General.—Such as they may prescribe.

Major general.—Two silver stars.

Brigadier general.—One silver star.

Colonel.—One silver spread eagle.

Lieutenant colonel.—One silver leaf.

Major.—One gold leaf.

Captain.—Two silver bars.

First lieutenant.—One silver bar.

Sleeve insignia of rank.
[See Figure 296.]

General officers.—See paragraphs 17 and 21.

Colonel.—A single knot composed of five strands of gold-wire lace, not exceeding ⅛ inch in width. To be applied to the sleeve of the full-dress coat below the elbow, the base resting on the gold band of the sleeve.

Lieutenant colonel.—Four strands, single knot.

Major.—Three strands, single knot.

Captain.—Two strands, single knot.

First lieutenant.—One strand, single knot.

Second lieutenant.—Without gold lace.

Chaplain.—Without gold lace.

The outside dimensions of the gold-lace insignia will be the same for all officers, the diminution being made by omitting strands from the interior.

Sleeve insignia of rank for overcoats, made of flat black mohair soutache braid ⅛ inch in width, will follow the form of the gold-lace insignia for full-dress coats, but be applied with the base resting at the lower end of the sleeve, except as prescribed in paragraph 21 for officers of the General Staff Corps.

UNIFORM FOR EVENING WEAR.
[See Figure 321 and Figure A on Uniform Color Plate VIII in Volume I.]

57. The commanding officer will designate the uniform for evening wear on all occasions of a general or official character occurring within the limits of his command.

For occasions of special formality, the uniform for evening functions shall be the prescribed full-dress dismounted uniform.

For other occasions of ceremony to which officers are invited in their official capacity, such as balls, official dinners, official receptions, etc., and formal mess dinners, the following special full-dress uniform is authorized, and officers are at liberty to wear it or the full-dress dismounted uniform:

An evening-dress coat of dark-blue cloth cut on the lines of the civilian dress coat, with the regulation gilt buttons of same number and placed as on sealed pattern in Quartermaster General's Office; the sleeves of this coat to be ornamented for all officers in the same manner as the sleeves of their full-dress uniform coats.

A waistcoat of dark blue or white, cut low with full open bosom, three small gilt regulation buttons, should be worn with this coat; also full-dress trousers by all officers except those of engineers, cavalry, artillery, and infantry, who will wear dark-blue trousers without stripes; patent-leather shoes, and full-dress cap. Shoulder ornaments for general officers will be epaulets or shoulder knots; for other officers, except chaplains, shoulder knots. On proper occasions, which are not official in character, officers are authorized to wear civilian evening dress.

MESS JACKET.
[See Figure 321 and Figure B on Uniform Color Plate VIII in Volume I.]

58. Officers of the staff corps and departments, the corps of artillery, and the regiments of cavalry and infantry are authorized to adopt a "mess jacket" distinctive of their corps, department, or regiment, which must conform in cut to the sealed pattern in the Quartermaster General's Office.

To be made of dark-blue cloth. Body of jacket to be cut like evening-dress coat, to descend to point of hips, slightly curved to a peak behind and in front; five buttonholes on lapels, three buttons of regulation coat size on each side, placed 1½ inches from bottom and spaced 2 to 3½ inches apart. Sleeves to be ornamented same as full-dress coat. Such

further distinctive ornamentation of this jacket, as may be desired by the organizations named, is authorized, but when once adopted the "mess jacket" for any particular organization shall not be changed without authority of the Secretary of War on the recommendation of a majority of the officers interested.

With this jacket will be worn the detachable shoulder knot provided for full-dress coat; also vests of the color of the coat, or white.

Commanding officers may, in the tropics or in the warm season, authorize the white trousers to be worn with this jacket.

Black shoes will always be worn with this jacket.

59. Professors and associate professors of the United States Military Academy holding permanent appointments as such, will wear the full-dress and dress uniforms of officers of The Military Secretary's Department, omitting the aiguillettes, with insignia as prescribed in paragraph 56.

UNIFORMS OF OFFICERS DETAILED FOR DUTY IN STAFF DEPARTMENTS, OR ON SPECIAL DUTY WITH INCREASED RANK, AND OF ACTING JUDGE ADVOCATES.

60. Officers detailed to fill vacancies in the General Staff Corps. The Military Secretary's Department, the Inspector General's Department, the Quartermaster's Department, the Subsistence Department, the Pay Department, the Ordnance Department, and the Signal Corps, and officers detailed as acting judge advocates will wear the uniform of the corps, department, or arm of service to which they permanently belong, omitting the insignia therefor on the sleeves of the full-dress coat and overcoat, the collar of the dress coat, service coat, and white coat, and substituting the insignia of the corps or department in which they are serving. Officers detailed in the General Staff Corps, The Military Secretary's Department, and the Inspector General's Department will wear the aiguillettes; those detailed in the Signal Corps will wear the shoulder belt.

Corresponding insignia will also be substituted for the regimental number or other insignia on the saddlecloth.

Officers detailed on duty carrying increased rank will wear the uniform of their permanent corps, department, or arm of service, with proper insignia to indicate the increased rank and their particular duty, as may be prescribed by the Secretary of War.

UNIFORM OF CONTRACT SURGEONS.

61. No full-dress uniform is authorized for contract surgeons; their dress, service, and white uniforms and overcoat will conform to those of medical officers, but without the shoulder straps or insignia of rank. The collar ornaments for their dress and white uniforms will be of silver instead of gold, and the letters "C. S." will replace the letters "U. S." The collar ornaments on their service uniform will be of dull-finish bronze metal, the letters "C. S." replacing the letters "U. S."

62. No full-dress uniform is authorized for dental surgeons; their dress, service, and white uniforms, and overcoat will be the same as those prescribed for contract surgeons, using the letters "D. S." in place of the letters "C. S."

UNIFORMS OF VETERINARIANS OF CAVALRY AND ARTILLERY
CORPS.
[See Figure 299.]

63. No full-dress uniform is authorized for veterinarians; their dress, service, and white uniforms and overcoat will conform to those of second lieutenants of cavalry or artillery, according to the arm of service, omitting the shoulder straps and the letters "U. S."; collar ornaments to consist of the device of arm of service with number of regiment or battalion in upper angle, of gold or gilt metal, and the foot of a horse, shod, with wings on sides, of white metal in lower angle, placed at a distance of 1 inch from each end of collar. For their service uniform, the collar ornaments will be of dull-finish bronze metal.

MISCELLANEOUS.

64. With the full-dress and dress uniforms, and with the service uniform when worn in garrison, officers will wear a plain white standing collar and plain white cuffs; the collar to show not to exceed ½ inch above the collar of the coat.

65. Officers and enlisted men are permitted to wear waterproof capes or overcoats, as nearly as practicable the color of the service uniform, when on duty involving exposure to rainy or other inclement weather.

66. The badge of military mourning is a knot of black crape upon the saber hilt for a period not to exceed thirty days. (A. R. 435.) [See officer on right in Figure 326.]

67. All officers pertaining to a garrison will, whenever within the limits of a post to which they belong, appear in some one of the prescribed uniforms. The wearing of civilian clothing will be restricted within the post to the necessary time required in entering and leaving same, except as provided in paragraph 57.

DESCRIPTION OF GARMENTS AND OTHER
ARTICLES OF UNIFORM FOR ENLISTED
MEN OF THE ARMY.

DRESS COAT.
[See Figures 301 and 302, and Figure F on Uniform Color
Plate VII in Volume I. See also Color Plate IX.]

68. A single-breasted sack coat of dark-blue cloth according to sealed pattern in the office of the Quartermaster General; fastened with six regulation buttons down the front; standing collar; shoulder loops, of the same material and color, let in at the shoulder seam and to button to the collar with a small regulation button; the sleeves to have a cuff, made according to sealed pattern, and ornamented with three small regulation buttons. The collar, shoulder loops, and cuffs to be piped with "cord edge braid" of the color of corps, department, or arm of service. The color of the braid

for Engineers, Ordnance, Hospital Corps, and Signal Corps to be mixed in alternate stripes.

Collar ornaments for enlisted men, of yellow metal similar to those for officers and according to sealed patterns in the office of the Quartermaster General, will be placed on this coat in the same manner as on the dress coat of the officers.

Musicians and trumpeters will wear the insignia of regiment or corps on their coat collars. Band musicians a lyre, same as worn on cap.

BREAST CORD.
[See Figure 302 and Figure F on Uniform Color Plate VII
in Volume I.]

69. Cords and tassels of mohair, of the color of the corps, department, or arm of the service, according to sealed pattern in the office of the Quartermaster General. To be attached to the dress coat, beginning at the button of the left shoulder loop, one cord passing in rear of the neck and the other in front, under the first button of the coat, crossing under the right shoulder loop and brought together under the right arm with a slide, then passing across the breast between the third and fourth buttons and attached to the left shoulder button.

SERVICE COAT.
[See Figures 301 and 303 and Color Plate IX.]

70. A sack coat of olive-drab woolen material or khaki-colored cotton material conforming in design and cut to the service coat for officers, according to sealed sample in the office of the Quartermaster General. The same collar ornaments will be placed on this coat as on the dress coat, except that all buttons and metal ornaments will be of dull-finish bronze metal.

WHITE COAT.
[See Figures 301 and 322.]

71. A sack coat of bleached cotton duck, according to sealed pattern in the office of the Quartermaster General. Collar ornaments to be the same as prescribed for the dress coat.

FATIGUE COAT.
[See Figure 316.]

72. *For all enlisted men.*—Of brown cotton duck according to sealed pattern in the office of the Quartermaster General.

OVERCOATS.
[See Figure 308.]

73. *For all enlisted men.*—Of olive-drab woolen material, general design and cut to be that of the officers' overcoat, the buttons to be of dull-finish bronze metal, according to sealed pattern in the office of the Quartermaster General.

DRESS TROUSERS.
[See Figures 301 and 302.]

74. *For all enlisted men.*—Of sky-blue kersey; to be cut and made in accordance with sealed standard pattern in the office of the Quartermaster General.

FIGURE 301. Top: 1902 pattern for both olive-drab-woolen and khaki-cotton service uniforms for enlisted men. Buttons (1902–11), dull bronze. Center: 1902 pattern for white summer sack coat and white trousers for enlisted men. In 1907 regulations prescribed this dress for members of the Hospital Corps only. Buttons, gilt. Bottom: 1902 pattern for dress coat, dark blue, and sky-blue-kersey dress trousers. Buttons, gilt.

FIGURE 302. Private, left, in the 1902-pattern dismounted-full-dress uniform; corporal, center, in the mounted-full-dress uniform; and first sergeant, right, in the dismounted-dress uniform. All 3 wear the same pattern of dress coat. Collar ornaments remained the coat of arms of the United States and crossed sabers until June 1, 1905, when General Order No. 197, War Department, directed that "the pre-scribed ornament shall be the letters 'U.S.' instead of the coat of arms of the United States," effective that date, and that the change would be completed throughout the Army by June 30, 1905. Coats are piped in yellow and two yellow bands on the cap identify the cavalry arm. Breeches on the corporal are olive-drab-wool service pattern. No sky-blue dress breeches were issued to enlisted mounted troops.

FIGURE 303. Private, squadron sergeant major, and lance corporal, Troop L, Third Cavalry (ca. 1904), in the new service uniform. The private wears the wool olive-drab uniform, while the squadron sergeant major and the lance corporal wear the summer khaki uniform, allowed only at tropical posts until a change in the regulations in 1907 permitted its wear during the summer months at all Army posts. The khaki helmet was issued for wear with the service uniform in summer by all troops for some duties until about 1907, when the supply was exhausted.

FIGURE 304. Chevrons for noncommissioned officers, pattern of 1902. Those for the dress coat were made with yellow facing cloth stitched to dark blue grounds. Chevrons for the olive-drab service uniform were olive-drab facing cloth on olive-drab woolen-cloth grounds; for the khaki service coat, of olive-drab facing cloth on khaki grounds; and for the white summer coat, of olive-drab facing cloth on grounds of white-bleached-cotton duck. Ranks for cavalry are shown here. Top Row: regimental sergeant major; regimental quartermaster sergeant; regimental commissary sergeant; squadron sergeant major; chief musician; chief trumpeter. Center Row: principal musician; color sergeant; first sergeant; drum major; sergeant; troop quartermaster sergeant. Bottom Row: corporal; lance corporal; cook; saddler; farrier and blacksmith.

STRIPES FOR TROUSERS.

75. Stripes to be of cloth of the following colors:
Cavalry.—Yellow.
Artillery.—Scarlet.
Infantry.—White.
Engineers.—Scarlet, piped with white.
Ordnance.—Black, piped with scarlet.
Post quartermaster sergeants.—Buff.
Post commissary sergeants.—Cadet gray.
Hospital Corps.—Maroon, piped with white.
Signal corps.—Orange, piped with white.

Army service detachment of the United States Military Academy, West Point, N. Y.—Buff.

All noncommissioned officers above the rank of corporal will wear stripes 1¼ inches in width, including pipings. All corporals will wear stripes ½ inch wide, including pipings.

Musicians and trumpeters will wear two stripes each ½ inch wide.

WHITE TROUSERS.
[See Figures 301 and 322.]

76. Of bleached cotton duck, without stripes, according to sealed pattern in the office of the Quartermaster General.

CANVAS FATIGUE TROUSERS.
[See Figures 308 and 316.]

77. Of brown cotton duck, without stripes, according to sealed pattern in the office of the Quartermaster General.

SERVICE BREECHES.
[See Figures 301 and 303.]

78. Of olive-drab woolen or khaki-colored cotton material to match the service coat. To be worn without stripes; to be made loose above the knee, fitting closely below the knee, extending to the tops of the shoes, and fastened with tapes or laces; to be worn with shoes and leggings.

For mounted use, to have a reenforce or saddle piece of the same material on seat and legs. The general design of the breeches will conform to the pattern prescribed for officers.

DRESS CAP.
[See Figure 302, Figure F on Uniform Color Plate VII in Volume I, and Color Plate IX.]

79. Of dark-blue cloth, of same pattern and shape as that prescribed for officers; between the two lower welts a band 1¾ inches wide, to be arranged as follows: A stripe of cloth of the color of the corps, department, or arm of service, at top and bottom, the intervening space of ¾ inch to be of the color of the cap; a black enameled leather chin strap, fitted with a stout fire-gilt slide and a leather keeper, secured at both ends by small gilt regulation buttons, one on each side immediately back of the ends of the visor.

Insignia of yellow metal, except where otherwise specified, and made according to sealed patterns in the office of the Quartermaster General, will be attached to the front of the cap, so that the top of the insignia will be slightly below the top of the cap. Designs as follows:

Cavalry.—Crossed sabers, number of regiment in the upper angle and letter of troop in lower angle.

Artillery.—Crossed cannons, with number of battery or company in the lower angle.

Infantry.—Crossed rifles, number of regiment in the upper angle and letter of company in lower angle.

Engineers.—The castle with letter of company above it.

Ordnance sergeants.—Shell and flame in white metal, inclosed in a wreath of gilt metal.

All enlisted men of the Ordnance Department.—A shell and flame in gilt metal.

Post commissary sergeants.—Crescent of white metal, the points up, inclosed in a wreath of gilt metal.

Post quartermaster sergeants.—Insignia of the Quartermaster's Department, in white metal, inclosed in a wreath of gilt metal.

Master signal electrician, master electrician, and electrician sergeants.—A symbol resembling forked lightning, of white metal inclosed in a wreath of gilt metal.

Enlisted men of the Hospital Corps.—Sergeants first class, a caduceus of white metal inclosed in a wreath of gilt metal. For sergeants, corporals, lance corporals, privates first class, and privates, a caduceus of gilt metal, without the wreath.

FIGURE 305. Cap and collar ornament for band musicians, pattern of 1902—gilt for dress coats and caps, and bronze for service coats and caps. Reproduced actual size.

Noncommissioned officers of the Signal Corps, except master signal electrician.—Two crossed signal flags and a burning torch of white metal, inclosed in a wreath of gilt metal. For all other enlisted men of the Signal Corps, two crossed signal flags and a burning torch of gilt metal.

Enlisted men of the Army service detachment at the United States Military Academy, West Point, N. Y.—The insignia of the Quartermaster's Department in gilt metal.

Band musicians.—A lyre of white metal. Engineers to have a castle of yellow metal in the center. Cavalry and infantry to have the number of the regiment, and artillery the number of the band, of yellow metal, in the center of the lyre. [See Figure 305.]

Musicians of Engineers.—A bugle of yellow metal, with a castle of white metal in the center of, and the letter of the company, in yellow metal, above the bugle.

Musicians of infantry and trumpeters of cavalry.—A bugle with letter of company or troop above the bugle, and number of regiment in center of bugle. [See Figure 322.]

Musicians of artillery.—A bugle with the number of the company or battery in the center.

SERVICE CAP (OLIVE DRAB).
[See Figures 308 and 324 and Color Plate IX.]

80. *For all enlisted men.*—Of olive-drab serge, according to sealed pattern in the office of the Quartermaster General. Pattern to conform to that of the olive-drab service cap for officers, omitting the band of lustrous olive-drab braid. Insignia to be of dull-finish bronze metal of same pattern as prescribed in paragraph 79, for the dress cap. Each cap to have an eyelet in the front seam of the flange of the cap, ⅝ inch from the edge of the crown, to receive the fastening of the insignia.

To be worn as prescribed, with the olive-drab service uniform.

SERVICE CAP (COTTON KHAKI).
[See Figure 303.]

81. *For all enlisted men.*—Of cotton khaki, U. S. Army standard, conforming in pattern to the olive drab serge service cap for enlisted men, according to sealed pattern in the office of the Quartermaster General. The top to be detachable, and each cap to be provided with two covers. To be worn as prescribed, with the cotton-khaki service uniform.

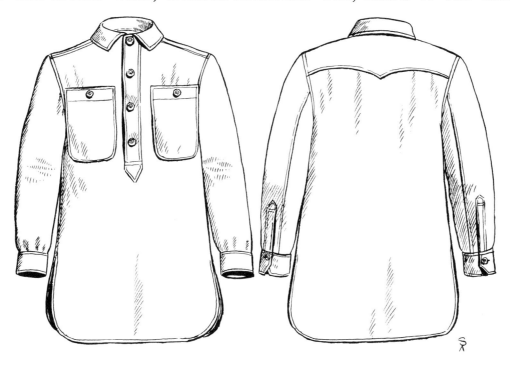

FIGURE 306. Light blue cotton-chambray shirt, pattern of 1902, to be worn under fatigue clothing for work details and stable duty.

SERVICE HAT.
[See Figure 303.]

82. *For all enlisted men.*—Of felt, of color of the service uniform as nearly as practicable, according to sealed pattern in the office of the Quartermaster General; with double hat cord 3/16 inch in diameter, of firm material, conforming in color to that of the corps, department, or arm of service; to be sewed fast to the hat. The number of the regiment and letter or number of the company, troop, or battery, made of dull-finish bronze metal, to be placed on the front part of the crown, the regimental number to be above the company letter or number. Enlisted men of field artillery will wear crossed cannons, with the number of the battery below them, all of dull-finish bronze metal. Post noncommissioned staff officers will wear the device in dull-finish bronze metal of their respective corps, as prescribed in paragraph 79, but without the wreath.

To have eyelets on each side for fastening a strap or cord, the use of which is authorized. The hat to be worn creased in the middle as issued.

WHITE CAP.

83. Same as prescribed for officers, omitting the white braid. The visor and cap strap to be the same as prescribed for the service cap, and the buttons to be small regulation, gilt. No ornaments will be worn on this cap.

SHOES.
[See Figure 311.]

84. According to sealed pattern in the office of the Quartermaster General.

Black calfskin shoes.—To be made in the Blucher style.

Marching shoes.—To be of russet tanned "grain calf" leather, thoroughly stuffed. They will be worn with the service uniform when so ordered by the commanding officer.

Garrison shoes.—To be of russet leather, made in the Blucher style.

Barrack shoes.—The uppers to be of brown cotton duck. They will be worn in barracks only.

LEGGINGS.
[See Figure 303.]

85. Of cotton duck or canvas, color of the service uniform, made in accordance with sealed pattern in the office of the Quartermaster General.

COLLARS.

86. *For all enlisted men.*—White linen collars, according to sealed pattern in the office of the Quartermaster General; to be worn with the full-dress and dress uniforms on all occasions and to show not to exceed 1/2 inch above the collar of the coat.

CRAVATS.

87. *For all enlisted men.*—Black, according to sealed pattern in the office of the Quartermaster General; the tie not to be worn outside of the opening of the collar of the coat.

BUTTONS.
[See Figure 300.]

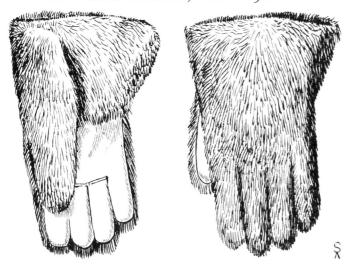

FIGURE 307. Muskrat-fur gauntlets, pattern of 1902.

88. *For all enlisted men.*—Of yellow metal, fire gilt and burnished or of dull-finish bronze, as prescribed, according to sealed standards in the office of the Quartermaster General, of same design as prescribed in paragraph 55 for all officers except Engineers.

CHEVRONS.
[See Figure 304.]

89. The rank of noncommissioned officers will be marked on the sleeves of the dress coat, overcoat, service coat, and white coat by chevrons, according to sealed patterns in the office of the Quartermaster General. The chevrons for the dress coat shall correspond in colors and pipings to those in paragraph 75, relating to stripes for trousers, placed upon a groundwork of dark-blue cloth. The bars or the embroidery of the chevrons for overcoats, service coats, and white coats shall conform in color to shade of olive-drab shirting flannel, placed upon a groundwork corresponding to the material of the respective garments.

The chevrons will be worn points up, midway between the elbow and shoulder, unless otherwise prescribed.

Rank will be indicated as follows:

Regimental sergeant major.—Three bars and an arc of three bars.

Regimental quartermaster sergeant.—Three bars and a tie of three bars.

Regimental commissary sergeant.—Three bars and a tie of three bars, having a crescent (points front); top of crescent ¼ inch below the inner angle and lower point of crescent ¼ inch above the first of the tiebars.

Color sergeant.—Three bars and a star.

Battalion of Engineers, quartermaster sergeant.—Three bars and a tie of two bars.

Squadron or battalion sergeant major.—Three bars and an arc of two bars.

Chief musician.—Three bars and an arc of two bars, with a bugle of pattern worn on caps in the center.

Chief trumpeter.—Three bars and an arc of one bar, with a bugle of pattern worn on caps in the center.

Principal musician.—Three bars and a bugle.

Drum major.—Three bars and two embroidered crossed batons.

Ordnance sergeant.—Three bars and an arc of one bar, inclosing a shell and a flame.

Sergeant of ordnance.—The same as for ordnance sergeant, omitting the arc.

Corporal of Ordnance.—Two bars, inclosing shell and flame.

First-class private of ordnance.—The shell and flame.

Post quartermaster sergeant.—Three bars and insignia of the Quartermaster's Department.

Post commissary sergeant.—Three bars and a crescent (points to the front); top of crescent to be ½ inch below the inner angle of chevron.

Sergeants, first-class, of the Hospital Corps.—Three bars and an arc of one bar, of maroon cloth, inclosing a caduceus 1¼ inches high, embroidered in maroon silk; the bars, arc, and caduceus to have a narrow white border.

Sergeants of the Hospital Corps.—The same as for sergeants, first-class, omitting the arc.

Corporals of the Hospital Corps.—The same as for sergeants, omitting one bar.

Lance corporals of the Hospital Corps.—A chevron of one bar of maroon cloth with white border, in addition to and placed just above the caduceus for a private, first-class.

Privates, first-class, of the Hospital Corps.—A device consisting of a caduceus 1¼ inches high embroidered in maroon silk and having a white border.

Master signal electrician.—Three bars and an arc of one bar of orange cloth, piped with white, inclosing a representation of forked lightning embroidered in white silk.

Sergeant of the first class of the Signal Corps.—Three bars and an arc of one bar, color orange, piped with white, inclosing a device consisting of crossed signal flags, red and white, and a burning torch in yellow.

Sergeant of the Signal Corps.—Same as for sergeant of the first class, omitting the arc.

Corporal of the Signal Corps.—Two bars, inclosing same device as for sergeant of the first class.

Private of the Signal Corps.—Device consisting of crossed signal flags, red and white, and a burning torch in yellow.

Master electrician.—Three bars and an arc of one bar of scarlet cloth, inclosing a representation of forked lightning, embroidered in white silk.

Electrician sergeant.—The same as for master electrician, omitting the arc.

CHEVRONS FOR COMPANY NONCOMMISSIONED OFFICERS.

First Sergeant.—Three bars and a lozenge.

Troop, battery, or company quartermaster sergeant.—Three bars and a tie of one bar.

Sergeant.—Three bars.

COLOR PLATE VII. The full-dress uniform prescribed for Indian scouts in 1890. Made more ornate than the dress uniforms for any other corps, the scout dress was designed to satisfy the Indian's love for color. The helmet plume, longer than that for other mounted men, had 4 strands of red horsehair mixed with the white. The eagle plate and the side buttons on the helmet had crossed arrows to distinguish the Indian scouts from the other branches of the Army.

Stable sergeant, Field Artillery.—Three bars and a horse's head.

Corporal.—Two bars.

Lance corporal.—One bar.

Cook.—A cook's cap of cloth conforming in color to corps, department, or arm of service.

Farrier and blacksmith.—A horseshoe of cloth 1⅜ inches long and 1⅛ inches wide, worn toe uppermost.

Saddler.—A saddler's round knife of cloth.

Mechanic and artificer.—Two crossed hammers of cloth.

Gunner.—An insignia of scarlet cloth, neatly piped and stitched; worn on the outside of the right sleeve, halfway between the point of the shoulder and the elbow, placed below the chevron; the shape to be that of an elongated cannon projectile 1½ inches long and ¾ inch wide, point up.

Gun commander.—A sergeant's chevrons, in the angle of which will be placed crossed guns of a suitable size, of scarlet cloth, stitched to the blue cloth of the chevron, the markings of hoops, trunnions, etc., to be outlined by black silk stitching.

Observer.—An equilateral triangle of scarlet cloth, ¾ inch on a side, base horizontal.

Master gunner.—The gunner's device encircled at the base by a wreath embroidered in yellow silk.

These devices shall be worn on both sleeves of coat and overcoat, placed and combined as follows:

Gun commander.—In the position prescribed for the chevron. If he is also a gunner, or master gunner, the corresponding device to be placed below the guns, with the point of the projectile up, and ¾ inch from the intersection of the guns.

Observer.—If a private and not a gunner, the triangle shall be worn on the sleeves of the coat and overcoat in the position adopted for the gunner's device. If a gunner, the triangle shall be worn with its apex ½ inch below the center of the base of the gunner's device. If a master gunner, the triangle shall be worn under the wreath with its apex ¼ inch therefrom. If a noncommissioned officer, the triangle shall be worn in the angle of the chevron, placed similarly to the lozenge in the first sergeant's chevron, apex up, base horizontal; in this case the device for gunner or master gunner, as the case may be, shall come beneath with the point of the projectile ¾ inch from the center of the base of the triangle.

Master gunner.—If a private or a noncommissioned officer not occupying one of the above positions, the device shall be worn as prescribed for that of gunner in each case.

First-class private, Engineers, to be distinguished by an insignia of a castle of red cloth, 1½ inches long and height in proportion; castle to be piped with white and worn on outside of right sleeve halfway between the front of shoulder and elbow.

SERVICE CHEVRONS.

90. All enlisted men who have served faithfully for one term of enlistment, for either three or five years, will wear as a mark of distinction upon both sleeves of the dress coat, below the elbow, a diagonal half chevron of cloth of the color of the corps, department, or arm of service in which they served, ½ inch wide, stitched upon a piece of dark-blue cloth of the color of the dress coat, extending from seam to seam, the front end being the lower and about 3½ inches from the end of the sleeve.

To indicate service in war: A diagonal half chevron of white cloth, ½ inch wide, with piping on each side ⅛ inch wide of cloth of the same color as the facings of the corps, department, or arm of service in which the soldier earned the right to wear it; those for the Engineers to have in addition a stitching of white silk on each side of the chevron. To be worn on both sleeves of the dress coat.

The following classes of enlisted men are entitled to wear the service-in-war chevron:

1. All enlisted men who served during the war of the rebellion and who were honorably discharged.

2. All enlisted men who served or may serve in the Army of the United States in war, or in such Indian or other campaigns approaching the magnitude of war, as may from time to time be so designated in orders from the War Department.

3. All enlisted men who served in the Regular or Volunteer Army of the United States between April 21, 1898, and April 11, 1899, and all who served in the Philippine Islands between April 11, 1898, and July 4, 1902, or with the China Relief Expedition.

The chevrons to indicate service and service in war, if more than one, will be worn one above the other in the order in which they were earned, ¼ inch space between them.

An enlisted man whose term of enlistment expired during the continuance of a war or campaign approaching the magnitude of a war, and who subsequently reenlisted, is entitled to wear the service-in-war chevrons for each enlistment in which there was war service; but in no instance will an enlisted man be allowed to wear the service-in-war chevron before his term of enlistment is completed; nor can two or more such chevrons be worn for service in wars during the same enlistment.

The service-in-war chevron will be worn in place of the service chevron for each enlistment in which the right to wear it was earned.

Service-in-war and service chevrons will be issued without charge.

GLOVES.
[See Figure 317.]

91. Of drab-colored leather or of white cotton or white wool, according to sealed patterns in the office of the Quartermaster General.

SPURS.

92. Of yellow metal, plain surface, with stuffed russet-leather straps, according to sealed pattern in the office of the Chief of Ordnance.

LEATHER BELT.
[See Figure 309 and Color Plate IX.]

93. Of stuffed russet leather, about 1½ inches in width, according to sealed pattern in the office of the Chief of Ordnance.

FIGURE 308. Enlisted men, Troop A, First Cavalry (ca. 1904). The man at left wears the pattern-of-1903 stable frock that superseded the longer 1879 pattern, the 1904 pattern service hat, and the 1904-pattern canvas fatigue trousers (a loose-fitting bib-overall garment) over his service uniform to protect it. The regimental sergeant major, center, wears the 1904 olive-drab overcoat and the olive-drab service cap. The man at right wears the blanket-lined canvas overcoat, 1895 pattern, muskrat cap and gauntlets, pattern of 1902, which differ only slightly from the 1879 patterns. He also wears the new 1904-pattern Arctic overshoes.

For troops armed with the saber, a similar belt with suitable slings will be provided for duty in garrison.

Belts and cartridge-carrying devices, when worn with the overcoat, will be worn outside the overcoat.

MISCELLANEOUS ARTICLES OF UNIFORM FOR OFFICERS, ENLISTED MEN, AND OTHERS, WITH REGULATIONS PERTAINING THERETO.

94. *Dispatch case for staff officers.*—Of pigskin, according to sealed pattern in the office of the Chief of Ordnance.

SADDLE.

95. To be complete, including cinch, quarter straps, coat straps, hooded stirrups, etc. Saddle and cinch straps to be of stuffed russet leather.

Trimmings to be of dull-finish brass.

General officers, aids-de-camp, officers of the Staff Corps and departments, and field officers may use the regulation saddle or a flat type of saddle similar to the Whitman or English saddle, covered with russet leather, open stirrups of white metal or steel finish.

All other officers will use the regulation saddle as furnished by the Ordnance Department.

SADDLECLOTHS FOR OFFICERS.

96. *For general officers.*—Of dark-blue cloth, according to sealed pattern in the office of the Chief of Ordnance, to be worn over the saddle blanket or pad and under the saddle; trimmed with two bands of gold lace 1 inch wide and 1½ inches apart, the outer band following the edge of the cloth; in each flank corner the coat of arms of the United States surmounted by stars indicating the rank of the general officer. General officers of the staff, except the General Staff Corps, will have the insignia of the corps or department instead of the coat of arms in the flank corners.

For officers permanently appointed in the Staff Corps and departments.—Of dark-blue cloth, according to sealed pattern in the office of the Chief of Ordnance, worn over the saddle blanket or pad and under the saddle, with an edging of gold lace 1 inch wide; in each flank corner the insignia of the Staff Corps or department, 2¼ inches high.

Aid-de-camp.—Same as other officers of his arm of service, except that the device shall be of the same design as the collar device prescribed herein. Dimensions same as for other officers.

For all other officers, except chaplains.—Of dark-blue cloth, lined with canvas, according to sealed pattern in the office of the Chief of Ordnance; worn under the saddle, number of regiment (except that for officers of engineers and artillery the metal insignia will be that prescribed for dress coats, 2 inches high) in enamel-leather figures, 2 inches in length on each flank corner; edges trimmed with enamel leather 1 inch wide; edges and figures of the same color as the facings of their respective arms.

For field officers of artillery.—The metal insignia will be that of the Coast or the Field Artillery, according to the branch to which assigned for duty.

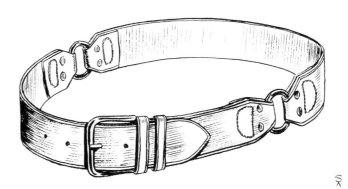

FIGURE 309. Dark russet waist belt, pattern of 1904, for wear with the full-dress and dress uniforms. The rings at the sides allowed the saber carrier to be hooked into the belt without the addition of a brass slide.

For chaplains.—Same as for line officers, with edging conforming to color of arm of service with which they are serving. A cross, 2 inches high, of white metal, placed diagonally in each flank corner.

Service saddlecloth for all officers.—A saddlecloth of the color of the service uniform, bound with russet leather, according to pattern in the office of the Chief of Ordnance.

For general officers the rank will be indicated by stars of dull-finish bronze metal.

For staff officers, artillery officers, engineer officers, and aids-de-camp the device will be of dull-finish bronze metal.

For regimental officers the number and for chaplains the cross will be as for the blue saddlecloth.

On mounted duty the dark-blue saddlecloth will be used with the full-dress or dress uniform, and the service saddlecloth with the service uniform.

97. All officers will provide themselves with arms and the articles of personal equipment or of horse equipments pertaining to their rank and duty, and maintain them in efficient order and condition.

Commanding officers will inspect and verify the arms and equipments of officers and enlisted men as often as they may deem necessary to assure themselves that all members of their commands are able to take the field fully equipped upon short notice.

LIST OF ARMS AND EQUIPMENTS TO BE IN POSSESSION OF OFFICERS.

General and Lieutenant General.
Such as they may prescribe.

All other mounted officers.
Horse equipments.—Saddle, complete; saddle blanket, blue saddlecloth, service saddlecloth, bridle, halter, watering bridle, nosebag, saddlebags, lariat, picket pin, currycomb, horse brush, and surcingle.

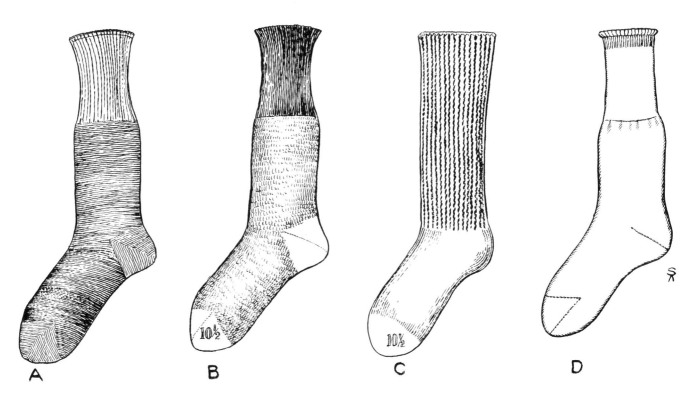

FIGURE 310. Model 1903 stockings. (A) Heavyweight cotton, light brown. (B) Lightweight cotton, brown and white mixed, with white heel and toe. (C) Heavy wool, gray and white mixed, with white toe. (D) Lightweight wool, made from worsted yarn.

FIGURE 311. At left are 3 views of the 1904 Blucher-style garrison shoe issued in black and russet calfskin to enlisted men. Officers' shoes were of the same pattern but were made of finer-grade leather and with higher-quality workmanship. At right is the issue campaign, or marching, shoe that was worn with leggings in the field and at mounted drills. Drawn from specimens in the author's collection.

122

FIGURE 312. Pajamas for enlisted men adopted June 1, 1904. Made of black-and-white-mixed cotton chambray, they were decorated with ¼-inch white tubular-braid frogs and pearl buttons. Truly the Army was softening a bit—providing a touch of creature comfort for its soldiers! Both pajama shirt and drawers were made and issued in 4 sizes.

Personal equipments.—Blanket, canteen, meat can, knife, fork, spoon, tin cup, saber belt, spurs, field glass, watch, compass, notebook, and pencils.

Arms.—Saber, revolver, and ammunition.

Staff officers and those acting as such will carry a dispatch case. Medical officers will carry a surgical case.

Mounted chaplains will be equipped as staff officers, but without arms.

Dismounted officers.

Personal equipment.—Blanket, canteen, tin cup, meat can, knife, fork, spoon, haversack, saber belt, field glass, watch, and compass.

Arms.—Saber, revolver, and ammunition.

The nature of the occasion will indicate the proper equipment of officers, which will conform to that of the men as prescribed by the commanding officer. For purpose of inspection the whole equipment may be required.

SADDLECLOTHS FOR ENLISTED MEN.

98. Saddlecloths of canvas similar in design to the officer's saddlecloth, color of the service uniform, with letter of troop and number of regiment in the flank corners, to be issued at such posts as may be designated.

BRASSARDS.

99. In time of war with a signatory of the Geneva Convention, by all persons in the military service neutralized by the terms of said convention, such as surgeons, members of the Hospital Corps, nurses, and chaplains, a brassard of white cloth 16 inches long and 3 inches wide, with a Geneva cross of red cloth 2 inches high and 2 inches wide in the center, will be worn on the left arm above the elbow while on duty in the field of operations.

SHIRTS, UNDERCLOTHING, AND STOCKINGS.
[See Figures 310, 312, 313, 314, 315, and 318.]

100. Olive-drab flannel shirts of light or heavy material, white muslin or other shirts of light texture, wool knit undershirts of light or heavy quality, cotton knit undershirts and drawers, canton flannel or jean drawers, woolen and cotton stockings, light or heavy weight, will be provided for enlisted men in conformity with the necessities of the service.

Whenever the coat is not worn no overshirts except the olive-drab flannel or chambray shirts furnished by the Quartermaster's Department will be worn with the service uniform.

WHITE-DUCK CLOTHING.

101. This clothing will be provided for all members of the Hospital Corps and is to be worn by them on ward duty when prescribed.

SUSPENDERS AND WAIST BELTS.

102. There will be issued to each enlisted man of the Army, annually, one pair of suspenders or one waist belt of

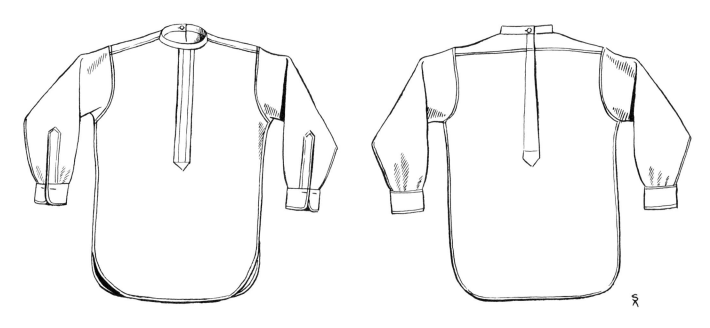

FIGURE 313. White muslin shirt for enlisted men, pattern of 1904, to be worn with the linen collar under the dress coat when worn for both dress and full-dress occasions.

FIGURE 314. Olive-drab flannel shirt, pattern of 1904, made and issued in 6 sizes for wear under the service coat and when the service coat was not worn for drill and field duty.

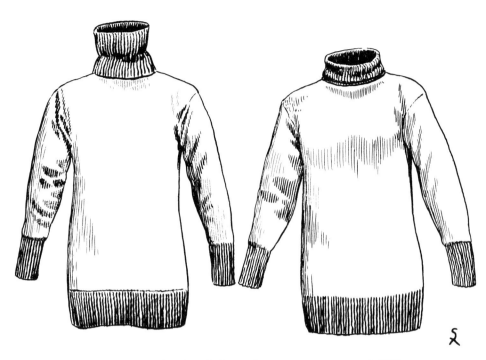

FIGURE 315. Olive-drab woolen sweater, pattern of 1904.

russet leather, according to sealed pattern in the office of the Quartermaster General. Suspenders, when worn, must not be visible.

ARCTIC OVERSHOES, ETC.
[See Figure 308.]

103. When the necessity for the issue is certified by the post commander, arctic overshoes, fur gauntlets, fur or blanket-lined canvas caps, and canvas or woolen mittens may be issued to enlisted men at cost price. These articles will conform to patterns in the office of the Quartermaster General and do not form part of the annual money allowance for clothing.

FUR OR BLANKET-LINED CANVAS OVERCOATS.
[See Figure 308.]

104. There will also be issued to troops stationed in extremely cold regions, when the necessity for such issue is certified by the post commander, fur or blanket-lined canvas overcoats, but only to men performing guard duty or field service, when exposure to weather would jeopardize life or limbs by freezing.

BAND UNIFORMS.

105. Bands will wear the general uniform of their regiments or corps. Commanding officers may, from the regimental or band funds, add such ornaments to the full-dress and dress uniform as they may deem proper and are not herein prohibited. Such ornaments will not include shoulder knots, shoulder straps, officer's trousers stripes, or any insignia of rank. Upon application to the Quartermaster's Department they will be supplied with music pouches.

Black lynx-skin shakos with plume and tassel of color of the corps or arm of service, and leather chin straps with brass scales and side buttons, will be issued for use on full-dress occasions by drum majors; to be made according to sealed pattern in the office of the Quartermaster General.

The shakos for drum majors of cavalry to be of smaller dimensions than those for the other arms.

Saber belt of enamel leather of color of corps or arm of service, and of regulation width.

Chevrons of cloth, according to rank, of the prescribed pattern.

Trousers of regulation patterns with stripes prescribed for musicians of their respective corps or arm of service.

Batons as per pattern, with silken cords and tassels of the color of the corps or arm of service. Only the dismounted drum majors will carry batons; drum majors of all mounted bands will carry sabers.

Articles of band uniforms, including shakos and saber belts, that do not form a part of the annual clothing allowance, may be issued, but will not be charged except in cases of loss or damage. The articles thus issued without charge remain the property of the United States.

FIGURE 316. Brown canvas fatigue clothing, pattern of 1904, made of 8-ounce cotton duck dyed brown. Issued to enlisted men for all fatigue duties that would ordinarily soil or damage the regular uniform. Made extremely loose, these garments were intended for wear over the service uniform.

COLOR PLATE VIII. Sergeant, U.S. Cavalry, in the new field uniform prescribed for enlisted men of cavalry in 1899. The yellow shoulder straps and chevrons distinguished him from other corps, and the issue of leggings marked the end of leather boots for cavalry until the new laced leather boots were prescribed in the 1930's.

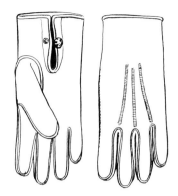

PATTERN OF 1905 ISSUE
BUCKSKIN GLOVES

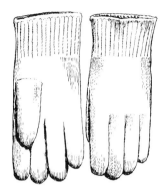

PATTERN OF 1903
WHITE WOOLEN GLOVES

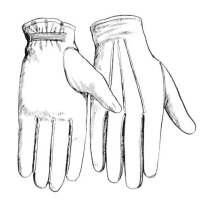

PATTERN OF 1904 WHITE
GLOVES THAT REPLACED
PATTERN WHITE BERLIN
FOR ENLISTED MEN.

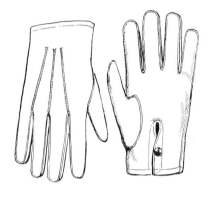

PATTERN OF 1905
YELLOW HORSEHIDE GLOVES
FOR FATIGUE DUTY

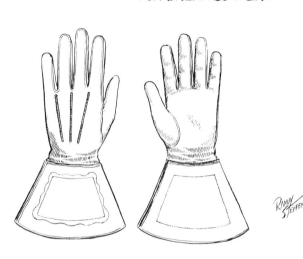

PATTERN OF 1904 BUCKSKIN
GAUNTLETS FOR ENLISTED MEN
OF CAVALRY AND LIGHT ARTILLERY

FIGURE 317. Gloves, 1903–05.

KHAKI HELMET.
[See Figures 303 and 319.]

106. The khaki helmet of the pattern now on hand in the Quartermaster's Department is prescribed as uniform for officers and enlisted men until the supply is exhausted, when its use will be discontinued. It will be worn in lieu of the service cap with the service uniform on occasions (*a*) and (*b*) (see Table of Occasions), from May 1 to September 30 at all posts in the departments of the Gulf and Texas, and from June 1 to September 30 at all other posts in the United States. At posts in the tropics it will be worn on occasions (*a*) and (*b*) throughout the year, except during the rainy season.

The price of this helmet is fixed at 40 cents.

WHITE HELMET.
[See Figure 322.]

107. The white helmet of the pattern now on hand in the Quartermaster's Department is prescribed in lieu of the white cap with the white uniform, for officers and enlisted men, until the supply is exhausted. Commanding officers are directed to permit it to be worn off duty in garrison with the service uniform, and to prescribe its use during the warm season with the full-dress and dress uniforms in lieu of the full-dress or dress cap. When the supply now on hand in the Quartermaster's Department is exhausted, the use of the white helmet as an article of uniform will be discontinued. Its price is fixed at 25 cents.

UNIFORMS FOR OFFICERS AND ENLISTED MEN ON DUTY AT
EMPLACEMENTS.

108. Officers when on duty at emplacements may wear a uniform of khaki-colored cotton or brown canvas, to be worn

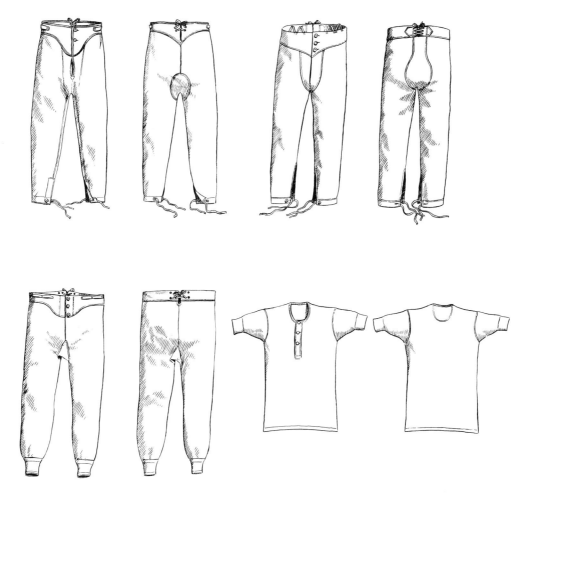

FIGURE 318. Top Row: Canton flannel drawers (cotton), pattern of 1903; Jean drawers, pattern of 1901, made of jean (cotton). The 1901 nainsook cotton drawers were identical in cut to jean drawers.

Center Row: This drawing illustrates the cut of the following drawers: 1904 cotton-knit drawers; 1904 heavyweight winter drawers, 60 per cent wool and forty per cent cotton; 1904 lightweight winter drawers, 60 per cent wool and forty per cent cotton; 1904 worsted merino and cotton summer drawers; 1904 cotton summer undershirt.

Bottom Row: 1901 nainsook undershirt made of nainsook checks; the next 2 drawings illustrate the 1904 worsted merino and cotton summer undershirt and the 1904 heavyweight collarette winter undershirt, 60 per cent wool and forty per cent cotton; 1904 lightweight collarette winter undershirt, 60 per cent wool and forty per cent cotton; the last drawing illustrates both the lightweight and heavyweight open-front undershirts for winter wear, both sixty per cent wool and forty per cent cotton, and both 1904 patterns.

FIGURE 319. Commissioned officers, Second Cavalry (ca. 1906), in the khaki summer uniform. Even though official approval for general wear within the Continental United States, except in coastal artillery emplacements, was not given until 1907, most officers were wearing the lightweight cotton uniform by late 1905. Collar insignia here is the "U.S." authorized the year before, which displaced the national coat of arms, for both officers and enlisted men. The second lieutenant, center, wears the khaki summer helmet, the supply of which, by now, is almost exhausted. The first lieutenant, right, wears an approved field crossbelt for officers, and the new Warnock hat guard, the forerunner of the later leather chin strap.

alone or over the cloth uniform, according to the weather. This uniform will conform to the present regulations prescribing the cut, insignia, etc., for service uniforms.

The saber belt will be worn outside the coat and officers may lay aside the saber after arriving at the guns, if necessary for the work in hand. Leggings may be worn on this duty.

Enlisted men, when at work or drill at the emplacements, may wear the brown fatigue uniform or the cotton service uniform, as the commanding officer may direct; rank to be shown by the usual chevrons.

Suitable leather gloves will be issued by the Quartermaster's Department to the enlisted men of the Coast Artillery and Ordnance to protect their hands while handling guns, machinery, and other appliances. These gloves will be

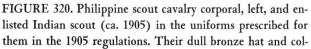

FIGURE 320. Philippine scout cavalry corporal, left, and enlisted Indian scout (ca. 1905) in the uniforms prescribed for them in the 1905 regulations. Their dull bronze hat and collar ornaments are shown above. The Indian scout wears the olive-drab mounted-service uniform; the Philippine scout wears the khaki cotton summer uniform.

FIGURE 321. First lieutenant, left, and captain, Eighth Cavalry (ca. 1906). The lieutenant wears the special uniform for evening wear with white tie and white waistcoat. The captain is dressed in the officer's mess jacket, with black tie and dark blue waistcoat. The white or dark blue waistcoat was permitted to be worn with either the evening coat or mess jacket. It was the individual officer's option to wear the full-dress-dismounted uniform or either of the special evening uniforms. Commanding officers were permitted to authorize the wearing of white trousers with the mess jacket in warm weather, but black patent leather shoes were always mandatory.

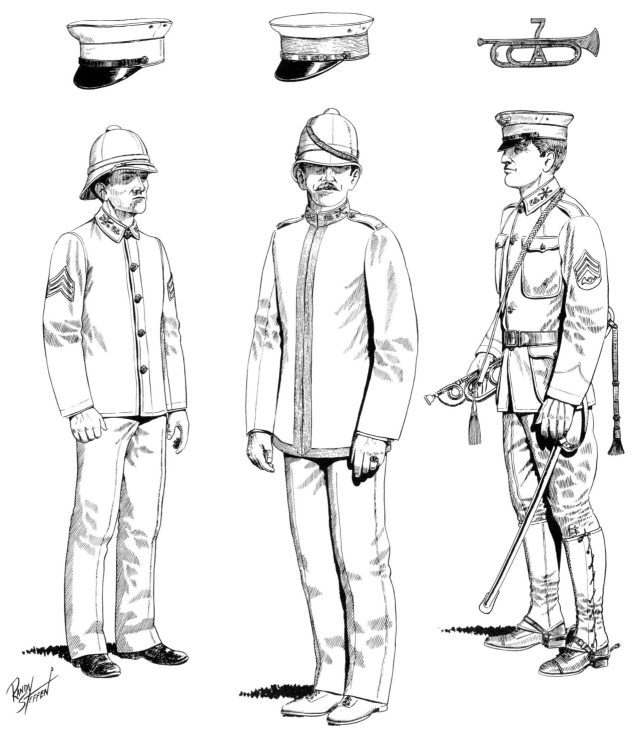

FIGURE 322. White summer dress for enlisted men, left, and officers, center (ca. 1906), showing the white helmets prescribed for wear instead of the white caps, until the supply of helmets was exhausted. Apparently most of the helmets were used up during this year, for the 1907 uniform regulations prescribe the white cap to be worn with the white uniform for all occasions—for officers only, since the white uniform for enlisted men was restricted to wear by members of the Hospital Corps only. The trumpeter, right, a principal musician, wears the summer khaki cotton service dress, with the distinctive trumpet insignia on his cap.

charged to the men at cost or invoice price, but the value of the same will not form a part of the annual clothing money allowance.

ENLISTED SCOUTS.

109. The uniform for enlisted scouts will, in general, be the same as the service uniform prescribed for enlisted men of the corresponding arm of service, the letters "U. S. S." in dull-finish bronze replacing collar ornaments and hat devices. [See Figure 320.]

110. *Uniform for officers and enlisted men of the Porto Rico Provisional Regiment of Infantry.*—Same as prescribed for infantry, excepting that the letters "P. R." of gothic design will replace the number of the regiment wherever it occurs. [See Figure 320.]

111. The uniform of *native troops in the Philippines* shall be the cotton service uniform of the infantry or cavalry, according to their organization, the letter "P." taking the place of the number of the regiment wherever it occurs.

TABLE OF OCCASIONS—COMPOSITION OF THE UNIFORMS OF OFFICERS OF THE ARMY, AND OCCASIONS ON WHICH THEY ARE TO BE WORN.*

FULL-DRESS UNIFORM.

Officers.	Articles.	Occasions.
General Officers; dismounted.	Full-dress coat, full-dress trousers, chapeau, epaulets, sash, white gloves, full-dress belt, saber, black shoes.	On state occasions at home and abroad; when receiving or calling officially upon the President of the United States, or upon the president, sovereign, or member of the royal family of other countries; and at ceremonies and entertainments when it is desirable to do special honor to the occasion, or when full dress is prescribed for enlisted men.
General Officers; mounted.	Full-dress coat, dress breeches, full-dress cap, shoulder knots, sash, drab-leather gloves, full-dress belt, saber, black boots, spurs.	On occasions as above requiring the officer to be mounted or following immediately after mounted functions.
Officers of Staff Corps and Departments; dismounted.	Full-dress coat, full-dress trousers, full-dress cap, white gloves, full-dress belt, saber, black shoes. Aiguillettes and shoulder belts for those authorized to wear them.	Same as stated above for dismounted general officers.
Officers of Staff Corps and Departments; mounted.	Full-dress coat, dress breeches, full-dress cap, drab-leather gloves, full-dress belt, saber, black boots, spurs. Aiguillettes and shoulder belts for those authorized to wear them.	Same as stated above for mounted general officers.
Officers of Cavalry, Artillery, Infantry, and Engineers serving with Engineer troops; dismounted.	Full-dress coat, full-dress trousers, full-dress cap, white gloves, full-dress belt, saber, black shoes. Aiguillettes for those authorized to wear them.	Same as stated for dismounted general officers.
Officers of Cavalry, Artillery, Infantry, and Engineers serving with Engineer troops; mounted.	Full-dress coat, dress breeches, full-dress cap, full-dress belt, saber, drab-leather gloves, black boots, spurs. Aiguillettes for those authorized to wear them.	Same as stated for mounted general officers.
Chaplains; dismounted.	Full-dress coat, full-dress trousers, chaplain's hat, white gloves, black shoes.	As stated for dismounted general officers.
Chaplains mounted.	Full-dress coat, dress breeches, chaplain's hat, drab-leather gloves, black boots, spurs.	As stated for mounted general officers.

DRESS UNIFORM.*

Officers.	Articles.	Occasions.
General Officers; dismounted.	Dress coat, dress trousers, dress cap, black shoes. Under arms, add dress belt (worn under coat), saber, and white gloves.	At reviews, inspections, parades, and other ceremonies when the troops are in dress uniform; at such other duties under arms as may be prescribed; on courts-martial, courts

COMPOSITION OF THE UNIFORMS OF OFFICERS OF THE ARMY,
AND OCCASIONS ON WHICH THEY ARE TO BE WORN—Continued.

Officers.	Articles.	Occasions.
		of inquiry, and boards of officers when prescribed. This uniform is also authorized as a mess dress, and for social occasions when full dress is not worn.
General Officers; mounted.	Dress coat, dress breeches, dress cap, drab-leather gloves, black boots, spurs. Under arms, add dress belt (worn under coat), and saber.	On occasions as above, requiring officers to be mounted.
Officers of Staff Corps and Departments; dismounted.	Dress coat, dress trousers, dress cap, black shoes. Under arms, add dress belt, saber, and white gloves.	Same as stated for dismounted general officers.
Officers of Staff Corps and Departments; mounted.	Dress coat, dress breeches, dress cap, drab-leather gloves, black boots, spurs. Under arms, add dress belt and saber.	Same as stated for mounted general officers.
Officers of Cavalry, Artillery, Infantry, and Engineers serving with Engineer troops; dismounted.	Dress coat, dress cap, dress trousers, black shoes. Under arms, add dress belt (worn under coat), saber, white gloves.	Same as stated for dismounted general officers.
Officers of Cavalry, Artillery, Infantry and Engineers serving with Engineer troops; mounted.	Dress coat, dress breeches, dress cap, drab-leather gloves, black boots, spurs. Under arms, add dress belt (worn under coat), and saber.	Same as stated for mounted general officers.
Chaplains; dismounted.	Dress coat, dress trousers, chaplain's hat, black shoes; white gloves when occasion requires gloves.	Same as stated for other dismounted officers.
Chaplains; mounted.	Dress coat, dress breeches, chaplain's hat, drab-leather gloves, black boots, spurs.	Same as stated for other mounted officers.

* NOTE.—When troops appear in the full-dress or dress uniform, as prescribed in these regulations, all officers on duty therewith or attached thereto in any capacity, shall wear the corresponding prescribed full-dress or dress uniform for officers.

WHITE UNIFORM.

For all officers; dismounted.	White coat, white trousers, white cap, white-canvas or black-leather shoes.	When authorized by the commanding officer, but will not be worn on occasions of duty with troops and will not be prescribed for such occasions.

SERVICE UNIFORM.

For all officers; dismounted.	(a) Service coat, service trousers, service cap, russet-leather shoes. (b) Under arms, add service belt, saber, drab-leather gloves. (c) Service coat, service breeches, leggings (of russet leather or canvas), russet-leather shoes, service hat, service belt, saber, and revolver, drab-leather gloves. Officers of the Signal Corps will wear russet-leather shoulder belt with uniform (b) and (c) when on duty requiring its use.	(a) For habitual wear in garrison. (b) For duty under arms in garrison, unless otherwise prescribed or authorized herein. (c) At drills (when prescribed), target practice, maneuvers, on marches, and in the field.
For all officers; mounted.	(a) Service coat, service breeches, service cap, russet-leather boots, or russet-leather shoes and leggings, spurs, drab-leather gloves. (b) Under arms, add service belt and saber.	(a) For habitual wear in garrison when mounted. (b) For mounted duty under arms in garrison unless otherwise prescribed or author-

COMPOSITION OF THE UNIFORMS OF THE OFFICERS OF THE ARMY, AND OCCASIONS ON WHICH THEY ARE TO BE WORN—Continued.

Officers.	Articles.	Occasions.
		ized herein.
	(c) Service coat, service breeches, russet-leather boots, or russet-leather shoes with russet-leather or canvas leggings, service hat, service belt, saber, and revolver, spurs, drab-leather gloves. Officers of the Signal Corps will wear the shoulder belt on occasions as above prescribed.	(c) At mounted drills (when prescribed), target practice, maneuvers, and on marches and in the field.

NOTE.—When troops appear in service uniform (a), (b), or (c), all officers on duty therewith or attached thereto in any capacity will wear the corresponding service uniform (a), (b), or (c).

COMPOSITION OF THE UNIFORMS OF ENLISTED MEN OF THE ARMY AND OCCASIONS ON WHICH THEY ARE TO BE WORN.

All enlisted men.	FULL-DRESS UNIFORM.	
Dismounted _____	Dress coat, breast cord, dress trousers, dress cap, black shoes, white gloves, russet-leather belt and cartridge box.	At reviews, parades, and other ceremonies under arms, unless otherwise prescribed by the commanding officer.
Mounted _____	Dress coat, breast cord, service breeches, dress cap, leggings, russet-leather shoes, drab-leather gloves, spurs, saber belt, and cartridge box (when prescribed.)	As above, when mounted.

	DRESS UNIFORM.	
Dismounted _____	Dress coat, dress cap, dress trousers, black shoes. Under arms, add white gloves, russet-leather belt and cartridge box.	When prescribed by the commanding officer.
Mounted _____	Dress coat, dress cap, service breeches, russet-leather shoes, leggings, spurs, drab-leather gloves. Under arms, add saber belt and cartridge box.	When prescribed by the commanding officer.

	WHITE UNIFORM.	
Dismounted _____	White coat, white trousers, white cap, white canvas or black-leather shoes.	When authorized by the commanding officer for off-duty wear; will not be prescribed for any occasion.

	SERVICE UNIFORM.	
Dismounted _____	(a) Service coat, service breeches, leggings, service cap, russet-leather shoes. (b) Under arms, add drab-leather gloves, russet-leather belt and cartridge box. (c) Service coat, service breeches, leggings, russet-leather shoes, service hat, field belt, drab-leather gloves.	(a) For habitual wear in garrison. (b) For duty under arms in garrison unless otherwise prescribed or authorized herein. (c) At drills (when prescribed), target practice, maneuvers, on marches, and in the field.
Mounted _____	(a) Service coat, service breeches, leggings, service cap, russet-leather shoes, drab-leather gloves, spurs. (b) Under arms, add russet-leather belt and cartridge box. (c) Service coat, service breeches, service hat, leggings, russet-leather shoes, spurs, field belt, and drab-leather gloves.	(a) For habitual wear in garrison when mounted. (b) For mounted duty under arms in garrison, unless otherwise prescribed or authorized herein. (c) At mounted drills (when prescribed), mounted target practice, maneuvers, on marches, and in the field.

COMPOSITION OF THE UNIFORMS OF ENLISTED MEN OF THE ARMY,
AND OCCASIONS ON WHICH THEY ARE TO BE WORN—Continued.

FATIGUE UNIFORM.		
All enlisted men.	Articles.	Occasions.
Dismounted _____	Fatigue coat, fatigue trousers, service hat, rus-set-leather shoes.	On fatigue.

NOTE.—With dismounted service uniform (*b*) noncommissioned staff officers equipped therewith will wear belt and saber or sword in lieu of belt and cartridge box.

With dismounted service uniform (*c*) noncommissioned staff officers equipped therewith will wear revolver and belt in lieu of saber or sword.

EXTRACT FROM ORDER OF THE PRESIDENT OF THE UNITED
STATES, DATED DECEMBER 30, 1902.

Throughout the military and naval services of the United States, whenever on occasions of ceremony officers of both services are required to appear together in uniform, the following schedule shall govern:

Uniform A _____ { Army, full dress.
Navy, special full dress.
Marine Corps, special full dress. }

Uniform B _____ { Army, dress.
Navy, service dress.
Marine Corps, undress. }

Uniform C _____ { Army, full dress or evening uniform.
Navy, evening dress A.
Marine Corps, special full dress. }

The following uniform will be worn by officers of the Army visiting the White House on occasions stated; in each case with saber; full-dress slings, white gloves, and the corresponding cap, except that side arms will not be worn with the "evening uniform."

State dinners _____ Full-dress uniform, dismounted.

Formal small dinner _____ { Full-dress uniform, dismounted, or evening uniform. }

Evening musical or dance { Full-dress uniform, dismounted, or evening uniform. }

New Year's and all other state receptions, daytime or evening. } Full-dress uniform, dismounted.

All other daytime functions (until 6 p. m.), including afternoon tea. } Dress uniform.

On August 14, 1907, the new regulations for the uniform, as prescribed in General Order No. 169, were published for the information of the Army. In these new descriptions and regulations were quite a few changes and modifications of the clothing and insignia that had been official in the 1902 and 1905 published regulations. Each of these changes will be covered in this section of Chapter 13.

Service and decoration *ribbons* were authorized for wear on the service uniform by the following section of the 1907 regulations:

6. Campaign badges, certificate of merit badges, and the sections of ribbons hereinafter prescribed are a part of the uniform for the officers and enlisted men to whom issued and will be habitually worn by them as follows:

On the full-dress coat and the dress coat the badges will be worn in the manner prescribed for badges of military societies in paragraph 8 of this order.

With the olive-drab wool service uniform a section of ribbon of the prescribed badges ⅜ inch long and of the full width of the ribbon will be worn in lieu of the badge by those entitled thereto; these ribbons to be sewed on the olive-drab wool service coat in a horizontal line in the position prescribed for badges and decorations on the full-dress coat in the following order from the line of buttons of the coat: The medal of honor ribbon, the certificate of merit ribbon, and the campaign ribbon in the order in which earned, without space between and without overlapping.

With the cotton khaki service uniform the section of ribbon, instead of being sewed on the coat, as prescribed herein for the olive-drab wool service uniform, will be sewed on a bar of the pattern in the office of the Quartermaster General, the bar to be secured to the coat by shanks on the bar passing through eyelets in the coat in the same manner as the buttons are secured to the service coat.

The badges and ribbons herein prescribed and the bars from which badges are suspended will be furnished by the Quartermaster's Department, and will be issued gratuitously to enlisted men at the rate of two bars during an enlistment and two sections of ribbon per year. Any issue of ribbons or bars in excess of this allowance will be charged to the soldier at cost price. These articles will be supplied to officers at cost price.

Neither badges nor ribbons will be worn by officers suspended from rank and command or by enlisted men serving sentence of confinement for more than five days.

Both officers and enlisted men were also directed to wear marksmanship badges as prescribed in the following paragraphs:

7. The various distinctive marks for excellence in small-arms practice and the badges for gunners and master gunners may be worn on the breasts of officers and enlisted men entitled to them on all occasions except on active duty in the field in time of war or during maneuvers, in the manner prescribed in paragraph 8; they will precede all badges of military societies (from the wearer's right to left) and will be preceded by badges of campaigns which may be adopted by the War Department.

8. *Badges of military societies.*—Officers and enlisted men who, in their own right or by right of inheritance, are members of military societies of men who served in the armies and navies of the United States in the war of the Revolution, the war of 1812, the Mexican war, the war of the rebellion, or the Indian wars of the United States, the Spanish-American war and the incidental insurrection in the Philippines, or the China relief expedition, or are members of the Regular Army and Navy Union of the United States, or of the Army and Navy Union of the United States, may wear on all occasions of ceremony the distinctive badges adopted by such societies, or such other medals as may be authorized by proper authority. Officers and enlisted men who served as officers, noncommissioned officers, privates, or other enlisted men in the Regular Army, volunteer or militia forces of the United States, during the war of the rebellion, and have been honorably discharged from the service, or still remain in the same, may wear on occasions of ceremony the distinctive army badge ordered for or adopted by the army corps or division, respectively, in which they served.

Badges to be worn on the left breast of the coat, suspended by a ribbon from a bar of metal passed through the upper ends and tops of the ribbons forming a horizontal line, the outer ends of which will be from 3 to 4 inches below the top of the shoulder, according to the height of the wearer.

9. Shoulder knots and shoulder straps will be worn by commissioned officers only. Shoulder straps will always be placed on the dress coat, as herein prescribed; their use on the full-dress coat is forbidden.

10. The uniform of general officers on the retired list is that prescribed for general officers of corresponding grade on the active list. If retired while serving as general officer in a corps or department, the insignia of such corps or department will be omitted. The uniform of an officer below the grade of brigadier general on the retired list is that prescribed for an officer of his rank in the corps, department, or arm of service in which he last served, except that the number of the regiment or insignia of corps or department will not be worn. A retired officer with brevet commission, either in the regular or volunteer service of the Army of the United States, may wear the uniform of his highest brevet grade, and a retired officer who has held a commission, not brevet, in the volunteer service, may wear the uniform of his highest grade in that service, except that the number of the regiment or insignia of corps or department will not be worn. Retired officers may, at their option, wear the pattern of uniform which was prescribed at the date of their retirement, or as prescribed herein, but the two uniforms will not be mixed.

In contrast to former regulations concerning the issue and wearing of the khaki service uniform by officers and enlisted men, the 1907 regulations now prescribed the lighter-weight summer wear for all troops in the United States, as well as in the tropics:

16. The service uniforms are made of wool or cotton. Except when otherwise ordered, the woolen uniform is prescribed for winter wear in the United States proper, including Alaska.

The cotton uniform is prescribed for tropical wear and for summer wear in the United States. It is also authorized for use at emplacements, as provided in paragraph 106.

17. It is not permitted to combine outer garments of wool with others of cotton in the service uniform of officers or enlisted men. This does not apply to the service hat.

A very important regulation and custom relative to the manner in which the sword or saber was worn when hooked up had been in the uniform regulations almost since the establishment of the regular mounted arm in 1833. Too many illustrators, in addition to almost *all* motion picture and television directors and technical advisers, portray the saber hooked up with the guard to the front—which is absolutely incorrect! The following excerpt from the 1907 regulations (and found in almost all other uniform regulations) makes the method of wearing the saber crystal clear. All the illustrations in this work show the saber worn hooked up in the prescribed manner.

14. The saber will be habitually worn hooked up when dismounted, guard to the rear; when worn with the overcoat, the belt will be inside and the saber outside of the overcoat. The proper saber knot will always be worn with the saber.

Descriptions of the officer's full dress coat in the 1902 and 1905 regulations called for distinctive button patterns and numbers on the breast. The 1907 regulations specify that *all* officers below the rank of brigadier general shall have 9 buttons in each row on the breast. The following paragraph contains the official description and limitation for conforming to the new regulation:

For officers of the various grades regulation gilt buttons will be placed on the breast of the coat as follows:

General.—Two rows, twelve in each row placed by fours, the distance between rows being from 8 to 10 inches at the top and from 4 to 5 inches at the bottom; rows and groups to be symmetrically disposed.

Lieutenant General.—The same as for the General, except that there will be ten buttons in each row, the upper and lower groups by threes and the middle groups by fours.

Major general.—The same as for the General, except that there will be nine buttons in each row, placed by threes.

Brigadier general.—The same as for the General, except that there will be eight buttons in each row, placed in pairs.

For all officers below the rank of brigadier general two rows of nine buttons each, the buttons to be placed at equal intervals.

Officers who now have full-dress coats with seven buttons are authorized to wear the coats until they become unserviceable.

The officer's service-coat pattern was not changed except for the addition of a band of brown braid above the cuff of each sleeve:

All officers except the General Staff Corps will wear a band of brown braid ½ inch wide on the sleeves of the service coat, the lower edge of the braid 3 inches from the end of the sleeves. For officers of the General Staff Corps the braid will be black. [See Figure 323.]

The officer on the left side of Figure 323 wears the new English-style overcoat approved for officers in June, 1907. Although this new pattern was not described in the 1907 uniform regulations, and was considered a nonregulation pattern, it was approved for optional purchase by the Secretary of War, and this style is advertised in the 1907 Warnock Military Goods catalog. The following year the new style was prescribed for both officers and enlisted men. (See Figure 324.)

In the 1907 paragraph describing the officer's overcoat, a new final sentence was added: "The overcoat will be worn over any uniform without change of headgear."

While the 1905 regulations prohibited the wearing of the coat-of-arms cap badge with the white cap for officers, the 1907 regulations specified that a gold or gilt cap badge in the form of the coat of arms of the United States, made of metal, and detachable, *should* be worn.

Paragraph 44 concerning gloves for officers was changed from paragraph 43 in the 1905 regulations so that mounted officers were authorized to wear leather gauntlets, and for dismounted duty, white gloves.

Enlisted men were issued drab-colored slickers for wear in rainy weather, and paragraph 66 of the 1907 regulations authorized their wear:

66. Officers are permitted to wear waterproof capes or overcoats, as nearly as practicable the color of the service uniform, when on duty involving exposure to rainy or other inclement weather. Enlisted men under similar conditions may wear the poncho or slicker issued by the Quartermaster's Department. [See Figure 324.]

Paragraph 72 abolished the white-bleached-cotton coat for wear by any but men of the Hospital Corps.

The 1905 regulations prescribed wearing the number of the regiment and the letter of the company on the front of the enlisted man's service hat, but the 1907 regulations made no mention of any insignia on this hat. Thus we can assume the numbers and letters were abolished.

SERVICE HAT.

83. *For all enlisted men.*—Of felt, of color of the service uniform as nearly as practicable, according to sealed pattern in the office of the Quartermaster General: with double hat cord ³⁄₁₆ inch in diameter, of firm material, conforming in color to that of the corps, department or arm of service; to be sewed fast to the hat.

Leather leggings were prescribed for wear by cavalry and artillery enlisted men in the 1907 regulations, in lieu of the canvas leggings formerly worn. The enlisted men in Figure 324 wear the new leather leggings.

LEGGINGS.

85. For enlisted men of cavalry and field artillery, of leather, and for all other enlisted men, of cotton duck or canvas, color of the service uniform, made in accordance with sealed patterns in the office of the Quartermaster General.

Paragraph 90, dealing with service chevrons, contains a change which specifies the method of wearing additional service chevrons beyond the first enlistment. This same paragraph also announces the eventual elimination of the service-in-war chevron, which is to be replaced by campaign badges to be worn on the breast:

SERVICE CHEVRONS.

90. All enlisted men who have served faithfully for a term of three years continuously or otherwise will wear as a mark of distinction upon both sleeves of the dress coat, below the elbow, a diagonal half chevron of cloth of the color of the facings of the corps, department, or arm of service in which they served, ½ inch wide, stitched upon a piece of dark-blue

FIGURE 323. Left: Captain, Sixth Cavalry (ca. 1908), in the new English-style olive-drab overcoat approved for officers in June, 1907 (Warnock Military Catalog, 1907). The sleeve insignia includes the bronze crossed-sabers device prescribed in the 1905 regulations. The detachable hood is not shown.

Center: First lieutenant, Sixth Cavalry (ca. 1908), in the 1907-pattern olive-drab service uniform. The strip of one-half-inch brown braid on each sleeve three inches from the end was prescribed in the 1907 uniform regulations, as were gauntlets for officers and enlisted men for mounted duty. The campaign bars above the left breast pocket are worn according to the current regulations.

Right: First sergeant, Troop D, Sixth Cavalry (ca. 1908), in the dress uniform for mounted duty prescribed in the 1907 regulations. He wears long sky-blue dress trousers inside russet strap leggings, instead of olive-drab service breeches, as formerly prescribed. The medals on his breast are, from left to right, the Certificate of Merit Badge, the Spanish-American War Medal, the Congressional Philippine Medal, and the Expert Marksman Badge.

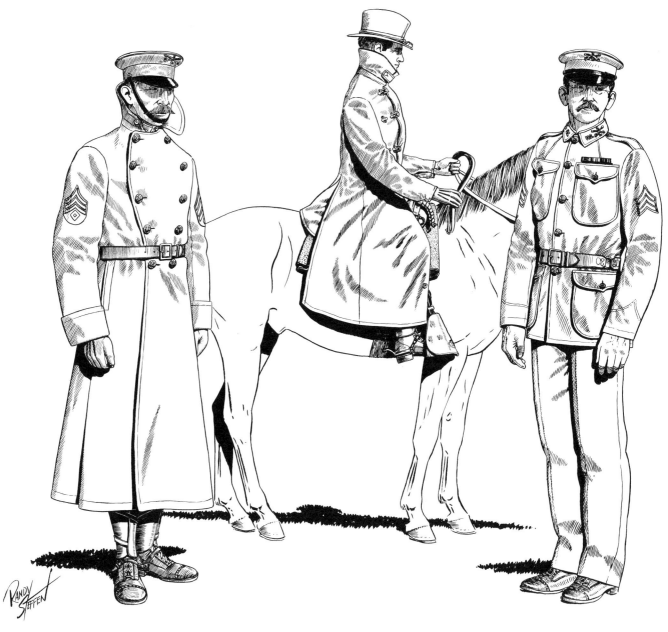

FIGURE 324. Enlisted men, Troop L, Second Cavalry (ca. 1908). The first sergeant, left, wears the new English-style olive-drab overcoat approved for officers in 1907 and for enlisted men the following year. Similar to the 1902 pattern, it has a more stylish curved opening at the chest, and an accordian pleat up the center of the back to make a less binding fit while retaining its military smartness. Its detachable hood is for wear in inclement weather only. The mounted man, center, wears the drab slicker authorized for enlisted men of cavalry and light artillery in the 1907 regulations. The sergeant, right, wears khaki trousers with the khaki service coat, authorized in 1907 for wear when not mounted and not on armed duty. He also wears the new decoration and campaign ribbons above the left breast pocket that were authorized in 1907 for wear on all but the full-dress and dress uniform coats in lieu of the diagonal half-chevron service stripes worn until now. From this period hence, service stripes were worn only on the dress coat.

cloth of the color of the dress coat, extending from seam to seam, the front end being the lower and about 3½ inches from the end of the sleeve. For each additional period of three years' faithful service, continuously or otherwise, an additional chevron will be worn, to be placed one above the other in the order in which they were earned, ¼ inch space between them.

Enlisted men now wearing the service-in-war chevrons are authorized to continue to wear them till the campaign badges heretofore authorized have been issued to the Army.

Paragraph 91 prescribes the issue and wearing of leather gauntlets for enlisted men on mounted duty. (See Figure 323.)

GLOVES.

91. Leather gauntlets for mounted duty, and white cotton or white wool for dismounted duty, according to sealed patterns in the office of the Quartermaster General.

No mention was made in the 1905 uniform regulations about the issue of dark-blue flannel shirts, so it can be assumed that, with the change from blues to olive-drab and khaki, blue shirts were no longer part of the prescribed uniform.

But paragraph 100 of the 1907 uniform regulations makes this assumption fact: "The blue flannel shirts now in stock will be exhausted by issue to the Coast Artillery Corps and for maneuver purposes."

Publication of the 1907 uniform regulations brought two more changes to the attention of the Army. While no mention of either is made in the text of the regulations, both are listed in the tables setting forth the composition of the uniforms of enlisted men, or in the footnotes that accompany these tables.

The first change is the listing of dress trousers for wear with leather leggings when the mounted-dress or full-dress uniform is prescribed. This meant that the trooper no longer wore the drab service breeches for mounted-dress parade. Now he was required to fold over the bottoms of his dress trousers for wear *under* the new leather leggings issued to cavalry and artillery. This change is listed in the accompanying 1907 tables under the headings of "Dress Uniform, Mounted," and "Full Dress Uniform, Mounted."

The second change is contained in the next-to-last footnote at the end of the Tables of Occasion: "Enlisted men of the mounted service may wear the khaki trousers when not mounted and not on armed duty." The sergeant on the right side of Figure 324 is dressed in accordance with the orders in this footnote.

Dress trousers, folded and worn under the leather leggings as described above, are illustrated in Figure 329 and on Figure C of Uniform Color Plate VIII (in Volume I).

The following 1907 tables show the changes from the previous Tables of Occasion (1905). All articles of uniform different from those listed before are italicized.

TABLE OF OCCASIONS.—COMPOSITION OF THE UNIFORMS OF OFFICERS OF THE ARMY, AND OCCASIONS ON WHICH THEY ARE TO BE WORN.

FULL-DRESS UNIFORM.

Officers.	Articles.	Occasions.
General Officers; dismounted.	Full-dress coat, full-dress trousers, chapeau, epaulets, sash, white gloves, full-dress belt, saber, black shoes.	On state occasions at home and abroad; when receiving or calling officially upon the President of the United States, or upon the president, sovereign, or member of the royal family of other countries; and at ceremonies and entertainments when it is desirable to do special honor to the occasion, or when full dress is prescribed for enlisted men.
General Officers; mounted.	Full-dress coat, dress breeches, full-dress cap, shoulder knots, sash, *leather gauntlets*, full-dress belt, saber, black boots, spurs.	On occasions as above requiring the officer to be mounted, or following immediately after mounted functions.
Officers of Staff Corps and Departments; dismounted.	Full-dress coat, full-dress trousers, full-dress cap, white gloves, full-dress belt, saber, black shoes. Aiguillettes and shoulder belts for those authorized to wear them.	Same as stated above for general officers dismounted.

COMPOSITION OF THE UNIFORMS OF OFFICERS OF THE ARMY,
AND OCCASIONS ON WHICH THEY ARE TO BE WORN—Continued.

Officers.	Articles.	Occasions.
Officers of Staff Corps and Departments; dismounted.	Full-dress coat, dress breeches, full-dress cap, *leather gauntlets*, full-dress belt, saber, black boots, spurs. Aiguillettes and shoulder belts for those authorized to wear them.	Same as stated above for general officers mounted.
Officers of Cavalry, Artillery, Infantry, and Engineers serving with Engineer troops; dismounted.	Full-dress coat, full-dress trousers, full-dress cap, white gloves, full-dress belt, saber, black shoes. Aiguillettes for those authorized to wear them.	Same as stated for general officers dismounted.
Officers of Cavalry, Artillery, Infantry, and Engineers serving with Engineer troops; mounted.	Full-dress coat, dress breeches, full-dress cap, full-dress belt, saber, *leather gauntlets*, black boots, spurs. Aiguillettes for those authorized to wear them.	Same as stated for general officers mounted.
Chaplains; dismounted.	Full-dress coat, full-dress trousers, chaplain's hat, white gloves, black shoes.	As stated for general officers dismounted.
Chaplains; mounted.	Full-dress coat, dress breeches, chaplain's hat, *leather gauntlets*, black boots, spurs.	As stated for general officers mounted.

Courts-martial, courts of inquiry, and boards of officers will hold their sessions in such uniform as the court or board shall decide.

DRESS UNIFORM.*		
General Officers; dismounted.	Dress coat, dress trousers, dress cap, black shoes. Under arms, add dress belt (worn under coat), saber, and white gloves.	At reviews, inspections, parades, and other ceremonies when the troops are in dress uniform; at such other duties under arms as may be prescribed. This uniform is also authorized as a mess dress, and for social occasions when full dress is not worn.
General Officers; mounted.	Dress coat, dress breeches, dress cap, *leather gauntlets*, black boots, spurs. Under arms, add dress belt (worn under coat), and saber.	On occasions as above, requiring officers to be mounted.
Officers of Staff Corps and Departments; dismounted.	Dress coat, dress trousers, dress cap, black shoes. Under arms, add dress belt, saber, and white gloves.	Same as stated for general officers dismounted.
Officers of Staff Corps and Departments; mounted.	Dress coat, dress breeches, dress cap, *leather gauntlets*, black boots, spurs. Under arms, add dress belt and saber.	Same as stated for general officers mounted.
Officers of Cavalry, Artillery, Infantry, and Engineers serving with Engineer troops; dismounted.	Dress coat, dress cap, dress trousers, black shoes. Under arms, add dress belt (worn under coat), saber, white gloves.	Same as stated for general officers dismounted.
Officers of Cavalry, Artillery, Infantry, and Engineers serving with Engineer troops; mounted.	Dress coat, dress breeches, dress cap, *leather gauntlets*, black boots, spurs. Under arms, add dress belt (worn under coat), and saber.	Same as stated for general officers mounted.
Chaplains; dismounted.	Dress coat, dress trousers, chaplain's hat, black shoes; white gloves when occasion requires gloves.	Same as stated for other officers dismounted.

* When troops appear in full-dress or dress uniform, as prescribed in these regulations, all officers on duty therewith or attached thereto in any capacity shall wear the corresponding prescribed full-dress or dress uniform for officers.

COMPOSITION OF THE UNIFORMS OF OFFICERS OF THE ARMY,
AND OCCASIONS ON WHICH THEY ARE TO BE WORN—Continued.

Officers.	Articles.	Occasions.
Chaplains; mounted.	Dress coat, dress breeches, chaplain's hat, *leather gauntlets*, black boots, spurs.	Same as stated for other officers mounted.
WHITE UNIFORM.		
For all officers; dismounted.	White coat, white trousers, white cap, white canvas or black leather shoes.	When authorized by the commanding officer, but not to be worn on occasions of duty with troops.
SERVICE UNIFORM—OLIVE-DRAB.		
For all officers; dismounted.	(*a*) Service coat, service trousers, service cap, russet leather shoes. (*b*) Under arms, add service breeches, service belt, saber, white gloves, russet leather leggings, omit trousers. (*c*) Service coat, service breeches, russet leather leggings, russet leather shoes, service hat, service belt, saber, revolver, canteen, field glass, watch, compass, notebook and pencils.	(*a*) For habitual garrison wear when not otherwise prescribed herein. (*b*) For habitual garrison duty under arms, also when changing station with troops by rail or water, and when not otherwise prescribed herein. (*c*) For field duty.
For all officers; mounted.	(*a*) Service coat, service breeches, service cap, russet leather boots or russet leather shoes and russet leather leggings, spurs, *leather gauntlets*. (*b*) Under arms, add service belt and saber. (*c*) Service coat, service breeches, russet leather boots or russet leather shoes and russet leather leggings, service hat, service belt, saber and revolver, spurs, *leather gauntlets, canteen, field glass, watch, compass, notebook and pencils.* Officers of the Signal Corps will wear the shoulder belt on occasions (*b*) and (*c*) as herein prescribed, when on mounted or dismounted duty requiring its use.	(*a*) For habitual garrison wear and when not otherwise prescribed herein. (*b*) For habitual garrison duty under arms, also when changing station by rail or water. (*c*) For field duty.

NOTE.—When troops appear in service uniform (*a*), (*b*), or (*c*), all officers on duty therewith or attached thereto in any capacity will wear the corresponding service uniform (*a*), (*b*), or (*c*).

Service uniform, khaki, same as above, when climate and weather require.

Olive-drab uniform for habitual wear when climate or weather does not require khaki.

The commanding officer may require officers on field service to be equipped with such additional articles of their prescribed equipment as conditions may make necessary.

COMPOSITION OF THE UNIFORMS OF ENLISTED MEN OF THE ARMY,
AND OCCASIONS ON WHICH THEY ARE TO BE WORN.

All enlisted men.	FULL-DRESS UNIFORM.	
Dismounted _____	Dress coat, breast cord, dress trousers, dress cap, black shoes, white gloves, russet leather belt, and cartridge box.	To be worn at all ceremonies in garrison (except inspection and guard mounting, and then if prescribed by the commanding officer), when climate and weather permit. To be worn at all ceremonies other than garrison when prescribed by proper authority.
Mounted _____	Dress coat, breast cord, *dress trousers*, dress cap, *russet leather leggings*, russet leather	As herein, when mounted.

COMPOSITION OF THE UNIFORMS OF ENLISTED MEN OF THE ARMY, AND OCCASIONS ON WHICH THEY ARE TO BE WORN—Continued.

All enlisted men.	Articles.	Occasions.
	or campaign shoes, *leather gauntlets*, spurs, saber belt, and cartridge box (when prescribed).	

DRESS UNIFORM.

All enlisted men.	Articles.	Occasions.
Dismounted _____	Dress coat, dress cap, dress trousers, black shoes. Under arms, add white gloves, russet leather belt, and cartridge box.	To be worn at retreat roll call and on pass, when climate and weather permit.
Mounted _____	Dress coat, dress cap, *dress trousers*, russet leather or campaign shoes, *russet leather leggings,* spurs, *leather gauntlets.* Under arms, add saber belt and cartridge box.	As herein, when mounted.

WHITE UNIFORM.

All enlisted men.	Articles.	Occasions.
Dismounted _____	White coat, white trousers, russet leather or black leather shoes.	*For enlisted men of the Hospital Corps only, as prescribed by the surgeon, for ward duty.*

NOTE.—*Leather leggings are prescribed for enlisted men of cavalry and light artillery only.*

SERVICE UNIFORM—OLIVE-DRAB.

All enlisted men.	Articles.	Occasions.
Dismounted _____	(*a*) Service coat, service breeches, leggings, service cap, russet-leather *or campaign shoes.*	(*a*) For habitual garrison wear when not otherwise prescribed herein.
	(*b*) Under arms, add *white gloves*, russet leather belt, and cartridge box.	(*b*) For habitual garrison duty under arms; also when changing station by rail or water and when not otherwise prescribed herein.
	(*c*) Service coat, service breeches, *olive-drab shirt*, leggings, russet leather *or campaign shoes*, service hat, field belt.	(*c*) For field duty.
Mounted _____	(*a*) Service coat, service breeches, *russet leather leggings*, service cap, russet leather *or campaign shoes, leather gauntlets, spurs.*	(*a*) For habitual garrison wear when not otherwise prescribed herein.
	(*b*) Under arms, add russet leather belt and cartridge box.	(*b*) For habitual garrison duty under arms; also when changing station by rail or water and when not otherwise prescribed herein.
	(*c*) Service coat, service breeches, *olive-drab shirt*, service hat, *russet leather leggings*, russet leather *or campaign shoes*, spurs, field belt, and *leather gauntlets.*	(*c*) For field duty.

NOTE.—With dismounted service uniform (*b*) noncommissioned staff officers equipped therewith will wear belt and saber or sword in lieu of belt and cartridge box.

With dismounted service uniform (*c*) noncommissioned staff officers equipped therewith will wear revolver and belt in lieu of saber or sword.

Leather leggings for enlisted men of cavalry and light artillery only.

Enlisted men other than cavalry and light artillery, mounted, or who may on occasions be mounted, will wear the canvas leggings.

Enlisted men of cavalry and light artillery may, when dismounted, wear the canvas leggings.

Olive-drab uniform for habitual wear when climate or weather does not require khaki.

SERVICE UNIFORM—KHAKI.

All enlisted men.	Articles.	Occasions.
Dismounted _____	(*a*) Service coat, service breeches or trousers, leggings (with breeches), service cap, khaki, russet leather or campaign shoes.	(*a*) For habitual garrison wear, including retreat roll call, and on pass.

COMPOSITION OF THE UNIFORMS OF ENLISTED MEN OF THE ARMY,
AND OCCASIONS ON WHICH THEY ARE TO BE WORN—Continued.

All enlisted men.	Articles.	Occasions.
	(*b*) Under arms, add white gloves, russet leather belt, and cartridge box. Omit trousers, but include service breeches and leggings.	(*b*) For habitual garrison duty under arms; also when changing station by rail or water.
	(*c*) Service coat, service breeches, olive-drab shirt, leggings, russet leather or campaign shoes, service hat, field belt.	(*c*) For field duty.
Mounted _____	(*a*) Service coat, service breeches, *russet leather leggings*, service cap, khaki, russet leather *or campaign* shoes, *leather gauntlets*, spurs.	(*a*) For habitual garrison wear.
	(*b*) Under arms, add russet leather belt and cartridge box.	(*b*) For habitual garrison duty under arms; also when changing station by rail or water.
	(*c*) Service coat, service breeches, *olive-drab shirt*, service hat, *russet leather leggings*, russet leather *or campaign shoes*, spurs, field belt, and *leather gauntlets*.	(*c*) For field duty.

FATIGUE UNIFORM.

Dismounted _____	Fatigue coat, fatigue trousers, service hat, russet leather shoes.	On fatigue and at stables.

NOTE.—With dismounted service uniform (*b*) noncommissioned staff officers equipped therewith will wear belt and saber or sword in lieu of belt and cartridge box.

With dismounted service uniform (*c*) noncommissioned staff officers equipped therewith will wear revolver and belt in lieu of saber or sword.

Leather leggings for enlisted men of the cavalry and light artillery only.

Enlisted men other than cavalry and light artillery, mounted or who may on occasions be mounted, will wear the canvas legging.

Enlisted men of cavalry and field artillery may, when dismounted, wear the canvas legging.

Enlisted men of the mounted service may wear the khaki trousers when not mounted and not on armed duty.

Khaki uniform for habitual wear when olive-drab uniform is not prescribed.

The years between 1907 and 1912 were marked by a great increase in the activities of the Army. A general pay increase approved by Congress in 1908 corrected the inequities which existed and made it possible for the regiments to be recruited up to near authorized strength.

President Teddy Roosevelt demanded that all field officers of the infantry, cavalry, and artillery demonstrate their physical fitness by riding 30 miles a day for 3 consecutive days. Those unable to meet the requirements of the test were retired either for length of service or by a special retiring board. All company-grade officers were required to take annual physical examinations.

There was still some trouble in the Philippines with the Moros, and the Regulars had to participate in actions to suppress them. Additional maneuvers in which the National Guard participated with units of the Regular Army brought to light existing defects in arms and equipment. Boards of officers were appointed to investigate and improve arms and equipment, and training facilities for both officers and enlisted men were enlarged and improved. Small military posts were abandoned and the posts retained were enlarged and improved.

The Corps of Cadets at West Point was increased by 25 per cent to bring more highly trained officers into the Army. Officers were detached from the Regular Army to serve as instructors for the National Guard; these vacancies allowed additional appointments of new second lieutenants, and a general advancement in grade took place for many officers in the various arms of the service.

In 1911 trouble along the Mexican border resulted

in a massive concentration of troops in that area, and almost all the units of the Regular Army were placed in a position for patrolling the border from the Gulf to the Pacific.

It was these activities that helped mark 1911 as the period of greatest contrast between the old Army and the new. The new spirit of progressiveness must have been responsible, in part, for the many changes that took place in the uniform and general equipment of the Army during 1912, and in the following years. (Ganoe, *The History of the United States Army*.)

Sometime during 1911 a uniform board was convened, and many changes were made in the cut and styles of the clothing for the army—more for officers than for enlisted men, but a considerable number for both. Publication of the 1912 *Regulations and Specifications for the Uniform of the United States Army* revealed the details.

For the first time, *Specifications for the Uniform* were published as a separate order from *Regulations for the Uniform*, and each was much more comprehensive than former publications covering the clothing and insignia for the Army.

New pattern dress and service breeches were prescribed for officers. Pegged wider than the old pattern, both dress and service breeches had "strappings," another name for reinforce, but of a new and different shape.

The following text with excerpts from both *Regulations* and *Specifications* cover the changes from the 1902–07 period.

5. BREECHES (DRESS).

The breeches will be cut loose in the thigh and tight from the knee down with ample length from the hip to the knee. To have a strapping of the same material on the contact surface on the inside of leg and knee, extending to a little below the leggin and from 6 to 8 inches of the crotch. To be fastened from the knee down with laces or buttons of appropriate size and color, either showing or concealed in a fly.

(*a*) General officers, except Chief of Coast Artillery, Chief of Engineers and Quartermaster General.—To be of dark blue elastique of adopted standard, without stripe, welt, or cord.

(*b*) Chief of Coast Artillery.—To be of dark blue elastique of adopted standard, with a stripe of scarlet cloth 1½ inches wide and welted at the edges.

(*c*) Chief of Engineers.—To be of dark-blue elastique of adopted standard, with a stripe of scarlet cloth 1½ inches wide with a piping of white cloth ⅛ inch in width at each edge.

(*d*) Quartermaster General.—To be of dark blue elas-

tique of adopted standard, with a stripe of buff cloth 1½ inches wide and welted at the edges.

(*e*) Officers below the rank of Brigadier General holding permanent appointments in the staff corps and departments, except Engineers, Quartermasters, and chaplains. To be dark blue elastique of adopted standard, without stripe, welt, or cord.

(*f*) Officers of Engineers.—To be of dark blue elastique of adopted standard, with a stripe of scarlet cloth 1½ inches wide with a piping of white cloth ⅛ inch in width on each edge.

(*g*) Officers of Quartermaster's Department.—To be of dark blue elastique of adopted standard, with a stripe of buff cloth 1½ inches wide and welted at the edges.

(*h*) Chaplains.—To be of black elastique without stripe, welt, or cord.

(*i*) Officers of Cavalry and Artillery.—To be of sky-blue elastique of adopted standard, with stripes 1½ inches wide and welted at the edges and of the color of arm of service.

(*j*) Officers of Infantry.—To be of sky-blue elastique of adopted standard, with stripes 1½ inches wide and welted at the edges. The stripes to be white.

6. BREECHES (SERVICE). [See Figures 325 and 326 and Figure F on Uniform Color Plate VIII in Volume I.]

To be of olive-drab woolen or cotton material, of adopted standard, to match the service coat, without stripe, welt, or cord. To be cut loose in the thigh and tight from the knee down, with ample length from the hip to the knee. To be fastened from the knee down with laces or buttons of appropriate size and color. *For mounted officers*, to have a strapping of the same material, or buckskin of the same color, on the contact surface on the inside of leg and knee, extending to a little below the leggin and from 6 to 8 inches of the crotch.

The old-pattern *dress* cap for officers, with the band of black mohair, was abolished, and the *full-dress* cap, in a new shape accomplished by stiffening in front, with the top falling without stiffening to the rear, was adopted for both dress and full-dress uniforms.

The new service cap for officers was made with the same shape as the dress cap, and the visor and chin strap were changed from black to russet leather. In addition, the former khaki service cap for wear with the khaki uniform was abolished and but a single service cap, of olive-drab woolen material, was prescribed for wear by officers.

9. CAP (DRESS).

(*a*) General officers except Quartermaster General and Chief of Coast Artillery.—To be made of dark blue cloth of adopted standard.

Badge.—Coat of arms of the United States embroidered in gold or gilt bullion in the front of the cap, taking in half of the upper part of velvet band and lower half of the two front quarters.

Band.—To be of blue-black velvet, about 1¾ inches wide, upon which is embroidered oak leaves of gold or gilt metal bullion. The leaves to be about 1 inch in length and each group of two leaves about ¾ inch in width. The velvet band with the gold leaves to encircle the entire cap.

Chin strap.—To be ⅜ inch in width and 9 inches long, of gold lace stitched on red Russia leather, edge to edge, fastened at each end of visor with a regulation small gilt button.

Crown.—Of dark-blue cloth of adopted standard, measuring about 10¼ inches from front to rear and 9½ inches from side to side; to be stiffened in front by means of haircloth springs sewed between the quarters and lining, falling without stiffening to the rear. To have two black japanned eyelets 1½ inches from the welt seam and about ¾ inch on each side of side seam of quarters.

Visor.—To be of black patent leather, cut to slope to an angle of about 45° when attached to cap. To be lined with embossed green hatter's leather, and on the outside two semicircles of oak leaves embroidered in gold or gilt bullion. The leaves to be about 1 inch in length and each group of two leaves about ¾ inch in width.

(*d*) Field officers.—Same as "General officers," par. 9 (*a*), p. 7.

Badge.—Same as "General officers."

Band.—A band consisting of two bands of gold lace about ½ inch in width on the top and bottom and in the center a silk band ¾ inch wide, of the color of the corps or arm of the service.

Chin strap.—Same as "General officers."

Crown.—Same as "General officers."

Visor.—Same as "General officers."

(*e*) Officers below the rank of field officers.—Same as "General officers."

Badge.—Same as "General officers."

Band.—Same as "Field officers."

Chin strap.—Same as "General officers."

Crown.—Same as "General officers."

Visor.—Same as "General officers", except that a plain visor will be substituted for the embroidered visor.

(*f*) Chaplain, veterinarian, dental surgeon, and acting dental surgeon.—Same as "General officers."

Badge.—Same as "General officers."

Band.—To be a plain band of black mohair braid about 1¾ inches wide.

Chin strap.—Same as "General officers."

Crown.—Same as "General officers."

Visor.—Same as "Officers below the rank of field officer."

10. CAP (SERVICE).

To be made of 13-ounce olive drab woolen material, of adopted standard, of same general design and pattern as the dress cap, par. 9, p. 7.

Badge.—Coat of arms of the United States in dull finished bronze metal, taking in half the upper part of mohair band and the lower part of front two quarters; to be attached

to front of cap by means of a threaded post inserted in an eyelet.

Band.—To be olive drab mohair braid about 1¾ inches in width around entire cap.

Chin strap.—*Russet leather*, about ½ inch in width and 9 inches long, fastened at each end of visor with a regulation small bronze button.

Crown.—Front to be *stiffened* by means of haircloth stiffening inserted between the lining and front quarter; crown to slope to rear without stiffening.

Visor.—*Top piece of russet leather*, lined with embossed green hatter's leather; to be waterproof.

The new pattern of white cap prescribed by the 1912 specifications is shown in Figure 327. Identical to the dress and service caps in shape, it now has removable covers. Chin strap and visor are essentially the same materials as in 1902 caps.

11. CAP (WHITE).—To be made of either linen or cotton duck of adopted standard of the same dimensions and pattern as the dress cap, par. 9, p. 7. The cap to be without lining. To have detachable covers which fit snugly over body band.

Badge.—Gold or gilt metal coat of arms of the United States, taking in the upper part of the band and the lower half of the two front quarters; to be attached to front of cover by means of a threaded post inserted in an eyelet.

Band.—To have a band of white braid about 1¾ inches wide entirely around the cap. Bottom of body band to be lined with dark-blue cloth entirely around.

Chin strap.—To be of gold lace stitched on patent leather edge to edge, ⅜ inch in width and 9 inches long, fastened at each end of visor with a small regulation gilt button.

Crown (cover).—Front to be stiffened by means of haircloth stiffening inserted in the front quarter; crown to slope to rear without stiffening.

Visor.—To be of black patent leather, lined with embossed green hatter's leather cut to slope about 45° when attached to cap.

New buttons with raised rims, in both gilt and bronze, were made standard by the 1912 regulations, and are shown in Figure 330. The same pattern was furnished for both officers and enlisted men in the two smaller sizes, but only for the overcoats of enlisted men in the large size. Officers' overcoats were fitted with buttons made of olive-drab-colored horn. (See Figure 326.)

7. BUTTONS (BRONZE).

(*a*) Officers, except Engineers.—To be of dull-finish bronze metal, well lacquered, and of permanent finish, circular and slightly convex in shape, with the coat of arms of United States clearly stamped thereon. To be 36 ligne for

FIGURE 325. Service uniform, pattern of 1912. Made from olive-drab woolen material for winter wear and olive-drab cotton material for summer wear, this pattern, with very minor modifications, remained issue until 1926. The officer service-uniform pattern was the same except for quality of material and workmanship.

FIGURE 326. Left: Lieutenant colonel, Eleventh Cavalry (ca. 1913), wearing the new pattern-of-1911 service uniform. The 5-inch-wide band of black cloth or crepe on his left arm is the approved symbol of family mourning for officers.

Center: Captain, Eleventh Cavalry (ca. 1913), with the new-size knots of ¼-inch black braid on the sleeves of his overcoat. The 1912 regulations omitted the metal crossed-sabers corps insignia below the knot on the overcoat sleeves, as it had been worn since 1907. No mention is made of the detachable hood in the 1912 regulations.

Right: First lieutenant, Eleventh Cavalry (ca. 1913), in the dress uniform prescribed for mounted occasions in the 1912 regulations. He wears the new dress cap, which is also the new full-dress cap, the former dark blue dress cap having been abolished with the uniform change in 1911. His shoulder straps are the new larger size, ¼ inch wider than the 1910 regulation. The black crepe saber knot is the badge of military mourning as prescribed in the 1912 regulations.

FIGURE 327. The white cap for officers, 1912 pattern. The coat-of-arms device is gilt metal, and the cover is removable.

large and 25 ligne for small buttons, rim and background, same as in gilt buttons.

8. BUTTONS (GILT).

(a) Officers, except Engineers.—To be of gold or gilt metal, circular and slightly convex in shape, with a polished raised rim, with the coat of arms of United States clearly stamped thereon in relief against a lined background. To be 36 ligne for large and 25 ligne for small buttons.

Considerable change was made in the service coats for both officers and enlisted men, as shown in Figures 325 and 326 and on Figure F of Uniform Color Plate VIII (in Volume I). The 1912 regulations did away with the khaki lightweight service coat for warm-weather wear and provided only one made of olive-drab woolen or cotton material.

The collar became a slightly stiffened standing collar fastened with hooks and eyes. Collar insignia remained the same as before, crossed sabers with the number of the regiment in the upper angle, of dull bronze, and the letters "U.S." of the same material for officers. There was a new pattern of bronze button for enlisted men, as shown in Figure 332.

The fit through the body of the coat was tighter and smarter than the 1902 pattern, and presented, generally, a much smarter and more military appearance.

16. COATS (SERVICE).

Body.—To be a single-breasted sack coat of olive drab woolen or cotton material of adopted standard; to fit closely at the waist and easy over the chest; buttoned down the front with five large coat buttons.

Buttons.—To be five large and six small bronze buttons. See "Button."

Collar.—To be standing collar of a suitable height, fastened with hooks and eyes.

Pockets.—Four outside patch pockets, two breast and two hip, slightly rounded at lower corners, and covered with a flap slightly rounded at the lower corners and coming to a point in the center, and buttoned by a small coat button.

Skirt.—To extend one-third the distance from the point of hip to the bend of knee according to height of wearer.

Shoulder loops.—On each shoulder a loop of same material as the coat let in at the sleeve head seam and reaching to the edge of the collar, buttoning at the upper end with a small coat button. Loops to be about 2 inches wide at the lower end and 1 inch wide at the collar end, and cross stitched down to shoulder about 2 inches from the lower end.

Ornamentation on sleeve.—Officers, except the General Staff Corps, will wear a band of brown braid ½ inch wide on the sleeves, and lower edge of the braid 3 inches from the end of the sleeve. For officers of the General Staff Corps the braid will be black.

While the pattern for the full-dress coat, the special evening-dress coat, and the mess jacket remained the same as to cut and style, a noticeable change was made in the size of the gilt-braid soutache and the soutache knot itself. The 1907 soutache braid had been ⅛ inch wide and formed a proportionately smaller soutache knot than the new ¼-inch-wide soutache braid, whose knot dimensions were set at 8½ inches from the upper edge of the gold band on the sleeve to the top of the knot, and 6¾ inches between the outside edges of the two loops. The new braid and larger knot are shown on the captain at the right of Figure 328.

The black soutache braid and the knot formed by it on the sleeve of the overcoat were similarly changed. The new braid increased from ⅛ inch in 1907 to ¼ inch in 1912, and the outside dimensions of the knot were proportionately increased, as indicated below. (See Figure 326.) The bronze crossed sabers were also abolished on the overcoat sleeve by the 1912 regulations.

FULL DRESS AND SPECIAL EVENING DRESS COAT AND MESS JACKET.

(c) Colonel.—A knot composed of three loops, one large upper and two small lower loops. Knot to be formed by five rows of ¼-inch gold or gilt soutache, ends of knot resting on gold band of sleeve. Outside dimensions of knot to be 8¼ inches from upper edge of gold band to top of upper loop and 6¾ inches across between outer edges, of lower loops. Insignia of corps, department, or arm of service will be worn in the center of space formed by the lower curves of the knot and the upper edge of the gold-lace band.

(d) Lieutenant colonel.—Same knot as for colonel, except that there will be four rows of gold or gilt soutache.

(e) Major.—Same knot as for colonel, except that there

FIGURE 328. Left: First lieutenant, Fifth Cavalry (ca. 1913), in field dress, wearing the issue olive-drab shirt without the service coat. His Model 1912 equipments on the regulation officer's belt are supported by the Model 1908 shoulder belt. His silver lieutenant's bars are pinned to his collar as prescribed by the 1912 regulations. His hat is the new Model 1911 service hat, the same pattern for officers and enlisted men.

Center: Private, Troop A, Fifth Cavalry (ca. 1913), in the new 1911-pattern service uniform with complete pattern-of-1912 cavalry equipments for service afoot as infantry, including canvas ration bags, intrenching tool with picket-pin

handle, the new bandoleer, and field cartridge belt. He also wears the new russet leather strap leggings selected by the 1910 cavalry board and the Model 1911 spurs made of nickel steel.

Right: Captain, Fifth Cavalry (ca. 1913), in the full-dress uniform that was slightly modified from the original pattern in 1907 and 1911. All officers below general grade now wear 9 buttons in each row on the breast, and the gilt soutache, or braid, forming the sleeve knot is ¼ inch instead of ⅛ inch, as formerly. Rank insignia is fastened to the shoulder knot in the same position as on the service-coat shoulder loops.

FIGURE 329. Left: Corporal, Twelfth Cavalry (ca. 1913), wearing the olive-drab flannel shirt without the service coat for summer duty. He wears the Model 1912 leather garrison belt.

Center: Regimental sergeant major, Twelfth Cavalry (ca. 1913), in the mounted-dress uniform. He wears the cap insignia prescribed for noncommissioned staff officers with only the number of the regiment attached to the crossed sabers. The service stripes on his sleeves are the new 3/8-inch width instead of the former 1/2-inch stripes and are for wear only on the dress coat.

Right: Bandsman, Twelfth Cavalry Band (ca. 1913), in service dress. He wears the prescribed lyre insignia on cap and collar, and carries the large size Model 1904 olive-drab cloth-covered music pouch over his shoulder. The service ribbon on his chest indicates he took part in the Philippine occupation in 1903, and the metal bar is the marksman's badge. He carries a bell upright alto band horn, and is dressed for garrison duty.

FIGURE 330. Buttons, pattern of 1912. They were made in both gilt and dull bronze in the two smaller sizes for officers and enlisted men, but were made in the large overcoat size only in dull bronze for enlisted men. Drawn from specimens in the author's collection.

will be three rows of gold or gilt soutache.

(f) *Captain.*—Same knot as for colonel, except that there will be two rows of gold or gilt soutache.

(g) *First lieutenant.*—Same knot as for colonel, except that there will be one row of gold or gilt soutache.

32. INSIGNIA ON SLEEVE OF OVERCOAT.

(a) *Officers below the rank of general, except officers of the General Staff Corps.*—A knot composed of three loops of one large upper and two smaller lower loops. Knot to be formed of ¼-inch black soutache. Ends of knot resting on bottom of sleeve. Outside dimensions of knot, 9¾ inches from lower edge of sleeve to top of upper loop and 7¼ inches across between outer edges of lower loops.

Specifications for the overcoat do not include any mention of the hood, so we can assume that the hood for the officer's overcoat had been abolished as an authorized article of uniform.

A new service, or campaign, hat took the place of the old pattern with the crease along the top of the crown. The crown of the new olive-drab fur-felt hat was pinched in what was termed a Montana peak. The brim was flat and stiff, and the hat, for both officers and enlisted men, was worn with the usual acorn-end hat cord—black-and-gold mix for officers, and yellow for enlisted men. Regulations made it mandatory for the cord to be sewed to the hat. The new service hats are shown in Figures 328 and 329.

The hat for chaplains was of the same style, but was made of black felt.

The gold-cord shoulder knots worn with the full-dress coat, special evening-dress coat, blue mess jacket, and new white mess jacket remained the same in pattern, but the new regulations prescribed wearing the metal insignia of rank on top of the knot, in the same position as worn on the shoulder loop of the service coat. (See Figure 328.)

45. SHOULDER KNOT.—To be of gold or gilt cord ¼ inch in diameter. The knot to be formed of 4 plaits of 3-cord and rounded at the top. A small gold or gilt coat button in the upper end of knot. Knot to be not more than 5½ inches long and 2½ inches wide, conforming to shoulder; to be stiffened on the underside with a flexible backing covered with cloth of the color of coat; to have attached to the strap a suitable attachment for fastening to the shoulder of coat. *Insignia of rank* to be placed in the same relative position as on the shoulder loop, par. 29, p. 20.

Shoulder straps for wear on the dress uniform coat were increased in width, from 1⅜ inches in 1902 to 1⅝ inches by the 1912 regulations. The captain in dress uniform at the right side of Figure 326 wears the new wider shoulder straps, as well as the new-pattern dress cap and the new sky-blue dress breeches. His black boots, with stiffened tops, are the approved pattern—similar to the pattern adopted in 1889, with stiffened tops—but the legs are narrower at the calf, and the toes are rounded.

46. SHOULDER STRAP.—To be 4 inches long and 1⅝ inches wide with a raised border of gold or gilt embroidery ⅜ inch wide; on the inside and outside of border to have a gold or gilt twisted wire ¹⁄₁₆ inch in diameter. The field of strap to be of cloth of the color of the facings of corps, department, or arm of service (see facings, par. 20, p. 16). Strap to be mounted on cloth of same color of coat and stiffened with a flexible backing.

Figure 326 shows the authorized badges of mourning for officers. Until 1912 only the black crepe knot on the saber had been authorized, but the new regula-

FIGURE 331. Left: The new-pattern (1912) dark blue mess jacket. It differed from the 1902 pattern in the yellow lapel facings and the wider (¼-inch) gilt soutache, or braid, forming the knot on the sleeve. Center: Cut of the back of both dark blue and white mess jackets. Right: The pattern-of-1912 white mess jacket. Cut exactly like the dark blue mess jacket, the ½-inch sleeve braid is gilt, while the ⅛-inch braid forming the sleeve rank knot is white. Service ribbons on both jackets are shown in the prescribed positions.

tions also included a band of crepe or plain black cloth 5 inches wide around the left arm above the elbow as a mark of family mourning. Both types are shown in Figure 326.

The dark blue mess jacket for officers was changed, and the optional distinctive ornamentation sanctioned in the earlier regulations was abolished. Instead, a regulation cut and decoration of lapels was prescribed, with lapel facings the color of the arm of service— yellow for cavalry. The soutache gilt knot on the sleeves was enlarged through the use of ¼-inch-wide soutache braid, as described earlier.

A white mess jacket was authorized for wear by officers in the 1912 regulations, the first time such a garment had been approved. It was cut exactly like the blue mess jacket, but the sleeve ornamentation was made from ⅛-inch-wide white soutache cord instead of ¼-inch cord, as was specified for all other such indications of rank on the 1912 uniforms. Figure 331 shows the cut and style of both dark blue and white mess jackets, and Figures D and E on Uniform Color Plate VIII (in Volume I) show them in their correct colors.

35. MESS JACKET, BLUE.—To be of dark blue cloth of adopted standard.

Body.—To be cut like special evening dress, to descend to point of hips, slightly curved to a peak behind and in front; two buttonholes on each front, below the turn of lapel, the lower hole being about 1½ inches from bottom of coat; three large gilt regulation coat buttons on each side beginning about 1½ inches from bottom of coat and spaced 2 to 3½ inches

FIGURE 332. Button-type collar insignia, pattern of 1912, for enlisted men's service coats and for shirt collars when shirts were worn without service coats in summer for duty in the field. (Circular No. 18, December 30, 1916). Drawn from specimens in the author's collection.

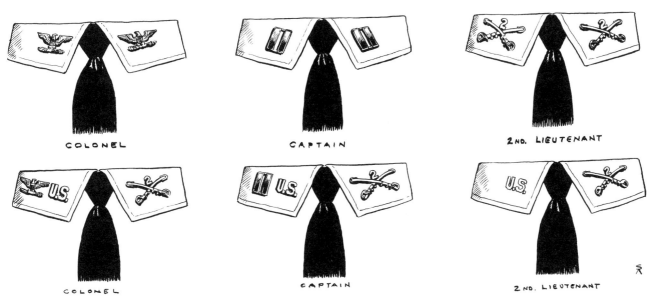

FIGURE 333. The top line shows insignia on collar of shirt when the shirt was worn without the coat, as prescribed by regulations from 1912 through December 30, 1916. At that time Circular No. 18 from the Adjutant General's Office directed all officers to conform to the arrangement of insignia shown in the bottom line. This order was rescinded by Circular No. 9, dated January 15, 1917, but regulations were changed back less than eight months later to the newer arrangement.

apart, following the line of outer edge of lapel; suitable shoulder-knot fastenings at upper and lower ends of shoulder.

Lapels.—To have three buttonholes on the turn, equally spaced, and a facing of cloth of color of facing of arm of service, outer edge of facing to be 1¼ inches from the edge of lapel and parallel to it, and follow the line of step and seam of collar.

Sleeves.—To be ornamented the same as sleeves of full-dress coat, par. 15 (*a–d*), p. 11–13.

36. MESS JACKET, WHITE.—To be of duck of adopted standard and conform in cut to the blue mess jacket, par. 35. The sleeve ornamentation to conform in design to that on the sleeves of the full dress coat, to be ½-inch white braid and ⅛-inch white cord. Buttons to be same.

The new regulations specified in paragraph 101 that the commanding officer could, at his discretion, prescribe the wearing of the olive-drab shirt without the coat at certain drills, and without the sweater in the field, at which time enlisted men would wear a belt instead of suspenders.

Officers were to wear the insignia of rank on the shirt collar, 1 inch from the edge of collar, as indicated in Figure 333 (without the necktie, or cravat, until authorized in the 1914 regulations), and non-

commissioned officers, chevrons denoting their grades on the sleeves of the shirt.

The olive-drab shirt was to be worn with the service coat at all times.

The new service uniform for enlisted men was of the same pattern as that prescribed for officers, but the material and workmanship were not as good. Figure 325 and Figure G on Uniform Color Plate VIII (in Volume I) show the cut and pattern of coat and breeches.

The disc, or button, collar insignia shown in Figure 332 are bronze, 1 inch in diameter, and are worn with the "US" 1 inch from the right side of the collar and the crossed sabers with number of the regiment and letter of the company 1 inch from the left side. See Figures 328, 329, and Figure G on Uniform Color Plate VIII.

Service and decoration ribbons were prescribed for wear on the service coat for both officers and enlisted men, as well as on the dress uniform, the special evening-dress coat, the mess jacket, and the white uniform. That paragraph from the 1912 regulations prescribing the correct wearing of these ribbons follows:

96. RIBBONS.

(*a*) The sections of ribbons are a part of the uniform and will be worn as prescribed in this order.

(*b*) By whom worn.—By those entitled to wear the corresponding badges or medal.

(*c*) When worn.—With the special evening dress, the dress, the mess jacket, the service and the white uniforms.

NOTE.—The medal of honor instead of the ribbon is worn with the special evening dress.

(*d*) How worn.—With the *cotton service*, the *white uniform*, and the *white mess jacket*, the ribbons, without space between them and without overlapping, will be sewed on a bar having a brooch-pin arrangement or eyelet shanks. In the latter case the bar will be secured to the coat in the same manner that the buttons are secured to the service coat. With the *woolen service*, the *dress*, the *blue mess jacket*, and the *special evening-dress* the ribbons may be sewed on the coat or on a bar as just described.

Ribbons will be worn on the left breast, in a horizontal line, about 4 inches below the middle point of the top of the shoulder.

In cases where the ribbons are sewed on the coat, enlisted men in full-dress uniform wearing badges will pin them just above the ribbons so as to exclude the ribbons from view. If the ribbons are not sewed on the coat they will be removed.

With the *special evening-dress*, the *blue mess jacket* and the *white mess jacket*, ribbons will be worn on the left breast of the coat, in a horizontal line about four inches below the middle point of the top of shoulder, the ribbon nearest the center of the body nearly touching the edge of the lapel. If necessary to have more than one line of ribbons, the other lines will be placed below and parallel to the first line, with a space of three-eighths inch between lines, the middle of each line being in the middle of the space between the edge of the lapel and the left side of the body.

With the *dress*, the *white* and the *service uniforms*, ribbons will be similarly worn except that the lines will begin nearer to the center of the body.

(*e*) Order in which worn.—Ribbons will be worn in the following order, from right to left:

(1) The medal of honor ribbon.

(2) The certificate of merit ribbon.

(3) The Philippine congressional medal ribbon.

(4) The campaign ribbons in the order of the dates of the campaigns.

(5) Army of Cuban Pacification ribbon.

(*f*) Not to be worn by officers suspended from command or enlisted men in confinement.—Ribbons will not be worn by officers suspended from rank and command, nor by enlisted men serving sentence of confinement.

(*g*) Not to be worn on shirt or sweater.—Ribbons will not be worn on the olive-drab shirt or the sweater.

Figures 326 and 329 show these ribbons worn correctly on the service uniform. Figures D and E of Uniform Color Plate VIII (in Volume I) show them worn on the mess jackets.

Actual decoration medals as well as campaign medals were worn on the full-dress coats for occasions of ceremony, and with the special evening dress in the case of the Medal of Honor only, according to the 1912 regulations:

56. BADGES AND MEDALS.

(*a*) Military badges and medals awarded by the Government.—The following are the different military badges and medals awarded by the Government: 1. The medal of honor; 2. The certificate of merit badge; 3. The Philippines congressional medal; 4. The campaign badges; 5. The Army of Cuban Pacification badge; 6. The various distinctive marks awarded for excellence in small-arms practice.

(*b*) Part of the uniform.—The badges and medals named above are a part of the uniform and will be worn as prescribed in these regulations.

(*c*) The badges of military societies and of corps and divisions that officers are authorized to wear are: 1. The badges of military societies commemorative of the wars of the United States, including the Philippine insurrection and the China relief expedition; 2. The badges of the Regular Army and Navy Union of the United States and of the Army and Navy Union of the United States; 3. The corps and division badges of the Civil War.

(*d*) Badges and medals enumerated in *a* and *c* not to be worn together.—The badges enumerated in paragraph *c* may be worn as prescribed in these regulations; will not be worn with the badges and medals named in paragraph *a* above, except with those named in *a*-6.

57. MEDAL OF HONOR.

(*a*) By whom worn.— By those to whom it has been awarded.

(*b*) When worn.—With the full-dress uniform and the special evening dress.

(*c*) How worn.—With the full dress the medal of honor will be worn pendant from the neck, the ribbon passing between the upper and lower hooks of the coat collar so that the medal proper shall hang about 1 inch below the opening of the collar; with the special evening dress it will be worn pendant from the neck, the ribbon passing around the neck under the collar so that the medal proper shall hang about 1 inch below the tie.

(*d*) The medal of honor will not be worn by officers suspended from rank and command, nor by enlisted men serving sentence of confinement.

(See "Philippine Scouts," par. 53 (m), p. 20.)

58. OTHER MEDALS AND BADGES.

(*a*) By whom worn.—*Badges and medals awarded by the Government* are worn by those entitled thereto by law and regulations. (For those entitled to campaign badges, see General Orders, No. 129, War Department, 1908, and General Orders, No. 23, War Department, 1911; for those entitled to wear the Army of Cuban Pacification badge, see General Orders, No. 96, War Department, 1909.)

(*b*) *Badge of military societies* may be worn by officers and enlisted men who, in their own right or by the right of inheritance, are members of military societies of men who served in the armies and navies of the United States in the War of the Revolution, the War of 1812, the Mexican War, the War of the Rebellion, or the Indian wars of the United States, the Spanish-American War and the incidental insurrection in the Philippines, or the China relief expedition, or are members of the Regular Army and Navy Union of the United States, or of the Army and Navy Union of the United States.

(*c*) *Corps and division badges of the War of the Rebellion.*—Officers and enlisted men who served as officers, noncommissioned officers, privates, or other enlisted men in the Regular Army, volunteer or militia forces of the United States during the War of the Rebellion, and have been honorably discharged from the service, or still remain in the same, may wear the distinctive Army badge ordered for or adopted by the Army corps or division, respectively, in which they served.

(*d*) When worn.—*Badges and medals* are worn with the full-dress uniform.

See "Philippine Scouts," par. 58 (m), p. 20.

(*e*) *The various distinctive marks awarded for excellence in marksmanship* may be worn with the full dress, the dress and the service uniforms. However, they will not be worn in the field.

(*f*) When worn with the ribbons, they will be worn as prescribed in par. *i*, p. 20.

(*g*) How worn.—*Badges and medals* will be worn on the left breast of the coat in a horizontal line, about 4 inches below the middle point of the top of the shoulder, those with ribbons being suspended from a bar of metal passed through the upper ends and tops of the ribbons. The badges and medals that have ribbons will be worn in but one line, overlapping, if necessary.

(*h*) *Distinctive marks awarded for excellence in marksmanship and corps and division badges of the War of the Rebellion*, are worn in a similar manner, except that they are not suspended from bars of metal passing through ribbons.

(*i*) When marksmanship badges are worn with ribbons, the badges will be worn under the ribbons, in a horizontal line parallel to and three-eighths-inch from the bottom of the ribbons.

(*j*) Order in which worn.—They will be worn in the following order of precedence, beginning at the right:

(*1*) Military badges and medals awarded by the Government.—1. The certificate of merit badge; 2. The Philippines congressional medal; 3. The campaign badges, in the order of the dates of the campaigns; 4. The Army of Cuban Pacification badge; 5. The life-saving medal; 6. The various distinctive marks awarded for excellence in small-arms practice. (See par. 58 (i), p. 20.)

(*2*) Badges of military societies and of corps and divisions.—1. Badges of military societies, commemorative of the wars of the United States, including the Philippine insurrection and the China relief expedition, in the order of the dates of such wars; 2. Badges of the Regular Army and Navy Union of the United States and of the Army and Navy Union

of the United States; 3. Corps and division badges of the Civil War. (See par. 56 (d), p. 18.)

(*3*) When worn in more than one line.—If necessary to have more than one line of badges and medals, the second line will be placed below the first line, the bars from which the badges and medals are suspended being parallel to the upper bar and three-eighths inch from the bottom of the lowest medal, the middle of the lower line of medals being in the same vertical line as the middle of the upper line.

(*k*) Life-saving medal.—Officers and enlisted men who have received, or who shall hereafter receive, life-saving medals from the Treasury Department, may wear them on occasions of ceremony as prescribed in these regulations.

(*l*) Organized Militia.—Officers and enlisted men of the active list of the Organized Militia, who have had service as indicated in paragraph 1, General Orders, No. 120, War Department, 1908, are entitled to campaign badges. (For instructions regarding preparation of requisitions, etc., see Circular No. 4, War Department, 1909.)

(*m*) Philippine Scouts.—Officers, including majors, and enlisted men of the Philippine Scouts, who are entitled thereto, will wear the medal of honor, the certificate of merit badge, the Philippine congressional medal, and the campaign badges with service uniform on all occasions of ceremony. The medal of honor will be worn as in the case of the full-dress uniform. (Par. 57 (c), p. 18.)

(*n*) Naval medals and badges will not be worn with the Army uniform, but an officer or an enlisted man of the Army who rendered, while an officer or enlisted man of the Navy or Marine Corps, service that would have entitled him to a campaign badge had it been rendered as an officer or enlisted man of the Army, is entitled to wear such campaign badge.

(*o*) First Field Army.—Officers and enlisted men of the First Field Army created by General Orders, No. 35, War Department, 1910, will, when in the field, wear on the left side of the service hat a badge in the form of a shield, the division being indicated thereon by a numeral. The badge forms a part of the uniform of the officers and enlisted men of the Regular Army and Organized Militia that are attached to the First Field Army, and will, when in the field, be worn by those officers and enlisted men as long as they are so attached. The badges will be issued gratuitously to enlisted men and at cost price to officers. If lost, the badges must be replaced, and in the case of enlisted men the cost price will be charged against them on the pay rolls of the organizations to which they belong.

For division headquarters troops, and for cavalry and field artillery, the background for the division numeral will be of red, white, and blue; for troops of the first brigade it will be of red; for those of the second brigade, of white; and for those of the third brigade, of blue.

(*p*) Coast Artillery Reserves.—Officers and enlisted men of the Coast Artillery Reserves will wear on the left side of the campaign hat a red shield charged with the Coast Artillery device in gilt. When the campaign hat is not worn the shield will be worn on the left breast of the coat immediately below the line prescribed for badges and medals.

(*q*) Badges and medals not to be worn by officers sus-

FIGURE 334. Specialist chevrons, pattern of 1912. The round grounds on which the designs of facing cloth were sewn were 2½ inches in diameter; they were worn on both sleeves above the elbow. Top—horseshoer, saddler, farrier; bottom—cook, wagoner. Drawn from specimens in the author's collection.

pended from command nor by enlisted men serving sentence of confinement.—Neither badges nor medals will be worn by officers suspended from rank and command nor by enlisted men serving sentence of confinement.

Badges and medals worn correctly are shown in Figures 323 and 328, as well as on Figure C of Uniform Color Plate VIII (in Volume I).

Five cavalry *specialist chevrons*, of a new and different pattern, were prescribed in the 1912 regulations. They were two and a half inches in diameter and had designs made of facing cloth sewed as shown in Figure 334. As with rank chevrons, the specialist symbols were yellow facing cloth on dark blue grounds for dress uniforms, and olive-drab facing cloth on wool or cotton olive-drab grounds for service coats, overcoats, and fatigue coats. The regulations specified that they be worn on both sleeves, midway between the elbow and top of the sleeve.

In addition to the specialist insignia, a sleeve patch, rectangular in shape, was authorized for the new rating of *first class private*. For cavalry this patch, worn in the same position as the specialist round patches,

had crossed sabers in facing cloth sewed to the ground. (See Figure 338.) All noncommissioned-officer-rank chevrons were prescribed by paragraph 84 (c) for wear on both sleeves of the overcoat, all uniform coats, the shirt when worn without the coat, and the sweater in the field.

Service stripes were reduced in width from ½ inch to ⅜ inch and were authorized for wear only on the sleeves of the dress coat. (See Figure 329.) Stripes were of yellow facing cloth and were given for each 3 years of faithful service, as before.

The 1902 regulations had increased the width of the sergeant's trouser *stripes* to 1¼ inches, including piping in the case of the noncommissioned staff. Of course, these stripes were worn only on the dress trousers—none on the olive-drab service trousers, or breeches.

This was the year the Army decided to eliminate the buckskin gauntlet as an item of uniform for both cavalry and artillery. Paragraph 33 of the 1912 regulations states, "Gauntlets.—Buckskin (until exhausted) and winter, as issued." Part b of paragraph

FIGURE 334A. Left: Cap and collar ornament for enlisted men of the cavalry detachment assigned to the U.S. Military Academy (ca. 1912). Right: Cap and collar ornaments (ca. 1912) for enlisted assistant inspectors of small-arms practice for organized militia cavalry. These were worn by noncommissioned officers from regular cavalry regiments who were attached to militia units as instructors and inspectors.

74 prescribes instead the wearing of "regulation riding gloves when mounted, and when prescribed." Part c directs that enlisted men shall wear, as prescribed by the commanding officer, white gloves or olive-drab woolen gloves for dismounted duty, and olive-drab woolen gloves with *any* of the uniforms when off duty. Photographs of this era prove that the supply of leather gauntlets was not exhausted for some time, and were worn by some troops for another 2 or 3 years.

The stable frock was to receive its *coup de grâce* in these regulations as well. Paragraph 119 directed that it was to be issued until the supply was exhausted. The canvas fatigue coat and trousers were to take its place. In another year or two the stable frock would no longer be seen along the picket line at morning stable call—the death knell for this symbol of the cavalryman for at least a century!

The wearing of shoes of specific type and color was covered in detail by the 1912 regulations. The following is the text of paragraph 102:

102. SHOES.

OFFICERS.

The russet leather shoes will conform in general style to the garrison and the marching shoes issued by the Quartermaster's Department. The high shoes of polished black leather, black enamel or patent leather, will have plain black leather or plain kid tops, with or without toe tips.

Full-dress and dress uniform (dismounted).—High shoes of polished black leather, black enamel, or patent leather.

Service uniform.—High russet leather shoe.

Special evening-dress and blue mess jacket.—High or low shoes or pumps, of black enamel, or patent leather.

White uniform.—Low white canvas shoes.

ENLISTED MEN.

Fatigue uniform and stable frocks.—Black, garrison or marching shoes.

Full-dress and dress uniform (dismounted).—Black shoes.

Full-dress and dress uniform (mounted).—Garrison shoes.

Service uniform.—The garrison shoe for garrison wear and the marching shoe for field service. (The use of the marching shoe in garrison will be prescribed by organization commanders to such extent as may be necessary to break them in thoroughly.)

White uniform.—Black or garrison shoes.

The gymnasium shoe will be worn in gymnasium work. It may be worn in barracks and may, when prescribed by the commanding officer, be carried in the surplus kit and used as a camp shoe.

The regulations were also specific about the color of socks to be worn with the various uniforms. Paragraph 106 states: "Black socks will be worn with the blue uniform dismounted and white socks with the white uniform." Stockings for enlisted men were olive drab in color, and on the few occasions olive-drab trousers were worn without leggings these stockings were worn. On mounted duty the leggings covered the stockings completely, so color was considered too unimportant to cover in the regulations.

Since cavalry officers wore boots with the service uniform on all occasions, the color of their socks or stockings was not covered in the regulations either, except as noted above for the blue or white uniforms worn for dismounted duty and on formal occasions.

Paragraph 107 directed that spurs were to be worn when boots were worn, whether mounted or dismounted. Black spur straps were to be worn with black boots, and russet straps with russet boots.

161

The same held true for enlisted men of cavalry. Spurs were to be worn when leggings were worn, and, since only russet spur straps were issued, there was no problem in that area.

Paragraph 109 reads, "SUSPENDERS may be worn, *but they must not be visible.*"

Sweaters were worn by both officers and enlisted men. Paragraph 110 of the regulations set forth specific rules for the wearing of this item:

110. SWEATER.—The sweater, as soon as issued by the Quartermaster's Department, will be worn by troops of the mobile army *in the field only*, when the weather is too cold to admit of the use of the flannel shirt alone. The collar of the shirt will be worn over that of the sweater.

Service coats will be packed and taken along by troops going into permanent or maneuver camps and issued on arrival. When troops are to take the field at other times, and, in the opinion of the commanding officer, conditions are likely to arise that will make the wearing of service coats desirable, he will order the coats of the enlisted men packed, and they may then or subsequently be sent forward and issued, being repacked when necessary.

When service coats are on hand, individual soldiers when out of camp will not wear the sweater as an outer garment, except by permission of the commanding officer in particular cases.

On the march and in other military formations officers will wear the sweater when the enlisted men do.

Sweaters will form a part of the surplus kit.

For insignia of rank on the sweater, see par. 85, p. 32.

Regulations for wearing white collars and cuffs by officers and enlisted men are covered in paragraph 114:

114. WHITE COLLARS AND CUFFS.

(*a*) Officers.—With the full-dress, the dress, and the white uniforms, and with the service uniform (except when in the field, at inspection in field equipment, drill, target practice, or on other duty involving physical exertion) officers will wear white cuffs and a plain white standing collar or white stock; the collar to show one-fourth inch above the collar of the coat.

With the special evening-dress and the mess jacket, either the standing or turned-down collar may be worn.

(*b*) Enlisted men.—With the dress and the full-dress uniform, and with the service uniform when worn on pass from garrison enlisted men will wear a plain standing white collar; the collar to show one-fourth inch above the collar of the coat.

Enlisted cavalrymen assigned as orderlies to regimental commanders, and those assigned as orderlies to brigade and higher commanders, were directed by paragraph 61 to wear a red brassard, furnished by the Quartermaster Department, on the right forearm.

Tables of Occasion governing the wearing of specific uniforms for specific occasions are detailed guides for the student of American military history. They describe not only the items of clothing prescribed for each duty and occasion, but accoutrements and decorations as well. The tables that follow are from the 1912 regulations:

TABLES OF OCCASIONS.

OFFICERS.

SERVICE UNIFORM AND EQUIPMENT.

Occasions.	By whom.	Articles.

A.

When dismounted:
1. Service cap.
2. Service coat.
3. Service breeches.
4. Russet-leather shoes (high).
5. Russet-leather or pigskin leggings. See par. 60 (a), p. 22; also par. 86, p. 32.
6. White collar or stock. } See par. 114 (a),
7. White cuffs. } p. 37.
8. Ribbons by those entitled thereto. (Marksmanship badges optional.)
9. Olive-drab woolen gloves when prescribed (when not on

Tables of Occasions—Continued.
OFFICERS—Continued.
SERVICE UNIFORM AND EQUIPMENT—Continued.

Occasions.	By whom.	Articles.
1. For habitual garrison wear until retreat, *not under arms.*	All officers, acting dental surgeons, and veterinarians.	duty the olive-drab woolen gloves or the regulation riding gloves may be worn).
		B.
		When mounted:
		Same as A, omitting "9. Olive-drab woolen gloves," and adding:
		1. Regulation riding gloves (optional when not on duty).
		2. Spurs, with russet-leather straps.
		C.
		When dismounted:
		Same as A, adding:
		1. Russet-leather belt.
		2. Saber, with service knot.
		D.
2. For habitual garrison duty, *under arms.*	All officers except chaplains.	*When mounted:*
		Same as A, omitting "9. Olive-drab woolen gloves," etc., and adding:
		1. Regulation riding gloves.
		2. Spurs, with russet-leather straps.
		3. Russet-leather belt.
		4. Saber, with service knot.
		A.
		When dismounted:
		1. Service hat, with hat cord sewed on (peaked, 4 indentations).
		2. Olive-drab shirt.
		3. Service coat (the sweater, as soon as issued by the Quartermaster's Department, will take the place of the service coat for field duty. See par. 110, p. 37).
		4. Service breeches.
		5. Russet-leather shoes (high).
		6. Russet leather, pigskin, or canvas leggings, or woolen puttees. See par. 60, p. 22; also par. 86, p. 32.
		7. Ribbons, by those entitled thereto (if coat is worn).
		8. Olive-drab woolen gloves, when prescribed (optional, when not on duty).
		9. Identification tag.
		10. Haversack (containing meat can, knife, fork, and spoon).
		11. Canteen (with canteen cover).
		12. Tin cup.
3. For field duty. _____	All officers, acting dental surgeons, and veterinarians.	13. First aid packet (with pouch).
		14. Watch.
		15. Notebook and pencils. See "C," page following.
		B.
		When mounted:
		Same as A, omitting "8. Olive-drab woolen gloves," etc.,

Tables of occasions—Continued.

OFFICERS—Continued.

SERVICE UNIFORM AND EQUIPMENT—Continued.

Occasions.	By whom.	Articles.
		and "10. Haversack (containing meat can, etc.)," and adding:
		1. Regulation riding gloves.
		2. Spurs.
		3. Saddle.
		4. Halter.
		5. Bridle.
		6. Saddle blanket.
		7. Saddlecloth.
		8. Saddlebags (containing meat can, knife, fork, and spoon).
		9. Surcingle.
		10. Nosebag.
		11. Horse brush.
		12. Currycomb.
		13. Lariat.
		14. Picket pin.
		See "D," page following
		C.
		When dismounted:
		Add to A, p. 40:
		1. Pistol (with holder, lanyard, and 20 rounds of ammunition).
		2. Pistol belt (to be worn over the coat).
		3. Field glass.[a] } See footnote 2,
		4. Compass. } p. 54.
		NOTE.—Company officers and battalion commanders of infantry will carry whistles. For dispatch cases; see par. 70, p. 24.
3. For field duty.	All officers except officers of the Medical Department and chaplains.	**D.**
		When mounted:
		Add to B, p. 40:
		1. Pistol (with holster, lanyard, and 20 rounds of ammunition).
		2. Pistol belt (to be worn over the coat).
		3. Field glass. } See footnote 2,
		4. Compass. } p. 54.
		NOTE.—Medical officers on duty with the sanitary units of the mobile army will carry field glasses and compass.

[a] The field glasses issued to organizations by the Signal Corps are not issued for the personal use of officers, and will not be used in lieu of the officers' personal field glasses.

NOTES.

1. Except by the officer of the day, the service uniform will not be worn after retreat by officers in garrison, unless prescribed by the commanding officer for some particular duty, nor will it be worn off the post except as authorized in the Table of Occasions of the dress uniform (dismounted), occasion 3, page 42.

2. Whenever necessary for personal protection, the personnel of the Medical Department may carry pistols.

3. Veterinarians when in the field will carry pistols and ammunition.

See Note 2, p. 50.

Tables of occasions—Continued.

OFFICERS—Continued.

DRESS UNIFORM (DISMOUNTED).

[Not required for the Tropics.]

Occasions.	By whom.	Articles.
1. For ordinary wear after retreat (in warm weather the white mess jacket or white uniform may be worn instead; in other weather the blue mess jacket or the special evening dress may be worn instead). 2. For social use before retreat (for functions before retreat the full dress may be prescribed). 3. When off the post, except that when riding or taking physical exercise the service uniform may be worn instead. In warm weather the commanding officer may prescribe the cotton service uniform for wear when off the post before retreat. 4. When dismounted dress uniform is prescribed for enlisted men and on such other occasions as may be prescribed. 5. As prescribed for White House.	All officers.	*When not under arms:* 1. Dress cap.[1] 2. Dress coat. 3. Dress trousers. 4. White collar or stock. 5. White cuffs. 6. Black shoes (high top). 7. Black socks. 8. White gloves when prescribed. (They may be worn on nonofficial occasions if desired.) 9. Ribbons by those entitled to wear them. (Marksmanship badges optional.) *When under arms:* Omit "when prescribed" after "8. White gloves;" add: 1. Saber (with full-dress slings and dress knot). 2. Belt (worn under coat). 3. Aiguillettes by those authorized to wear them.

[1] The former "full dress cap" is designated in this order as the "dress cap," except in the case of chaplains, acting dental surgeons, and veterinarians, in which case the "dress cap" is the same as the former "dress cap." See specifications issued by the Quartermaster General.

DRESS UNIFORM (MOUNTED.)
[Not required for the Tropics.]

Occasions.	By whom.	Articles.
1. When the mounted dress uniform is prescribed for enlisted men and on such other occasions as may be prescribed. 2. When riding off the reservation it may be worn. 3. As prescribed for White House.	All officers.	*When not under arms:* 1. Dress cap. 2. Dress coat. 3. Dress breeches. 4. Black boots. 5. White collar or stock. 6. White cuffs. 7. White leather gloves. 8. Spurs, with black straps. 9. Ribbons by those entitled to wear them. (Marksmanship badges optional.) *When under arms, add:* 1. Saber (with full-dress slings and dress knot). 2. Belt (worn under coat). 3. Aiguillettes by those authorized to wear them.

Note.—The dress uniform, mounted, may be prescribed for mounted officers on dismounted occasions.

Tables of occasions—Continued.

OFFICERS—Continued.

FULL-DRESS UNIFORM (DISMOUNTED.)
[Not required for the Tropics.]

Occasions.	By whom.	Articles.
1. State occasions at home or abroad. 2. When receiving the President of the United States. 3. When receiving or calling officially upon the president, sovereign, or member of the royal family of other countries. 4. Ceremonies and entertainments when it is desired to do special honor to the occasion. 5. When full dress, dismounted, is prescribed for enlisted men. 6. Social or official functions of a general nature, when prescribed. (If after retreat, the special evening dress will be prescribed instead, unless the occasion be one of special ceremony.) 7. As prescribed for White House.	General officers when dismounted.	1. Chapeau (or dress cap when shoulder knots are worn. See par. 71 (b), p. 24). 2. Full-dress coat. 3. Full-dress trousers. 4. Black shoes (high top). 5. Black socks. 6. White collar or stock. 7. White cuffs. 8. Saber, with dress knot. 9. Full-dress belt for officers above the grade of brigadier general; belt of black webbing (with full-dress slings), for brigadier generals, to be worn under the sash. 10. Plain white gloves (except white cotton). 11. Epaulets (shoulder knots may be worn when capes or overcoats are worn in inclement weather). 12. Sash. 13. Medals, badges, aiguillettes, and shoulder belts by those authorized to wear them. (Marksmanship badges optional.)
	All other officers except chaplains when dismounted.	1. Dress cap. 2. Full-dress coat. 3. Dress trousers (full-dress trousers for officers of the staff corps and departments, except the Quartermaster's Department and Corps of Engineers). 4. Black shoes (high top). 5. Black socks. 6. White collar or stock. 7. White cuffs. 8. Saber, with dress knot. 9. Full-dress belt. 10. Plain white gloves (except Berlin). 11. Shoulder knots. 12. Medals, badges, aiguillettes, and shoulder belts by those authorized to wear them. (Marksmanship badges optional.)
	Chaplains when dismounted.	1. Chaplain's hat. 2. Full-dress coat. 3. Full-dress trousers. 4. Black shoes (high top). 5. Black socks. 6. White collar or stock. 7. White cuffs. 8. Plain white gloves (except white cotton). 9. Medals and badges by those entitled to wear them.

Tables of occasions—Continued.

OFFICERS—Continued.

FULL-DRESS UNIFORM (MOUNTED).
[Not required for the Tropics.]

Occasions.	By whom.	Articles.
1. When full-dress, mounted, is prescribed for enlisted men. 2. Social or official functions of a general nature when prescribed. (If after retreat, the special evening dress will be prescribed instead, unless the occasion be one of special ceremony.) 3. As prescribed for White House. *On the following occasions when required that the officer be mounted:* 1. State occasions at home or abroad. 2. When receiving the President of the United States. 3. When receiving or officially calling upon the president, sovereign, or member of the royal family of other countries. 4. Ceremonies and entertainments when it is desired to do special honor to the occasion.	General officers.	1. Dress cap. 2. Full-dress coat. 3. Dress breeches. 4. Black boots. 5. White collar or stock. 6. White cuffs. 7. Saber, with dress knot. 8. Full-dress belt for officers above the grade of brigadier general; belt of black webbing (with full-dress slings) for brigadier generals, to be worn under the sash. 9. White leather gloves. 10. Shoulder knots. 11. Sash. 12. Spurs, with black straps. 13. Medals, badges, aiguillettes and shoulder belts by those entitled to wear them. (Marksmanship badges optional.)
	All other officers except chaplains.	1. Dress cap. 2. Full-dress coat. 3. Dress breeches. 4. Black boots. 5. White collar or stock. 6. White cuffs. 7. Saber, with dress knot. 8. Full-dress belt. 9. White leather gloves. 10. Shoulder knots. 11. Spurs, with black straps. 12. Medals, badges, shoulder belts and aiguillettes by those entitled to wear them. (Marksmanship badges optional.)
	Chaplains.	1. Chaplain's hat. 2. Full-dress coat. 3. Dress breeches. 4. Black boots. 5. White collar or stock. 6. White cuffs. 7. White leather gloves. 8. Spurs, with black straps. 9. Medals and badges by those entitled to wear them.

NOTE.—The full-dress uniform, mounted, may be prescribed for mounted officers on dismounted occasions.

167

Tables of occasions—Continued.

OFFICERS—Continued.

SPECIAL EVENING DRESS.

[Not required for the Tropics.]

NOTE.—All officers will provide themselves with the special evening dress by July 1, 1912. Until that time the full dress may be worn on occasions for which the special evening dress is prescribed.

Occasions.	By whom.	Articles.
1. Social or official functions of a general nature occuring in the evening. (If the occasion be one of special ceremony the full dress may be prescribed instead.) In warm weather the white uniform may be prescribed instead. 2. For private formal dinners and other private formal social functions occurring in the evening. (The mess jacket may be worn instead.) 3. For ordinary evening wear.	All officers except chaplains.	1. Dress cap. 2. Special evening-dress coat. 3. Special evening-dress trousers by officers of the Infantry, Cavalry, and Artillery; dress trousers by officers of the Quartermaster's Department and Corps of Engineers; full-dress trousers by all other officers. 4. High or low shoes, or pumps, of black enamel or patent leather. 5. Black socks. 6. White evening dress shirt with standing or turned-down collar and plain gold shirt studs. 7. White vest with small regulation buttons of gold or gilt. 8. Evening dress tie of black silk. 9. Plain white kid gloves (compulsory at dances; optional on other occasions). 10. Medal of honor by those entitled thereto. 11. Ribbons, except medal of honor ribbon, by those entitled thereto. 12. Aiguillettes, by those authorized to wear them (optional with general officers; other officers will wear them when directed by their commanders).

BLUE MESS JACKET.

[This uniform is optional and can not be prescribed by the commanding officer.]

Occasions.	By whom.	Articles.
In the United States: 1. For private formal dinners and other private formal social functions occurring in the evening (the special evening dress may be worn, and in warm weather the white mess jacket). 2. For ordinary evening wear (the dress uniform may be worn, and in warm weather the white mess jacket or the white uniform).	All officers except chaplains.	1. Dress cap. 2. Blue mess jacket. 3. Dress trousers[1] by officers of Infantry, Cavalry, Artillery, Quartermaster's Department and Engineers; full-dress trousers by all other officers. 4. High or low shoes, or pumps of black enamel or patent leather. 5. Black socks. 6. White evening dress shirt with standing or turned-down collar and plain gold shirt studs. 7. White or blue vest, with small regulation buttons of gold or gilt. 8. Evening dress tie of black silk. 9. Plain white kid gloves (compulsory at dances; optional on other occasions). 10. Ribbons, by those entitled to wear them.

Tables of occasions—Continued.
OFFICERS—Continued.

Occasions.	By whom.	Articles.
		11. Aiguillettes, if desired, by those authorized to wear them.

¹ The dress trousers worn with the mess jacket will have no pockets, side or hip, and will be cut high in the waist, without buckle in the back. These trousers may be worn with the full dress and the dress uniforms.

WHITE MESS JACKET.

[In the United States, including Alaska, this uniform is optional and can not be prescribed by the commanding officer.]

Occasions.	By whom.	Articles.
In the Tropics: 1. For private formal dinners and other private formal social functions occurring in the evening. 2. For evening functions, social or official, of a general nature. 3. For ordinary evening wear (the white uniform may be worn instead.) *In the United States* (optional): In warm weather for ordinary evening wear and for private formal dinners and other private formal social functions occurring in the evening.	All officers except chaplains.	1. White cap. 2. White mess jacket, with shoulder knots. 3. White trousers. 4. Low white canvas shoes. 5. White socks. 6. White evening dress shirt with standing or turned-down collar and plain gold shirt studs. 7. White vest with small regulation buttons of gold or gilt. 8. Evening dress tie of black silk. 9. White gloves of lisle thread (compulsory at dances; optional on other occasions). 10. Ribbons by those entitled to wear them. 11. Aiguillettes, by those authorized to wear them (optional with general officers; other officers will wear them when directed by their commanders).

WHITE UNIFORM.
[Not to be worn on duty with troops under arms.]

Occasions.	By whom.	Articles.
In the Tropics: 1. Until retreat, when prescribed by the commanding officer. 2. For ordinary wear after retreat (the white mess jacket may be worn instead). 3. For official occasions, under arms, after retreat, when prescribed by the commanding officer. *In the United States in warm weather* (optional): 1. For ordinary wear after retreat. 2. For social use before retreat. 3. When off the post.	All officers, acting dental surgeons, and veterinarians.	*Not under arms:* 1. White cap. 2. White coat. 3. White trousers. 4. Low white canvas shoes. 5. White socks. 6. White collar or stock. 7. White gloves of lisle thread at dances only. 8. Ribbons, by those entitled to wear them. *Under arms, add:* 1. Aiguillettes, by those authorized to wear them. 2. Saber, with dress knot. 3. Belt (under coat) with full dress slings. 4. White gloves, of lisle thread.

WHITE HOUSE.

Occasions.	Uniform.
(a) Official occasions. When calling by appointment upon the President of the United States.	Full dress, dismounted.
New Year's and other state receptions (until 6 p. m.).	Full dress, dismounted, for dismounted officers.

Occasions.	Uniform.
Tables of occasions—Continued. OFFICERS—Continued. WHITE HOUSE—Continued.	
	Full dress, mounted, for officers of cavalry and field artillery; full dress, mounted or dismounted, for all other mounted officers, and retired officers of the mounted service.
State receptions (evening). _____	Full dress, dismounted.
State dinners. _____	Full dress, dismounted.
(*b*) *Social occasions.*	
When calling by appointment on the President and wife of the President (until 6 p. m.).	*Unless white uniform with side arms be indicated:* Dress, dismounted, with side arms, for dismounted officers.
All other daytime functions, including luncheons, afternoon teas, garden parties, etc.	Dress, mounted, with side arms, for officers of cavalry and field artillery; dress mounted or dismounted, with side arms, for all other mounted officers and retired officers of the mounted service.
Unofficial dinners. _____	Special evening dress. ⎫ Retired officers may wear the
Evening musicale or dance. _____	Special evening dress. ⎭ full dress, dismounted.

SCHEDULE OF UNIFORMS WHEN OFFICERS OF BOTH SERVICES APPEAR TOGETHER.

Throughout the military and naval services of the United States, whenever on occasions of ceremony officers of both services are required to appear together in uniform, officers of the Army will be governed by the following schedule.

Uniform A:
> *Army, full dress.*
> Navy, special full dress.
> Marine Corps, special full dress.

Uniform B:
> *Army, dress.*
> Navy, service dress.
> Marine Corps, undress.

Uniform C:
> *Army, special evening dress.*
> Navy, evening dress A.
> Marine Corps, special full dress.

Whether the full dress, mounted or dismounted, or the dress, mounted or dismounted, shall be worn, will be determined by the nature of the occasion as set forth in the Tables of Occasions.

ENLISTED MEN.

SERVICE UNIFORM.

Occasions.	All enlisted men.	Articles.
		A.
		1. Service cap.
		2. Service coat.
		3. Service breeches.
		4. Garrison shoes. (The use of the marching shoe will be prescribed by organization commanders to such extent as may be necessary to break them in thoroughly.)
	When dismounted.	5. Leggings.
		6. White collar, (See par. 114 (b), p. 38.)
1. For habitual garrison wear until retreat when *not under arms.*		7. Ribbons by those entitled thereto. (Marksmanship badges optional.)
		8. Olive-drab woolen gloves, when prescribed (optional when not on duty).

Tables of occasions—Continued.
ENLISTED MEN—Continued.
SERVICE UNIFORM—Continued.

Occasions.	All enlisted men.	Articles.
	When mounted.	**B.** Same as A, omitting "8. Olive-drab woolen gloves," etc., and adding: 1. Regulation riding gloves, when prescribed (optional when not on duty). 2. Spurs.
2. For habitual garrison duty *under arms*. 3. For inspection and guard mount, when prescribed by the commanding officer. See occasion 2, p. 51, and occasion 1, p. 52. 4. For all other ceremonies when climate or weather will not permit the use of the dress or full dress.	When dismounted.	**C.** Same as A, adding: 1. Russet leather belt. 2. Cartridge box. (When the new garrison belt is issued, it will be worn instead of the russet leather belt and cartridge box.)
	When mounted.	**D.** Same as A, omitting "8. Olive-drab woolen gloves," and adding: 1. Regulation riding gloves, when prescribed. 2. Spurs. 3. Russet leather belt. 4. Cartridge box.
5. When changing station by rail or water.	Dismounted. _____	**E.** Same as C.
6. For field duty. _____	When dismounted.	**F.** 1. Service hat, with hat cord sewed on (peaked, 4 indentations). 2. Olive-drab shirt. 3. Service coat. (The sweater, as soon as issued by the Quartermaster's Department, will take the place of the service coat for field duty. See par. 110, p. 37.) 4. Service breeches. 5. Marching shoes. 6. Leggings. 7. Identification tag. 8. Brassards, by those entitled to wear them. 9. Ribbons by those entitled thereto. (Ribbons will not be worn on the sweater or olive-drab shirt.) 10. Olive-drab woolen gloves, when prescribed (optional when not on duty). 11. Field belt.
	When mounted.	**G.** Same as F, omitting "10. Olive-drab woolen gloves," and adding: 1. Regulation riding gloves, when prescribed. 2. Spurs.

NOTE.—The personal equipment of enlisted men will be as prescribed in orders and regulations.

Tables of occasions—Continued.
ENLISTED MEN—Continued.
SERVICE UNIFORM—Continued.

NOTES.

1. Except by members of the guard, the service uniform will not be worn out of barracks after retreat by enlisted men in garrison, unless prescribed by the commanding officer for some particular duty, or authorized as stated in note 3, below.

2. There are two service uniforms, the woolen olive-drab and the cotton olive-drab. The woolen olive-drab uniform will be prescribed for habitual wear when the climate or weather does not require the cotton olive-drab.

3. The cotton olive-drab will be prescribed by commanding officers for soldiers on pass in warm weather and also for use in garrison in warm weather when out of barracks after retreat. The woolen olive-drab will not be worn by soldiers on pass from commands supplied with the dress uniform.

4. When under arms, every enlisted man will carry the arms pertaining to his grade and branch of service.

5. With dismounted service-uniform, in garrison under arms and when changing station by rail or water, noncommissioned staff officers will wear belt and saber instead of belt and cartridge box.

6. With dismounted service-uniform, in the field, noncommissioned staff officers will carry the pistol instead of the saber.

7. The service cap is not authorized for enlisted men in the Philippines; the service hat will be worn for field duty, and the helmet will be worn at other times.

8. When troops are traveling by rail, the train commander may cause the arms and equipments not required for the necessary guard duty en route to be properly secured and stored in a property or baggage car. (Par. 246, Field Service Regulations, 1910.)

DRESS UNIFORM.

[Not required for the Tropics.]

Occasions.	All enlisted men.	Articles.
1. For retreat roll call; for habitual garrison wear after retreat, and when on pass from commands supplied with the dress uniform (in warm weather the commanding officer will prescribed the cotton olive-drab instead). 2. For parade and other ceremonies (except inspection and guard mounting, and then if prescribed by the commanding officer), when weather and climate permit. (The full-dress uniform may be prescribed instead). (See occasions 3 and 4, p. 49.)	Dismounted. _____ Mounted. _____	**A.** *Not under arms:* 1. Dress cap. 2. Dress coat. 3. Dress trousers. 4. Black shoes. 5. White collar. 6. Ribbons by those entitled to wear them. (Marksmanship badges optional.) **B.** *Under arms or with side arms, add to A:* 1. White gloves or olive-drab woolen gloves, as prescribed by the commanding officer. 2. Russet-leather belt. 3. Cartridge box. (When the garrison belt is issued it will be worn instead of the russet-leather belt and the cartridge box.) **C.** *Not under arms:* 1. Dress cap. 2. Dress coat. 3. Dress trousers. 4. Russet-leather shoes. 5. White collar. 6. Leggings. 7. Regulation riding gloves. 8. Ribbons and marksmanship badges by those entitled to wear them. 9. Spurs.

Tables of occasions—Continued.

ENLISTED MEN—Continued.

DRESS UNIFORM—Continued.

Occasions.	All enlisted men.	Articles.
		D.
		Under arms or with side arms, add to C:
		1. Russet leather belt.
		2. Cartridge box. (As the garrison belt is issued it will be worn instead of the russet leather belt and the cartridge box.)

FULL-DRESS UNIFORM.

[Not required for the Tropics.]

Occasions.	All enlisted men.	Articles.
1. For parade and all other ceremonies in garrison (except inspection and guard mounting, and then if prescribed by the commanding officer) when climate and weather permit. (The dress uniform may be prescribed instead.) (See occasions 3 and 4, p. 49;) 2. For all ceremonies other than garrison, when prescribed by the commanding officer.	Dismounted. _____	A. 1. Dress cap. 2. Dress coat. 3. Dress trousers. 4. Black shoes. 5. White collar. 6. Medals and badges by those entitled to wear them. (Marksmanship badges optional.) 7. Breast cord. 8. White gloves or olive-drab woolen, as prescribed by the commanding officer. 9. Russet leather belt. 10. Cartridge box. (When the garrison belt is issued it will be worn instead of the russet leather belt and cartridge box.)
	Mounted. _____	B. Same as A, omitting "4. Black shoes," "8. White gloves or olive-drab woolen gloves," and adding: 1. Russet leather shoes. 2. Leggings. 3. Regulation riding gloves. 4. Spurs.

WHITE UNIFORM.

Occasions.	By what enlisted men worn.	Articles.
When working in kitchen or bakery.	Cooks and bakers. _____	1. White coat (for members of the Hospital Corps, gilt collar ornaments same as those of the dress coat).
In wards, dispensaries, post-mortem rooms, operating rooms and mess rooms; also by Hospital Corps men while on duty assisting dental surgeons.	Members of the Hospital Corps.	2. White trousers. 3. Russet leather or black shoes.
In summer, when posted at the main entrance of recruiting stations, when on duty in parks and squares, and when otherwise directed by recruiting officers.	Members of general recruiting service.	1. White cap. 2. White coat (with gilt collar ornaments same as those of dress coat). 3. White trousers. 4. White web belt, with plate. 5. Black shoes.

Tables of occasions—Continued.

ENLISTED MEN—Continued.

FATIGUE UNIFORM.

Occasions.	By what enlisted men worn.	Articles.
On fatigue at stables and at mountain battery drills, involving packing and unpacking. (Mounted troops to whom stable frocks and overalls have been issued will wear them on stable duty instead of the fatigue uniform.)	All enlisted men, except of the Coast Artillery.	1. Fatigue coat. 2. Fatigue trousers. 3. Service hat. 4. Russet leather or black shoes.
On fatigue or at work or drill at emplacements. (Fatigue clothing will not be worn by enlisted men at drill in range towers or plotting rooms.)	Enlisted men of the Coast Artillery.	1. Fatigue coat. 2. Fatigue trousers. 3. Blue denim hat. 4. Black or russet leather shoes, as may be prescribed by the commanding officer. 5. Leather gloves by those whose work requires it.

NOTE.—Noncommissioned officers in charge of working parties will not wear the fatigue uniform unless their duties be such as to make it necessary.

Changes prescribed by the *1914 Regulations for the Uniform* were concerned mostly with the *wearing* of the uniform, and not with the *pattern* of the different items of clothing and insignia. The changes evident in the published regulations for this year are listed as they appear in War Department Document No. 468 from the Office of the Chief of Staff, and are treated here in the order in which they appear:

Mourning.—The badge of military mourning is now prescribed as *both* the 5-inch-wide band of black crepe around the left arm above the elbow *and* the black crepe knot on the saber when the saber is worn. It is now restricted for wear at funerals only, or when otherwise prescribed by the War Department. The black crepe arm band is still the approved symbol for family mourning, as before.

Swordsman's Badge.—Prescribed by General Order No. 16 in the 1914 series; it is shown in Figure 335. The regulations governing its issue and award follow:

70. Swordsman's badge.—1. A badge for excellence in swordsmanship, to be known as the swordsman's badge, conforming to the approved design in the office of the Chief of Ordnance, has been adopted. These badges will be issued by the Ordnance Department, at the rate of two badges for each troop and one badge for the noncommissioned staff of each regiment of Cavalry, to the best swordsmen in each organization as determined by the regimental commander by actual test made once in each calendar year.

2. A badge when once awarded becomes the property of the soldier and will be worn as provided in Uniform Regulations. An additional badge will not be awarded to a man who qualifies as swordsman in any subsequent year.

If lost by the owner, or in transmission to him, or if it becomes unsightly from long wear, the badge may be replaced without cost to the owner upon proper evidence that no negligence can be imputed to him.

4. Requisitions for such additional badges as may be required for award after the first year will be forwarded to the Chief of Ordnance when the number required shall have been determined.

5. In order to secure uniformity throughout the Cavalry in awarding the swordsman's badge, the following test is prescribed, to be conducted under the direction of regimental commanders:

6. Five competitors will be selected from each troop and two from the noncommissioned staff. These competitors in each organization will be tested over the course herein prescribed, under the direction of a field officer of the regiment.

The organization commander will be guided in selecting his competitors by the results of "tryouts," so that the five competitors will be, in his opinion, the five best qualified to make a high score in the course prescribed.

7. A track, as shown in the accompanying diagram, will be laid out on open ground and the competitors required to ride the course on their own mounts, attacking dummies as indicated. They will not be allowed to practice over the ground used for the test.

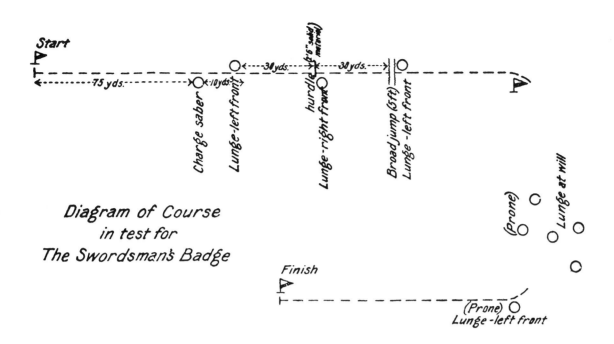

Diagram of Course
in test for
The Swordsman's Badge

8. The first 75 yards will be covered at a charging gallop, the rest at a maneuvering gallop.

The time for the course will be determined by taking the time of an officer who will gallop over the course at the prescribed gaits but without attacking dummies, being careful, however, to go sufficiently near each to attack it. The distance from the last dummy to the finish may be covered at speed.

9. Credit the trooper with 100 points. Deduct 2 points for each period of 5 seconds he is slower than the established time. Deduct 5 points for any dummy he fails to touch. Also deduct from 1 to 5 points for incorrect form at each dummy.

For example, if the trooper gets No. 1 fairly and in good form his score is 0. If he strikes it but is not leaning down enough, deduct, say, 2 or 3 points—his score will be minus 3. If he lunges properly but misses, his score will be minus 5. If he misses and also lunges badly, his score could be as much as minus 10.

10. The isolated dummies should be attacked in the manner indicated in the diagram, and the five in the group, in any order and from any direction, at the judgment of the trooper. Proper form, however, will be insisted upon in whatever manner he chooses to attack.

(*Par. I, G. O. 16, 1914—2093855, A. G. O.; G. O. 88, 1914—2093855 B. A. G. O.*)

Paragraph 58(e) authorized the wearing of the new swordsman's badge, as well as badges awarded for excellence in marksmanship, under any decoration or campaign ribbons worn, on the left breast; these badges were to be worn in a line parallel to and ⅜

inch under the ribbons.

Rain Cap Covers for officers were authorized by paragraph 64, which specified that they may be worn in stormy weather, a black cover over the dress cap and an olive-drab one over the service cap.

Service Hat.—Paragraph 66(c) authorized the service hat to be worn by officers and enlisted men with the service uniform *other than for field duty* under exceptional or severe climatic conditions, but only when the post commander ordered such a deviation from the ordinary and prescribed wearing of the service hat.

Chin Straps on Dress and Service Caps.—Paragraph 66(f) prescribed that "at all mounted formations of ceremony, and such other occasions as may be necessary, the chin strap on dress and service caps will be used."

Black Neckties.—Paragraph 69(c), under the heading of *CRAVATS*, prescribed that

when off duty, in permanent and maneuver camp and out of camp, when service uniform with olive-drab shirt and without coat is authorized, officers and enlisted men will wear a plain black cravat tied as a four-in-hand. No other style or color of cravat will be so worn.

First-aid Field Packet.—The first-aid field packet

FIGURE 335. The Army Swordsman's badge authorized by General Order No. 16, March, 1914, for issue at the rate of two badges for each troop and one badge for the noncommissioned staff of each regiment of cavalry, to the best swordsmen in each organization as determined by the regimental commander by actual test made once in each calendar year. Awarded to enlisted men only.

first became an issue item in 1912, and the regulations for that year instructed officers to carry it in front of the right hip, attached to the field belt. Enlisted men wearing the field belt were to carry it under the second pocket, to the right of the belt fastener. The 1914 regulations were more specific about cavalry troopers carrying the packet on their belts: "Soldiers armed with the revolver or pistol will carry the first-aid packet on the *left* side toward the front of the belt."

Service Hat.—Paragraph 77(c) in the published 1914 uniform regulations prescribed that the service hat was to be worn with the service uniform for field duty and target practice, as formerly. In addition:

It will also be worn with the fatigue uniform and with stable frocks. . . . it may be worn in garrison when slickers are worn, or when, in the opinion of the post commander . . . severe climatic conditions would make the wearing of the caps endanger the health of his command.

Change No. 3, November 10, 1914, added, "also with the cotton service uniform by all troops in the U.S. when stationed south of parallel 35° north latitude, and by all troops in the Philippine Islands, Hawaii, and the Canal Zone."

Hat Strings.—Paragraph 77(d): "At all mounted formations of ceremony, and such other occasions as may be necessary, the hat strings provided on service hats will be used, tied either under the chin or as chin straps on the point of the chin."

Insignia of Rank on Sweater.—Paragraph 86:

(a) When the sweater is worn by officers, the insignia of rank will be worn on the collar of the sweater, similarly placed as prescribed for the collar of the shirt. [See Figure 333.]

(b) The insignia of rank of noncommissioned officers will be worn on the sleeve of the sweater. . . .

The 1912 regulation that allowed enlisted men not on duty to wear service *trousers* without leggings was rescinded in the 1914 regulations, and only those enlisted men actually on duty in offices were permitted to go without breeches and leggings, and then *only* during the hours in which they were actually engaged in office duty.

In 1915 there were more changes in the uniform regulations. The flat braid on the officer's dark blue dress coat was widened to 1½ inches from the 1¼-inch width it had been since 1895, when this pattern was first adopted as the *undress* coat for officers.

There were some changes in the size of the metallic shoulder-loop insignia for officers' service coats and olive-drab shirts. Generals' silver stars were made larger, and the silver and gold leaves for majors and lieutenant colonels were increased from ¾ inch in width and length in 1912 to 1 inch in these regulations.

The ¼-inch-wide black-and-gilt soutache flat braid on officers' overcoats, full-dress coats, special evening-dress coats, and dark blue mess jackets were reduced to ⅛-inch-wide flat braid. Apparently the wide braid made the soutache knots too large and heavy-looking for a neat military appearance, even though the outside dimensions of the knots were retained in the larger size as changed in 1912.

The regulations governing the wearing of the first-aid field packet were again changed for cavalry. Change No. 13, dated July 26, 1915, states:

First Aid Packet and Magazine Pocket.—The first-aid packet will be worn with the cavalry field rifle belt in front of the left hip under the first rifle cartridge pocket to the left of the belt fastener. The magazine pocket, double, web, will be worn on the cavalry field rifle belt in front of the left hip between the first-aid packet and the belt fastener. When the pistol belt is worn with field equipment the magazine pocket, double, web, and the first-aid packet will be worn in front of the left hip, in the order named to the left of the belt fastener. Officers will wear them in corresponding positions.

Officers' Dress Belts and Saber Slings.—A change had been made in the printed 1915 uniform regulations concerning the design of the gold-lace dress belts, but 4 months later, before many, if any, officers had bought belts conforming to the change, another change took place. The new pattern for field officers of cavalry had belts of black enameled leather, 1¾ inches wide, with the outside covered with one piece of 2-vellum gold or gilt lace. Belts for company grade officers had the outside covered with 4-vellum gold or gilt lace interwoven with 3 black silk stripes.

Dress saber slings for both field and company grade officers were embroidered to correspond with their respective belts.

Leggings.—Change No. 3, dated October 3, 1915, changed the 1915 uniform regulations and specifications concerning leggings for enlisted men, which were then canvas, to read, "Leggings, cavalry and field artillery—Oak-tanned, full grained, russet, cowhide leather, as issued." These were the leather leggings worn until 1917 when the leather-faced canvas leggings were issued to mounted troops.

While no uniform regulations or specifications were published in 1916, many of the changes memoranda were; these were circulated to the Army, where they were to be pasted in the 1915 published regulations. The following are those that affected the appearance of the cavalryman in 1916.

Cavalry machine-gun units were issued the bolo knife for cutting brush for machine-gun emplacements. Change No. 18, dated December 30, 1916, established a uniform method of carrying the bolo, mounted. It created paragraph 59½ to be inserted in the regulations:

> Bolo.—Enlisted men armed with the bolo will wear it suspended from the waist belt on the left side, as prescribed in orders from the War Department (par. I, G.O. No. 172, W.D., 1908). When mounted the wearer should carry the bolo on the left hip far enough forward so as not to mar the saddle.

The same order, Change No. 18, revised the regulations for wearing rank insignia on the collar of the officer's olive-drab shirt. Figure 333 shows the approved insignia from 1912 to the date of this order on the top row, and the approved insignia *after* the change on the bottom row. By another change a few weeks later the arrangement reverted to that shown on the top row, but within the year the new arrangement was reinstated.

Until Change No. 18, enlisted men wore no insignia on the collars of their shirts when the shirt was

FIGURE 336. The short overcoat, pattern of 1916, prescribed for officers in Circular No. 18, December 30, 1916. Made of drab moleskin cloth and lined with sheepskin, it had a 6-inch rolling sheepskin collar dyed beaver shade, and was provided with 2 lower pockets. It was authorized for wear in the field only, and saw service in the United States and France during and after World War I.

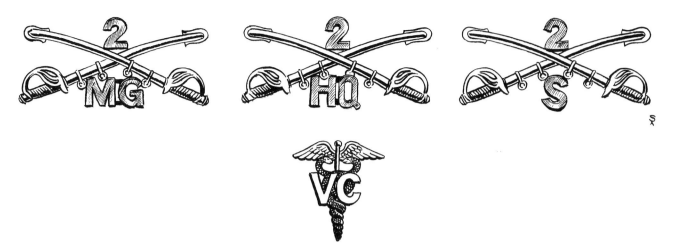

FIGURE 337. Top: Cap and collar ornaments (ca. 1916) for the new troop designations recently made a part of each regiment of cavalry. Prescribed in Circular No. 6, October 12, 1916, they designated machine-gun, headquarters, and supply troops. Bottom: The new collar caduceus ornament for offi-cers of the Veterinary Corps, as prescribed in 1916. Formerly the insignia for veterinarians were crossed sabers with the number of the regiment in the upper angle and a silver winged horse's hoof in the lower.

worn without the service coat. But paragraph 82 of the 1915 regulations was changed, and wearing the button insignia on the shirt collar when the shirt was worn without the coat was prescribed, arranged as on the collar of the service coat, "US" on the right, crossed sabers on the left.

The wearing of noncommissioned-officer chevrons on the issue sweater was abolished by Change No. 16, September 11, 1916, as was the wearing of metallic officer-rank insignia on the collar of the sweater.

A new short overcoat was prescribed for officers in Circular No. 18, dated December 30, 1916. Subparagraph d was added to paragraph 92 of the published 1915 regulations, which read:

(d) When in the opinion of the commanding officer the climatic conditions make it advisable, officers may be permitted to wear, *in the field only*, a short double breasted overcoat of drab moleskin cloth lined with sheepskin and with a six inch rolling sheepskin collar dyed beaver shade and provided with two outside lower pockets.

Although the wearing of this coat is permissible under the conditions named above, it should not be so construed by commanding officers as to result in a part of the officers of a regiment wearing, at a formation under arms in the field, this short coat and others at the same time wearing the olive-drab overcoat. All should wear it or none. The wearing of mixed uniforms at formations under arms is not permissible.

The new short overcoat is shown in Figure 336.

With the revised regimental organization for cavalry in 1916 came additional insignia for enlisted men. Collar ornaments for men of machine-gun troops had crossed sabers, in both gilt and bronze, with the letters "MG" in the lower angle. Men in the new headquarters troop had crossed sabers with the letters "HQ" in the lower angle, and men attached to supply troops had the letter "S" attached to the crossed sabers in the lower angle. Figure 337 shows the new insignia.

A new collar insignia for veterinarians was also prescribed. It is shown below the enlisted men's crossed sabers in Figure 337.

Circular No. 6, October 12, 1916, listed insignia and cap ornaments for cavalry *buglers* instead of "trumpeters." So this may be taken as official terminology for cavalry field musicians from the date of this circular.

Heretofore veterinarians had been authorized to wear only the service and white uniforms prescribed for second lieutenants, but without insignia of rank. The 1916 regulations changed this, and prescribed that the uniform for veterinarians should be the same as that for medical officers, but with the letters "VC" on the caduceus. Medical officers wore regular officers' uniforms, even to the full dress, dress, and those for

TROOP

FIRST
SERGEANT

SERGEANT
MESS SERGEANT
SUPPLY SERGEANT
STABLE SERGEANT

CORPORAL

COOK

HORSESHOER

SADDLER

PRIVATE
FIRST CLASS

HEADQUARTERS TROOP

REGIMENTAL
SERGEANT MAJOR

SQUADRON
SERGEANT MAJOR

FIRST SERGEANT
DRUM MAJOR

COLOR
SERGEANT

SERGEANT
MESS SERGEANT
SUPPLY SERGEANT
STABLE SERGEANT
BAND SERGEANT

BAND
CORPORAL

SADDLER   HORSESHOER

PRIVATE
FIRST CLASS

BAND
LEADER

SERGEANT
BUGLER

ASSISTANT
BAND LEADER

SUPPLY TROOP

REGIMENTAL
SUPPLY SERGEANT

FIRST
SERGEANT

MESS SERGEANT
STABLE SERGEANT

CORPORAL

COOK

SADDLER

HORSESHOER

WAGONER

FIGURE 338. Dress chevrons, pattern of 1916, for all cavalry noncommissioned grades. Chevrons for service uniforms were identical in pattern except they were made of olive-drab facing cloth on grounds of uniform material (olive-drab cotton or wool) instead of yellow on dark blue. (Circular No. 6, October 12, 1916.) Drawn from specimens in the author's collection.

179

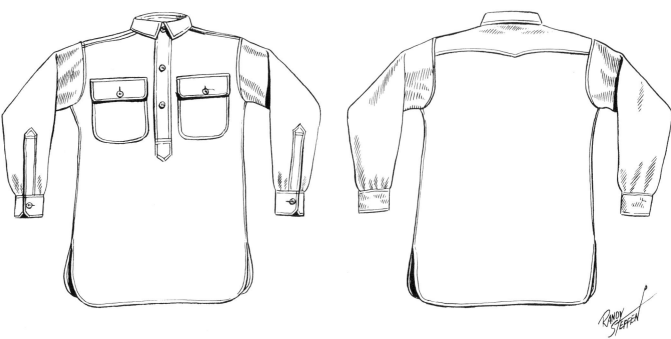

FIGURE 339. The olive-drab shirt, pattern of 1916. It differed from the 1912 pattern only in the quality of the flannel cloth and the addition of pocket flaps. It was also made from olive-drab cotton material for wear in summer.

formal evening wear, including the mess jackets.

The printed regulations are really not clear concerning this point, and I hesitate to state that at this time veterinarians also had this right.

ARMS

Weapons issued to and used by the cavalry regiments during this period, particularly after 1912, were pretty well standardized until horse cavalry was abolished during World War II.

The .38-caliber Colt revolver had been purchased in large numbers for issue during and after the Spanish-American War, but it was not until this lighter bullet failed to knock down the Moros in the Philippines that the War Department realized that replacing the .45-caliber single-action Colts with the .38 double-action had been a mistake. The big-caliber Colts that had played such an important role in subjugating the Indian were, at last, taken out of storage and shipped to the Pacific, where they were issued in exchange for the later-model double-action revolvers.

In a tardy effort to exchange single-action pistols for double-actions, the Army made hurried purchases of the large-frame Model 1878 Colt .45-caliber double-action revolver. A considerable number of these had been purchased toward the end of the century for use in Alaska. Fitted with large trigger guards so heavy gloves and mittens could be kept on the hands while firing them, these double-action Colts had been unofficially termed the Alaskan model, although records seem to indicate that few ever saw service in that far northern territory.

By the time contracts were made and deliveries started, the single-action army model Colts that had been stored in arsenals had been issued to the troops in the Philippines. It is doubtful, judging by Ordnance Department records, that more than a few, if any, of the double-action Colts ever got to the site of the action against the Philippine rebels. Figure 340 shows the Colt Model 1878 double-action .45-caliber "Alaskan model" pistol.

The Colt New Service Model 1909 was the next revolver adopted by the Ordnance Department for issue to the Army. This large-frame double-action arm was made in .45 caliber, and, while a quantity of the long-barreled version of this model was issued to and carried by cavalry troops, it did n~*

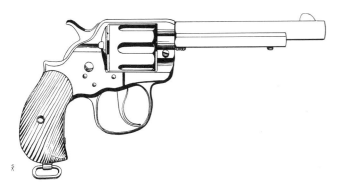

FIGURE 340. The Colt double-action army revolver (first manufactured by Colt in 1878). Not until 1902 did the Ordnance Department purchase any substantial number of this .45-caliber revolver. In that year 5,000 were ordered and delivered. The large trigger guard undoubtedly was to provide space for fur-gauntleted hands to manipulate this weapon efficiently. Sometimes called the Alaskan model, its purchase was to replace the .38-caliber revolvers that had proved less-than-sure manstoppers in the Philippines, although this arm never was used in the land of the Moros. Drawn from a specimen in the West Point Museum collection.

James E. Serven's account of the development of the Colt automatic pistol in his *Colt Firearms, 1836–1960* (Santa Ana, Serven Books, 1954) is a fascinating story of John Browning's genius and the manufacturing skill of the Colt company. The first Colt-Browning automatic pistol produced was the Model of 1900, and the Army purchased several hundred in that year for issue to cavalry for field trial. This was a .38-caliber arm with a 6-inch barrel. Four hundred .45-caliber Colt automatics were purchased by the Ordnance Department in 1907 for tests, and in 1911 the Army ordered more than 44,000 of the standardized Model 1911.

From that time on it can be said all U.S. Cavalry troops were armed with the Model 1911 or Model 1911 A1 automatic pistol. Limited issues of other hand guns were made for trial, but the adopted pistol for cavalry remained the Colt automatic until cavalry was unhorsed.

Figure 343 shows the Model 1911 with the lanyard loop on the magazine floor plate as it was issued to cavalry.

After more than a decade of use, the Krag-Jorgensen U.S. magazine rifle and carbine models with which the Army had been equipped were replaced by a new arm based on the German Mauser. A board of

to replacing all the single-action Colts with which the cavalry regiments had been rearmed since 1902. Figures 341 and 342 show the revolver and the holsters made for it, both the long- and short-barreled versions.

Most issues to cavalry units were of the long-barreled version, but some officers seemed to prefer the shorter barrels. Holsters, of the same design and construction as the Model 1879, were made for both barrel lengths, and are shown in Figure 342. Lanyard rings in the butts of these arms were standard, and lanyards were prescribed for issue and use by both enlisted men and officers in the regulations. The thong attached to the ring at the bottom of the holster was for tying down the holster to the upper part of the leg to limit its motion when mounted. For dismounted wear this thong was done up in a neat roll and allowed to dangle at the end of the holster.

The Colt Model 1911 .45-caliber automatic pistol was the standard sidearm of all regular cavalry from 1912 until the end of United States horse cavalry. Some cavalry troops were issued this pistol in 1911, but it was not until the next year that most wore the new automatic at their hips.

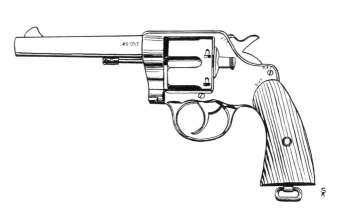

FIGURE 341. The Colt New Service Model of 1909 used by Cavalry in limited numbers. Chambered for the .45-caliber Colt cartridge, it replaced the single-action and the Model 1878 double-action army Colts that had been reissued after the .38-caliber Model 1892 revolvers had proved ineffective against the Moros in the Philippines. This arm was replaced as a cavalry weapon in 1912 and 1913 by the .45-caliber Model 1911 Colt automatic pistol. Drawn from a specimen in the author's collection.

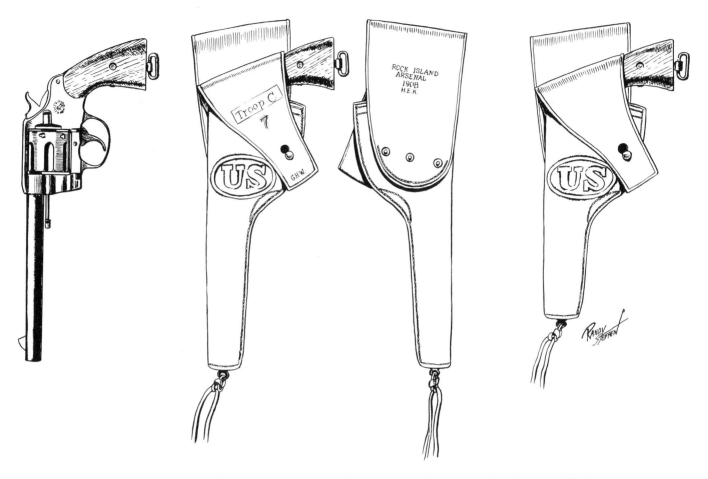

FIGURE 342. The Colt New Service Model 1909 .45-caliber revolver, long barrel, and holsters.

officers, convened in 1900, tested rifles of different designs and recommended the adoption of the Mauser-type weapon.

Five thousand of the new type were ordered manufactured in 1901, but before they could be made up another board of officers made further studies, and additional improvements were recommended. Finally approved in 1903, the new rifle was produced at the Springfield Armory, and was generally issued to the Army about 1905.

The cavalry regiments were armed with the same weapon as the rest of the Army, for it had been decided to standardize on one rifle for all units of the Army.

The Springfield Armory produced 741,815 Model 1903 rifles from 1904 to 1922, and the Rock Island Arsenal turned out 291,685 from 1905 to 1918.

Figure 344 shows the Springfield Model 1903 as it was issued to cavalry. Not until World War II was it replaced completely by the Garand M1 semiautomatic rifle.

When the general change of uniform occurred in 1902, a new saber was adopted for *all* officers of the Army. For the first time in the history of the U.S. Army, there was a single pattern of saber for all officers of all arms of the service.

Figures 345 and 346 show the new-pattern sabers for officers and enlisted men, as well as scabbards and saber-hanger details.

In 1905 the chief of ordnance authorized the publication of a manual containing illustrations and detailed descriptions of adopted horse equipments and equipments for officers and enlisted men. Much of the detail for both text and illustrations in this chap-

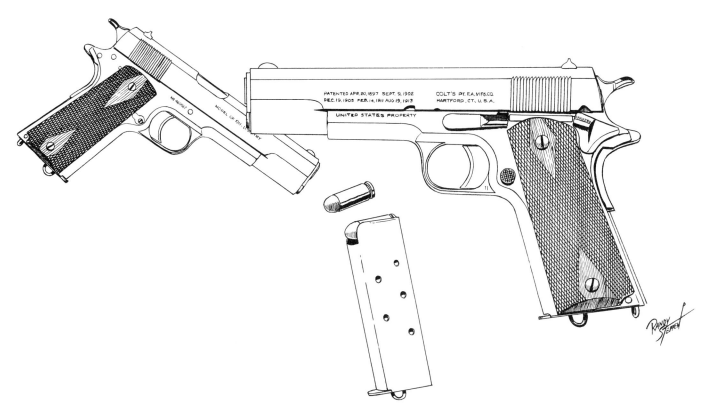

FIGURE 343. The Colt Model 1911 .45-caliber automatic pistol, first issued to some cavalry in late 1911. It remained the service sidearm for cavalry until all cavalry was dismounted in 1943. The loop on the magazine floor plate was for attachment of a lanyard to prevent loss of the magazine by mounted troops. (M. D. Waite, National Rifle Association) Drawn from a specimen in the author's collection.

ter comes from this source. (Document No. 1719, *Horse Equipments and Equipments for Officers and Enlisted Men,* dated May 10, 1905, revised July 3, 1908, 1917 edition.)

The following description of the 1902 officers' saber is from this document:

OFFICERS' SABER AND SCABBARD.

The parts are—
>Blade.
>Tang.
>Pommel.
>Guard.
>Grip.
>Ferrule.
>Nut.
>Washer.

and of the scabbard—
>Body, with tip, bands, and rings.
>Mouthpiece, with screws.
>Linings.

The blades are made from tool steel in lengths of 30, 32, and 34 inches. The tang or support for the hilt is made of soft iron welded to the base of the blade.

The pommel, guard, and ferrule are of German silver. The pommel covers the end of the hilt and extends along the back of the grip, the lower end being held by a ferrule, while the upper end is secured by heading down the tang, which passes through all parts of the hilt when the latter is assembled with the blade.

The guard is of the basket form with four branches, plate, and hook. The ends are slotted for the tang, the lower end abuts against the shoulder of the blade, and the upper end fits into a notch in the front of the pommel. It has a slot near the upper end for attaching the sword knot.

The ferrule passes around the pommel and grip just above the lower end of the guard, holding them securely together. The grip is of black bone shaped to fit the fingers of the hand.

The scabbard is made from sheet steel formed to shape and brazed, after which the tip and bands for rings, also of steel, are brazed to the scabbard. The bands are drilled to receive the 1-inch rings made from 0.166-inch steel wire.

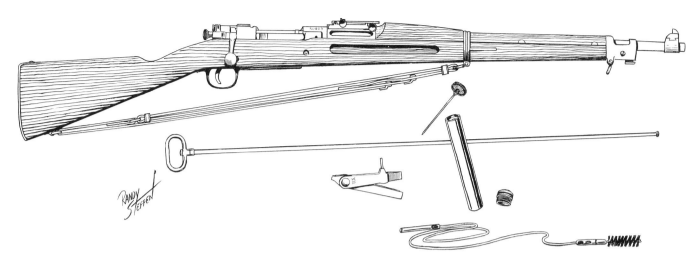

FIGURE 344. The U.S. magazine rifle, Model of 1903 (modified 1905). This is the world-famous Springfield 1903 that won honor and distinction in two great wars and during more than 20 years of peace between those wars. Made to fire the caliber-.30-06 cartridge, it was patterned after the efficient Mauser action. It is shown here as issued, with accessories including leather sling, oiler, thong case, and cleaning rod. Also issued, but not shown here, were the bullet-jacket extractor and a headless-shell extractor. Cavalry was not issued the bayonet until some time in the 1920's. (Description and rules for the management of the U.S. magazine rifle, Model of 1903, caliber .30, April 18, 1906.) Drawn from a specimen in the collection of Donald D. Gold, Jr., Vero Beach, Florida.

The steel mouthpiece is secured to the body by two screws and has a spring which extends inside the scabbard and grips the sides of the blade to secure it in the scabbard. Two lining strips of wood held between the mouthpiece and the sides of the scabbard, protect the point in sheathing the saber. The scabbard is nickel plated.

Sometime between 1902 and 1906 the Ordnance Department decided to issue a new cavalry saber. The saber it was to replace had been in use since 1861, when the light cavalry saber had replaced the Model 1840 heavy dragoon saber. The new pattern, issued only in limited numbers to a portion of the then existing 10 regiments, had the same shape and size of guard, grips, and blade as the Model 1861, but the guard of the new model was made of steel instead of the traditional brass. The saber, with its saber knot, scabbard, and issue saber belt and hanger is shown in Figure 346.

The following text is the Ordnance Department description found in the 1917 edition of Document No. 1719 cited above:

CAVALRY SABER AND SCABBARD.

The parts are nearly the same as for the officer's saber, but all are much heavier, and the scabbard has no wood lining strips.

The blade of steel is 36 inches long, with a moderate degree of curvature, as it is intended for both thrusting and cutting. The guard is of steel and has three branches instead of four, as in the officer's saber.

The pommel is of malleable iron brazed to a sheet-steel ferrule, which extends part way down the grip. The grip is of wood, covered with leather and wound with brass wire. The hilt is secured by the tang, which passes through the guard, grip, and pommel, being headed down on the latter.

The scabbard is formed and made in the same manner as that for the officers' saber, but browned by the same process used for rifle barrels, instead of being nickel plated.

Figure 347 shows the cavalry saber, Model of 1913—the last saber issued and used by the U.S. Cavalry. Its design is credited to Lieutenant George Patton, old "Blood and Guts" Patton of World War II fame. No doubt this young cavalry lieutenant, who was master of the sword at the Mounted Service School, did work out the final straight-blade design, but the general pattern of the Model 1913 saber was the result of long, hard, and serious work by the members of the Cavalry Equipment Board.

The board's design for the saber to be part of the

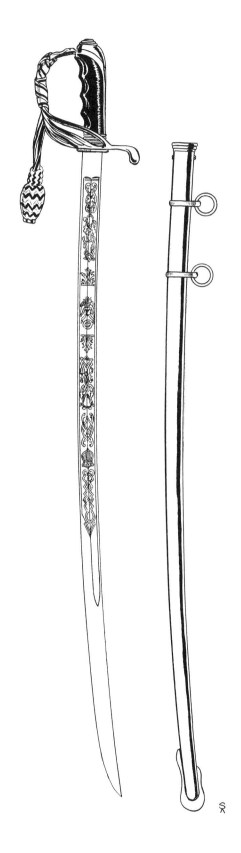

1912 cavalry equipments was very similar to the so-called "Patton" saber, except for its straight blade and slightly different-shaped pressed-steel guard. The grips were wood instead of steel, as in the adopted Model 1913, but the similarity is too strong to be coincidental.

The following text is from an article by Captain Edward Davis, Thirteenth Cavalry, and a member of the 1912 Cavalry Equipment Board. It was entitled, "The New Cavalry Equipment," and appeared in the September, 1912, edition of the *Journal of the United States Cavalry Association*.

THE SABER.

The saber designed by the Board is a cut and thrust weapon, being about thirty-eight inches long, overall, and weighing two pounds. While the opinions of experts in dismounted fencing were considered it was borne in mind that a cavalryman's saber was desired. In endeavoring to produce a saber well adapted to both cutting and thrusting, the Board combined the best qualities found in sabers especially designed for cutting and other sabers especially designed for thrusting. The point of the blade is on the median element thereof, thus favoring accuracy in thrusting, and the blade for some distance back from the point is double edged in order to facilitate penetration. It was recommended that this saber be issued sharp and kept in that condition. The steel guard is dark finished, presents and unbroken surface to cuts and thrusts and gives ample protection. The grip is of wood, shaped to the closed hand and covered with shark skin wired down.

This saber is a service weapon and it was recommended that paragraph 1544 A. R., 1910, be amended so that this saber and its scabbard can be drawn by officers from stores as is now the case with the rifle, revolver, etc. It was also recommended that the present officer's saber and scabbard be retained for use in garrison.

FIGURE 345. The Model 1902 saber for all commissioned officers of the Army. Both guard and scabbard are steel with a dull nickel finish. Grips are black horn and the blade is ornately etched on both sides with "U.S." and floral designs on one side, the national coat of arms and floral designs on the other. The blades are made in different lengths, according to the height of the individual officer. This saber is regulation today for all occasions when wearing a saber is prescribed. The saber knot shown here is the dress saber knot—gilt and black. Drawn from specimens in the author's collection.

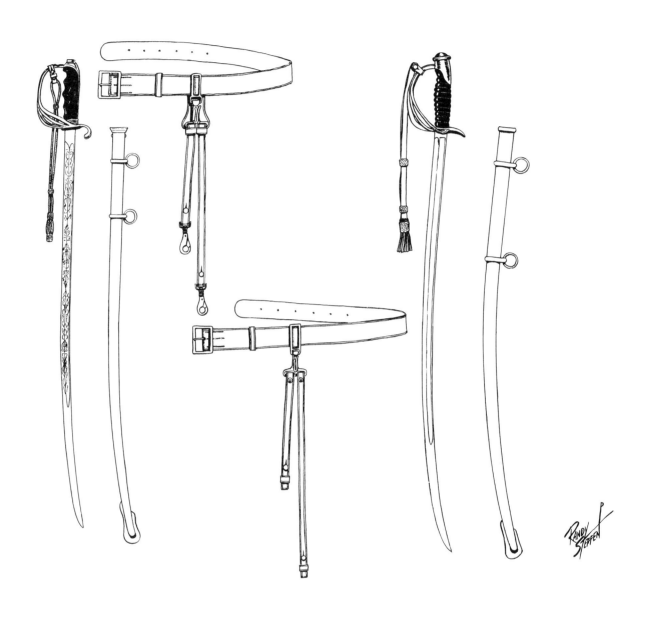

FIGURE 346. Officer's (left) and enlisted man's sabers, scabbards, saber belts, and service saber knots (ca. 1906).

Recently, items have appeared in service periodicals mentioning a new saber developed by the Ordnance Department. Inasmuch as the Board's model of saber was worked on by the Ordnance Department for almost two years, it is supposed that the saber recently mentioned in service periodicals is the one recommended by the Board or a slight modification thereof as it is not thought that the Ordnance Department has designed and produced an entirely new saber within the comparatively few weeks which have elapsed since the Board's model was produced.

The Saber Scabbard.

The saber scabbard is of wood treated with oil and covered first with raw hide and then with waterproofed olive drab canvas, this canvas covering being woven after the manner of hosepipe covering, the seam being thereby eliminated with consequent gain in wearing quality and appearance. The mouth of the saber scabbard is a dark finished, bell shaped, metal funnel, the opening being two and one-half inches by one and three-eighths inches inside measurement. The opening in the mouth of the present service saber scabbard is one and one-fourth by one-half inches. The increased area in the mouth of the scabbard facilitates returning the saber, and the change in shape combined with the dark finish of the metal gives an acceptable appearance. The dark finished metal tip of the scabbard is drawn down and reduced so that it forms a point which fits into the grommets of the shelter half, the intention being to dispense with the shelter half pole and to use the saber in its scabbard, guard down, as a substitute for the pole.

It is apparent that Captain Davis was at least partially aware of the work being done by someone on a modified design of the 1912 board recommendation, for he mentions in his article that he believes the published items refer to a slight modification of the saber recommended by the board.

And he was correct, for the Patton saber, except for its straight blade, is almost a dead ringer for the curved-blade model described above by Captain Davis. Even the tip of the scabbard of the first issues of the straight-blade saber was the same—intended to make the saber in its scabbard take the place of the folding poles for the shelter half. This tip is shown in Figure 347.

The nickel-plated scabbard next to the saber itself in Figure 347 was called the officer's garrison saber scabbard, Model of 1913, and was intended for attachment to the saddle for garrison and parade duty only. Following is a more complete description of the scabbards and saber, taken from the 1914 manual, *Description and Directions for Use and Care of Cavalry Equipment, Model of 1912* (Document No. 1715, October 5, 1914).

THE CAVALRY SABER, MODEL OF 1913.

The cavalry saber, model of 1913, has a straight two-edged *blade*, with a chisel point. The blade is of forged steel; extreme length, including grip, being approximately 41½ inches. The blade proper tapers from a width of 1.175 inches and a thickness of 0.298 inch at the guard to a width of 0.58 inch and a thickness of 0.162 inch, 1.8 inches from the point, and from the latter section forward is tapered to the chisel point. The blade has a groove running down each side to within 4¾ inches of the point. Both edges are sharp, except that the back is dulled to a width of 0.03 inch for a distance of 18 inches from the guard and the front edge for a distance of 12 inches from the guard.

The grip end of the blade is shaped to take the *pommel*, which is a steel forging forming the back of the grip. This piece is checked with diagonal milling cuts 11 per inch and has a checked thumb depression. This pommel is fastened to the back of the blade and to the sides are fastened the right and left *grips* of black hard rubber checked with 13 per inch checking. The rubber grips are fastened on with two grip screws about 1 inch long, passing through grips and blade. The pommel is secured to the blade by a pommel screw at the extreme rear end 1¼ inches long, which screws into the blade.

The *guard* is of sheet steel 0.042 inch thick, pressed to form a complete protection for the hand and stiffened by three grooves pressed into it. The guard is fastened at its rear end by being brazed to a connection plug which enters the pommel piece, and is held therein by the pommel screw passing through it. The guard is further stiffened by the edges being rolled inward all around the guard. Just below the guard on the blade is a sheet *steel washer* and below that a *leather washer* to protect the guard against the saber scabbard.

The guard and pommel are given a brown finish and the blade is left bright and polished.

The saber will be issued sharp, and should be kept in that condition. The metal portions of the hilt should not be brightened by polishing. If rust gathers upon them, rub it off with an oiled rag. The saber is carried in the saber carrier, edge to the rear, secured by the billet on the carrier through loop on the scabbard.

THE SERVICE SABER SCABBARD.

This scabbard is made up of a hickory body, thoroughly seasoned and dipped in oil and white lead; a *rawhide cover*, sewed up with a rawhide string and drawn on tightly, when wet, so as to dry in place, making a firm covering, and then thoroughly coated with shellac; an *outer covering* of tubular olive-drab webbing; a *tip* of drawn steel, forced on, riveted with three through rivets and crimped to the body; a *mouthpiece* of pressed steel, welded at the seams and having a ring on each side for attaching saber attachment, the mouthpiece riveted to scabbard by three bifurcated rivets and crimped. Inside this mouthpiece is a flat spring, which bears on the saber so as to hold it firmly in place, but at the same time admitting of easy withdrawal of saber.

The metal parts have a dull bronze finish, and the web cover is given two coats of shellac to render it waterproof,

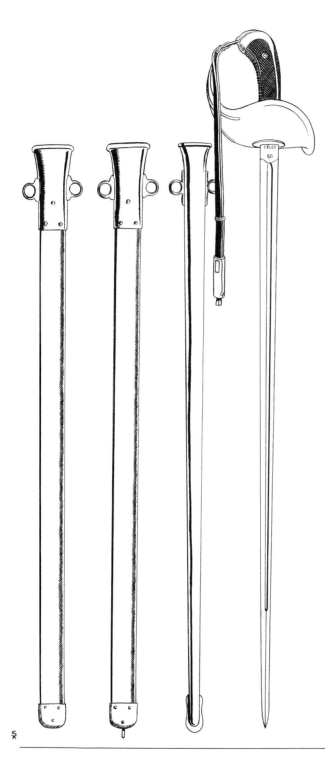

FIGURE 347. The cavalry saber, Model of 1913. While actually a straight blade designed primarily as a thrusting weapon, it was, nevertheless, designated a "saber" in all official publications. Purportedly designed by Lieutenant George Patton in 1912 and 1913, it superseded the curved blade that had been standard since the beginning of the American mounted service. The guard was stamped steel in full basket form with 3 reinforcing ridges in the region of the knuckle bow. Grip and guard were blackened. Three different scabbards were made for this saber. To the immediate left of the saber in this drawing is the nickel-plated officers' scabbard. To its left is the first model of service scabbard, with a protruding steel tip at the end that allowed the scabbard to serve as a shelter-half pole. The second model of scabbard, as shown here, and the one used from 1917 until the saber was discontinued as a cavalry weapon in 1934, is at the extreme left. This saber was designed to be attached to the saddle and was never worn by the trooper. The nickel scabbard was drawn from a specimen in the collection of R. A. Bennett, Jr., of Salem, Oregon. Saber and service scabbards from the author's collection.

rusty, clean them with an oiled rag. The canvas cover should not be soiled by smearing oil or grease upon it.

THE SABER KNOT.

The saber knot consists of two ½-inch body straps, 13½ inches long, on which are two movable slides. At one end a 3⅝-inch button loop is attached by means of a button, and at the other end is secured a blind tassel body composed of a compact roll of leather about 2¾ inches long by ⅝ inch in diameter.

OFFICER'S GARRISON SABER SCABBARD, MODEL OF 1913.

The officer's garrison saber scabbard is made of sheet steel and is lined with pine. The mouthpiece of the scabbard forms a spring which grips the saber and prevents rattling. Near the mouth, at equal distances therefrom and on opposite edges, rings are secured which are used to hold the scabbard in the saber carrier and with which the saber attachment is engaged. The scabbard has a nickel-plated finish.

of uniform appearance, and not easily soiled. The tip has a point with a hole for drainage, the tip being of proper size to fit the grommets of the shelter tent, so that the scabbard with saber in it can be used for a shelter-tent pole.

Metal parts of the scabbard must not be polished. If

HORSE EQUIPMENTS AND CAVALRY ACCOUTREMENTS

One of the most noticeable changes in horse equipments that resulted from the 1902 uniform change was the switch from black leather to russet, or fair,

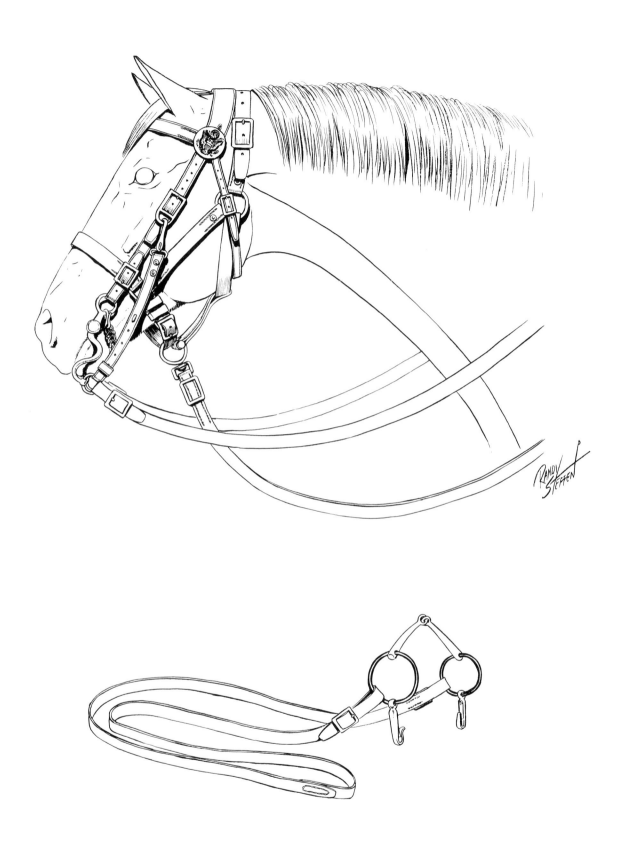

FIGURE 348. Model 1902 curb bridle (top) and watering bridle.

leather for all horse equipments, and all leather uniform items except cap visors and chin straps for officers and enlisted men, dress shoes, and officers' dress boots.

This change was well received by the cavalry regiments, for keeping the leather horse equipments looking good with blacking was a chore, and the black stains on uniforms from the blacking rubbing off was eliminated. With the new natural finish, only applications of castile soap were necessary to keep the articles of equipment in presentable condition.

Just as ordnance boards were set up for constant improvement of arms, a new permanent cavalry board and an infantry board were established under direction of the Secretary of War. The following General Order made the authorization of these boards known to the Army:

General Orders No. 45

Headquarters of the Army
Adjutant General's Office
Washington, March 31, 1903

By direction of the Secretary of War, boards are established as hereinafter described, to be known as the *Infantry Board* and the *Cavalry Board*, respectively, to which may be referred, from time to time, subjects relating to the operations and equipment to the infantry and cavalry arms, respectively, upon which their opinions and recommendations may be desired.

The field officers of cavalry and the two senior captains of that arm stationed at the School of Application for Cavalry and Field Artillery, Fort Riley, Kansas, shall constitute the Cavalry Board.

By Command of Lieutenant
General Miles

H. C. Corbin
Adjutant General
Major-General, U.S. Army

Even before the establishment of permanent equipment boards, much work had been done by special boards in the improvement of cavalry equipment. You will recall the mention of a kit, issued for trial, intended for troop saddler alteration of the quarter straps on the Model 1885 McClellan saddle to adjustable types (March, 1900).

Shortly after the turn of the century, a special cavalry equipment board modified the cavalry curb bridle and designated it the Model 1902. Figure 348 shows this bridle as it is illustrated and described in the manual published in 1905 showing horse equipments for officers and enlisted men. The Model 1902 watering bridle is also shown.

Notice the difference between the new curb bridle and the Model 1885 shown in Figure 253. The Model 1892 bit is substituted for the Shoemaker; a brass buckle with an attached loop provides a new means of attaching the new-pattern link strap to the headstall cheek instead of to the halter ring, as formerly; a curb chain has replaced the Model 1885 curb strap made of leather, which dried and curled in time, causing pinching of the horse's lips at the corners of the mouth; and a new bronze rosette with the United States coat of arms has replaced the old target-shaped brass rosette that had been standard since 1874.

The watering bridle, in the 1902 version, utilizes the same snaffle bit with the spring snaps for attaching to the halter squares, but now the reins are buckled to the bit rings instead of being sewn permanently to them.

The 1902 bridle is made of fair, or russet, leather, as are the watering bridle reins—the most obvious change from the former black leather bridles.

The 1904 McClellan saddle, with its adjustable quarter straps, had quite a few distinct changes, especially in the shape and cross-section dimensions of the tree components. The shape of the cantle, as seen from the rear, became a segment of a circle, whereas the 1885 pattern had been more elliptical. The side-bars, narrowed at the point where the stirrup loops were riveted in 1885, reverted to their former shape, and the iron reinforcing pieces at both pommel and cantle arches were improved in shape and strength.

A few saddles with the improved tree and the adjustable quarter straps, but covered with *black* leather, were made at the arsenals prior to 1902 for issue to cavalry and for trial in use. Such a black saddle, identical in every other respect to the Model 1904, is in the author's collection. This demonstrates most conclusively that the 1904 McClellan was the result of several years of intensive thought and much experimentation and test.

The following page from the 1905 edition of Document No. 1719 lists the equipment for officers and enlisted men that made up the 1904 cavalry horse equipments:

HORSE EQUIPMENT.

A complete set of horse equipments for enlisted men regularly consists of—

1 cavalry saddle, McClellan pattern
1 saddle cover
1 saddlebag
1 saddle blanket
1 curb bridle, model of 1902
1 watering bridle
1 halter
1 link
1 surcingle
1 lariat
1 lariat strap
1 picket pin
1 nosebag
1 horse brush
1 currycomb
1 scabbard for United States magazine rifle, model of 1903
2 saber straps
1 service saddlecloth
and, when especially required—
1 combination halter bridle, experimental
1 cavalry bridle, model of 1906, experimental
1 horse cover, or horse cover blanket lined, according to climate
1 stirrup with guidon socket
For officers only are added—
1 dress saddlecloth
1 service saddlecloth
1 breast strap and martingale, hunting design
1 Whitman saddle
for which the equipments are the same in material and finish, except as noted.

The following illustrations and descriptions are of the 1904 equipments listed above that were official for cavalry during this period:

CAVALRY SADDLE, McCLELLAN PATTERN.
[See Figure 349.]

A complete saddle is composed of—
1 saddletree (covered).
1 set saddle trimmings.
6 coat straps.
1 quarter strap (adjustable) complete.
2 stirrup straps.
2 stirrups (hooded).
1 cincha (hair).
SADDLETREE.
The parts are—
1 pommel.
1 cantle.
2 side bars.
1 pommel iron.
2 stirrup-strap loops.
The pommel consists of two pieces of selected ash (rough size, 1½ by 3 by 14⅝ inches) framed together at the top,

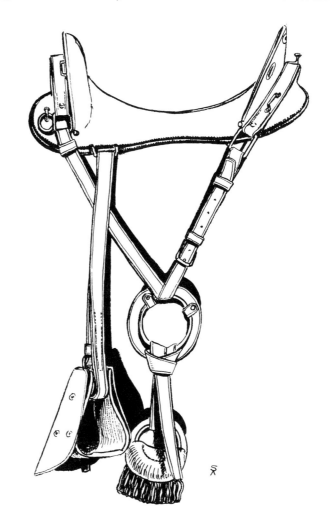

FIGURE 349. Model 1904 cavalry saddle.

glued and properly shaped. It is fastened to the side bars with two 1½-inch and two 1¾-inch No. 12 wood screws, and has one slot for coat strap.

The cantle is made of two pieces of selected ash (rough size, 1½ by 4¾ by 14½ inches) framed together at the top, glued and properly shaped. It is fastened to side bars with two 1½-inch and two 1¾-inch No. 12 wood screws, and has three slots for coat straps.

Each side bar is made from one piece of selected basswood (rough size, 2½ by 6¼ by 22¼ inches) turned to shape and gained for stirrup-strap loop.

The pommel iron is made from decarbonized sheet steel 0.065-inch thick, pressed to shape, and secured to pommel with three 1¼-inch No. 8 iron rivets, and to side bars with four—two in each.

The cantle iron is made from decarbonized sheet steel 0.065-inch thick, pressed to shape and secured to cantle with four 1¼-inch No. 8 iron rivets, and to side bars with six—three in each.

The stirrup-strap loops made from 0.284-inch decarbonized steel wire welded, are attached to the side bars by straps of decarbonized sheet steel 0.049 inch thick, each strap being fastened to the bar by three $1\frac{1}{2}$-inch No. 8 iron rivets. The loops have their lower edges inclined from the horizontal upward and to the front, and swing freely in the straps for the better adjustment of the stirrup straps when the rider is in the saddle.

Saddletrees are made in three sizes, in the following proportions:

15 per cent with 11-inch seat.
50 per cent with $11\frac{1}{2}$-inch seat.
35 per cent with 12-inch seat.

The size of seat, $11\frac{1}{2}$ and 12 inches, is the inside measurement, on the bare tree, between the intersections of cantle and pommel with the side bars. The actual measurements between these points is 0.17 inch larger than the above figures, to allow for the thickness of cover. After the saddle is covered with rawhide and leather the position of these points at intersection can not be accurately determined, but can be measured with sufficient precision to definitely fix the size of the saddle.

The length of the side bars alone varies with the different sizes of saddles, the other parts of the saddletree remaining the same for all sizes. These side bars are turned in copying lathes which produce duplicates of the forms used as guides; two forms, one right and one left, being required for each size of saddle. After turning, the centering ends of the side bars are cut off and the bars placed in forms which detect any defects in form due to warping or other causes, and which also insure great exactness in the distance between the side bars and the positions of cantle and pommel, these being fastened to the side bars while the latter are firmly held in forms. A separate form is used for each size of saddle, thus insuring exact uniformity in all essential dimensions.

The cantle and pommel irons are pressed to the shape required to fit the angles between the side bars and the pieces which they support. The principal surfaces of contact are near the tops of the cantle and pommel, where they best sustain the strains. Both irons are cut away toward the lower edges of the side bars so that they will not interfere with the holes for lacing thongs described below.

FINISHING AND COVERING THE SADDLETREE AFTER ASSEMBLING.

The front and rear ends of the side bars are carefully finished and shaped down by hand; holes for lacing thongs are bored through the bars along junctions of pommel and cantle, front and rear, and the bars grooved underneath in line with these holes so that the thongs used will not project below the under surface of the slide bars.

The tree is finished smooth and then coated by dipping into a mixture of white lead in oil, which protects and preserves the wood. It is then covered with hard rawhide made from calfskin. This skin is cut to shape under dies, is then soaked, and while wet, stretched and secured in place with wet rawhide (hard cowhide) thongs passing through the holes in front and rear of pommel and cantle. The top and bottom covers are then trimmed down and drawn together with light wet rawhide (hard calfskin) thongs, the seams being confined to the top and upper edges of the side bars so that no ridges are formed on the under bearing surfaces.

When this rawhide dries and shrinks it forms a smooth, hard cover, which prevents the wood from splitting and binds the parts of the tree into a strong, rigid, and serviceable unit that will retain its shape even after the wood itself is considerably decayed.

The rawhided tree is now covered with russet collar leather weighing 6 to 7 ounces per square foot. The seams around the pommel and cantle are reinforced with welts of leather and the seams in center of top covers have light welts; the seams on the edges of side bars are so placed that they will not chafe the horse or rider. The bottoms are lined with sheepskin, having wood $\frac{1}{2}$ inch long, which is sewed to same before attaching to saddle. Four wrought-iron saddle nails, $1\frac{1}{4}$ inches long, with heads $\frac{1}{2}$-inch in diameter, japanned to color of leather, are placed in the side bars at the points of the pommel and cantle to cover and protect the ends of the seams.

SADDLE TRIMMINGS.

Saddle trimmings are made of brass, as it does not rust, is amply strong, and is easily cast and formed into the required shapes.

A complete set includes—

4 $1\frac{1}{4}$-inch rings.
2 foot staples (semicircular), with screws.
4 foot staples (low), with screws.
2 foot staples (high), with screws.
7 ovals, with screw pins.
1 shield, with screw pins.
1 saddlebag stud, with rivets.

Located as follows:

Two $1\frac{1}{4}$-inch rings of cast brass are on front end of side bars, and two on rear of cantle.

The semicircular foot staples, made of cast brass, are fastened to the front ends of the side bars with four 1-inch No. 6 brass screws and secure two of the $1\frac{1}{4}$-inch rings.

The low foot staples are made of cast brass and used for holding the coat straps, two being placed on the front of pommel and two on the rear of cantle. Each is secured with two $\frac{7}{8}$-inch No. 6 brass screws.

The high foot staples, made of cast brass, are used on the rear end of saddle bars for attaching the saddlebags. They are secured to the side bars through the rear quarter strap by two 1-inch No. 6 brass screws.

The ovals are made from sheet brass 0.028 inch thick and are placed around the slots for coat straps as follows: One on front of pommel, three on front and three on rear of cantle. Each is secured with two $\frac{3}{4}$-inch No. 2 brass screw pins.

The shield is made of sheet brass 0.028-inch thick, pressed to shape, punched with slot for coat strap, stamped with size of saddletree, and secured to pommel, over slot, with three $\frac{3}{4}$-inch No. 2 brass screw pins.

The saddlebag stud is made of cast brass and secured

to cantle iron, through rear quarter strap, with one ⅜-inch No. 10 brass rivet, and to saddletree, through quarter strap and cantle iron, with one 1-inch No. 8 oval-head brass rivet.

COAT STRAPS.

These are six in number—
  3 for pommel, 33 inches long.
  3 for cantle, 45 inches long.

They are made from russet collar leather, 7 to 8 ounces per square foot. They pass through the slots and foot staples and have leather stops riveted on them 10½ inches from buckle, with ³⁄₁₆-inch tubular iron rivet and cap. One ⅝-inch cast-brass center bar buckle, with tongue of brass wire 0.120-inch diameter, is securely sewed to each strap.

QUARTER STRAP.

This is made from medium russet harness leather, the parts of one complete adjustable strap being—
  1 pommel quarter strap.
  1 cantle quarter strap.
  2 side quarter straps and sliding loops.
  2 quarter strap safes, lined.
  2 quarter strap rings, 4-inch.
  2 cincha straps.

The pommel quarter strap is passed over pommel iron and secured at the center to top of saddletree with two No. 8 1-inch oval-head brass rivets and burs. Each end is sewn into a 1¼ by 1⅜ inch halter square and riveted with a ⅜-inch tubular iron rivet and cap.

The cantle quarter strap is passed over cantle iron, and center of the strap secured to top of saddle with one 1-inch No. 8 oval-head brass rivet and bur (which also secures the saddlebag stud) and with two 1-inch No. 8 oval-head brass rivets and burs, one placed each side about 3 inches from saddlebag stud. It is secured to lower edges of side bars by the foot staples, which are fastened with four 1-inch No. 6 brass screws. Each end is sewn into a 1¼ by 1⅜ inch halter square and riveted with a ⅜-inch tubular iron rivet and cap.

The side quarter straps are made from russet collar leather 7 to 8 ounces per square foot, have one 1¼-inch malleable-iron barrel roller buckle sewn on one end, and have one standing loop and two sliding loops. The billet end has eight holes spaced 1¾ inches apart for adjusting the length of strap.

To ASSEMBLE THE SIDE STRAP.—First. Pass the billet under the ring on the safe between the ring chapes and draw up until the buckle is about 12 inches from the ring; then pass it through the halter square on pommel strap from the under side, again through ring on safe, thence through halter square on cantle from under side, and then through buckle, adjusting the length required.

The quarter strap safes are made of two thicknesses of medium russet harness leather, stitched together and lined with sheepskin with wool ½ inch long and secured to quarter strap rings with leather chapes and two ⅝-inch No. 10 brass rivets and burs.

The cincha straps are made from russet collar leather

7 to 8 ounces per square foot, and securely stitched to quarter strap ring; the stitching being reinforced with one ³⁄₁₆-inch tubular iron rivet and cap.

The 4-inch quarter strap rings are made from 0.284-inch decarbonized steel wire, as brass is not strong enough to retain its shape under the strain of the cincha.

STIRRUP STRAPS.

These, two in number, are made of medium russet harness leather, with one 1⅜-inch malleable-iron center-bar buckle securely sewed on one end, and have a standing loop on the upper side made sufficiently high to take the billet end after the strap has been passed through. The buckle is sewed on reversed so that when the stirrup is assembled the strap is given a quarter turn to throw the opening of the hood somewhat out from the horse for convenience in mounting.

To ASSEMBLE STRAP WITH RIGHT OR OFF STIRRUP.—Place stirrup on floor with opening of hood toward you. Pass free end of strap through the small opening in top of hood, and out of large opening in rear, rough side of leather bearing on the wooden crossbar. Grasp free end of strap in right hand and buckle end in left. Pass free end of strap around right side of buckle end and through the loop at buckle end from the bottom toward the top, rough side of leather of free end against the smooth side of leather of buckle end. Pull the free end of strap up until the buckle end slides down so that double thickness of leather is around wooden crossbar. From the outside pass free end of strap through top of right stirrup-strap loop on saddle, rough side of leather bearing on the loop. Buckle free end of strap, passing what remains of free end after buckling through opening at end of buckle and down center of loop between the two portions of stirrup strap already encircled by loop.

To ASSEMBLE STRAP WITH LEFT OR NEAR STIRRUP.—Pass free end of strap through opening in top of stirrup, rough side of strap to wooden crossbar and out at rear, as above explained. Grasp the buckle end in right hand, and free end in left. Pass free end around left side of strap and through loop near buckle, rough side of free end bearing against smooth side of buckle end. The remainder of the operation is the same as for right stirrup strap.

When assembled, the buckle lies on inside of strap, the opening of hood is to the rear, and the strap lies flat against the shin.

STIRRUPS.

A pair of stirrups consists of—
  2 stirrup staves with rivets.
  2 stirrup spreaders.
  4 crescentric washers, with rivets.
  2 stirrup hoods.

STAVES.—To be made from selected white oak (rough size, 5 by 24 inches); they may be either sawed or split; if sawed, they must be ⅝ inch thick and sawed parallel to the grain of the wood; if split, they must be ¾ inch thick. They must be of tough, live wood, of best quality, entirely free from knots and all defects, and after steaming must be capable of being quickly bent around a curve to form them into stirrups without developing splints, cracks, breaks, or checks.

Staves are cut to size, planed, gained for riser, and steamed, before bending. After bending they are thoroughly kiln-dried and then properly shaped.

The spreaders, made from clear ash, are placed between the upper ends of the bent staves for attaching the stirrup strap. Each is secured by one 2¾ by ³⁄₁₆ inch iron rivet and bur, and one 3 by ³⁄₁₆ inch iron rivet, which also passes through the middle of the crescentric washers.

The crescentric washers are made of decarbonized sheet steel 0.05 inch thick, each being secured to stirrup with one 3 by ³⁄₁₆ inch iron rivet and bur passing through stave and spreader, and with two ⅝-inch No. 10 iron rivets passing through stave only.

The crescentric washers prevent the stave from splitting through the plane of the spreader rivets, and the wings by extending down over the section of greatest curvature, strengthen the stave where it is most likely to break. Due to the tendency to straighten after bending, stirrups vary in curvature, and the washer is given its particular form so it can be more easily adjusted and fitted to the stirrup than if oval or triangular in shape.

Stirrup hoods, made of russet harness leather with letters "U. S." stamped in an oval on center of front, are riveted to stirrup with four ⅝-inch and two ¾-inch tubular iron rivets, brown japan finish. They are made of two thicknesses of leather sewed around the edge. The bottom of the hood projects ¾ inch below the plane of underside of stirrup.

CINCHA.

The parts are—
    1 cincha body.
    2 cincha safes.
    2 cincha covers.
    2 cincha 4-inch rings.

They are made 20 inches in length, this being the actual measurement of cincha unstretched, from inside to inside of the outer ends of the rings.

The cincha body is made of 24 strands of 6-ply spun and twisted horsehair rope, knotted on the cincha ring. The body is 8 inches wide in center when finished. A three-strand horsehair rope is woven across the body near each ring, and in two places across the middle to keep the strands from spreading.

Safes are made of medium russet harness leather, and placed under the rings. The knots of the cincha are protected by a cover of the same weight of leather, which is secured to safe and cincha rings with stitching and with one ⅝-inch No. 10 brass belt rivet and bur.

The cincha rings are the same as those for the quarter straps, made of decarbonized steel wire 0.284-inch diameter, welded. Their inside diameter is 4 inches.

SADDLE COVER.
[See Figure 350.]

The parts are—
    1 body (in halves).
    3 billets.

3 buckles and chapes.

The body is made of two pieces of No. 9 olive-drab cotton duck with edges turned under and sewed around sides and bottom, forming a bag and having the top hemmed. The top is closed and held by three billets and buckle chapes of medium harness leather, each of which is reinforced with scrap leather and secured to the body by stitching, and one tubular rivet and cap. The billets and buckle chapes are ⅞-inch wide and are fastened on outside of body on opposite sides. The buckle chape has a ⅞-inch barrel roller buckle, brown japan finish, and a standing loop.

SADDLEBAGS.
[See Figure 350.]

The finish of metal parts of saddlebags is bronze for officers and brown japan for enlisted men.

The components of a complete pair are—
    2 pouches, with flaps.
    1 seat.
    1 set linings.
    1 salt bag.
    2 coffee and sugar bags.
    2 side straps.

For each pouch, 1 flap, 1 front, 1 back, 3 flap billets, 3 buckle chapes, 1 ring chape, and 1 gusset are required. The near-side pouch is for rations and the off-side for clothing.

The flaps are made of russet bag leather, 5 to 6 ounces per square foot, have letters "U. S." within an oval stamped on center of face. Three flap billets, made of russet collar leather, pass through slots in the flap.

The fronts are made of russet bag leather 5 to 6 ounces per square foot, and two metallic buttons are fastened inside near top of "front" for securing the linings. Three ¾-inch brass-wire buckles with chapes and standing loops of russet collar leather are sewed to lower part of "front" for fastening down flaps by billets mentioned.

The backs are made of russet bag leather 5 to 6 ounces per square foot, and have two metallic buttons fastened near top for securing the linings. Side straps are used to fasten the saddlebags to cincha rings to prevent flapping, and are attached to lower front corner of saddlebag backs by a ⅞-inch brass ring and chape of russet collar leather.

The gussets are made of russet bag leather, 5 to 6 ounces per square foot. Front, back, and gusset are joined together and stitched, with folded welt inclosed in seam. The back of the pouch is reinforced on each side with a trianguler piece of russet bag leather. To prevent ripping or tearing the ends of gusset are reinforced with a strip secured to the gusset by two ³⁄₁₆-inch tubular iron rivets and caps, and to the front with one ³⁄₁₆-inch tubular iron rivet and cap, and to back, through triangular reinforcement, with one ¼-inch tubular iron rivet and cap. Pouch and flap are joined separately to seat with stitching and with two ⁵⁄₁₆-inch tubular iron rivets and caps.

The seat, made of russet collar leather 7 to 8 ounces per square foot and fastened to pouches and flaps, as stated above, is designed to fit smoothly over cantle and side bars of the saddle, and has one hold through center for the saddlebag stud, with a slot on each side for the foot staples (high) to pass through. These slots are reinforced with two brass ovals 0.035 inch thick, each secured to seat with two ⅜-inch No. 12 brass belt rivets. Two key billets are riveted to "seat" near slots, each with ⁵⁄₁₆-inch tubular iron rivet and cap.

LININGS.

The parts of one set are—
    2 front linings.
    1 back lining, off side.
    1 back lining, near side.
    1 gusset lining.

All the linings are made from No. 9 olive-drab cotton duck, and each back lining has two buttonholes near the top for fastening to the pouches. The back lining of near side has two pockets of the same kind of duck, for the knife, fork, and spoon. The front, back, and gusset linings of each pouch are joined and stitched with No. 25 olive-drab linen thread.

The coffee, sugar, and salt bags, three in number, are made from white cotton drill. 8 ounces per square yard, with a draw string of No. 12 cotton chalk line, 20 inches long, run through hem.

The side straps are made of russet collar leather, 7 to 8 ounces per square foot, with ¾-inch brass-wire buckle and two standing loops of same material as strap.

Saddle Blanket.

specifications.

1. Wool.—The blankets will be made of pure wool; no Colorado wool, or what is known as "carpet wool," or kemp, to be used. The yarn to be evenly spun with a moderate twist and free from lumps or shreds.

2. Color.—To be a mixture of olive-drab shade, the various colors required to produce the mixture to be dyed in wool and thoroughly cleaned before mixing. They must be sufficiently fast to withstand milling and climatic influences, such as sunlight, air, and the exposure incident to military service.

3. Border.—An olive-brown border of two stripes, as shown in drawing. The wool in the border to be of the same grade as the body of the blanket, and to withstand the tests for permanency of color.

4. Threads.—The finished blanket to have not less than 26 threads per inch in the warp and 36 threads per inch in the woof, and to weigh not less than 5 pounds.

5. Strength.—The blankets must be moderately combed and stand a strain of at least 80 pounds per inch in the direction of the warp, and 90 pounds per inch in the direction of the woof.

6. Size.—The blankets to be rectangular, 72 by 84 inches, with straight edges.

7. Ordnance Department Brand.—Each blanket to have the letters "U. S." and the bursting shell as shown in drawing. The letters, insignia, color, and method of working same in the blanket to be the same as that shown upon the drawing.

8. Color Test.—The permanency of the color of the blanket will be tested by subjecting one blanket in every ten to the following test:

If the tested blankets do no conform to the requirements of the specifications, all the blankets delivered in that lot will be rejected.

Test No. 1.—Boil for ten minutes in a solution composed of 80 grains of Ivory soap to one pint of water.

Test No. 2.—A second sample shall be taken and boiled ten minutes in solution containing 10 grains of dry carbonate of soda to one pint of water.

Test No. 3.—Soaking twelve hours in a solution composed of 3 drams of citric acid to two fluid ounces of water, temperature about 70° F.

Test No. 4.—Soaking twenty-four hours in lactic acid, sp. gr. 1.21 U. S. P., temperature about 70° F.

Test No. 5.—An exposure to the weather (roof test) for thirty days.

To correctly judge the results, the specimens that have been subjected to the above tests must be washed in a weak solution of Ivory soap and tepid warm water. No change of color must appear. The olive-brown borders must also stand the above test without change.

9. Workmanship.—The blankets to be manufactured in a thoroughly workmanlike manner and when finished must be free from grease, must smell sweet, present a bright, clear appearance, and be perfectly dry when presented for inspection. They must be of uniform quality and not show any stops in weave when held against the light or any other defects in workmanship. The ends to be secured from raveling by a gimp and elastic overlock stitch as shown upon the standard sample. The gimp and thread employed to conform in shade to the body of the blanket.

Curb Bridle, Model of 1902.
[See Figure 348.]

The components are—
    1 curb bit, model of 1892.
    1 curb chain, model of 1904.
    1 rein.
    Headstall—
        2 cheek pieces.
        1 crownpiece.
        1 brow band.
        1 throatlatch.
        2 brow-band ornaments.

All bridle trimmings, except brow-band ornaments, are of bronze; bronze finish for officers, brown japan for enlisted men.

The curb bit, model of 1892, is made of best quality shear steel and has dull nickel finish. The branches are drop-forged and electrically welded to the mouthpiece, which is made of soft decarbonized steel. A loop is forged on upper part of each branch for attaching the curb-chain hook and cheek piece, and an eye on lower end of each branch into which is welded the rein ring, made of 0.203-inch decarbonized steel wire. The bits are made regularly in three sizes, which differ only in length of mouthpiece, the proportions being:

Number.	Length of mouthpiece.	Proportion of manufacture.
	Inches.	*Per cent.*
1	4.5	15
2	4.75	75
3	5	10

A larger size, No. 4, with mouthpiece 5.25 inches long, is occasionally made to fill special requisitions.

The curb chain, model of 1904, is a special steel chain with links and hooks finished in dull nickel.

The curb-chain hooks, model of 1904, are made right and left, of spring-steel wire, 0.165 inch diameter, tempered, and have dull nickel finish. The left hook is formed with the eye and hook in the same plane, while the right hook has the eye twisted at a right angle to the hook. The hooks are closed so as to offer a resistance of 10 to 16 pounds to disengaging from a ring of 0.134-inch diameter wire.

All leather parts of the bridle are made from russet bridle leather weighing 9½ to 10½ ounces per square foot.

The reins are made of two pieces of russet bridle leather sewed together in the middle. One rein billet, with one ⅞-inch bronze center-bar buckle, is securely sewed to each end of rein.

The cheek pieces are made of russet bridle leather. For officers' bridles they are alike, but for enlisted men they are right and left. They differ in that the right cheek piece has a ¾-inch bronze center-bar buckle, while the left cheek piece has a ¾-inch bronze "Saalbach" buckle securely sewed to upper end. This buckle has a loop at the lower end which takes the snap of the link when the link is carried on the bridle. Both cheek pieces have billets with ¾-inch bronze center-bar buckles securely sewed to lower end. To admit fine adjustments, the holes in the crownpiece for the cheek-piece buckles are spaced ½ inch apart, while those in billets are ⅞ inch.

The crownpiece is made of russet bridle leather with ends split for a distance of 8 inches and a ⅛-inch strip taken out of the center, forming a cheek and throat strap billet on each end.

The brow band is made of russet bridle leather. A loop is formed on each end by doubling over and stitching the ends of the piece.

The throatlatch is made of russet bridle leather and has a ⅝-inch bronze center-bar buckle securely sewed on each end.

The brow-band ornaments are made from sheet copper 0.035 inch thick for enlisted men and 0.109 inch thick for officers; both are bronzed and bear the coat of arms of the United States in relief. Loops of 0.109-inch soft brass wire, to receive the brow band, are soldered to the rear sides.

WATERING BRIDLE.
[See Figure 348.]

The parts are—
　　1 watering bit.
　　2 bit snaps.
　　1 rein.

The watering bit has dull nickel finish.

The mouthpiece is made in two parts. Each is slightly curved and tapers from 0.59 inch diameter just inside of the rein ring to 0.4 inch diameter at base of eye, being forged from a soft decarbonized steel bar 0.625 inch in diameter. The ends of the two pieces have holes 0.34 inch in diameter and are joined together, as shown on Plate III, by having the eye in one piece cut and closed into the other. The other ends of the mouthpiece are drilled with holes 0.31 inch diameter, into which are welded the rein rings, 2.75 inches in diameter, made of 0.25 inch decarbonized steel wire.

Bit snaps are dull nickel finished after assembling. The body is drop-forged from a soft, decarbonized steel bar $\frac{7}{16}$ inch diameter; the spring is made of sheet spring steel 0.0218 inch thick, and is secured in place by two projections on snap body, which are clenched over spring and by punching metal into a depression on body.

The reins are made from two pieces of russet bridle leather, 9½ to 10½ ounces per square foot, sewed together at middle. One rein billet with one ⅞-inch bronze center-bar buckle, brown japan finish, is securely sewed to each outer end.

HALTER.
[See Figure 348.]

The parts of a complete halter are—
　Headstall—
　　　1 crown strap.
　　　1 crown chape.
　　　2 cheek pieces.
　　　1 noseband.
　　　1 chin strap.
　　　1 throat strap and swivel ring.
　　　1 throatband.
　　　1 halter strap.

All leather parts except the halter strap are made from medium russet harness leather.

The crown strap has one end secured to upper ring of off cheek piece with stitching and one ⅜-inch tubular iron rivet and cap, while the billet end of strap fastens into buckle of crown chape.

The crown chape has one end secured to upper ring of near cheek piece, while to the other is stitched a 1⅛-inch malleable-iron center-bar buckle. The ends of chape are folded over and fastened with stitching and one $\frac{7}{16}$-inch tubular iron rivet and cap.

One end of each cheek piece is secured to the halter square of nose-band with stitching and a ⅜-inch tubular iron rivet and cap, while the other end is secured in the same way to a malleable-iron ring 1⅝ inches diameter.

The noseband has a malleable-iron halter square, 1¼ by 1⅜ inches, secured to each end with stitching, and a ⅜-inch tubular iron rivet and cap.

The chin strap has a 1⅛-inch malleable-iron center-bar buckle and 2 standing loops, sewed to one end. Two sliding loops are also provided.

The throat strap is folded on itself, making three thicknesses, and stitched, forming a loop at the top for the throatband. Held in its fold at the bottom end is one 1¼-inch halter

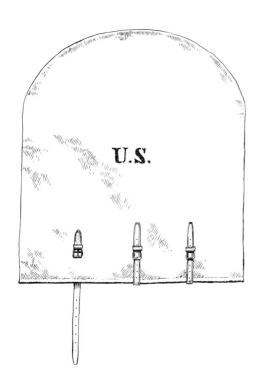

A.   SADDLE COVER

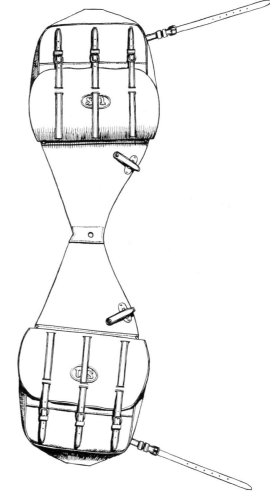

B.   SADDLEBAGS M1904

C.   SABER STRAP

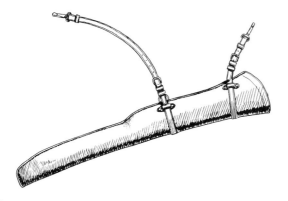

D.   RIFLE SCABBARD FOR:
       U.S. MAGAZINE RIFLE M1903
       U.S. MAGAZINE CARBINE M1896
       U.S. MAGAZINE CARBINE M1899

FIGURE 350. Horse equipments (ca. 1904).

belt, around which passes the ring of the swivel ring; two $\frac{7}{16}$-inch tubular iron rivets and caps reinforce the stitching.

The swivel ring is made of malleable iron and consists of one $1\frac{1}{8}$-inch halter square swiveled on a $1\frac{3}{4}$-inch ring.

The throatband passes through the loop in throat strap and is secured to each cheek ring with stitching and one $\frac{3}{8}$-inch tubular iron rivet and cap.

The halter strap is made of heavy russet harness leather, tapered at one end to facilitate tying; to the other end is attached, by stitching and riveting, a $1\frac{1}{8}$-inch tongueless malleable-iron center-bar buckle.

The halter for officers' equipment differs from the above in the metal parts, which are cast bronze bronzed, instead of malleable-iron with brown japan finish.

LINK.
[See Figure 348.]

The strap is made of medium russet harness leather. A 1-inch malleable-iron snap, German, bronzed, is sewed to one end, and adjustment to fit cheek piece is provided by a sliding loop and a hook of 0.15-inch brass wire, which is riveted to the other end of the strap with two $\frac{3}{8}$-inch No. 14 brass belt rivets. The link is used by enlisted men only.

SURCINGLE.
[See Figure 353.]

The body of the surcingle is made of linen webbing $3\frac{1}{2}$ inches wide, blue for cavalry and scarlet for artillery. A $1\frac{1}{2}$-inch iron barrel roller buckle, brown japan finish, with chape and standing loop of medium russet harness leather, is securely sewed to one end, and a $1\frac{1}{2}$-inch billet, with swell and reinforce, of medium russet harness leather, to the other end. Two leather loops of medium russet harness leather are sewed on web to take the billet. Surcingles are manufactured in three sizes and in equal proportions, as follows:

Size.	Length of webbing.	Total length, including billet.
	Inches.	Inches.
No. 1	48	74
No. 2	63	81
No. 3	63	93

LARIAT.

The body is a $\frac{3}{8}$-inch linen braided rope, of twenty strands, glazed, and 26 feet long. To each end is attached a link and hook, the rope being protected from wear by a thimble, around which the end of the rope is passed and secured by being wrapped in two places with soft copper wire of 0.035 inch diameter. One end of hook is closed around the link, while the other forms the hook. It has a spring made from sheet spring steel 0.028 inch thick and tempered.

LARIAT STRAP.
[See Figure 351-C.]

This is made from russet collar leather, 7 to 8 ounces per square foot. It is $\frac{7}{8}$ inch wide and has at one end a

bronzed 1-inch malleable-iron snap, German, fastened with one No. 10 brass belt rivet, the other end having a standing loop fastened with two No. 10 brass belt rivets.

PICKET PIN.
[See Figure 351-D.]

The parts are—
  1 pin.
  1 crossbar.
  1 loop.
  1 ring and eye.
All parts, except the ring, are drop-forged from soft decarbonized steel.

The pin is made 0.6 inch in diameter, with the head sufficiently strong to resist upsetting when struck to drive the pin into the ground. The crossbar swivels around head of pin, while the loop is riveted to the crossbar so as to turn freely. The eye is riveted into loop, so as to swivel easily, and the ring, made of decarbonized steel wire $\frac{1}{4}$ inch diameter, is welded into eye. The complete picket pin is painted black.

NOSEBAG.
[See Figure 351-A.]

The parts of the nosebag are—
  1 body.
  1 bottom.
  1 headband with reinforce.
  1 buckle and chape.
  1 ventilator.
The body is made of No. 9 olive-drab cotton duck, hemmed at the top and stitched to the bottom, which, to resist wear, is made of two thicknesses of russet harness leather.

The headband, made of $1\frac{1}{2}$-inch olive-drab cotton halter webbing, with No. 0 brass grommets, is fastened to top of off side of nosebag by stitching and one $\frac{7}{16}$-inch tubular iron rivet, while a $1\frac{1}{2}$-inch iron roller buckle, brown japan finish, with chape of olive-drab cotton halter webbing, is fastened in the same manner to near side of nosebag.

The ventilator, made of russet collar leather, 7 to 8 ounces per square foot, is sewed to front side of nosebag and then perforated with $\frac{1}{4}$-inch holes, as shown. The letters "U. S.", $1\frac{1}{2}$ inches high, are stenciled on body of nosebag above ventilator.

HORSE BRUSH.
[See Figure 351-B.]

The body, oval in shape, consists of a top or veneer piece and a sufficient number of thicknesses of scrap leather resulting from other manufactures, glued together, making a thickness of 0.53 inch. It is drilled with 510 holes 0.132 inch in diameter, which are filled with an excellent grade of Okatka or Turkish bristles drawn with a 0.016-inch soft brass wire. After the brush is drawn, the veneer piece is glued on and hand strap and veneer piece are stitched to body, as shown. The hand strap is embossed with the letters "U. S." within an oval and stitching reinforced by four $\frac{3}{8}$-inch tubular iron rivets and caps.

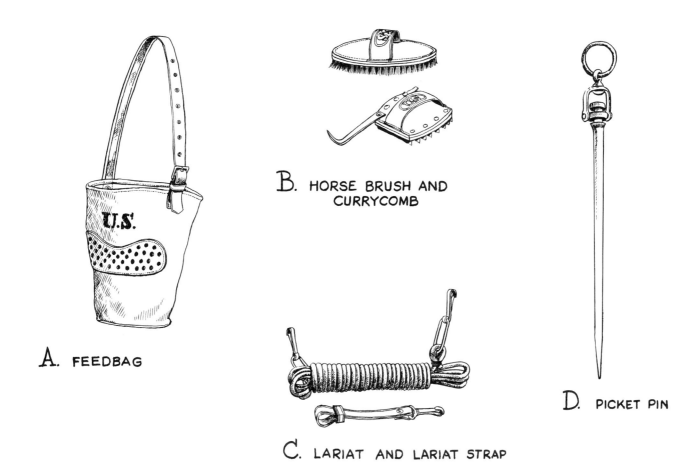

A. FEEDBAG

B. HORSE BRUSH AND CURRYCOMB

C. LARIAT AND LARIAT STRAP

D. PICKET PIN

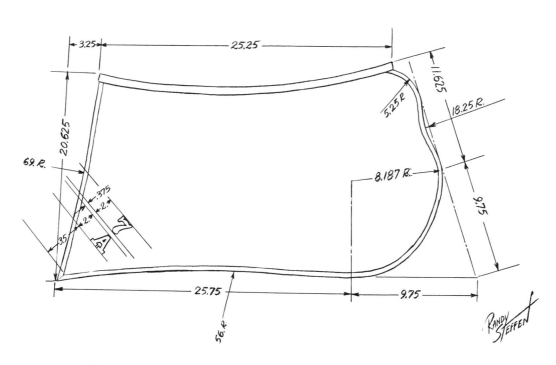

E. PATTERN FOR SADDLECLOTH (OFFICERS AND ENLISTED MEN)

FIGURE 351. Horse equipments (ca. 1904).

CURRYCOMB.
[See Figure 351-B.]

The parts are—
- 1 back.
- 4 tooth bars.
- 1 dust iron.
- 1 hook iron.
- 1 strap.
- 1 hook.

The back is made of two thicknesses of russet collar leather, 7 to 8 ounces per square foot, glued together and stitched, as shown.

Four tooth bars, blanked from decarbonized sheet steel 0.035 inch thick, bent into an inverted U shape, making seven rows of teeth and one dust plate, are secured to back with eight ⅜-inch No. 8 rivets.

The hook and dust irons, made of decarbonized steel ⅞₆ by 0.095 inch, are secured to body, through tooth plates with one ½-inch No. 8 rivet and one ½-inch No. 8 countersunk rivet.

The strap, made of russet collar leather, 7 to 8 ounces per square foot, with letters "U. S." within an oval, stamped thereon, is secured to back through tooth plates by four ½-inch No. 8 flathead rivets.

The hook is of steel ¼ inch thick and when not in use closes and lies along the top of the back. It is fastened through the hook iron with one ⅝-inch No. 8 rivet.

SCABBARD.
[See Figure 350-D.]

For United States magazine rifle, model of 1903.
The parts are—
- 1 body and mouth reinforce.
- 2 springs.
- 2 straps with sliding loops and snaps.
- 4 loops.
- 1 ring.

The body is made of medium russet harness leather, cut and stitched as shown. Mouth of scabbard is reinforced with a piece of medium russet harness leather. One ⅞₆-inch tubular iron rivet and cap, brown japan finish, is riveted through scabbard just below swell, to reinforce stitching, as this is the seat of the lower band swivel and carries a large part of the weight of the rifle.

Two springs, made of sheet spring steel 0.028 inch thick, with holes punched for stitching, are fastened in bottom of scabbard to strengthen the scabbard against the end thrust of rifle, and to form a hole for the escape of water.

The rifle scabbard straps are made of medium russet harness leather, with ⅞-inch barrel roller buckle, brown japan finish, two standing loops of the same material as straps, which are secured to each strap by stitching and one sliding loop.

The upper strap passes around scabbard and through two loops, while the lower passes around scabbard and through an inch ring and two loops. The straps are provided with snaps, so that the scabbard can be quickly removed from the saddle.

The loops are made of same material as the straps, and each secured to scabbard with two ⅜-inch tubular iron rivets and caps, brown japan finish.

The ring is 1 inch in diameter, made of malleable iron, brown japan finish. It is placed around the ring reinforce and secured in the seam of scabbard by stitching, and one ⅜-inch tubular iron rivet and cap, brown japan finish.

SABER STRAPS.
[See Figure 350-C.]

These are made of russet collar leather, 7 to 8 ounces per square foot, with ⅝-inch brass center-bar buckle, and standing loop of same material as strap, secured to strap with stitching. Buckle is finished in bronze for officers and brown japan for enlisted men.

SERVICE SADDLECLOTH FOR ENLISTED MEN.
[See Figure 351-E.]

The service saddlecloth for enlisted men is made from No. 9 olive drab cotton duck and lined with No. 2 olive drab cotton duck. Saddlecloth is made in halves and held together by 1¼-inch olive drab cotton webbing placed over the seam and stitched through both thicknesses of duck. Around the edge is a binding of 1¼-inch olive drab cotton webbing, showing on outside ⅝ inch. In each flank corner is placed the number of the regiment, and "band," "N. C. S.," or the company letter, the letters and figures being of enameled leather 2 inches high and color to suit arm of service—yellow for cavalry, light blue for infantry, scarlet for artillery. The engineers have a scarlet letter two inches high outlined with a white letter, both being of enameled leather.

COMBINATION HALTER BRIDLE.
EXPERIMENTAL.
[See Figure 352.]

The components are—
- 1 curb bit, model of 1892.
- 1 curb chain, model of 1904.
- 1 rein.
- 2 bridle cheek pieces.
- 1 crownpiece.
- 2 halter cheek pieces.
- 1 nose and chin strap.
- 1 gullet.
- 1 brow band.
- 2 brow band ornaments.
- 1 halter strap.

All trimmings, except brown band ornaments, are of malleable iron; bronze finish for officers and brown japan finish for enlisted men.

The curb bit and curb chain are the same as are used on the curb bridle, model of 1902.

All leather parts are made from russet harness leather.

The rein is 1 inch in width, made in two pieces and sewed together in the middle. Each part ends in a rein billet having a 1-inch barrel roller buckle and one standing loop.

The bridle cheek pieces are alike, the upper end of each

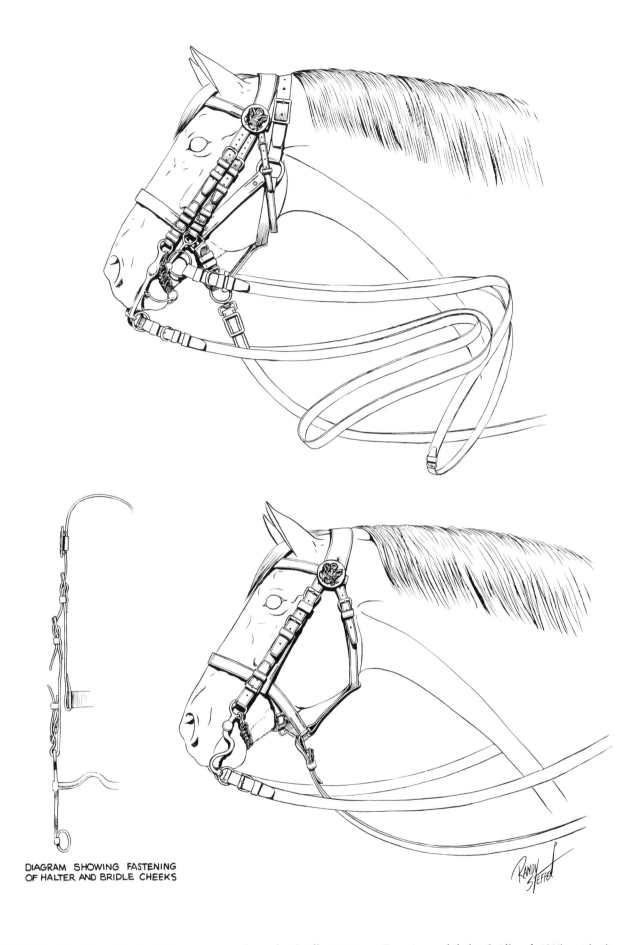

DIAGRAM SHOWING FASTENING
OF HALTER AND BRIDLE CHEEKS

FIGURE 352. Top: Model 1906 experimental cavalry bridle. Bottom: Experimental halter-bridle of 1905, with diagram showing fastening of halter and bridle cheeks.

having a 1-inch barrel roller buckle and standing loop, and the lower end having a billet with a 1-inch barrel roller buckle and one standing loop.

The crownpiece is made from one piece of leather 1⅞ inches wide with both ends split in two for a distance of 7½ inches from the end, forming three billets and one buckle piece. The latter is ⅞ inch in width and extends 13¼ inches beyond the end of billet and forms the throatlatch, ending in a ⅞-inch barrel roller buckle and one standing loop. To the 1-inch billets are attached first, the halter cheek piece, and then the bridle cheek piece.

The halter cheek pieces are alike and are made of two thicknesses of leather sewn together and forming a loop at the lower end, through which the nose and chin strap passes, and having sewed to the upper end of 1-inch barrel roller buckle and one standing loop for attaching to the crownpiece.

The nose and chin strap is made in two parts: an outer strap 1 inch wide with ends sewn into a 1 by 1¼ inch halter square, and an inside chin strap ⅝ inch wide, consisting of a billet and buckle piece, which fastens under the halter square with a ⅝-inch barrel roller buckle and standing loop. The nose and chin strap passes through the loops in lower end of the halter cheek pieces in assembling.

The gullet is folded on itself, making three thicknesses and stitched, forming a loop at the top for the throatlatch and holding the halter square above mentioned in a fold at the bottom.

The brow band is made with a loop in each end through which the crownpiece passes and is formed by doubling over the end and stitching.

The brow-band ornaments, made from sheet copper 0.035-inch thick for enlisted men and 0.019 inch thick for officers, are the same as are used on the curb bridle, model of 1902.

The halter strap is made of 1-inch width, tapering at the end. The upper part ends in a billet having a 1-inch barrel roller buckle and one standing loop for attaching to the halter square.

CAVALRY BRIDLE, MODEL OF 1906.
EXPERIMENTAL.
[See Figure 352.]

This consists of a curb bridle, model of 1906, experimental, and a bridoon bridle, model of 1906, experimental, made from russet collar leather 7 to 8 ounces per square foot and assembled together.

The components of the curb bridle are—
    1 curb bit, model of 1906, experimental.
    2 curb hooks.
    1 curb chain, model of 1906, experimental.
    1 curb bit thong.
    1 rein.
  Headstall—
    2 cheek pieces.
    1 crownpiece.
    1 brow band.
    2 brow band-ornaments.

All bridle trimmings, except brow-band ornaments, are made of bronze; bronze finish for officers, brown japan finish for enlisted men.

The curb bit, model of 1906, has dull nickel finish. The branches are drop-forged from best quality shear steel and electrically welded to mouthpiece, which is made of soft decarbonized steel. A loop is forged on upper part of each branch for attaching the cheek piece and curb hook, the latter being of shear steel, bent around the loop. The lower end of each branch is straight, tapering from 5/16-inch diameter below the mouthpiece to 0.28 inch above the bottom end, which is forged to the rear at a right angle and into which is welded the rein ring, made from 0.203-inch decarbonized steel wire. Near the middle of the lower branch an eye is forged for attachment of the curb bit thong.

The curb chain, model of 1906, is the model of 1904 chain with an additional ring in the middle, through which the curb-chain thong passes.

The curb-bit thong is of soft rawhide and is passed through middle link of curb chain and has the ends tied into the middle eye on each branch of the curb bit.

The rein is ¾ inch in width, made in two pieces, and sewed together in the middle. Each part ends in a rein billet having a ¾-inch bronze buckle and three standing loops.

The cheek pieces are alike, the upper end of each having a ¾-inch bronze buckle, one standing loop and one sliding loop, and the lower end having a billet with ¾-inch bronze buckle and three standing loops.

The crownpiece is 1¼ inches in width with both ends split in two for a distance of 7¾ inches from the end, and forming three billets and one buckle piece. The latter is ½ inch in width and extends 14½ inches beyond the end of billet, forming the throatlatch and ending in a ½-inch bronze buckle with one standing loop and one sliding loop.

The brown band is made by doubling over each end and stitching so as to form two loops through which the crown-pieces of both bridles pass when assembled.

The brow band ornaments are made from sheet copper, 0.035 inch thick for enlisted men, and 0.109 inch thick for officers; both are bronzed and have loops of 0.109 inch soft brass wire soldered to the rear sides to receive the brow band.

The bridoon bridle, model of 1906, is composed of the following parts:
    1 bridoon bit, model of 1906, experimental.
    1 rein.
    1 cheek piece.
    1 crownpiece.

The bridoon bit, model of 1906, has dull nickel finish. The mouthpiece is forged in two parts from a soft decarbonized steel bar 0.625 inch in diameter, and joined at the center, the ends having holes 0.38 inch in diameter, one of which is cut through and closed into the other. The other ends are closed around the rein rings. The rein ring and curved branch with loop for cheek piece and crownpiece are drop forged in one piece. The ring section varies in diameter from 0.35 inch at the mouthpiece to 3/16 inch diametrically opposite. The branch tapers to 0.32 inch diameter below the loop, which measures 0.75 inch diameter inside and has circular section of 0.2 inch diameter at upper part.

The rein is ⅞ inch wide, made in two parts, and joined together in the middle, the ends being narrowed to ⅝ inch and being secured with a ⅝-inch bronze buckle and standing loop. One rein billet with one ⅞-inch bronze buckle and three standing loops are securely sewed to each outer end.

The cheek piece is the same as is used on the curb bridle, model of 1906, and is fastened at the upper end to the crownpiece.

The crownpiece is ¾ inch in width and is provided at the billet end with eight holes for adjustment in fastening to the cheek piece. The lower end has a billet, ⅞-inch bronze buckle, and three standing loops for attachment to the loop bit.

HORSE COVER.
[See Figure 353.]

The parts of a complete horse cover are—

  1 cover.
  2 billets, with reinforces.
  2 buckles, with chape and reinforces.
  1 surcingle.
  1 crupper, with reinforces.

The cover is made of olive-drab cotton duck No. 9, cut and stitched as shown. It has two slits, reinforced with olive-drab cotton webbing, through which the surcingle passes. For cold climates the cover is blanket lined.

The billets are made of medium russet harness leather. Each has two reinforces of same material as billet, and is fastened to front of cover on off side, with stitching and one No. 10 brass belt rivet and bur.

Two 1-inch barrel roller buckles, brown japan finish, with chapes of medium harness leather, are secured to front of cover on near side through reinforces, each chape being fastened to cover with stitching and No. 10 brass belt rivet and bur.

The surcingle is made of olive-drab cotton duck No. 9, doubled and stitched, as shown. One 1½-inch barrel roller buckle, brown japan finish, with russet harness leather chape, is securely sewed to one end, and a billet of medium russet harness leather to the other.

The crupper is made of manila rope 0.25 inch in diameter, covered with 1½-inch olive-drab cotton webbing, and is fastened to the inside of the cover. The cover is reinforced outside and inside at the points of attachment with russet leather disks.

STIRRUP WITH GUIDON SOCKET.

The guidon socket is used with the regulation stirrup to form the guidon stirrup, and consists of—

  1 socket.
  1 top strap and reinforce.
  1 bottom strap.

The socket is made of medium russet harness leather and secured to stirrup hood by the two straps.

The top strap is made of medium russet harness leather, reinforced, sewed around socket, and riveted to hood with

two ⁷⁄₁₆-inch tubular iron rivets and caps, brown japan finish. Two ⁷⁄₁₆-inch tubular iron rivets and caps, brown japan finish, through strap and reinforce, in addition to stitching, give necessary stiffness.

The bottom strap is made of medium russet harness leather, sewed around socket, to which it is also secured with two No. 12 brass belt rivets and burs. It is fastened to the stirrup hood by two ⁷⁄₁₆-inch tubular iron rivets and caps, brown japan finish.

SADDLECLOTHS.
[See Figure 351-E.]

The dress saddlecloth for general officers is made of dark-blue cloth, Army standard, with an inner lining of buckram and an outer lining made from black enameled No. 1 duck, 54 inches wide, weighing about 24 ounces per linear yard. Saddlecloth is made in halves, neatly joined and held together by a strip of black enameled leather placed over the seam and stitched through the cloth and lining. Around the edge is a binding of black enameled leather, showing on the outside a width of ⅜ inch. The cloth is trimmed with two bands of gold lace, 1 inch wide and 1½ inches apart, the outer band next to the enameled leather. In each flank corner is placed the coat of arms of the United States surmounted by stars, indicating the rank; coat of arms dull gold, stars of dull silver. General officers of the staff corps and departments will have the insignia of the corps or department in flank corners, instead of the coat of arms.

The dress saddlecloth for permanent officers of the staff corps or departments is made of dark-blue cloth, Army standard, with an inner lining of buckram and an outer lining made from black enameled No. 1 duck, 54 inches wide, weighing about 24 ounces per linear yard. Saddlecloth is made in halves, neatly joined and held together by a strip of black enameled leather placed over the seam and stitched through the cloth and lining. Around the edge is a binding of black enameled leather showing, on the outside, a width of ⅜ inch. It is trimmed with gold lace 1 inch wide next to the enameled leather, with the insignia of the staff corps or department in each flank.

Dress saddlecloth for officers of the Engineer Corps is the same as for the other staff corps, except that the edging of gold lace is replaced by scarlet enameled leather 1 inch in width, with a piping of white ⅛ inch wide.

The dress saddlecloth for line officers is made of dark-blue cloth, Army standard, with lining made from No. 2 white cotton duck, 22 inches wide. Saddlecloth is made in halves, neatly joined and held together by a strip of black enameled leather placed over the seam and stitched through the cloth and lining. Around the edge is a binding of enameled leather (scarlet for artillery, yellow for cavalry, and light blue for infantry), showing 1 inch on the outside of the cloth. In the flank corners of the saddlecloth is placed the number of the regiment (except for officers of Coast Artillery, who will wear the metal insignia as prescribed) 2 inches in length, of enameled leather same color as binding.

Officers of the line on the General Staff, serving as aid-

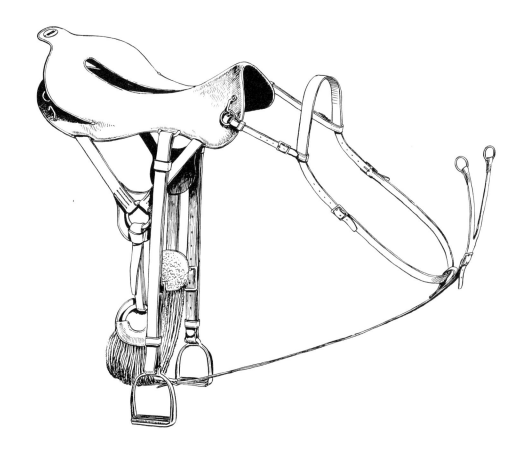

FIGURE 353. Whitman officer's saddle (russet) with breast strap and martingale. The surcingle and horse cover are shown below.

de-camps or detailed in the staff corps or departments, will have the regulation saddlecloth of their arm, except that the numbers will be replaced by the proper insignia.

Dress saddlecloths for chaplains are the same as for line officers, with edging conforming to color of arm of service with which they are serving, and having in each flank corner a white-metal cross.

Specifications for Dark-Blue Cloth, Army Standard.

Wool to be of pure long staple, American fleece wool of three-quarters and full blood mixed in equal proportions, free from shoddy, flocks, reworked wool, or any other impurities.

Width to be 54 inches.

Threads to contain not less than 66 threads of warp and 60 threads of filling in each square inch.

Weight: To weigh not less than 20 ounces to the linear yard.

Strength: To be capable of sustaining a strain of 50 pounds to the inch in width of warp, and 42 pounds to the inch in width of filling.

Color: To be of same shade of dark blue as standard sample, and to be dyed in the wool with pure indigo, best quality (unless otherwise authorized in writing by the contracting officer).

The service saddlecloth for enlisted men is made from No. 9 olive drab cotton duck and lined with No. 2 olive drab cotton duck. Saddlecloth is made in halves and held together by 1¼-inch olive drab cotton webbing placed over the seam and stitched through both thicknesses of duck. Around the edge is a binding of 1¼-inch olive drab cotton webbing showing on outside ⅝ inch. In each flank corner is placed the number of the regiment, and "Band," "N. C. S.," or the company letter, the letters and figures being of enameled leather, 2 inches high, and color to suit arm of service—yellow for cavalry, light blue for infantry, scarlet for artillery. The engineers have a scarlet letter 2 inches high outlined with a white letter, both being of enameled leather.

Service saddlecloth for all officers is made from No. 9 olive drab cotton duck, 22 inches wide, and lined with No. 2 white cotton duck, 22 inches wide. Saddlecloth is made in halves, neatly joined and held together by a strip of russet collar leather placed over the seam and stitched through both thicknesses of duck. Around the edge is a binding of russet collar leather, showing on the outside a width of ⅝ inch. In each flank corner is placed for line officers (except for officers of Engineers and Coast Artillery, who will wear the prescribed bronze metal insignia, and chaplain, who will wear a white metal cross) the number of the regiment, 2 inches high, same color as the trimmings of their respective arms; for officers of the General Staff, staff corps or departments, and aid-de-camps the proper insignia in bronze, and for general officers stars in bronze indicating their rank.

Breast Strap and Martingale.
hunting design.
[See Figure 353.]

The parts are—

1 neck strap.
2 saddle straps.
2 shoulder strap billets.
2 shoulder strap buckle pieces.
1 martingale rear end.
1 martingale buckle piece.
1 martingale front end.

All trimmings have bronze finish.

All leather parts are made from russet bridle leather, 7 to 8 ounces per square foot.

The neck strap is 1¾ inches wide and has a 1.3-inch brass ring attached to the upper side of each end by a ring chape ¾ inch in width, which is secured by stitching.

The saddle straps are ¾ inch wide and have on one end a ¾-inch center-bar brass buckle and standing loop. In assembling, the free end of strap is passed through ring of neck strap from upper side and through standing loop, being drawn as close as desired, then through ring of saddle from under side and buckled, the loop at saddle ring being held by a sliding loop.

The shoulder strap billets are ⅞ inch wide and each is secured by stitching to the ring on neck strap.

The shoulder strap buckle pieces are ⅞ inch wide and each has stitched to the upper end a ⅞-inch brass center-bar buckle with sliding loop. The lower ends are secured by stitching to a 1.81-inch brass ring, which is stitched to the martingale rear end.

The martingale rear end is 1¼ inches wide. One end has a 1¼-inch malleable iron barrel roller buckle and standing loop, through which the body is passed, forming an adjustable loop to receive the cincha. The other end forms a loop, holding the 1.81-inch ring above mentioned, which is provided with a safe, the latter and the two thicknesses of body being stitched together.

The martingale buckle piece is ⅞ inch wide. It is fastened by a ⅞-inch brass center-bar buckle to the martingale front end, and forms a loop to receive 1.81-inch ring of martingale rear end.

The martingale front end is 1⅝ inches wide. By removing from the center a piece ⅛ inch in width two parts ¾ inch wide are formed, the end of each being fastened by stitching to a 1½-inch brass ring. The other end of martingale forms a billet ⅞ inch wide, which fastens into the ⅞-inch center-bar buckle on martingale buckle piece.

Whitman Saddle.
[See Figure 353.]

A complete saddle consists of—
1 saddletree (covered).
1 set saddle trimmings (bronzed).
5 coat straps.
1 quarter strap, complete.
2 stirrup straps.
2 stirrups (German silver).
1 cincha (horse hair).

This saddle is for officers and has all exposed metal parts bronze finish.

SADDLETREE.

The parts of the saddletree are—
- 1 cantle.
- 1 pommel block.
- 2 side bars.
- 1 pommel iron.
- 1 cantle iron.
- 1 pommel strap.
- 2 stirrup-strap loops (bronzed).

The cantle is made of two pieces of poplar, fitted together with a halved joint and glued. It is fastened to the side bars with two 1¾-inch and two 1½-inch No. 12 wood screws.

The pommel block is made of poplar, placed in a form and glued to the front ends of the side bars.

Each side bar is made from one piece of selected basswood (rough size 3½ by 6⅝ by 24 inches), turned to shape and tested and gained for stirrup-strap loop, quarter straps, pommel iron, and pommel strap.

The pommel iron is made from decarbonized sheet steel 0.065 inch thick, drop-forged and fitted flush with top of pommel block and side bars, to which it is fastened with four ¾-inch No. 8 wood screws.

The cantle iron is made from decarbonized sheet steel 0.065 inch thick, pressed to shape and fastened to cantle and side bars with eight 1¼-inch No. 8 iron rivets.

The pommel strap is made of steel ⅛ by 1 inch, and formed to shape required; it fits into the under side of pommel block and side bars and is fastened with four 1½-inch No. 8 iron rivets.

The stirrup-strap loops are the same as for the McClellan saddle, and are attached to the side bars in a similar manner.

Saddletrees are made in three sizes and are measured from top of pommel in front to the slot for coat strap. The sizes and measurements are as follows:
- 11-inch measures 16 inches.
- 11½-inch measures 17 inches.
- 12-inch measures 18 inches.

The finishing and covering of the saddletree with rawhide is nearly the same as for the McClellan saddle, the boring of holes and grooving for lacing thongs being at the base of cantle only. The rawhided tree is covered with russet collar leather 6 to 7 ounces per square foot.

The top covers and rear cantle pieces are each seamed with light welts of the same leather. Two bronzed wrought-iron saddle nails 1¼ inches long, with heads ½ inch in diameter, are placed in the side bars at the base of the cantle to protect the end of the seams.

SADDLE TRIMMINGS.

A complete set includes—
- 4 1¼-inch rings.
- 4 foot staples (low) with screws.
- 2 foot staples (high) with screws.
- 2 ovals, with screw pins.
- 1 saddlebag stud, with rivets.

Placed as follows:

Two 1¼-inch rings, of cast brass, are on front end of side bars and two on rear of cantle.

The low foot staples are made of cast brass, and each is fastened with two 1-inch No. 6 brass screws, and secures a 1¼-inch ring and a coat strap.

The high foot staples are made of cast brass and are used on the rear end of side bars for attaching the saddlebags. Each is secured with two 1-inch No. 6 brass screws.

The ovals are made from sheet brass 0.028 inch thick and are placed in front and rear of cantle around slot for coat strap, the one in front being stamped with the size of saddle, and each being fastened with two ¾-inch No. 2 brass screw pins.

The saddlebag stud is made of brass and secured to the cantle iron with two ⅜-inch No. 10 brass belt rivets, being attached before the saddletree is covered with rawhide.

COAT STRAPS.

These are five in number—
- 2 for pommel, 33 inches long.
- 2 for cantle, 45 inches long.
- 1 for cantle (double), 45 inches long.

They are made from russet collar leather, 7 to 8 ounces per square foot.

The single coat straps are the same as those used on the McClellan pattern. The double coat strap is the same as two cantle straps cut from one piece of stock, except that at 6 inches from buckle end 2 inches remain uncut.

QUARTER STRAP.

This is made from medium harness leather and is not adjustable. The parts are—
- 2 pommel quarter straps.
- 2 cantle quarter straps.
- 2 quarter-strap rings, 2-inch.
- 2 quarter-strap safes.
- 2 cincha straps.

The upper ends of the quarter straps fit into the grooves gained in the side bars and each is fastened with four 1-inch No. 6 brass screws.

The lower ends form loops which hold the 2-inch quarter-strap rings and are securely sewed to the quarter-strap safes.

The quarter-strap rings are of cast brass, 2.1 inches inside diameter and of circular section 0.328 inch in diameter.

The quarter-strap safes are made from one piece of medium harness leather and are sewed with three rows of stitching to the quarter straps under the quarter-strap ring.

The cincha straps are made from russet collar leather, 7 to 8 ounces per square foot, and securely stitched to the quarter-strap ring with three rows of stitching.

STIRRUP STRAPS.

These are the same as for the McClellan saddle.

To Assemble Strap with Right or Off Stirrup.—Place the stirrup on floor with loop for stirrup strap pointing toward you. Pass the free end of strap through the loop of stirrup from the far side, rough side of leather next to the loop; grasp strap and complete the assembling as directed for the McClellan saddle.

To Assemble Strap with Left or Near Stirrup.—
Place the stirrup on floor as above described and assemble as
directed for the McClellan saddle.

STIRRUPS.

A pair of stirrups consists of—
  2 stirrup bodies.
  2 treads.

The body is of cast German silver and has the base hollowed out to receive the tread. The arch of the stirrup tapers toward the top, where it forms a loop with opening (for the stirrup strap) ¼ by 1⅜ inches on the rear side, and somewhat wider on the front, the loop being inclined to the rear. The body is polished and stamped on the bottom with the letters "U. S." and place and year of manufacture, after which it is nickel plated.

The tread is of soft rubber with top surface corrugated. It is fitted to the shape of the opening in the base of stirrup to which it is secured by three German silver rivets passing horizontally from front to rear and finished flush with outside of base.

CINCHA.

The cincha is the same as for the McClellan saddle, but has the cincha ring bronzed.

When so ordered the underside of saddle and inside of quarter-strap safes are lined with sheepskin, having wool ½ inch long.

Figure 354 shows the last type of Whitman saddle sold to officers by the Ordnance Department. The exact date of the change from nonadjustable quarter straps to adjustable ones is not known to me, but it is apparent, by the 1912 and later regulations, that the Whitman saddle was no longer considered an approved saddle for officers' field use.

Accoutrements are discussed in Ordnance Department Document No. 1719, listing horse equipments and equipments for officers and enlisted men, dated May 10, 1905, revised July 3, 1908, and published by the Government Printing Office in 1917.

REVOLVER HOLSTERS, COLT'S CALIBER .38 AND CALIBER .45, LONG AND SHORT BARREL.
[See Figure 342.]

There are three revolver holsters of the same general design. They are for the Colt's caliber .38, the Colt's caliber .45 long-barrel, and the Colt's caliber .45 short-barrel revolvers.

All of these are made of russet collar leather, weighing 9 to 9½ ounces per square foot.

The parts are—
  1 body.
  1 billet.
  1 loop.
  1 holster button, washer, and safe.
  1 ring, stud, and washer.

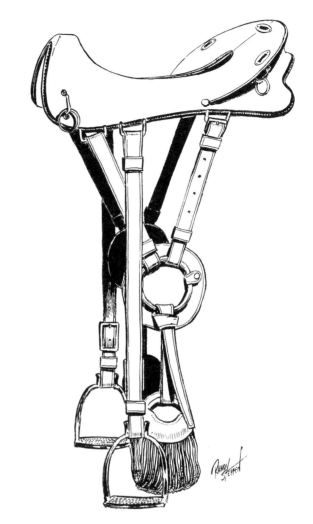

FIGURE 354. Whitman officer's saddle (ca. 1905).

The body is stamped on the front with the letters "U. S.," surrounded by an oval, and is punched near the bottom on the inside with a small hole for drainage. A bronzed button for fastening the billet is riveted to the body, the inside washer being covered by a leather safe, stitched in place. The seam at the top of the body is reinforced by a piece of leather stitched inside across the seam. A circular bottom is sewed in flush with the body, and into this is riveted an eye and ring, of bronzed brass, for attaching the elk-skin leg thongs.

The billet is fastened to the body with three No. 12 brass belt rivets, to the loop with two, and is provided with a hole and slit for button.

The loop is doubled and stitched to the body, the stitching being reinforced by three No. 12 brass rivets passing through both thicknesses and the body, and three through the inner fold and body in addition to the two which fasten it to the flap. The loop is made large enough to pass over the woven rifle cartridge belt when filled with cartridges.

CARTRIDGE BELT, MODEL OF 1903, FOR .30 CALIBER MAGAZINE
RIFLE, AND SUSPENDERS, MODEL OF 1907, FOR CARTRIDGE BELTS.

[See Figure 355-A.]

SPECIFICATIONS FOR BELTS.—Each woven cartridge belt
to be straight and 3½ inches wide, having nine pockets each,
of the required size for holding two clips, each clip containing five cartridges. Each pocket shall be woven with its top
even with the top edge of the belt body, and shall be provided with a substantial flap extending the full depth of the
pocket, or substantially to the bottom. The pockets may, in
the discretion of the department, be made with woven partitions for separating the clips. Each pocket will be fastened
to the belt body by three metallic eyelets or rivets, equally
spaced, as shown on drawing, with centers 0.28 inch from top
edge of belt, and its outer end be fastened to the pocket by a
secure and serviceable glove fastener. The fasteners must be
capable of withstanding 5,000 fastenings and unfastenings
without losing their usefulness as such. The bottom of each
pocket shall be woven to the belt body and shall for a distance
of 1 inch from the lower edge of pocket be reinforced to a
double thickness, either by interwoven linen threads or by an
extension of the flap, the raw edge of which shall be sewed by
two rows of stitching to the pocket proper. The raw edges of
the top of the flap shall be turned under and sewed. The nine
pockets must be of equal dimensions and be equally spaced
in a length 26.2 inches. At each end of the pocket section
there shall be 10.5 inches of plain webbing, the width of
which shall be the same as that of the body of the belt, to
which the belt fastener, furnished by the Ordnance Department, will be attached. Ends of billets shall be completely
incased in metal and a hook shall be attached to each end of
the belt, and two metallic eyelets shall be inserted between
adjacent pockets for the three outer pockets only, two outside
of each end pocket, and sets of two at intervals of 2 inches
therefrom toward the end of the belt, into which the hooks
may be inserted to permit the length of the belt to be adjusted, as shown in drawings. Metallic eyelets will also be
inserted in the body of the belt, near both edges, between the
adjacent pockets and outside of each end pocket. These eyelets shall be located with their centers ⅜ inch from the edge
of belt, and shall have washers on their front faces. The diameter of the flanges of these eyelets shall be not less than 0.4
inch and diameter of washers shall be not less than 0.45 inch.
For all eyelets the threads shall be separated, the eyelet then
inserted and clinched without previous forming of a hole by
the cutting of threads. All metallic eyelets shall be permanently secured in the belt without fraying it and be amply strong
to support a dead load of not less than that which may be
sustained by the fabric of which the belt is made. The interior
diameter of the hole in the eyelets shall be 0.2 inch.

Fifteen per cent of the belts, and no more, shall be made
4 inches longer than the standard belt, but the number and
position of the eyelets shall remain the same as in the standard belt except that the four inner eyelets for the end hooks
will be omitted. A tolerance of plus or minus 2 per cent will
be permitted upon the dimensions of the belt shown upon
the drawing.

SPECIFICATIONS FOR SUSPENDERS.—Each pair of suspenders for woven cartridge belts for ball cartridges, model
of 1907, shall consist of two straps crossing in the back
through a seamless drawn bronze or copper guide. The straps
shall be of folded tape or of webbing woven to shape. The
two ends at the back must be provided with hooks for attaching them to the belt. To each front end there must be attached
two branches, the upper ends of which are joined to a buckle
or other device which can be adjusted on the shoulder strap,
and the lower ends of which are provided with hooks for
attaching them to the belt. The shoulder pieces should be 2¼
inches in width where they bear on the shoulders, and be reduced in width in front and rear thereof to about 1 inch, a
tolerance of plus or minus 0.10 inch being allowed. The hooks
for attaching the suspenders to the belt must be of such size
as can be readily inserted in 0.2-inch holes in the metallic
eyelets of the belts, and each hook must sustain a pull of not
less than 100 pounds. A tolerance of plus or minus 2 per cent
will be permitted upon the dimensions of the suspenders
shown on the drawings, except where other tolerances are
prescribed.

All metal parts, including glove fasteners, eyelets, etc.,
shall be dull-finish bronze or of metal fire gilt and burnished,
and of the same shade of color as that prescribed for the buttons on the service uniforms of the United States Army.

The belts and suspenders must be well milled, thoroughly clean, free from crocking, closely shorn, water-repellant,
and free from streaks or other imperfections of dye, weave,
and finish. The thread used in these belts and suspenders
must be dyed an olive-drab color of the same standard shade
as prescribed for the olive-drab colored uniform of the United
States Army. The color must pass the tests prescribed in paragraph 6 of "Instructions to bidders and special specifications
governing the manufacture and inspection of woven rifle
cartridge belts, model of 1903, and suspenders, model of 1907,
No. 480."

The rifle cartridge-belt fastener is made in two parts,
male and female, from bronze bronzed.

To fit the belt for cavalry a ring of 0.135-inch soft brass
wire is fastened to it by a chape of russet collar leather, which
is secured by two No. 10 brass belt rivets passing through
the eyelets between the second and third pockets from the
left end.

CANTEEN STRAP.
[See Figure 355-A.]

This consists of a body, two hooks, two clips, and a canteen snap hook.

The body is made of 1-inch olive-drab webbing, three
ply, to which are fastened by brass eyelets the hooks, each
composed of a clip made from sheet brass 0.016 inch thick,
and a hook of 0.134 inch soft brass wire bronzed. The canteen snap hook is held in position by a tubular iron rivet
passing through the body of the strap.

OFFICERS' SABER BELT.
[See Figure 346.]

The parts are—

1 belt body with buckle and sliding loop.

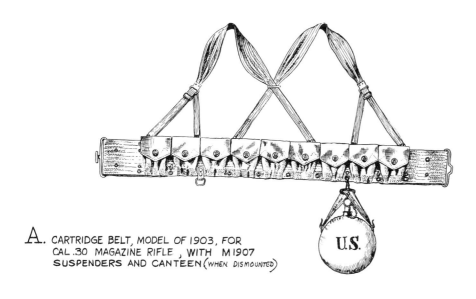

A. CARTRIDGE BELT, MODEL OF 1903, FOR
CAL .30 MAGAZINE RIFLE , WITH M 1907
SUSPENDERS AND CANTEEN (WHEN DISMOUNTED)

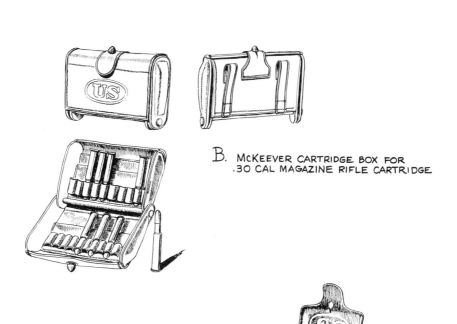

B. McKEEVER CARTRIDGE BOX FOR
.30 CAL MAGAZINE RIFLE CARTRIDGE

C. CARTRIDGE BOX FOR CAL .38 AND .45
REVOLVER AMMUNITION . BOX FOR .38
CARTRIDGE SHOWN; BOX FOR .45 CAL
DOES NOT HAVE WOOD BLOCK.

D. M 1903 CARTRIDGE BELT FOR COLT'S .38 CAL. REVOLVER

FIGURE 355. Cartridge belts and cartridge boxes.

1 officers' saber belt slide.

1 slide safe.

1 officers' saber attachment.

The belt body is made from russet collar leather 7 to 8 ounces per square foot, or of two thicknesses of pigskin stitched together. It is provided with a sliding loop of the same material and a 1¾-inch bronze center-bar buckle, bronzed, which is secured by stitching.

The belt slide is made of bronze bronzed with a loop at the lower end for hook attachment, and is provided with a safe to protect the clothing from wear.

The length of the saber belt is measured from the buckle end of belt body to the last hole, and is 3 inches shorter than the over-all measurement. Officers' saber belts are regularly made in four sizes, the proportions being as follows:

> 38 inches over all, with adjustment between 27½ and 35 inches, 35 per cent.
>
> 43 inches over all, with adjustment between 32½ and 40 inches, 53 per cent.
>
> 48 inches over all, with adjustment between 37½ and 45 inches, 10 per cent.
>
> 53 inches over all, with adjustment between 42½ and 50 inches, 2 per cent.

The officers' saber attachment consists of the following parts:

> 1 officers' hook attachment.
>
> 1 long strap.
>
> 1 short strap.
>
> 2 officers' saber-belt snap hooks.
>
> 2 buttons for officers' saber attachment.

The hook attachment consists of a hook of cast bronze riveted to a spring plate of half-hard brass, 0.049 inch thick. A loop of bronze, for attaching the straps, is inclosed in lower part of spring plate.

Each strap is made from russet collar leather 7 to 8 ounces per square foot, or from two thicknesses of pigskin stitched, and has a standing loop of same material. One end of strap is passed through loop of hook attachment and standing loop on strap, and is then passed through loop on snap hook and fastened by a brass button, bronzed, which engages in slits in the strap.

The snap hooks are made of bronze, with tongue of same material actuated by a spring made of special steel wire 0.035 inch in diameter. A lock nut is placed on hook near the swivel, so that the tongue can be locked in position after snap hook is engaged in ring of saber scabbard. The upper part of hook is riveted into the loop of swivel, which is of sheet brass 0.083 inch thick. A pin of soft-brass wire 0.134 inch in diameter is riveted through upper part of loop for attaching strap, as explained. All metal parts are bronzed.

ENLISTED MEN'S SABER BELT.
[See Figure 346.]

The parts are—

> 1 belt body with buckle and sliding loop.
>
> 1 enlisted men's saber-belt slide.
>
> 1 enlisted men's saber attachment.

The belt body is made from russet collar leather 7 to 8 ounces per square foot, with sliding loop of the same. The buckle is the same as for officers, while the belt slide differs somewhat in shape and dimensions.

Enlisted men's belts are made 38 and 47 inches over all, in equal proportions; the former with adjustment between 24½ and 35 inches, and the latter with adjustment between 33½ and 44 inches.

Belts for the enlisted men of the Hospital Corps are provided with two holes, with eyelets, to receive the double hook of the pouch for first-aid packet.

One enlisted man's saber attachment consists of the following parts:

> 1 enlisted men's hook attachment.
>
> 1 long strap with sliding loop.
>
> 1 short strap with sliding loop.
>
> 2 buttons for enlisted men's saber attachment.

The hook attachment consists of a hook of bronze riveted to a spring plate of half-hard brass 0.049 inch thick, which is slotted in lower part to receive the straps.

Each strap is made from russet collar leather 7 to 8 ounces per square foot and has a sliding loop. One end of strap is passed through the slot in hook attachment and is fastened with a No. 10 brass belt rivet; the other end is passed through the ring on saber scabbard and sliding loop, and is fastened by a brass button engaging in slits in the strap. All metal parts are bronzed.

SABER KNOTS FOR OFFICERS.
[See Figure 346.]

The parts are—

> 1 sling.
>
> 2 sling sliding loops.
>
> 1 tassel.
>
> 1 button piece.
>
> 1 button-piece sliding loop.
>
> 1 saber-knot button.

The body is made from russet collar leather 5½ to 6 ounces per square foot, cut and braided around a core of chalk line so as to form a soft, pliable cord, which is doubled, the ends being fastened to a tassel, which is made from the same leather as the body, split and rolled. The ends of the tassel are stitched through sling and wrapped with waxed shoe thread, over which russet collar leather is braided.

The button piece, made from 5½ to 6 ounce russet collar leather, secures the sling strap to the saber. It is fastened by a bronzed saber-knot button of brass fitting into slits in the loop.

SABER KNOT FOR ENLISTED MEN.
[See Figure 346.]

The parts are—

> 1 sling strap.
>
> 2 sliding loops.
>
> 1 tassel.
>
> 1 button piece.
>
> 1 saber-knot button.

The sling strap is a single flap strap, with two sliding loops, all made from 6 to 7 ounce russet collar leather. The ends are passed through a loop on the tassel and stitched together, then passed through the two sliding loops, a hole punched, and slits made for the saber-knot button, which fastens the sling strap and button piece together.

The tassel, of the same leather as the body, is slit, then made into a roll ¾ inch in diameter and wrapped with waxed shoe thread. A loop is then sewed on, after which the tassel is again wrapped with waxed thread, over which russet collar leather is braided.

The button piece, made from the same leather as the body and tassel, doubles around the guard of the saber, and is fastened to the sling strap by the saber-knot button of bronzed brass.

SPURS.
[See Figure 356-A, B.]

The parts are, for one pair—
2 spur bodies.
2 rowels.

The bodies of officers' spurs are made of polished white metal, with bar loop and stud for spur strap on each side. The rowels, made from sheet spring steel 0.049 inch thick, have 24 teeth, are 0.75 inch in diameter, and fastened into body by a rivet of soft steel wire 0.109 inch in diameter.

Spurs for enlisted men are made of bronze, with loops and studs for the spur strap. The rowels, made from soft decarbonized sheet steel 0.0625 inch thick, are 0.875 inch in diameter, with ten teeth, and are fastened into body in the same manner as those for officers.

SPUR STRAPS.
[See Figure 356-A, B.]

Officers' spur straps are made from russet collar leather 5½ to 6 ounces per square foot. They are narrowed at the ends and fitted with ⅝-inch white metal buckles.

Enlisted men's spur straps are made from russet collar leather 7 to 8 ounces per square foot, are uniform in width, and fitted with ¾-inch brass wire buckles.

CANTEEN.
[See Figure 355-A.]

The components are—
1 body.
1 neck.
1 boss.
1 cork and safety.
1 cover, olive-drab duck.
1 cover, felt.

The body, made of IX sheet tin, bright finish, is formed by a die in two pieces, which are then soldered together. A triangular loop of 0.148-inch tinned iron wire, with a clip of the same tin as the body, is soldered on each side. The neck is a single piece of white metal, soldered to the canteen by a tin boss.

The cork is 1.25 inches long, tapering from 0.9375 to 0.8125 inch in diameter, and has a cap of IX tin covering the top.

A No. 00 brass safety chain, 3 inches long, is attached to a ring of 0.095-inch brass wire, which passes around the neck. The other end is fastened to the loop of the cork pull, which

passes through the cork and is held in by a tin washer and galvanized-iron nut.

The canteen is first covered, for protection and coolness, with gray wool felt 0.25 inch thick, and over this with No. 9 olive-drab duck. The letters "U. S." are printed on the front.

MCKEEVER CARTRIDGE BOX, CALIBER .30.
[See Figure 355-B.]

The parts are—
1 front.
1 back.
1 hinge.
2 belt loops.
1 thumb piece.
1 large end, plain.
1 small end, plain.
1 large pressed end for screw driver.
1 small pressed end for screw driver.
1 button and washer.
1 hinge rod and washer.
1 large body piece.
1 small body piece.
1 large bellows piece.
1 small bellows piece.

The body is made of russet collar leather 9 to 9½ ounces per square foot, cut and stitched, as shown. The front and back, connected by a leather hinge, rotate on a bronzed brass hinge rod 0.165 inch in diameter, which is held in position by brass washers, riveted to the ends. A swell is pressed in the right-hand end of the box, across which a strap is stretched to form a recess for carrying a screw driver.

The front is stamped with the letters "U. S." and is fastened to the back at the top by a leather thumb piece, sewn to the back, which fits over a bronzed brass button riveted to the front. Two waist-belt loops are fastened to the back by stitching at the lower ends and No. 12 brass rivets at the upper.

The cartridges are held in loops of 1-inch webbing sewed to a bellows of No. 9 olive-drab duck. The bellows, by allowing the heads of the cartridges to incline forward when the box is open, facilitates their insertion and extraction.

MEAT CAN.
[Figure 356-C.]

The parts of the meat can are—
1 body.
1 cover.
1 handle.

The body, formed in a die, is made from soft decarbonized steel, 0.025 inch thick, thoroughly pickled, annealed, and capable of being drawn, without further annealing, into shape shown. After forming, the body is tinned by immersion in a bath of melted tin. A hinge for attaching the handle is riveted to the body by three ³⁄₁₆-inch No. 10 tinned iron rivets.

The cover is formed in a die from the same material used for the body, and is also tinned. For convenience in removing the cover, a D ring of 0.109-inch tinned iron wire is attached

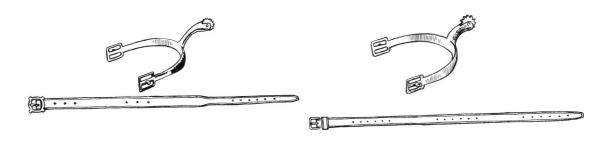

A. OFFICER'S SPUR AND SPUR STRAP
WHITE METAL, HALF-CONCEALED ROWEL

B. ENLISTED MAN'S SPUR AND SPUR STRAP
BRONZE WITH 10-POINT STEEL ROWEL

C. M1906 CUP
ALUMINUM

M1908 CUP
EXPERIMENTAL

KNIFE, FORK,
SPOON

MEAT CAN AND COVER

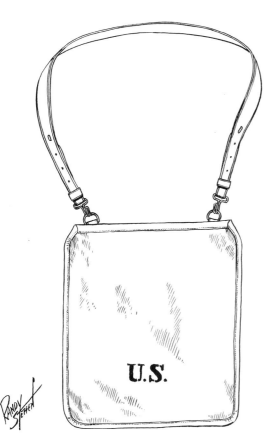

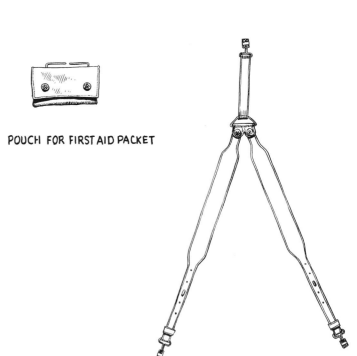

D. POUCH FOR FIRST AID PACKET

E. HAVERSACK FOR CAVALRY
WITH CARRYING STRAP

F. OFFICER'S SHOULDER BELT

FIGURE 356. Miscellaneous accoutrements (ca. 1908).

to it with a tin clip and ³⁄₁₆-inch rivet 0.134 inch in diameter.

The handle is formed from soft decarbonized steel 0.12-inch thick, then tinned and secured to the hinge by pin 0.134 inch in diameter. When the meat can is assembled, the handle folds over the cover and the end of it engages the rim of the body, holding the cover firmly in place.

CUP, MODEL OF 1908.
[See Figure 356-C.]

The parts are—
  1 body.
  1 handle.
  1 upper insulator.
  1 lower insulator.

The body is made from sheet aluminum 0.04 inch thick and drawn by two operations into a cup 4.8 inches in diameter and 2½ inches deep. The top of the cup is rolled to form a strong, stiff rim.

The handle is made from same material as the body and is completed in six operations. It is stamped with the letters "U. S." and "R. I. A." and year of manufacture. The edges are folded for stiffness and a slot is punched to receive the tines of a fork for handling cup over a fire. It is separated by fiber board insulators 0.05 inch thick from the body, to which it is fastened by three aluminum rivets of 0.15 inch diameter.

CUP, MODEL OF 1906.
[See Figure 356-C.]

The parts are—
  1 body.
  1 handle.
  1 upper insulator.
  1 lower insulator.

The body is made from sheet aluminum 0.04 inch thick and drawn by three operations into a cup 4 inches in diameter by 4.13 inches deep. The top of the cup is rolled to form a strong, stiff rim.

The handle is made from decarbonized sheet steel 0.022 inch thick in three operations. It is stamped with the letters "U. S." and "R. I. A." and year of manufacture, the edges folded for stiffness, and a slot punched to receive the tines of a fork for handling cup, after which it is aluminized. It is separated by fiber board insulators 0.05 inch thick from the body, to which it is fastened by three aluminum rivets of 0.15 inch diameter.

KNIFE.
[See Figure 356-C.]

The knife blade, blanked from special double-bevel cutlery steel, is straightened and tempered. The aluminum handles are then cast on, after which the blades are ground, polished, and tinned, the handles finally being stamped with the letters "U. S." and "R. I. A." and year of manufacture.

FORK.
[See Figure 356-C.]

The fork is blanked by three operations, after which it is formed to shape, with letters "U. S." on handle, tempered, polished, and tinned. It is then stamped with letters "R. I. A." and year of manufacture.

SPOON.
[See Figure 356-C.]

The spoon is blanked and formed with letters "U. S." on handle at a single operation, after which it is polished and tinned. It is then stamped the same as the fork.

CARTRIDGE BOX FOR CALIBERS .38 AND .45 REVOLVER AMMUNITION.
[See Figure 355-C.]

The parts are—
  1 body.
  2 end pieces.
  1 bottom reinforce.
  2 belt loops.
  1 revolver cartridge-box button and washer.
  1 block.

The body is made from a single piece of russet collar leather 5½ to 6 ounces per square foot, cut to shape by a die, after which it is stamped with letters "U. S." It is then made up with ends and bottom reinforce stitched in place. A bronzed brass button, for fastening flap, is riveted through bottom, and two waist-belt loops secured to back by stitching at the bottom and riveting at the top. A poplar block, bored for 12 cartridges and reinforced by leather to prevent splitting, is inserted in the box when used for caliber .38 cartridges.

REVOLVER LANYARD.

The parts are—
  1 body.
  1 sliding hoop.
  1 chape.
  1 bag snap hook.

For officers the body is made from russet leather 6 to 7 ounces per square foot, cut and braided around a core of chalk line so as to form a cord. The cord is doubled, provided with a sliding loop, and the ends fastened to a ⅝-inch bronzed bag snap-hook by a chape of 8 to 9 ounce russet collar leather.

For enlisted men the body is made from No. 5 olive-drab sash cord with sliding loop of leather covered with thread to match. The ends are fastened to a ⅝-inch brown japanned bag snap hook by a russet leather chape, to which they are strongly stitched.

HAVERSACK, MODEL OF 1908.
[See Figure 356-E.]

The parts are—
  1 back.
  1 reinforce.
  1 front pouch.
  1 front pouch bottom.
  1 front pouch flap.
  1 rear pouch.
  1 rear pouch bottom.
  1 salt bag.
  2 sugar and coffee bags.
  2 knife and fork pockets.

1 knife scabbard.
1 fork scabbard.
1 fastening strap.
1 buckle chape.
2 hook chapes.
2 haversack snap hooks.

The back is made from No. 4 olive-drab cotton duck. The reinforce, rear pouch, rear pouch bottom, front pouch, front pouch bottom, front pouch flap, and knife and fork pockets are made from No. 9 duck. The knife and fork scabbards are from scrap leather; the salt bag and sugar and coffee bags from 8-ounce white cotton drill, and the fastening strap, buckle, and hook chapes of olive-drab webbing.

The top edges of both pouches and the lower edge of the front pouch flap are bound with 1-inch olive-drab cotton webbing, and the flap is held down by two soft rawhide thongs.

The front pouch and bottom are sewn together and seam felled, and with fastening strap and front pouch flap is stitched to the reinforce, the latter being then stitched with a felled seam across the wider portion of back, so that the top of the haversack is covered with two thicknesses of duck, after which the edges are bound with 1-inch olive-drab cotton webbing extending an inch beyond seam.

The hook chapes are sewn on outside of back, the two haversack snap hooks being for attachment to rifle cartridge belt.

The rear pouch bottom, with buckle chape and knife pockets sewn in place, is stitched to rear pouch and seam felled after both edges of bottom have been bound with tape. These form a pouch with knife and fork pockets across the ends when stitched to inside of back. The letters "U. S." are stenciled on outside of back.

The salt and coffee and sugar bags are three in number and are provided with draw strings of No. 12 cotton chalk line, 20 inches long.

CANTEEN-HAVERSACK STRAP.

The parts are—
1 body.
2 sliding loops.
2 brass wire end hooks.
2 brass wire double hooks.

The body is cut by a die from russet collar leather 7 to 8 ounces per square foot. The ends form loops through the double hooks, and are fastened by the end hooks, which are held in place by the sliding loops. Holes in the body admit of adjustment for length. The end hooks are made of brass wire 0.148 inch in diameter. The double hooks are made of brass wire 0.134 inch in diameter and have their ends twisted through 45° to permit the strap being used with haversacks having either the old D rings or the new snap hooks.

CARTRIDGE BELT, MODEL OF 1903, FOR COLT'S .38 CALIBER REVOLVER.

SPECIFICATIONS.—Each woven belt to be straight and 2¼ inches wide, to have eight pockets, each of the required size for holding six caliber .38 revolver cartridges. Each pocket shall be provided with a substantial flap, with the outer end fastened to the pocket by a secure and serviceable glove fastener. The fasteners must be capable of withstanding 5,000 fastenings and unfastenings without losing their usefulness as such. The eight pockets must be of equal dimensions and be equally spaced in a length of 23.25 inches. At each end of the pocket section there shall be 11 inches of plain webbing, the width of which shall be the same as that of the body of the belt, to which the fastener furnished by the Ordnance Department will be attached. Ends of billets shall be completely incased in metal and a hook shall be attached to each end of the belt and two metallic eyelets shall be inserted between adjacent pockets, two outside of each end pocket, and sets of two at intervals of 2 inches therefrom toward the end of the belt, into which the hooks may be inserted to permit the length of the belt to be adjusted, as shown in drawings. For eyelets the threads shall be separated, the eyelet then inserted and clinched without previous forming of a hole by cutting of threads. All metallic eyelets shall be permanently secured in the belt without fraying it and be amply strong to support a dead load of not less than that which is sustained by the fabric of which the belt is made. The interior diameter of the hole in the eyelets shall be 0.2 of an inch.

The general specifications as to metal parts and the kind, quality, and tests of the material from which the belt is made are the same as those for the rifle cartridge belt.

The cartridge-belt fastener is similar to that of the rifle cartridge belt, except that it is the proper size for the narrow web of the revolver cartridge belt, and the inside loop of the female is straight. Where this belt is prescribed as part of the equipment for mounted men a ring of soft brass wire for saber attachment is fastened to it by a chape of russet collar leather, which is secured by two brass rivets passing through the lower edge of the belt between the second and third pockets from the left end.

POUCH, MODEL OF 1907, FOR FIRST-AID PACKET.
[See Figure 356-D.]

The parts are—
1 body.
1 double hook.

The body is made of one piece of No. 9 olive-drab cotton duck, the flap and top having double thickness for attachment of the glove fasteners and eyelets for the double hook. The latter is of half-hard brass wire 0.019 inch in diameter, passes through the eyelets, and has the ends bent into a form suitable for attaching to the cartridge belt.

SHOULDER BELT.
[See Figure 356-F.]

The parts are—
2 shoulder straps with sliding loops and end hooks.
1 rear centerpiece.
1 loop piece.
1 loop.
3 clamps.

This is made from russet collar leather 7 to 8 ounces per square foot. The shoulder straps are cut and punched with seven holes for adjustment. One end of each is doubled into a loop for the clamp, which is held to place by a sliding loop, and has an end hook of soft brass wire 0.148 inch in diameter fastened by two No. 14 brass belt rivets. The other end is attached to the loop piece by a No. 10 brass belt rivet passing through a No. 151 brass eyelet.

The loop is of cast bronze and joins the rear centerpiece to the loop piece, the latter being stitched across close to loop. A clamp is secured by stitching to the other end of the rear centerpiece.

This belt is made from pigskin when so requested.

WAR DEPARTMENT,
    OFFICE OF THE CHIEF OF ORDNANCE,
          Washington, July 3, 1908.
May 10, 1905.
Revised July 3, 1908.
Form No. 1719.

The next 6 pages of illustrations show the equipments covered by the preceding descriptions on the mounts of both officers and enlisted men, equipped for garrison duty, and packed for duty in the field.

About the time the Springfield Model 1903 rifle was issued to cavalry, the position of the rifle on the field pack was changed from the near side to the off side of the saddle, and the position of the saber was also reversed. Other items of the pack were also changed from their positions on the saddle in the 1890's, and are shown as regulations prescribed them to be.

Figure 357 shows an officer in service uniform wearing the saber, as regulations prescribed, and riding the Whitman officer's saddle. The bridle on his horse is the 1906 experimental bridle with double reins to bit and bridoon.

Figures 358 and 359 show troopers in service dress equipped for garrison duty. They ride the Model 1904 McClellan saddle. Bridles are the Model 1902, and saddlecloths are as described in the 1905 equipment publication.

Figure 360 illustrates the field dress and equipment of a field officer. He rides the Whitman saddle, packed according to regulations with his field equipment. The bridle on his horse is the issue Model of 1902.

Figures 361 and 362 illustrate the proper uniforms and equipment for enlisted men for field duty. The 1904 McClellans are packed in the prescribed manner for this period.

While the rifle scabbard and saber remained as shown in this group of illustrations for use with the McClellan saddle until the late 1920's, other items of equipment were shifted to various parts of the pack from time to time.

With the introduction of the Model 1912 horse equipments for extensive field trial, the field pack and most other articles of horse equipment were completely changed.

The Model 1909 cavalry bridle, used only in limited numbers before 1916 or 1917, is shown on Figure 363. Except for the method of attaching the bridoon or snaffle bit to the cheeks of the headstall, it is identical to the Model 1902 headstall, with the Model 1909 curb bit and the Model 1909 snaffle bit.

The first complaints registered against the McClellan saddle seemed to have come right after the Civil War. Ever since then officers had growled and grumbled about the McClellan, several times loud enough and in numbers large enough to prompt the convening of boards whose purpose was to recommend a replacement for the service saddle of the McClellan pattern. This happened in 1879 and in 1884. But economy, and especially the large number of McClellans left over from the war and in storage, forestalled adoption of any other pattern.

The clamor for a change between 1885 and 1911 must have increased considerably, for the 1911 Cavalry Equipment Board went to work with intense vigor and seriousness. Captain Davis' article ("The New Cavalry Equipment," *Journal of the United States Cavalry Association*, September, 1912) reveals that this board

had before it some three or four thousand documents representing the opinions and recommendations of hundreds of officers of the mounted service. It had also, for inspection, the horse equipment of the following nations: Great Britain, Germany, France, Russia, Austria, Italy, Spain, Holland, Denmark, Norway, Sweden, Belgium, Switzerland, Japan, and Mexico. Supplementing the Board's advantage in actually inspecting these equipments, were the reports on foreign cavalry equipment, including photographs, drawings, compilations of statistics, etc., provided by the American military attachés at London, Berlin, Paris, St. Petersburg, Vienna, Tokyo, Peking, Buenos Aires, Chile, and Peru. Further evidence was found in the proceedings of earlier boards on cavalry equipment notably those of 1884, 1878, 1874, of 1884, 1878, 1874, 1872, 1859, 1857, and 1847. These documents constitute the main portion of the recorded history of American cavalry equipment. Consultation was also had with experienced and successful business firms and manufacturing institutions engaged in the production and sale of first-class saddlery and kindred articles. These men of commerce, were as a rule quite eager to meet the government's representatives more than half way and gave many valuable suggestions. In

FIGURE 357. First lieutenant, Seventh Cavalry (ca. 1906), in service uniform and equipped for garrison duty under arms.

FIGURE 358. Corporal, Fifth Cavalry (ca. 1906), in service uniform and equipped for garrison duty under arms. Near side.

FIGURE 359. Private, Fifth Cavalry (ca. 1906), in service uniform and equipped for garrison duty under arms. Off side.

218

FIGURE 360. Major of cavalry (ca. 1906), in service uniform and with full equipment for field service.

FIGURE 361. Private, Seventh Cavalry (ca. 1906), in service uniform and with full pack for duty in the field. Near side.

220

FIGURE 362. Sergeant, Seventh Cavalry (ca. 1906), in service uniform and with full pack for duty in the field. Off side.

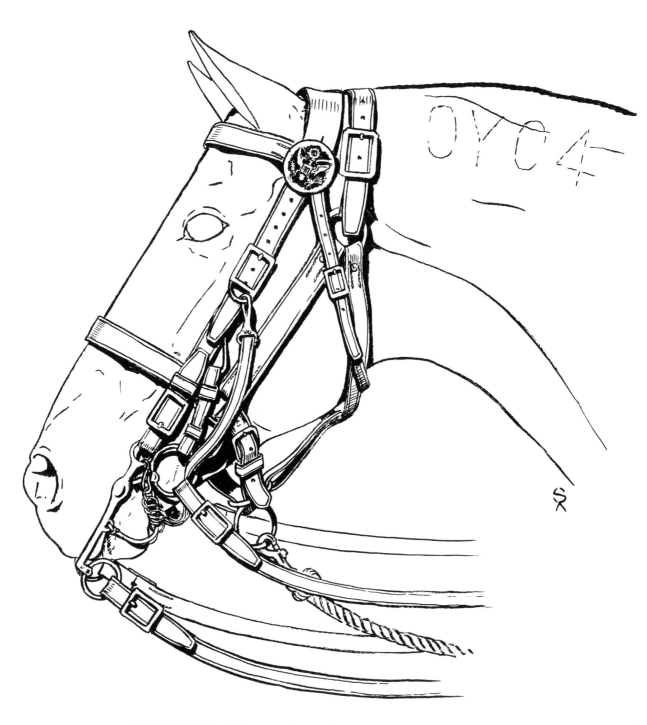

FIGURE 363. Model 1909 cavalry bridle with link strap and Model 1904 halter.

its actual work of design and development of equipment, the Board had at its disposal the resources of the personnel and plant of the Rock Island Arsenal and the active and generous support of the Chief of Ordnance.

Captain Davis, a member of this board, as mentioned earlier, admits that the design of the saddle itself was the most difficult problem they had before them. The selection and development of the rifle-carrier pattern proved to be almost as difficult, although basically it was influenced by the British rifle bucket then in service.

The 1912 saddle, with its adjustable sidebars to accommodate itself to the back of any troop horse whose size and shape was prone to change with his physical condition throughout a long march or demanding campaign, was not original with this board. Both the Campbell and Jones saddles submitted to the 1854 and 1859 boards had this feature, although each was accomplished in completely different ways that proved unsatisfactory for cavalry use. Great Britain, the Netherlands, Austria, and Russia had experimented with adjustable saddles.

The self-adjusting feature of the new United States cavalry saddle was accomplished by joining the sidebars to the bases of the pommel and cantle arches by hinges instead of the usual rigid joints. For the first time since 1847, the American service saddle went uncovered by rawhide.

The general form of the new saddle was much like that of an English-type riding saddle, and it was felt that such a saddle would promote generally better horsemanship than former patterns. Heavy wooden stirrups with the unwieldy leather hoods were replaced by open steel stirrups, and an English-type stranded girth, whose position on the horse could be adjusted by a method taken from the English, took the place of the hair cinch on the McClellan.

A pattern for enlisted men, termed the service saddle, and a modified version for officers were developed. In addition, completely new and different appendages for the field pack and the arms of the trooper appeared.

On October 5, 1914, the Ordnance Department published Document No. 1715, a manual titled, *Description and Directions for Use and Care of Cavalry Equipment, Model of 1912*. The descriptions of the 1912 equipments that follow here are from that manual. Illustrations were drawn from saddles in the Quartermaster Museum at Fort Lee, Virginia, from

specimens in the author's collection, and from the photographic illustrations in the above-cited ordnance manual.

It was the serious intention of the Ordnance Department to abolish the McClellan saddle and replace it throughout the service with the Model 1912 equipments. Substantial numbers of the new pattern were manufactured and issued to some troops of the various regiments. Production and procurement of the McClellan saddle and its related equipments were halted in anticipation of the changeover.

When the so-called "punitive expedition" after Pancho Villa was undertaken (1916), a large number of the 1912 equipments outfitted the troopers and mounts of some of the units led by General Pershing, and the rigors of a deadly serious campaign under the most exacting and devastating conditions revealed defects that prevented the new-pattern saddle and equipments from being universally adopted for all U.S. Cavalry.

Ordinarily less space would be devoted to equipment never officially adopted, but the push for a change from the McClellan was so serious in the case of the 1912 equipments that it is felt a comprehensive coverage is necessary.

The following text and illustrations describe the equipments fully. Text is from the above-cited manual.

DESCRIPTION AND DIRECTIONS FOR USE AND CARE OF CAVALRY EQUIPMENT, MODEL OF 1912.

CAVALRY BRIDLE.
[See Figure 364.]

This article of equipment is a combination of a curb bridle, bridoon bridle, and halter, and is intended to serve as a bridle both in garrison and in the field. In the latter instance it is also used as a halter. It is not intended to be used as a stable halter in garrison, but should be kept by the trooper to whom issued on the peg with the rest of his equipment. A stable halter is provided for stable and corral use in garrison, and the bridle can thus always be kept presentable.

The bridle consists of the following essential parts:

A *cheek piece*, which is a plain strap of 9½ to 10½ ounce bridle leather 1 inch wide and 78 inches long. This strap passes twice over the head of the horse, thus forming a long loop on each side of the head. At the bottom point of each of these loops the noseband is suspended from the cheek piece by means of the noseband slides. The cheek piece is adjusted to length by means of a buckle and six holes on the near side of the bridle just below the brow band.

A *brow band*, of medium harness leather 18 inches long and 1⅜ inches wide in the middle and tapering to ⅞ inch

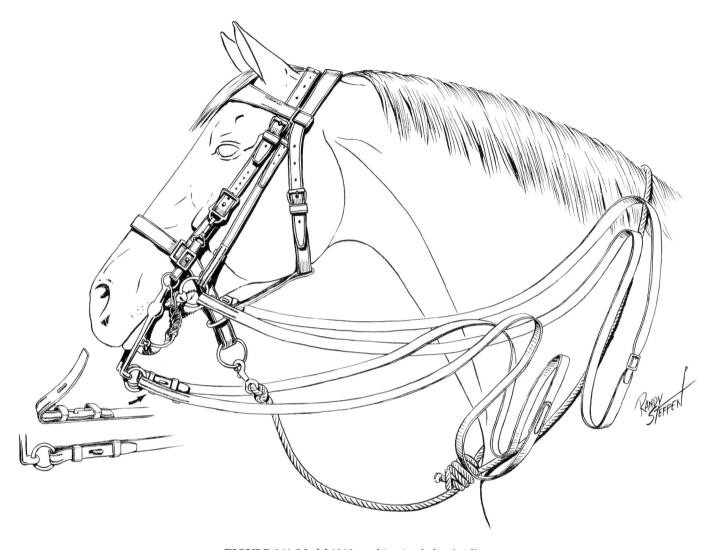

FIGURE 364. Model 1912 combination halter-bridle.

wide at each end, where loops 2¼ inches long are stitched to encircle the cheek piece, bridoon crown piece, and throat latch on each side of the head. Onto these loops are slipped ⅞-inch brass-wire loops which separate the cheek piece from the throat latch and bridoon crown piece.

The *throat latch*, a plain strap of medium harness leather 1 inch wide and 43⅝ inches long, passes up through the loops in the brow band in rear of the cheek piece and directly over the bridoon crown piece and down under the throat of the horse, passing through the upper loop in the throat strap, and ending in a common buckle on the near side, where six holes are punched for adjustment.

A *nose band*, of medium harness leather 41 inches long and 1⅛ inches wide, made into an endless band by a 5½-inch stitched lap. This band is suspended from the cheek piece on each side by passing through the noseband slide, and in the rear it passes twice through the 2³⁄₁₆-inch small iron

ring in the lower end of the throat strap and once through the similar ring for attaching the halter tie rope.

A *throat strap*, of medium harness leather ⅞ inch wide, about 18 inches long, folded upon itself twice so as to form a billet 6 inches long of three thicknesses sewed together, with 1-inch loop for the throat latch at its upper end and a 2³⁄₁₆-inch small iron ring at its lower end, which ring passes over the looped rear end of the noseband.

A *bridoon crown piece*, a plain strap of collar leather, 7 to 8 ounces, 25⅛ inches long and ¾ inch wide, with five holes at each end. This strap passes up through the rear loops in the brow band and lays directly under the throat latch, to which it is stitched for a distance of 1 inch on the top to secure it in position.

Two bridoon straps, of 6 to 7 ounce collar leather ¾ inch wide and 13⅝ inches long. A buckle in the upper end of each strap secures it to the bridoon crown piece on either side.

224

The lower end of each strap passes through the ring of the bridoon bit and back through two standing loops (sewed to the strap above the bit) and over a stud hook on the side next to the animal.

Two bit straps, each a plain strap of 7 to 8 ounce collar leather ⅝ inch wide, 10⅜ inches long, with a hole in the center and one 9/16 inch from each end. This strap carries at its center the bit strap retainer (a double loop with a stud hook in the center bar). The two ends of the strap double back and fasten over the stud hook, so that the strap when assembled forms two loops, the upper one carrying a ⅝-inch snap hook and the lower loop passing through the upper loop in the curb bit.

The snap hook engages in the lower loop of the cheek slide. These slides, one on either side of the bridle, are adjustable on the cheek piece by 6 holes in the cheek piece.

The *halter tie rope* is a plain manila rope ½ inch in diameter and 100 inches long; at one end an eye splice is formed by means of which a bronze swivel bolt snap is attached, which snaps into the 2³⁄₁₆-inch small iron ring on the rear of the noseband.

The *bridoon reins* are of 7 to 8 ounce collar leather ⅞ inch wide and cut 57¾ inches long. Three and one-fourth inches from the bit ends of the reins a 4½-inch lap is stitched onto the inside (flesh side) of the reins. Approximately midway on this reinforcing piece is a stud hook pointing to the rear, and on each side of the hook is a standing loop. Two and one-fourth inches from the extreme bit end of the reins a hole with slit is punched, so that to assemble the rein to the bit ring the end is passed through the ring under the first standing loop, the stud hook passed through the hole in the rein, and the end carried on under the rear standing loop; the reinforcing piece above described is sufficiently long to give two thicknesses of leather where it loops through the bit ring.

The rear ends of the bridoon reins are connected by a ⅝-inch buckle.

The *curb reins* are of 7 to 8 ounce collar leather ¾ inch wide and cut 55¼ inches long. The method of attachment at the bit ring is the same as for the bridoon reins. The reins are stitched together at the bight with a 1½-inch lap, with rounded ends skived down. The reins assembled carry a sliding loop ⅜ inch wide just in front of the bight.

The *bridoon* is the model of 1909 bit, which has been revised to use a 2¼-inch ring in place of a 2-inch, and is now made of 27 per cent nickel steel.

The *curb bit* is the present model of 1909 bit of 27 per cent nickel steel.

The *curb chain* is model of 1912 and differs from former models in that it is a single twist chain composed of 15 links of 27 per cent nickel steel 5⁄32-inch wire. When issued with bit the off curb hook is brazed together, thus making the chain a part of the complete bit.

The *lip thong* is of soft rawhide, medium weight, 18 inches wide by 14¼ inches long.

To fit the bridle, unsnap, unbuckle, and remove all bit straps, and first adjust the halter so that the noseband will stand at the desired height. To do this unbuckle the cheek strap, and then lengthen or shorten cheek strap and distribute the gain or loss on both sides of headstall, so that the cheek slides that support bit straps will stand at the same level. Punch new holes, if necessary, in noseband for the noseband slides. Wet the leather in the vicinity of the cheek loop thoroughly and shape snugly by pressure or blows; the cheek will then remain smoothly in position. Once the halter is adjusted to a particular horse, do not change it from that adjustment for the bits, but adjust them to proper height in mouth by means of the adjustment provided for the cheek slides. The bridoon is readily adjusted by its buckles. Always remove bit and bridoon before taking off halter. Never try to put on halter with bits attached to it. To secure halter tie, pass end around neck loosely, lay a double turn of about 6 inches in length along standing part, loop to the front, and free end to the rear, wind the free end three or four times about both loop and standing part, thrust free end through loop and draw tight.

In case it becomes necessary to replace the snap hook, or the rope itself, proceed as follows: Pass the end of the rope through the eye of the snap, unravel about 7 inches of the end, place the eye of the snap close to the unraveled strands, open a strand on the standing portion of rope near to eye, pass middle strand, No. 2, of unraveled portion through opening on standing part and draw tight. Next untwist the strand at the left of the middle one, pass No. 1 strand through the opening and draw snug. Now turn the rope over, untwist the remaining strands, pass No. 3 strand through opening, and draw snug. Now draw the strands more snugly against the standing part of the rope and, commencing with either one of the three strands, pass each one in turn, as before, from right to left, between its mates, following the twist of the rope, until the operation has been performed three times. Now place the rope on the floor and roll it under foot until the splice is smooth, then neatly trim away useless ends.

To still further finish this splice, wrap it throughout its length toward the snap with shoe thread, well waxed, then return to starting point by passing needle and thread between strands at each one-half inch, and finally secure all ends snugly. If preferred, this eye splice may be made up without passing it through the eye of the snap bolt. After completion, pass the free end of the tie rope through the snap hook eye and then through the eye splice and draw up snugly. The tie rope shown in the cut of the bridle is assembled in this way:

To finish free end of rope tie, use the Daly wrap[1] as follows: Untwist the strands for about 7 inches, then take a single cord of each strand and untwist to the same point. Now take No. 1 cord from the left, and lay it across the nearer side of the rope just below the junction of the untwisted portions, and lay No. 2 cord over No. 1 cord. Now carry No. 2 cord well to the farther side of the rope out of the way.

Bring No. 3 cord over No. 2 cord, pass No. 3 cord under No. 1 cord, between it and the rope near the point where it leaves the rope, and draw all three cords snugly. This operation leaves the strands standing upward and the cords downward, the strands thus being secured in the center. Now pass

[1] So named after Chief Packer Henry W. Daly, who first introduced its detailed description into military works.

each cord from right to left between the twisted strands of the rope itself until each has been so passed through for three times, precisely as was done with the unraveled strands in making the snap splice above. Finish in a manner similar to that there described, and cut off the unraveled strands about ½ inch above grasp of cord.

This wrapping may be still further finished by waxed thread as described under the snap splice.

To tie the horse to a hitching post or rail, never tie by the reins, but slip the loop of the rope tie over the horse's head, pass the doubled end of loop through the ring or once or more times around the rail; unsnap the hook and pass it through the free end of the loop, pulling taut; then snap hook to halter ring; adjust the reins so that they will not catch on the post or be trampled under foot. To untie, reverse the process.

No link is provided for this bridle. To secure horses of Nos. 1 and 2 for fighting on foot, tie them by the bridoon reins, each to the halter ring of the horse on its left.

Small detachments of 2 to 8 men, and larger bodies at times, can secure their horses advantageously by "coupling" them, as this eliminates the necessity of horse holders. To couple the horses each set of two men dismount and bring their horses close together, near side to near side, head to croup. Then each man makes fast the bridoon reins of the other to the attaching strap of the saber carrier as tight as possible with a slip knot. The horses can then only circle round.

The Service Saddle.
[See Figure 365.]

The saddle consists of the following essential parts:

A *frame* of pressed steel ⅟₁₆ inch thick. This frame has pressed into it three ribs running longitudinally around the frame for stiffness.

Two *pommel hinges*, one right, one left, the upper half of each hinge being of bronze riveted to the steel frame. The lower half of each hinge, of cast aluminum, is bolted to the wooden side bars.

Two *pommel* hinges, one right, one left, the upper half of each riveted to the steel frame and the lower half bolted to the wooden side bars. These hinges are so shaped and located that the axis of the pommel and cantle hinge lies in a straight line on each side of the saddle, thus allowing free movement of the side bars around this line as an axis.

Two *stirrup-strap loops*, each suspended from the frame by a steel strap which is riveted to the frame. The loops are shown clearly in Plate II and are provided at the rear ends with a safety loop for holding the stirrup strap in the stirrup-strap loop, but which will allow the strap to slip out in case of a violent pull to the rear, as in case of a fall in which the rider's foot might catch in the stirrup to drag him. The safety loop is convenient also for removing the stirrup straps for cleaning, etc. This loop should be kept clean and oiled frequently.

Two *rear girth strap loops* riveted rigidly to the frame in rear of the stirrup strap loop.

Two *forward girth strap loops*, suspended from the for-

ward end of the frame by a metal strap riveted to the frame.

Two *cantle loops*, one right and one left, for rifle carrier, boot and saber carrier. These are bronze loops riveted to the frame just outside of the cantle hinges.

Two *wooden side bars*, one right and one left, shaped on the under side to fit the horse's back. These are of basswood, natural finish and varnished.

One *cantle roll support*, a casting of aluminum riveted to the cantle of frame and extending out to the rear having down through it a slot for roll strap.

A *ground seat of sole leather* formed in a press to fit the metal frame accurately and riveted to same.

Two *pieces of straining webbing*, passing under the sole leather ground seat from cantle to pommel, securely riveted to the steel frame and stretched so as to support the leather seat.

A *seat*, of 6 to 7 ounces collar leather, embossed to imitate pigskin, pressed in a die to the exact shape of the ground seat. This seat passes up over the aluminum cantle roll support and around the cantle is stitched so a facing leather underneath the steel frame and forward from the cantle is stitched to the jockeys by a welted seam, the jockeys being of similar material to the seat. The seat is also stitched to the under facing of the pommel.

Two *skirts*, one right, one left, cut to shape, and embossed to imitate pigskin, made of medium harness leather riveted to the steel saddle frame. The skirt has a loop riveted to it near its upper forward corner, through which passes a strap of the pommel pocket, thus holding the latter down in its proper position.

The *side bar pads* are of olive-drab felt, about ½-inch thick. These pads are cut to the shape of the under sides of the side bars. A piece of light collar leather is stitched to the forward and rear ends of the pads forming pockets, these pockets fitting over the side bars and holding the pads snugly to the side bars. Small straps are provided to facilitate removal of the pads from the bars when necessary.

Stirrup straps.—These are of light harness leather, 1⅜ inches wide and 56½ inches long over all when complete. At one end is a 1⅜-inch bronze center-bar buckle sewed to the strap by a 2-inch pointed lap, flesh side out. The free end is pointed and punched with 12 oblong holes 1¼ inches apart, each hole being numbered.

The *stirrups* are issued in two sizes, varying in width ¼-inch.

Girth-strap adjusters [see Figure 372].—These pieces are designed to vary the location of the girth relative to the saddle. The adjuster consists of a piece of 7 to 8 ounce collar leather a little wider than the girth and about 12 inches long. This is reinforced for the upper 6 inches with a back of similar leather stitched to the front around the edges. There are four loops formed in the adjuster by slots cut in the outer piece; between each pair of loops is riveted a ⅗₁₆-inch bronze stud. Each girth strap passes through a pair of these loops, and the stud enters one of the holes in the girth strap.

The *girth* is made of olive drab, hard laid No. 60 cotton seine twine woven in the center and at each end near the

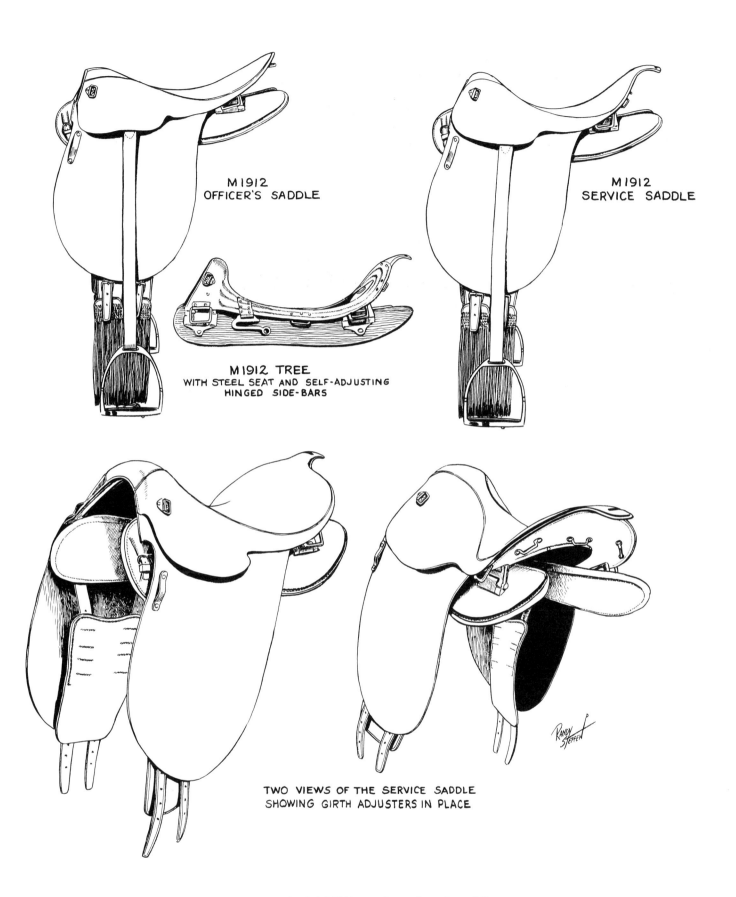

M 1912
OFFICER'S SADDLE

M 1912
SERVICE SADDLE

M 1912 TREE
WITH STEEL SEAT AND SELF-ADJUSTING
HINGED SIDE-BARS

TWO VIEWS OF THE SERVICE SADDLE
SHOWING GIRTH ADJUSTERS IN PLACE

FIGURE 365. Model 1912 experimental cavalry saddle.

THE HORSE SOLDIER, 1881–1916

buckles with No. 16 olive drab cotton seine twine. There are two buckles at each end of special design. The upper ends of these special buckles are 1 9⁄16-inch roller buckles, and the lower ends of the buckles are widened to take the strands of the girth. The forward buckle on each side takes 17 strands and the rear buckle 18 strands, the strands being in one continuous piece, making two half turns and a half hitch each time it passes through the loop of a buckle.

The woven center band of the girth consists of eight rows of chain stitching, and stitched upon this band is a chape of leather carrying a 1¼ by ¾ inch buckle of 0.18-inch soft brass wire. This buckle points to the rear and secures the carrier strap, elsewhere described.

Two double-buckle, *pommel coat straps* and three single-buckle, *cantle coat straps* are issued for use in packing the saddle. These straps are ¾ inch wide, of 7 to 8 ounce collar leather.

The cantle straps are each 20 inches long. The pommel straps are 27½ inches long, the second strap being sewed on at a point 17⅜ inches from the pointed end and extending equally with the strap proper.

For the purpose of property accountability these straps are considered as a part of the saddle complete.

The saddle is made in two sizes, 15 and 16 inches, measured on the frame from the rear face of the pommel arch to the front face of cantle arch.

DIRECTIONS FOR USE AND CARE.

Although this saddle is made to withstand severe treatment, it is recommended that it be subjected to no greater degree of neglect and abuse than circumstances may require. Its beauty and finish will amply warrant the best of care. To saddle, place it upon the blanket so that the front edge of the side bar approaches closely to the shoulder blade without pressing upon it. The saddle will tend to remain in that position and will give little trouble by shifting. The saddle adjusts itself automatically to the horse's back, in so far as the bearing surfaces of the side bars are concerned, and no adjustment in this respect is required. This automatic feature is brought about by applying all weight that comes upon the side bars through their center of rotation, thus leaving the side bar of the loaded saddle entirely free to adapt itself to the horse's back. In order to preserve this freedom, no attachments of any kind should be placed on the side bar other than as issued, and no weight borne by the saddle should be permitted to rest upon the side bars, except as transmitted to them through their proper hinges. The cantle roll support and straps have been devised especially to raise the roll and keep all weight off the surface of the side bars.

The girth should ordinarily be about 4 inches in rear of the point of the elbow, varying somewhat with the conformation of the horse. It is readily adjusted in this respect by the girth-strap adjusters [see Figure 372]. To move the girth relatively forward, shorten the front girth straps, or lengthen the rear girth straps, or both. To move the girth relatively to the rear, reverse this method. By this means the saddle may be held in different positions if found desirable. Habitually the studs should be in the corresponding holes in both front

and rear straps. A variation of one hole is usually sufficient to set the saddle forward or back to conform to the needs of an ill-shaped horse or a sore back. Three lengths of girth are issued, to wit, 28, 32, and 36 inches. Considerable latitude is also allowed on the girth straps for lengthening and shortening. It is desirable, however, that the proper length of girth be obtained, rather than to try and fit all horses with a single length. Habitually the buckles of the girth on either side should rest upon the corresponding girth-strap adjuster. This is designed to act as a safe to these buckles and prevent their injuring the horse. A sufficient number of holes is provided in the girth straps to permit of the lowering the adjusters to serve this purpose.

When not needed, the coat straps should be disposed of as follows: The double buckle straps may be either removed and placed within the pommel pockets or, if the latter are worn on the saddle, the free ends of the double buckle straps may be passed through their usual staples above the pommel pockets, from rear to front, flesh side up, thence forward, down in front of pommel-pocket gusset, under pommel-pocket attaching strap, and back to buckles, drawn up snugly, and buckled to both buckles; the remaining single buckle coat straps may be either rolled or twisted as heretofore on the McClellan saddle.

The stirrups are attached by loops that permit their ready removal from the saddle. This is done rather for reasons of convenience than of safety. If the latch fails to open readily with the fingers, put a thong through its eye and pull on the thong. The stirrups are issued dark colored and are not to be brightened by polishing. If rust gathers upon them, remove it by an oiled rag. The stirrup straps are purposely placed with flesh side out—this prolongs their life. They are worn with the buckles drawn up against the safety loops on saddle, buckles on outside.

When unsaddling in the field, fold the skirts and carrier straps with their attachments under the saddle before placing it on the ground.

In garrison the saddle should be hung on a bracket sufficiently wide so that the saddle rests on its side bars. If a narrower support is used, the saddle will rest on the low point in its leather seat and soon become badly misshapen.

SADDLE BLANKET.

To fold the saddle blanket, proceed as follows:

The blanket, after being well shaken, will be folded into six thicknesses, as follows: Hold it well up by the two corners, the long way up and down; double it lengthwise (so the fold will come between the "U" and "S"), the folded corner (middle of blanket) in the left hand; take the folded corner between the thumb and forefinger of the right hand, thumb pointing to the left; slip the left hand down the folded edge two-thirds its length and seize it with the thumb and second finger; raise the hands to the height of the shoulders, the blanket between them extended; bring the hands together, the double fold falling outward; pass the folded corner from the right hand into the left hand, between the thumb and forefinger; slip the second finger of the right hand between the folds, and seize the doublefolded corner; turn the left

228

(disengaged) corner in, and seize it with thumb and fore-finger of the right hand, the second finger of the right hand stretching and evening the folds; after evening the folds grasp the corners and shake the blanket well in order to smooth the folds; raise the blanket and place it between the chin and breast; slip the hands down halfway, the first two fingers out-side; the other fingers and thumb of each hand inside; seize the blanket with the thumbs and first two fingers; let the part under the chin fall forward; hold the blanket up, arms ex-tended; even the lower edges; seize the middle points between the thumbs and forefingers; and flirt the outside part over the right arm; the blanket is thus held before placing it on the horse.

THE COOLING STRAP.
[See Figure 374.]

This strap is made of olive-drab webbing, is $87\frac{1}{2}$ inches long and is fastened with a tongueless bar buckle. The horse's back should not, when heated, be immediately exposed, after unsaddling, to the hot sun or to the cool air. The saddle blanket should be left upon it for a reasonable period. To keep the blanket properly in place, the cooling strap has been provided. When not in use, fold the strap carefully and re-place it in the compartment therefor in the rear of the off pommel pocket.

THE RIFLE CARRIER BOOT.
[See Figure 366-A, B.]

This piece of equipment has two essential parts—(1) a *leather bucket* in which the butt of the rifle fits quite snugly, and (2) a *standing part*, which supports the bucket and serves to attach the whole boot to the saddle.

As will be seen from the cuts, the bucket is a flask-shaped cup about 9 inches high. The body is of 7 to 8 ounce collar leather and has a sole-leather lining. Between the lining and outside there are two flat steel springs so shaped and located as to cause the flat sides of the boot to press moderately against the sides of the rifle butt, thus steadying it and preventing excessive movement. The bottom of the bucket is of sole leather, oval shaped, and pressed into the form of a shallow cup, the sides of which are riveted to the bucket sides by 24 brass belt rivets with burs. There is a bottom lining of gray felt $\frac{1}{2}$ inch thick to deaden the pounding of the rifle butt.

The standing part of the boot consists of a stiff body about $17\frac{1}{2}$ inches long and varying in width from 4 to 6 inches, made up of two thicknesses of bridle leather $9\frac{1}{2}$ to $10\frac{1}{2}$ ounces, stitched together all around the edges and hav-ing between them a thin sheet steel spring of approximately the same shape for stiffness. In addition to this spring there is a thin cast aluminum alloy reinforce piece for added strength at the bottom where the bucket is attached. The at-taching strap, a plain strap of heavy harness leather, is riveted onto the top of the standing part, then passes upward through a loop near the near cantle hinge of the saddle, back down to a stud in the back of the standing part where adjustment is obtained, thence on downward to the carrier strap which passes under the horse.

The bucket is attached to the standing part by means of a swivel on the lower end of the standing part which engages with a staple riveted into the bottom of the bucket. The whole weight of the rifle and bucket rests on this swivel. The bucket is maintained in an upright position by a retaining strap which is riveted into the wall of the bucket but is held to the standing part by friction only, so that if the bucket is violently forced away from the standing part, as in case of a man falling from his horse on the near side, the retaining strap will slip out of the standing part and allow the bucket to swing freely from the swivel.

In order to obtain sufficient friction on the retaining strap it passes up between the front and back leathers of the stand-ing part for a distance, then doubles back on itself under a metal spring loop which holds the strap firmly enough to maintain the bucket upright unless an abnormal force is used to free it.

This article of equipment supports the rifle while it is on the saddled horse. Before "Standing to horse" the trooper at-taches his rifle to his belt by passing the muzzle up through the belt ring and engaging the snap hook of the belt ring strap into the trigger guard. [See Figure 368.] To insure that the trigger guard screws may not work out due to this meth-od of slinging the rifle to the belt, tighten the trigger guard screws periodically.

At "Stand to horse," the rifle being slung to the belt, the trooper then has both hands free to use for any purpose. Being at "Stand to horse," upon any preparatory command, except for mounting or linking horses, at once unsling rifle from belt ring and take position of "Order arms," removing bridoon reins from horse's neck and passing right arm through them, if necessary. If the command is for linking horses, link first, and then unsling rifle. To mount, proceed as though without rifle. [See Figure 368.] When seated in saddle, with left hand grasp rifle at bolt, barrel to the front, slip butt of the rifle into the bucket, steadying the latter with left foot if desired, and take the position of the trooper mounted. To dismount, at preparatory command, seize the rifle with left hand at the bolt, give it a quick, forcible pull, lifting butt from the bucket, and let rifle hang from the belt. After this preparation dismount as though without rifle, except that as the right foot passes over the croup, bring it beside the left foot, still in the stirrup, and make a slight pause. This permits rifle to come to rest in a vertical position and prevents its unnecessary swinging as trooper descends to the ground.

The rifle carrier is fastened to the saddle horse by passing the end of the attaching strap downward through the loop on near cantle hinge, and securing by its proper stud and loop on back side of standing portion of the boot. The free end of this strap below the stud forms a depending billet which at-taches to the near buckle of the carrier strap. The boot is adjusted to the particular trooper by placing him on the saddle horse, his rifle in the bucket, and raising or lowering the boot to suit his convenience. [See Figure 366-C.] The retaining strap is purely a safety device. In case the trooper should be thrown toward the near side, the retaining strap will be forcibly pulled from its loop, the bucket will fall and release the rifle butt. [See Figure 366-B.] The trooper will thus be disengaged from his horse. When thrown in any other direc-

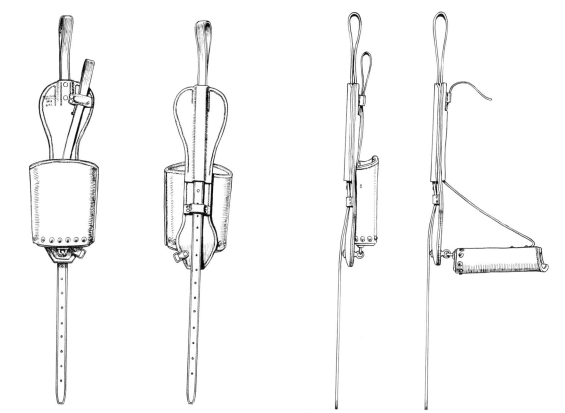

A. FRONT AND REAR VIEWS OF M1912 RIFLE CARRIER BOOT (BUCKET)

B. EDGE VIEWS OF BUCKET SHOWING HOW BUCKET RELEASES BUTT OF RIFLE AUTOMATICALLY IN EVENT OF A FALL

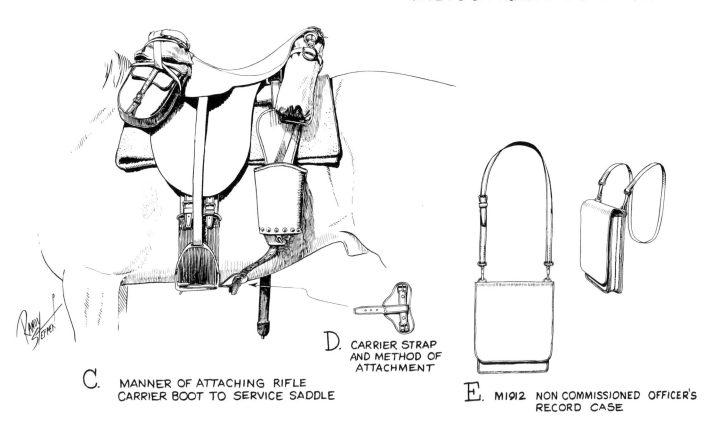

C. MANNER OF ATTACHING RIFLE CARRIER BOOT TO SERVICE SADDLE

D. CARRIER STRAP AND METHOD OF ATTACHMENT

E. M1912 NON COMMISSIONED OFFICER'S RECORD CASE

FIGURE 366. Model 1912 cavalry equipments.

tion, this act will of itself withdraw the rifle from the bucket. Once the retaining strap is withdrawn from its loop from any cause, the trooper before mounting should replace it. This is easily done. Pass the free end up through leather facing of standing part, if necessary, then through metal loop, and draw bucket into vertical position against standing part of boot. Turn free end of retaining strap on itself, and pass back through metal loop, above previous part, then downward through leather loop on outside face of standing part, and draw it sufficiently snug *to bring fold to within about ½ inch of metal loop.*

It is impracticable with this carrying device to "advance rifle."

STOCK COVER.
[See Figure 367-A.]

This is essentially a protecting band of collar leather, 7 to 8 ounces, which clamps snugly around the rifle stock just above the rear sight and extends forward along the stock for a distance of about 9⅞ inches. The object of the cover is to prevent injury to the rifle where it comes in contact with the belt ring, and further to prevent injury to the belt ring by the sling swivel of the rifle moving up and down through it. It is practically a plain cylinder of leather, except that it is cut away where it passes over the lower band and swivel and sling of the rifle, and a protecting flap, called the swivel safe, is sewed on at this point. The cover is kept in place by a spring bolt and lock riveted into the overlapping edges. The swivel safe above mentioned has two slots cut in it, through which the sling of the rifle may be passed.

To place, lock the cover together just above its position on the rifle, slip it down to its proper position, and secure it there by passing the gun sling through lower slot from outside inward, then through swivel from below upward, then through upper slot from inside outward, thence back to sliding loop on gun sling and draw taut to press swivel against stock below the band.

RIFLE COVER.
[See Figure 367-B.]

This article is made of olive-drab cotton duck, 8 ounces per square yard in weight, fiber dyed. It is of one single piece, except for a reinforce band at the muzzle and 4 inches wide. There is a drawstring of cotton seine twine. The length of the cover made up is 34 inches, which length is determined by the fact that the trigger guard must be exposed to permit of attachment of belt-ring snap. The cover is practically waterproof, and makes up in a measure for the loss of protection to the rifle in storms, formerly furnished by the old-pattern rifle scabbard. The proper authority will determine on what occasions it will be made use of. When not worn on the rifle, it can be conveniently carried in the cantle roll.

THE CAVALRY SABER, MODEL OF 1913.
[See Figures 369 and 347.]

The cavalry saber, model of 1913, has a straight two-edged *blade*, with a chisel point. The blade is of forged steel; extreme length, including grip, being approximately 41½ inches. The blade proper tapers from a width of 1.175 inches

and a thickness of 0.298 inch at the guard to a width of 0.58 inch and a thickness of 0.162 inch, 1.8 inches from the point, and from the latter section forward is tapered to the chisel point. The blade has a groove running down each side to within 4¾ inches of the point. Both edges are sharp, except that the back is dulled to a width of 0.03 inch for a distance of 18 inches from the guard and the front edge for a distance of 12 inches from the guard.

The grip end of the blade is shaped to take the *pommel*, which is a steel forging forming the back of the grip. This piece is checked with diagonal milling cuts 11 per inch and has a checked thumb depression. This pommel is fastened to the back of the blade and to the sides are fastened the right and left *grips* of black hard rubber checked with 13 per inch checking. The rubber grips are fastened on with two grip screws about 1 inch long, passing through grips and blade. The pommel is secured to the blade by a pommel screw at the extreme rear end 1¼ inches long, which screws into the blade.

The *guard* is of sheet steel 0.042 inch thick, pressed to form a complete protection for the hand and stiffened by three grooves pressed into it. The guard is fastened at its rear end by being brazed to a connection plug which enters the pommel piece, and is held therein by the pommel screw passing through it. The guard is further stiffened by the edges being rolled inward all around the guard. Just below the guard on the blade is a sheet *steel washer* and below that a *leather washer* to protect the guard against the saber scabbard.

The guard and pommel are given a brown finish and the blade is left bright and polished.

The saber will be issued sharp, and should be kept in that condition. The metal portions of the hilt should not be brightened by polishing. If rust gathers upon them, rub it off with an oiled rag. The saber is carried in the saber carrier, edge to the rear, secured by the billet on the carrier through loop on the scabbard.

THE SERVICE SABER SCABBARD.
[See Figures 369 and 347.]

This scabbard is made up of a hickory body, thoroughly seasoned and dipped in oil and white lead; a *rawhide cover*, sewed up with a rawhide string and drawn on tightly, when wet, so as to dry in place, making a firm covering, and then thoroughly coated with shellac; an *outer covering* of tubular olive-drab webbing; a *tip* of drawn steel, forced on, riveted with three through rivets and crimped to the body; a *mouthpiece* of pressed steel, welded at the seams and having a ring on each side for attaching saber attachment, the mouthpiece riveted to scabbard by three bifurcated rivets and crimped. Inside this mouthpiece is a flat spring, which bears on the saber so as to hold it firmly in place, but at the same time admitting of easy withdrawal of saber.

The metal parts have a dull bronze finish, and the web cover is given two coats of shellac to render it waterproof, of uniform appearance, and not easily soiled. The tip has a point with a hole for drainage, the tip being of proper size to fit the grommets of the shelter tent, so that the scabbard with saber in it can be used for a shelter-tent pole.

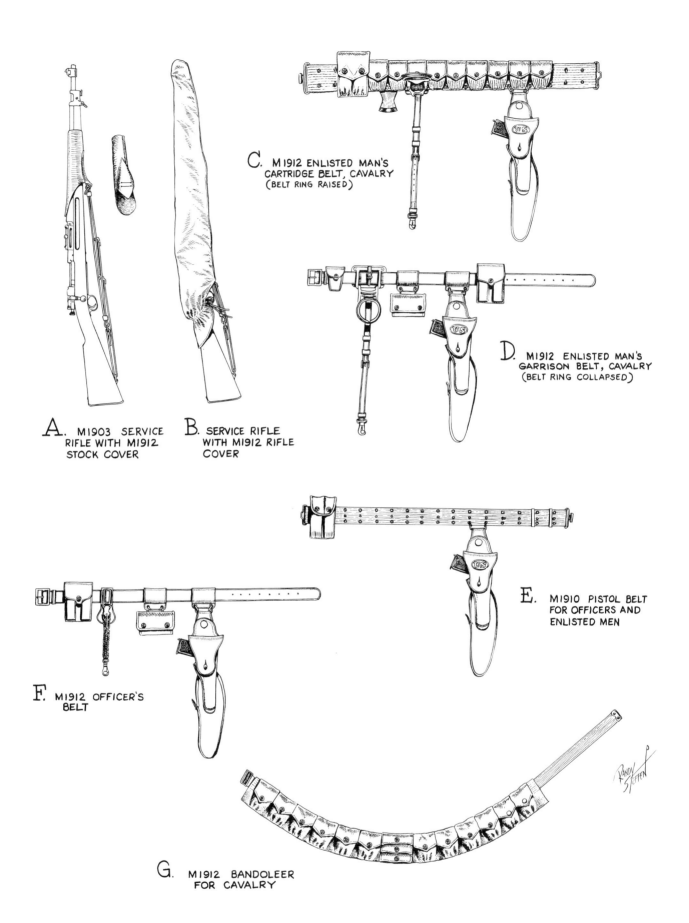

C. M1912 ENLISTED MAN'S CARTRIDGE BELT, CAVALRY (BELT RING RAISED)

D. M1912 ENLISTED MAN'S GARRISON BELT, CAVALRY (BELT RING COLLAPSED)

A. M1903 SERVICE RIFLE WITH M1912 STOCK COVER

B. SERVICE RIFLE WITH M1912 RIFLE COVER

E. M1910 PISTOL BELT FOR OFFICERS AND ENLISTED MEN

F. M1912 OFFICER'S BELT

G. M1912 BANDOLEER FOR CAVALRY

FIGURE 367. Model 1912 cavalry equipments.

FIGURE 368. Preparing to mount, with rifle. Suspended from the belt by the supporting strap and contained within the ring of the Model 1912 rifle carrier, the rifle does not interfere with the trooper in the act of mounting.

Metal parts of the scabbard must not be polished. If rusty, clean them with an oiled rag. The canvas cover should not be soiled by smearing oil or grease upon it.

THE SABER KNOT.
[See Figures 369 and 347.]

The saber knot consists of two ½-inch body straps, 13½ inches long, on which are two movable slides. At one end a 3⅜-inch button loop is attached by means of a button, and at the other end is secured a blind tassel body composed of a compact roll of leather about 2¾ inches long by ⅝ inch in diameter.

SABER CARRIER, SERVICE.
[See Figures 369 and 371-B.]

The saber carrier consists of two principal parts, a base piece and the saber loop. The loop is essentially a tube of medium harness leather 6 inches long and of oval cross section to conform to the scabbard which is carried in it. The loop is lined with a light collar leather.

The loop is hung from the base piece by means of a large bronze joint or swivel, which is so designed as to permit of motion relative to the base piece only in one plane, i. e., the vertical plane parallel to the axis of the animal. This motion is itself restricted by stops in the swivel suitably located so that the loop carrying the scabbard and saber can swing about 40° to the front or rear.

The loop has stitched onto its outside a saber loop billet, a strap of 7 to 8 ounce collar leather, which serves to fasten the scabbard in place in the saber loop.

The base piece is made up of two pieces of leather about 12¼ inches long and 5⁹⁄₁₆ inches wide at widest part, the upper corners rounded and the lower end tapered down to 1¼ inches wide. These two pieces are stitched together all

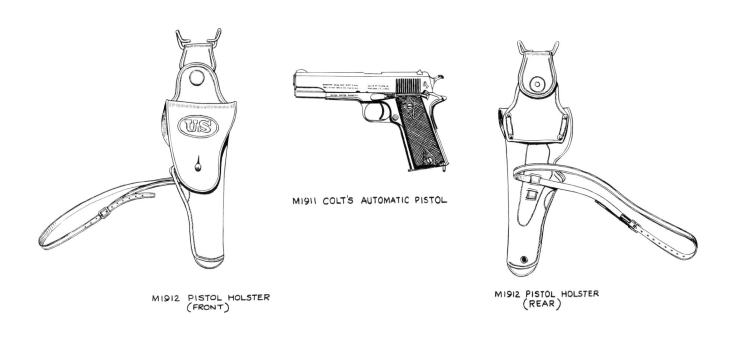

M1911 COLT'S AUTOMATIC PISTOL

M1912 PISTOL HOLSTER
(FRONT)

M1912 PISTOL HOLSTER
(REAR)

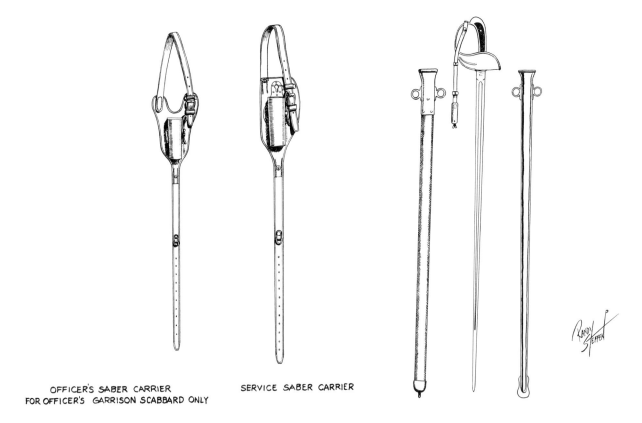

OFFICER'S SABER CARRIER
FOR OFFICER'S GARRISON SCABBARD ONLY

SERVICE SABER CARRIER

CAVALRY SABER M1913
LEFT: SERVICE SCABBARD M1913
RIGHT: OFFICER'S GARRISON SABER SCABBARD
(FOR SERVICE SABER)

FIGURE 369. Model 1912 cavalry equipments.

around the edges, and the outer one has a 2.8-inch hole where the stationary part of the swivel protrudes. At the upper corner of the base piece is riveted and stitched an attaching strap or billet of medium harness leather 1¼ inches wide. This strap is 23¼ inches long, and after passing up to the off suspension loop on the cantle of the saddle returns to a 1¼-inch bronze-finished barrel roller buckle on the base piece.

Extending from the tapered-down bottom of the base piece is a depending billet, a strap of medium harness leather 1¼ inches wide and 21¾ inches long, which passes under the animal and is buckled to the carrier strap.

In the base piece just above the swivel is a key slot cut through the swivel plate and leather of the base piece which is for attaching the intrenching tool carrier to the saber carrier.

The *officers' saber carrier* differs from the above in several particulars; the base piece is lighter and padded with goat hair next to the animal where the swivel would be apt to chafe. The attaching and depending billets are of 7 to 8 ounce collar leather ⅞ inch wide; the loop is lighter and slightly longer; the swivel is of lighter construction and permits slightly less swing to front and rear.

This carrier is designed to carry the bright metal officers' garrison scabbard only. In the field officers will use the service scabbard.

The scabbard is placed on the off side of the saddled horse and held in place by passing its attaching strap through the loop on the off cantle hinge. The depending billet buckles to the carrier strap. Adjust so that saber shall swing in a vertical plane. Keep swivel well oiled. Do not brighten metal parts.

If it is desired to be armed with the saber mounted, but without the rifle carrier boot, or the special picket pin carrier, as the case may be, remove the carrier strap wholly from the equipment. Then buckle the depending billet of the saber carrier into the swivel buckle on the girth and adjust to proper tension. It is probable that this billet end will not pass into the standing loop beyond the swivel buckle, on account of the angle made by this billet. This need cause no inconvenience— dispose of the billet end by tucking it in between the strands of the girth, which will answer just as well.

When separating from the horses for extended fighting on foot, if the horses are to be led any material distance or over rough ground, then the saber should be secured to its scabbard by the saber knot.

THE CARRIER STRAP.
[See Figure 366-D.]

This is a leather safe, trilobular in shape, about 6½ inches wide and 5 inches long. To the forward lobe is attached a strap of 9½ to 10½ ounce bridle leather, 1½ inches wide by 12 inches long, which connects the carrier to the girth by means of the buckle in the center of the girth. To each side lobe of the carrier strap is attached by a leather chape a 1¼-inch malleable-iron roller buckle, bronzed, the leather chape carrying a standing loop. These buckles serve as means of

attaching the depending billets of the saber carrier and rifle carrier boot, or special picket pin carrier.

The purpose of this article is to retain the rifle boot, or special picket pin carrier, as the case may be, and the saber carrier snugly against the flanks of the horse, thus avoiding all flapping, swinging, and unnecessary motion of whatever kind. It should be drawn sufficiently snug to accurately accomplish this purpose and no more. It serves in no sense as a rear girth—the saddle needs no rear girth—and it should not be employed for any such purpose. The strap attaching it to buckle in girth admits of easy adjustment to accommodate horses of different conformation.

THE INTRENCHING TOOLS.
[See Figure 370.]

The shovel.—This consists of a blade only, the trooper's picket pin supplying the handle. [See Figure 370-A, B.]

The shovel is of sheet steel 0.058 inch thick. It is 7⅝ inches long and 6⅞ inches wide at the top. The top edge is bent over toward the concave side of the shovel so as to form a stiffening rib ⁵⁄₁₆ inch wide along the top edge of two thicknesses of metal.

On the front of the shovel is a socket made of forged steel riveted on with six ³⁄₁₆-inch rivets. This socket fits the small end of the picket pin. A short 5-link steel chain is fastened to the shovel near the socket, and this chain carries at its outer end a split pin which enters a hole in the picket pin, thus securing the latter when in its place as a shovel handle.

To assemble, slip the pin into the socket in the blade, turn the pin gently till the hole in the web of the pin is nearest the cotter pin of the blade. Insert this cotter pin in the hole in the web and turn the picket pin handle till the chain binds. To detach, reverse the process. Do not use blows or violence. Keep the picket pin clean and free from rust and there will be no difficulty. Carry the shovel, on the march, in the outer compartment in the intrenching tool carrier, convex surface outward. To go on the dismounted firing line the trooper assembles his shovel in the tool frog of his belt, concave surface next him, carries the depending strap of his belt ring across on the outside of the shovel blade from rear to front, and engages its snap hook upon the upper edge of the belt just in front of the magazine pocket on the left side.

The Pick.—This is a single, chisel-pointed pick, made of tool steel; the pick, consisting of head only is 6¼ inches long over all, 1 inch wide at the blade, tapering back 4½ inches to ⅝ inch wide. Thickness at base of bevel ³⁄₁₆ inch, tapering back 4⅛ inches to ⁷⁄₁₆ inch. The eye for the handle is forged in the head to fit the larger end of the picket pin snugly. The pick is ground to an edge, tempered, and painted olive drab all over. Weight when finished 9½ ounces.

This article, as the above, utilizes trooper's picket pin for its handle. Introduce the pin through the eye of the pick from the front toward the rear, hammer face of pin toward back of pick. The pick is issued along with the shovel blades in the proportion of one pick to three shovels. On the horse it is

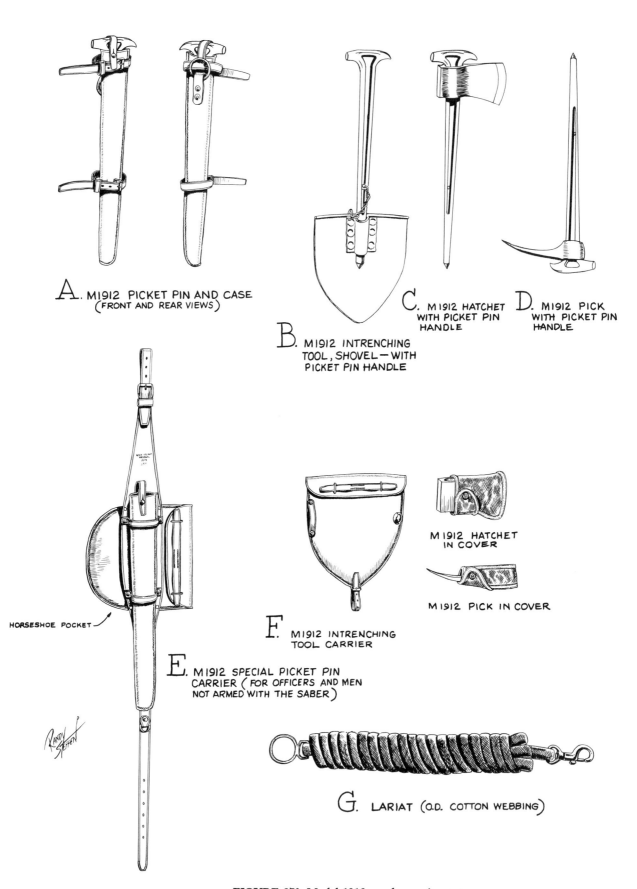

A. M1912 PICKET PIN AND CASE
(FRONT AND REAR VIEWS)

B. M1912 INTRENCHING
TOOL, SHOVEL — WITH
PICKET PIN HANDLE

C. M1912 HATCHET
WITH PICKET PIN
HANDLE

D. M1912 PICK
WITH PICKET PIN
HANDLE

HORSESHOE POCKET

E. M1912 SPECIAL PICKET PIN
CARRIER (FOR OFFICERS AND MEN
NOT ARMED WITH THE SABER)

F. M1912 INTRENCHING
TOOL CARRIER

M1912 HATCHET
IN COVER

M1912 PICK IN COVER

G. LARIAT (O.D. COTTON WEBBING)

FIGURE 370. Model 1912 cavalry equipments.

carried in the intrenching-tool carrier. To carry dismounted, assemble, slip point of pin handle down through loop of tool frog, edge to the front, and secure belt-ring strap as explained in case of the shovel. [See Figure 370-D.]

The *pick cover* remains constantly upon the pick except when the latter is in use; the trooper then puts the cover in his pocket for the time being. [See Figure 370-F.]

The Hatchet.—This consists of the head only and is 4⅞ inches long centrally, measured on the face of the blade, the back of the head being rectangular and 2¼ inches by ¾ inch. The eye is forged in the head to fit the larger end of the picket pin snugly. The edge is ground sharp and tempered, and the head is painted olive drab all over except the cutting edge for ½ inch wide. The hatchet finished weighs 20 ounces.

As above stated, the head only is finished. Place the picket pin in the eye of the hatchet from front to rear, face of hammer head on same side as back of hatchet head. A slight blow or jar on extreme hammer end will tighten the hatchet on pin handle. To loosen it jar the point end of the pin. This tool is issued to troops at the rate of one for each sergeant, omitting the first sergeant. It is carried in the intrenching tool carrier, in the same compartment as the shovel or pick of the other troopers. To carry dismounted, assemble, slip point end of pin down through loop of tool frog, edge to the front, and secure belt-ring strap as explained in case of the shovel.

The hatchet cover remains constantly upon the hatchet except when the latter is in use; the trooper then puts the cover in his pocket for the time being. [See Figure 370-F.]

THE INTRENCHING-TOOL CARRIER.
[See Figure 370-F.]

The *intrenching-tool carrier* is a leather pocket conforming to shape of shovel, made of a front and back of medium harness leather stitched together around the edges. The back piece is longer than the front and doubles over to form a flap, which flap is locked by two staples protruding through the flap and double-ended billet passing through the staples. The pocket has a partition of 5 to 6 ounce collar leather, thus forming a large inside pocket for carrying horseshoes, nails, etc. There is a small nail pocket of 3½-ounce collar leather 3⅛ by 2¼ inches wide, which can be removed from the shovel carrier, but is attached thereto by a short thong.

This article of the equipment is for the purpose of carrying either the shovel, the pick, or the hatchet, as the case may be, in its outer compartment, and the trooper's extra horseshoe and nails in the inner compartment. It is attached to the saddled horse by means of the saber carrier and the loop at the rear of the off girth-strap adjuster. To attach it to the saber carrier, turn the saber carrier till the axis of its slot is parallel to and just over that of the lock stud on the intrenching-tool carrier. Slip the stud through the slot and turn the saber carrier on this stud so that when the axis of the base piece of the saber carrier is vertical, and its depending billet extending downward, that of the intrenching-tool carrier will be horizontal, and slip the billet of the saber carrier through the loop on the lower edge of intrenching-tool carrier. The saber carrier is then attached to the saddle and carrier strap by its

proper billets, and the billet at point of intrenching-tool carrier is buckled through loop on girth-strap adjuster into its proper buckle.

THE CAVALRY PICKET PIN AND LARIAT.
[See Figure 370-B, C, D.]

The *picket pin* is a forging of medium-grade crucible steel. It is 13¾ inches over all length and is slightly tapering from a width of 1¼ inches under the head to ½ inch diameter ¾ inch above the point. The shank of the pin is of channel section, for lightness, from the head to 3½ inches from the point with a web ³⁄₁₆ inch thick. The head of the pin is shaped like a claw hammer, so that the pin can be used as such when desired. The point and head are given a mild temper.

The *lariat* is made of olive-drab cotton webbing, ⅝-inch wide, oval in section. At one end is a ⅞-inch swivel eyebolt snap, bronze finish, and at the other end a double eye. The double eye is of bronze, and the part engaging in the loop of the lariat is a ¾-inch D, while the other part is a ring 1¼ inches diameter. The lariat assembled is 15 feet long, exclusive of the snap and double eye. [See Figure 370-G.]

The picket pin serves as a handle for the several intrenching tools, also a shoeing hammer and a clinching iron in emergencies, as well as its usual purpose of aiding in tethering a horse. To use it with the lariat, snap the hook of the latter into the halter ring, and drive the pin through the ring of the double eye on the lariat, leaving the hammer head slightly above the surface of the ground. The ring will then work around the pin as the horse feeds, giving a swivel effect. In case the horse pulls up the pin, the loop will draw off the pin, and the latter should be found near the point it was driven. The pin is carried on the march either in its case on the saber scabbard or in the special carrier, as the case may be.

THE PICKET PIN CASE.
[See Figure 370-A.]

The *picket pin case* is a slightly conical tube of 7 to 8 ounces, collar leather, 13½ inches long, shaped to fit the picket pin quite closely. There are two straps with buckles which encircle it and secure it to the saber scabbard, the upper one ¾ inch wide and the lower ⅝ inch wide, both of 7 to 8 ounce collar leather. A billet piece at the top passes over the head of the pin and secures it.

The case carries the picket pin for those troopers armed with the rifle. The upper strap passes around the scabbard through the carrier rings thereon. The lower strap passes around the scabbard.

THE RATION BAGS.
[See Figure 371-A.]

These bags, one right and one left, forming a pair, are made of a heavy fiber dyed duck, No. 1, which weighs 28 ounces per square yard. The *back piece* is approximately 21 inches long and 7 inches wide, the lower 11½ inches being double in thickness. This piece is bound around the edges with cotton webbing ³¹⁄₁₀₀ ounce per yard and ¾ inch wide.

To this back piece is stitched the *pocket body*, made of

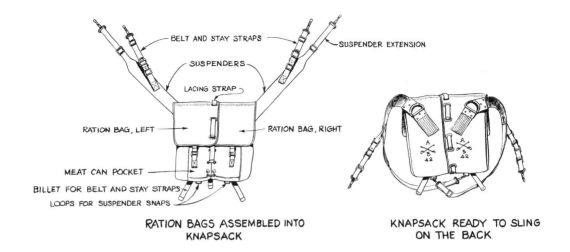

BELT AND STAY STRAPS — SUSPENDER EXTENSION

SUSPENDERS

LACING STRAP

RATION BAG, LEFT — RATION BAG, RIGHT

MEAT CAN POCKET

BILLET FOR BELT AND STAY STRAPS

LOOPS FOR SUSPENDER SNAPS

RATION BAGS ASSEMBLED INTO
KNAPSACK

KNAPSACK READY TO SLING
ON THE BACK

METHOD OF CONNECTING RATION BAGS BEFORE PLACING ON CANTLE
END OF SIDE BARS

A. RATION BAGS, M1912

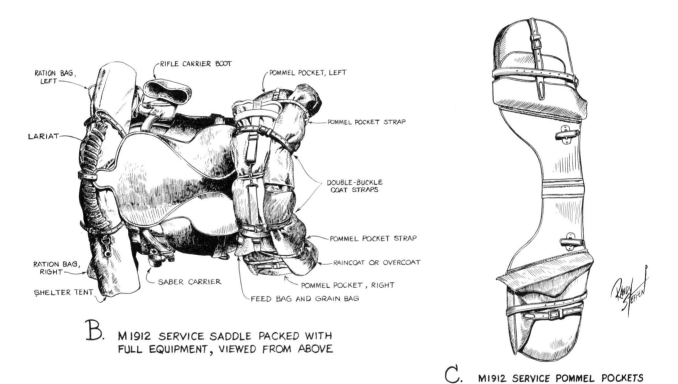

RATION BAG,
LEFT

RIFLE CARRIER BOOT

POMMEL POCKET, LEFT

POMMEL POCKET STRAP

LARIAT

DOUBLE-BUCKLE
COAT STRAPS

POMMEL POCKET STRAP

RATION BAG,
RIGHT

RAINCOAT OR OVERCOAT

SHELTER TENT

SABER CARRIER

POMMEL POCKET, RIGHT

FEED BAG AND GRAIN BAG

B. M1912 SERVICE SADDLE PACKED WITH
FULL EQUIPMENT, VIEWED FROM ABOVE

C. M1912 SERVICE POMMEL POCKETS

FIGURE 371. Model 1912 cavalry equipments.

238

one piece of the No. 1 duck, the pattern being cut to include the front, side gussets, bottom, and gusset flaps at the top, the whole forming, when stitched to the back piece, a pocket approximately 6 inches wide, 11 inches long, and 3 inches deep. On the back of each back piece is fastened a *suspender* of cotton webbing 2 inches wide. This suspender is so attached to the back piece that it can swing out at the proper angle for slinging over the shoulder (about 40°), or can swing over in a line parallel with the axis of the bag when used to connect the two bags for slinging over the cantle of the saddle.

The forward side of each bag is so arranged that the back piece extends out from under the pocket; these extensions, when overlapped, serve as a means for connecting the bags together to form a knapsack, as shown assembled in plate.

When used as a knapsack the belt and stay strap shown in plate are attached to the billet on the suspender body. When the bags are arranged to sling over the cantle of the saddle these belts and stay straps are removed from the suspender billet and attached to a billet at the bottom of each bag and serve to connect the bags to small D-rings on the rifle boot and saber carrier to steady the bags in place.

To the outside of the pocket of each bag is stitched a flap of the No. 1 duck, 10½ by 4⁷⁄₁₆ inches; this piece is stitched only along its bottom edge and rear edge, the front and top edges being free. The front edge is provided with six grommets for lacing, so that when the two bags are assembled into the knapsack these flaps are laced up to form the meat-can pocket.

The ration bags are intended for campaign use and will carry two haversack rations and one emergency ration (packed after the manner of the present issue of rations), although their ordinary contents will be one haversack ration and one emergency ration. These rations will distribute quite evenly, both as to weight and volume, between the two bags.

The bacon bag is an accessory of the ration bags and is intended to carry the portion of a trooper's haversack ration of bacon remaining after he has broken open the can and consumed some of it. Place the bacon in the bag without the can. It is not probable the can could be gotten in the bag, and in any case it would only strain and tear the bag. The enamel lining has been analyzed and found harmless.

Four leather thongs are supplied each trooper for securing his blanket when dismounted, or for other purposes. They are carried in the ration bags. Keep them clean, soft, and pliable.

(1) To pack the ration bags with two haversack rations and one emergency ration when bacon is furnished as a meat component, place in the rear ration bag two hard-bread packages, on the side next to the horse, and one can of bacon on the outside, with the flat side of the bacon can against the hard-bread packages. If the bacon is in a short or Morris can, push it to the bottom of the bag and put the two grocery components above it. If the bacon is in a long or Dold can, the two grocery components placed flat side down will just fit in level on top of the bacon and the hard bread. Then in the off ration bag put one emergency ration flat side down in the bottom of the bag. Next put in two packages of hard bread on the side next to the horse and one can of bacon on

the outside. If this can is a Morris can, it will only fill the lower half. If it is a Dold or long can, it will reach to the top of ration bag. Packed in this way the off bag is 1½ ounces heavier than the near bag, as near to a balance as the contents will permit.

(2) When canned corned beef is carried instead of bacon the same system of placing the hard bread and canned meat is followed, as above, except that the long pyramidal can of corned beef will extend to the bottom of each ration bag where its sharp edges will wear out the canvas unless a wadding of paper or hay is first thrust into the bag. In carrying this particular can of meat, care must always be taken to protect the bottom of the bag in the manner mentioned. The emergency ration in the off pocket should not be placed in the bottom but should be brought up and put alongside the corned-beef can in order to give a better shape to the bag. The balance will be the same as when bacon is carried, although the rations weigh 11 ounces more.

(3) If the issue of the meat component happens to be one-half bacon and one-half corned beef, the bags are packed with three hard-bread packages, two grocery components and one emergency ration on the near side and one hard bread, one bacon, and one corned-beef can on the off side. This makes the off bag 1½ ounces heavier than the near bag, exactly as before.

(4) To pack the ration bags with one haversack ration and one emergency ration when the meat component of the former is bacon, place one hard-bread carton, one grocery component, and one emergency ration in the near bag. The off bag is then 2 ounces heavier than the near bag, as nearly as the contents can be made to balance. In order to keep the bag in shape, stuff with hay, oats, or grass.

(5) As rations are consumed, rearrange remaining contents so as to keep the balance. If one side must be heavier than the other, let it be always the off side, thus aiding in counterbalancing the weight of the rifle. To hold remaining contents in place, stuff bags with paper or extra oats and lace the grommets with small thong. When only the emergency ration remains, put it and bags in cantle roll.

To place the filled bags on the saddled horse, first buckle a belt and stay strap to the billet depending downward and forward from each bag and couple the bags together, the lacing grommets of each bag to the rear, by engaging the hook at the extremity of each suspender into the little D ring on the upper portion of the opposite bag, then adjust suspenders to minimum length. Having first placed the shelter-tent roll and lariat across the bars just in rear of the cantle, then place over them the suspenders of the bags and pull the ends of the shelter-tent roll through the suspenders on each side so that these ends will rest on top of the bags. Fasten the pack by the center or cantle-roll coat strap lightly, and then step behind the horse and verify the balance of the pack, adjusting as necessary; then tightly grasp and bind the cantle roll, lariat, and suspenders with all coat straps, so that the pack entire rides snugly and well up above the back. Finally, engage the snap hooks of the belt and stay straps into the small D rings on the saber carrier and the rifle-carrier boot, first having made a trial adjustment of each, so that when engaged the bags will ride snugly in the correct position. When the ration bags are not needed, roll them inside the cantle roll or place them with the roll in the wagon, as the circumstances may permit.

To use the ration bags dismounted, place them side by side on the ground or on some convenient support, one set of lacing grommets superposed upon the other, and draw the lacing web snugly through these grommets. It will be retained there by friction. Place the meat can, with knife, fork, and spoon, inside in the pocket for that purpose, lace the pocket together with the thong provided, and secure covering flaps. The two bags have now formed a single knapsack. [See Figures 371-A and 328.] Place the knapsack on the trooper's back, above the bandoleer in case that article is worn, suspenders up; bring the billet ends of the suspenders down in front of the shoulders, carry them under the respective arms and shoulders of the trooper, and engage the hook at the end of each into the rectangular loop at the lower end of the ration bag, either the loop on same bag with suspender or the loop on the other bag, as found more convenient. Attach the belt and stay straps to the billet pieces placed on body of suspender, if not already there, engage the hooks on these straps each into an eyelet on the cartridge belt, and adjust both the suspenders and the belt and stay strap to the particular trooper's convenience.

To add the blanket to the dismounted trooper, form it into a convenient roll about 42 inches long, place it symmetrically on top of knapsack, break down the ends about the upper corners of the knapsack, and secure the roll snugly to the top and sides of the knapsack by the thongs provided for this purpose. When the blanket roll is inclosed in the shelter half the ropes of the latter can be used to secure the free ends of the roll to the sides of the knapsack.

THE SERVICE POMMEL POCKETS.
[See Figure 371-C.]

The pommel pockets are made of bag leather, 5 to 6 ounces per square foot in weight, the near and off pockets being stitched onto a base of medium harness leather, so shaped as to fit over the pommel of the saddle and suspend the pockets therefrom on either side. This base piece is made in halves, each half approximately $17\frac{1}{2}$ inches long and $7\frac{1}{2}$ inches wide at widest part where pocket is mounted upon it, and tapering down to about $3\frac{5}{8}$ inches wide where it passes over pommel. The two halves are joined together at the narrow part, the joint being reinforced with a strip of medium harness leather $1\frac{3}{4}$ inches wide and $3\frac{5}{8}$ inches long. The base piece above described forms the inner wall of each pocket, and the walls or gussets of the pockets and the top flaps, all of bag leather, are stitched to the base piece.

The pockets are approximately 10 inches long, $7\frac{1}{2}$ inches wide, and $3\frac{1}{2}$ inches thick, the bottom ends being semicircular in shape.

They are attached to the saddle by engaging the high foot staples on the pommel through the slots in the base piece of the pockets and fastening them in that position, either by the billets on the base piece or by passing the double buckle coat straps through them, as will be explained later, and then passing the attaching strap on each pocket through the loop at forward end of skirt near that pocket, buckle tongue pointing to the front, drawing snug, and buckling. The near pocket contains canteen with cover and cup, in main compartment, wire cutters in smaller compartment. The off pocket contains meat can, knife, fork, and spoon in canvas bag, grooming outfit above, and sponge, soap, and calkins, and extractor, when carried, below in main compartment, and cooling strap in its proper compartment. The small outside compartment opening from below is for the trooper's personal needs, pipe, tobacco, etc.

THE GROOMING CLOTH.

While the condemned saddle blankets furnish the principal source of the grooming cloth, the burlap grain sack makes an excellent grooming cloth. This source will doubtless always be abundant. The cloths may be cut of any convenient size for use in garrison, but should be limited for field service to the available space for carrying the cloth in the pommel pockets. The grooming cloth is not an article of issue.

KNIFE, MODEL OF 1910.

This is made of a blade of cutlery steel and a handle of aluminum cast onto the blade. The blade is ground and polished and handle stamped "U. S." and "R. I. A." and year of manufacture. This article is identical with the infantry knife.

FORK, MODEL OF 1910.

The fork is made of one piece of noncorrosive metal stamped to shape. It has the letters "U. S." and "R. I. A." and year of manufacture stamped into it. This article is identical with the infantry fork.

SPOON, MODEL OF 1910.

The spoon is made of one piece of noncorrosive metal stamped to shape. It has the letters "U. S." and "R. I. A." and year of manufacture stamped into it. This article is identical with the infantry spoon.

MEAT CAN, MODEL OF 1910.

This article is identical with the Infantry meat can and is made of an aluminum body and cover, both of which are formed in dies and have the rim rolled over for stiffness. Riveted to the body is the hinge and handle, and to the cover is riveted the loop. When the meat can is assembled the handle folds over the cover and the hooked end of it engages the rim of the body, holding the cover firmly in place.

THE CANTEEN COVER, MODEL OF 1910.
[See Figure 374-D.]

The aluminum canteen, model of 1910, consists of the following parts:

One body, aluminum; one collar, noncorrosive metal; one shackle, noncorrosive metal; one cap chain, German silver; one cap rivet, German silver; one cap, aluminum; one gasket. The body of the canteen is of pure sheet aluminum, which is formed into the shape of a bottle, having one con-

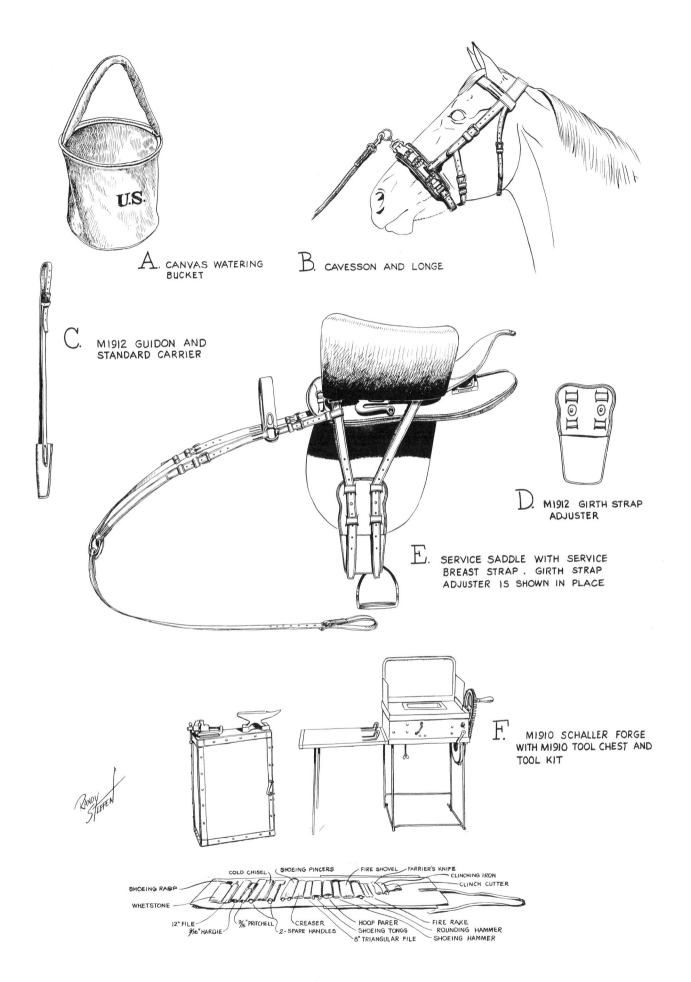

A. CANVAS WATERING BUCKET

B. CAVESSON AND LONGE

C. M1912 GUIDON AND STANDARD CARRIER

D. M1912 GIRTH STRAP ADJUSTER

E. SERVICE SADDLE WITH SERVICE BREAST STRAP . GIRTH STRAP ADJUSTER IS SHOWN IN PLACE

F. M1910 SCHALLER FORGE WITH M1910 TOOL CHEST AND TOOL KIT

SHOEING RASP

WHETSTONE

COLD CHISEL — SHOEING PINCERS — FIRE SHOVEL — FARRIER'S KNIFE

CLINCHING IRON

CLINCH CUTTER

12" FILE

9/16" HARDIE

9/16" PRITCHELL

CREASER

2 - SPARE HANDLES

HOOF PARER

SHOEING TONGS

8" TRIANGULAR FILE

FIRE RAKE

ROUNDING HAMMER

SHOEING HAMMER

FIGURE 372. Model 1912 cavalry equipments.

cave side and a capacity of approximately 2 pints. The collar is assembled to the canteen neck, and the cap is attached to the canteen collar by means of the chain, shackle, and sliding ring. The shackle is so designed that, should the chain break, the shackle can be opened, the detached links threaded to that portion of the chain remaining attached to the cap, and the entire chain connected to the sliding ring by means of the shackle. Shackles are issued separately for purposes of repair when desired, as are also caps and chains.

The Cup, Model of 1910.

The cup, model of 1910, consists of the following parts:

One body, aluminum; one handle, noncorrosive metal; one sliding lock, noncorrosive metal; one hinge, noncorrosive metal; one hinge pin. The cup is drawn seamless from sheet metal, the upper edge of the cup being stiffened by a bead formed on the body. The cup is so shaped as to fit over the bottom end of the canteen, and the handle is so formed that when it is not in use it fits snugly around the cup. The handle contains a slot into which the fork may be fitted when it is desired to lengthen the handle. Both the canteen and cup are identical with those of the Infantry equipment.

The Canteen, Model of 1910.
[See Figure 374-D.]

This cover is made of olive-drab cotton duck No. 9, fiber dyed, and is lined with a blue-gray felt. The cover has two flaps which pass over the top of the canteen on either side of the neck and are provided with snap fasteners. These fasteners, like all of this type used on service equipment, are so designed that they will open easily if pulled in a direction of the longitudinal axis of the fastener (which is oval in shape), but will not open if pulled in any other direction, thus avoiding trouble from opening by brushing against objects, clothing, or other men.

On the back of the cover is a web strap which carries a double-end wire hook, by means of which the canteen is suspended from the belt when used by dismounted trooper.

Currycomb, Model of 1913.
[See Figure 374-B.]

This article differs from those of previous issue mainly in being metal throughout, except the strap, which is of olive-drab cotton webbing.

Horse Brush.
[See Figure 374-B.]

The horse brush has an oval back piece of russet collar leather 4.67 by 7.25 inches and a hand strap of the same material. This brush is about ½ the size of that formerly issued.

Wire Cutters, Model of 1910.
[See Figure 374-C.]

These cutters, shown in Plate VII, are forged from a good grade of tool steel. They are 8¼ inches long over all and have a leverage at the cutting edges approximately ten times the power applied at handle.

The handles are insulated with hard rubber so as to with-stand a voltage of 5,000 volts. The extreme ends of the handles are provided with soft-rubber tips, because the hard rubber is very brittle and would break if the cutters were dropped on hard ground.

These articles are to be issued to each officer below the grade of major and to each enlisted man. They are carried in their special compartment in the near-pommel pocket.

Individual Soap Box.

This box is made of tin, coated with yellow enamel, is ¾ inch deep, including lid, with 2¹¹⁄₁₆ inches diameter, both outside measurements. The top edge of the box is rolled inward to form a smooth, round rim. The box will hold 2 ounces of saddle soap.

This article is for the purpose of supplying each man an individual allowance of soap for cleaning his equipments. It is carried on the march in his off pommel pocket. When its contents are exhausted it should be refilled from stores in bulk, and not thrown away as useless.

The 4-inch Sponge.

This is provided for the individual use of the trooper and should not be cut. If cut it would soon fray out and be used up. It is carried in the off pommel pocket.

The Care of the Equipment.

This general subject is entitled to a greater degree of consideration than it has usually received in times past. It should be made a matter of instruction as well as one of administration. The general principles upon which the proper care of leather is based, as well as the proper method of treatment, should be taught to noncommissioned officers in their regular school as are the subjects of Guard Duty, Drill Regulations, etc. The cleaning and oiling of the equipment should, whenever practicable, be superintended by a commissioned officer as is stable duty. Leather properly cared for remains soft and pliable until absolutely worn out, probably many years; if uncared for or improperly cared for it soon dries out, becomes brittle, and its fibers are then easily broken and the equipment rendered useless. Under such conditions it lasts only a comparatively short time, a few years at the most, and even during that period is stiff, difficult of adjustment, and generally unsatisfactory.

It is a very simple matter in principle to properly care for leather equipment—in practice, considerable skill is required. Two agents only are needed to keep the equipment in first-class condition—soap and oil. The soap for the purpose of removing all dirt and the other matter that would serve as an obstacle to the penetration of the oil, the latter for softening and preserving the leather. Two varieties of soap are ordinarily used—Castile and harness soap. Castile soap is a powerful cleanser, frequently containing an excess of free alkali that renders it an active agent in removing dirt, but it has no tendency of itself to soften and preserve the leather, as does good harness soap, which has no free alkali, but, on the other hand, frequently has a greater or less percentage of uncombined fatty substance available for softening and preserving purposes. Other agents are not only wholly unnecessary but frequently absolutely injurious and should never be made use of.

When new equipment is received it should, before use, be given a light application of oil. The necessity for this step is occasioned by the fact that leather frequently remains a considerable period of time in store in the arsenal, constantly drying out and parting with its oil. Upon issue this oil should be replaced. As new equipment is already clean, no application of soap is necessary in this instance. All that is needed is that the leather be slightly moistened, and that the oil be lightly and quickly applied. As far as practicable the oil should be applied on the flesh side, as it penetrates much more readily from this side than from the grain side. It should be applied by a rag or cotton waste, moistened in it to prevent an undue amount being used. A larger amount would do the leather no injury, but any amount above what the leather would readily absorb and retain would not only be wasted, but would continually ooze out under the action of the heat of the sun and soil the clothing. In order that no more oil than is really necessary be applied, it should be measured out in the beginning, and should rarely exceed the soap box cover full, about 1 ounce, for a trooper's entire equipment. It should be lightly applied for a similar reason. If much force is used, the portions first receiving the application get too much oil. If not applied quickly, the same holds true—portions where the rag is allowed to rest too long take up too much. A light, evenly distributed application should be the aim. Neat's-foot oil is furnished by the Ordnance Department for this purpose, and no other oils should be used. After the equipment has been thus oiled it should, if possible, be permitted to remain in a warm, dry place for 24 hours, if practicable, and then be rubbed thoroughly with a coarse, dry cloth to remove any unabsorbed oil.

The equipment is now ready for use, and will be found much improved in pliability by this initial treatment, but a single treatment is insufficient to attain the desired end. As time goes on, if proper care and treatment is given, the equipment will continue to improve both in flexibility and appearance until it is a delight to eye and fingers.

Daily, or as often as used, the equipment should be wiped off with a cloth slightly dampened in water, merely to remove mud, dust, or other foreign substance, and the bits and other metal portions wiped off with a rag slightly moistened with oil to prevent rust. This takes but a few minutes after each daily use, and maintains the appearance of the equipment. It is, however, insufficient of itself to properly preserve it.

At intervals of from one to four weeks, depending upon circumstances, it is essential that the equipment be thoroughly cleaned. To do this properly every detachable piece should be separated—all billets unbuckled and the entire equipment reduced to its simplest elements. The trooper should then form a thick lather by moistening his sponge in clean water, squeezing it out and working it vigorously upon the Castile soap. When a thick, creamy lather is thus obtained he should thoroughly clean each piece of his leather equipment, working the sponge upon every portion, and drawing each strap its entire length through the lathered sponge, so as to actually remove the salt, sweat, dirt, or whatever may be, from each leather piece. After the leather parts are thus made approxi-

mately clean by the use of the Castile soap he should go over them again similarly with the harness soap in order to obtain a fine surface dressing and finish, the former being better adapted to cleansing, the latter to softening and preserving the leather. After the leather has been allowed to become partially dry, but not to harden, it should be rubbed thoroughly with a soft cloth. If the foregoing has been carefully executed, the appearance of the equipment should now be perfect, and if the leather is thoroughly soft and pliable nothing further is required. In general, however, it will be found desirable to apply a small amount of oil. This is done precisely as in the case of the new equipment, care being taken to avoid an excess, and thoroughly rub with a dry cloth before use.

All metal parts, except bits and spurs, need ordinarily only to be wiped clean with a cloth slightly moistened in oil; they are purposely issued dark, and it is desired they be retained in that condition. The use of warm water on the bits, stirrups, or similar portions to remove hardened saliva, sweat, mud, etc., is frequently advantageous. The bit, chain, and spurs may also be polished, but all dark metal should be cleaned and oiled only and should never be attacked with eroding agents.

THE FEED BAG AND GRAIN BAG.
[See Figure 373-C.]

The feed bag is a canvas cylinder, open at one end, suspended from the horse's neck when in use in a horizontal position, thus spreading the grain over a considerable area. There are two web suspending straps, one over the head and one near the withers on the neck. The body of the bag is of olive-drab duck No. 9, approximately 22¼ inches long. The supporting straps are of heavy 1-inch olive-drab cotton webbing, and are fitted with bronzed snaps and adjustable buckles.

The grain bag is of unbleached drilling formed into a long cylinder, 30½ by 8 inches, open at one end. There are two soft cotton binding cords sewed to the outside of the bag, one at the open end and one at the center, the first to close the bag when full and the second to equalize the loaded bag into two parts for slinging across the pommel of the saddle. [See Figure 373-B.]

The grain bag is used to avoid spilling grain while carrying it on the march. (The capacity of the bag is 10 pounds.) Place the amount of grain desired to be carried within the bag, tie the choke securely, divide the grain into two approximately equal portions by the string in the middle, place the bag inside the feed bag, press the grain bag well over toward the side of the feed bag opposite the webbing straps, fold the elliptical end piece of the feed bag in over the end of the grain bag, turn the extra canvas on the side of the webbing straps over upon the opposite side and secure it, first by the thong attached midway of the feed bag and then by the webbing straps of the latter, taking a half hitch, with each around its own end of the roll thus formed, then turning the roll over and bringing the free ends of these web straps out from the under side of their respective ends of the roll, then up over these ends, under the half hitches, and snapping the hooks thereon into each other. Place the grain roll thus formed upon the pommel, hooks upon upper surface, and secure by the

243

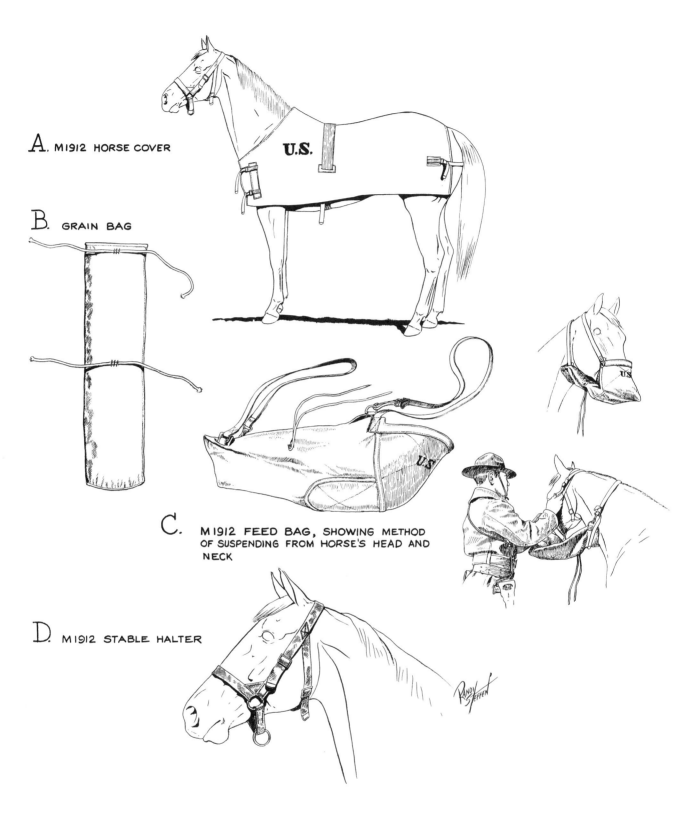

A. M1912 HORSE COVER

B. GRAIN BAG

C. M1912 FEED BAG, SHOWING METHOD OF SUSPENDING FROM HORSE'S HEAD AND NECK

D. M1912 STABLE HALTER

FIGURE 373. Model 1912 cavalry equipments.

two double-buckle straps furnished for that purpose, the grain roll being attached by the buckle at the extremity, the rain coat being attached immediately in front of the grain roll by the second buckle. To feed, take the grain roll off the pommel and remove grain bag from interior of feed bag. Untie grain bag and empty such portion of grain as is desired to feed therefrom into feed bag. Place grain bag in any desired position of safety while horse is feeding. Place the feed bag on the horse so that the opening will be immediately under his nose and the body of the bag under his neck. Snap the hooks into the corresponding D rings to support bag in this position. Adjust by making the steadying strap across the front of the horse's nose just sufficiently taut to allow the horse to feed easily, with a portion of his nostrils always above the opening. It is important that this adjustment be carefully made, as in the event of the horse not feeding well from the bag it will in most cases be due to the lack of adjustment of this strap. Adjust the remaining two straps by shortening them to a convenient height. The rear one should be drawn up well back on the neck about as high as comfort will permit. Once adjusted to any given horse no further adjustment will be needed until used on a horse of materially different dimensions.

By use of a second grain bag, or by carrying grain in the feed bag without a grain bag and using the regular grain bag for this purpose, an additional 10 pounds of grain can, in emergencies, be carried in the cantle roll.

In camp or on the march grain is fed morning, noon, and evening. The men are to remain near their horses until they have finished eating.

PACKING THE SADDLE.
[See Figures 371-B and 366-C.]

This should be done, whenever practicable, after the horse is saddled. When impracticable to pack after saddling, pack the saddle beforehand, and have each packed saddle placed accurately upon the horse by two troopers, one on either side of the animal. It is a virtual impossibility for the ordinary trooper, unaided, to properly place his packed saddle upon his horse. His attempts to do so result usually in placing the saddle inaccurately upon the back and either riding all day with it in such undesirable position or, making matters worse, by shoving it into the proper position after it has been placed, thus insuring folds and wrinkles in the layers of blanket or pad below, all of which evils can be readily avoided by carrying out the simple directions above.

To Form the Cantle Roll.—Lay the shelter tent on the ground and turn in triangle to lie flat. Turn under from 6 inches to 8 inches from end opposite the triangle. Spread the articles to be carried, viz, six tent pins, necessary underclothing and toilet articles, uniformly along the triangle edge over a range not exceeding 28 inches in length, leaving a vacant space of about 4 inches in the middle part to enable the roll to break nicely when completed. Turn over the two sides of the tent till they nearly meet in the center. Roll snugly from the triangle seam toward the other end. On reaching the other end, bend the roll and bring the underfold neatly over the

roll to bind and secure it in a snug, compact form. This gives a roll about 30 inches long. The roll, when the ration bags are packed, should rest its ends on top of the bags, holding them snug.

If the bed blanket is to be carried on the horse, fold it neatly to six layers, each the size of the folded saddle blanket, and place it accurately upon the latter.

Place the pommel pockets, with their prescribed contents, upon the saddle as indicated under their description and pass the tapered end of a double-buckle coat strap through one staple, above the pommel-pocket oval, from front to rear, flesh side up. Place the grain roll, formed as indicated under description of that article, symmetrically upon the pommel, passing one of its center thongs under the base piece connecting the two pockets and tying both center thongs by a slipknot. Pass the second double-buckle coat strap correctly through its staples and then snugly secure the grain roll in position by the buckle on the main part of each double-buckle coat strap.

Place the raincoat or the overcoat, as the case may be, properly folded, just in front of the pommel pockets, and secure it in that position, first, by the additional buckles on the double-buckle coat straps, taking care to keep these straps toward the center so that the raincoat when placed will readily break down in front of the pommel pockets, and, second, by the attaching straps of the pommel pockets, the billet of each of which passes from the loops on underside of pocket around in front of the lower part of the raincoat on its respective side, then between the webbing strap and the feed bag at its respective end of the grain roll, and by then buckling into its own buckle secures pommel pockets and all snugly to the loop on front edge of saddle skirt.

Place the rifle carrier boot, saber carrier, intrenching tool carrier with its prescribed contents, and carrier strap as indicated, and attach the saber and picket pin in its case, all as indicated under the respective descriptions of these several articles.

Place the ration bags, if carried, as stated under their description.

Form the lariat into a snug roll about 14 or 15 inches long, place this roll upon the upper surface of the cantle roll, middle point of lariat roll over middle point of cantle roll, and secure the combination thus formed to the cantle by the three coat straps pertaining thereto, the cantle roll to be symmetrically disposed as regards the median plane of the animal, the coat straps to include in their grasp the suspender straps of the ration bags, if the latter are carried, so that all will form a compact cargo, well raised above the back of the horse and side bars of the saddle.

In order to reduce the burden upon the horse, in a measure, whenever practicable, the bed blanket and the cantle roll should be carried in wagons.

CARTRIDGE BELT, CALIBER .30; CAVALRY.
[See Figure 367-C.]

This belt is woven of olive-drab cotton duck, fiber dyed. The belt is 4 feet 4 inches long, extreme length. The middle

245

section has nine interwoven pockets, each pocket to hold two clips of five United States rifle caliber .30 cartridges, belt between pockets and in end sections to be woven one ply. The upper portion of the belt is woven two ply to form slit housing for the pocket flaps; these flaps fasten down over the pocket by means of a snap fastener, which bears the United States coat of arms. Each pocket has an interior retaining strap three-fourths inch wide, which also snaps down in place.

At the ends are end fasteners riveted to the belt. These have two short metal hooks pointing toward each other, which lock into the eyelets in the body of the belt so as to give an adjustable-length belt. The end sections, being turned back and fastened by the end fasteners to give the desired length of belt, carry the belt fastener—a male on the right and female on the left side—which form a quickly manipulated connecting buckle. There is room on the left end section to carry a double web magazine pocket for pistol ammunition. To the belt on the left side is riveted a leather tool frog.

The *belt ring* is a large ring, 3½ inches inside diameter, supported on two standards, which are hinged to the base so that the ring may be held out in a horizontal plane when in use, or when not in use may be hung down close to the trooper's body. The ring and standards are supported when horizontal by a supporting brace, which assumes approximately an angle of 45°, and is locked in position by a double-spring latch on the standards. The ring is raised to a horizontal position by the hand, and when it reaches this position the supporting brace snaps over the latch without further assistance. When it is desired to collapse the ring, the two halves of this spring latch are squeezed together by the fingers, aided by two lugs on the latch for this purpose, thus withdrawing the latch halves and freeing the supporting brace.

The ring is faced inside with leather. The base supports the ring standards and supporting brace and is riveted to the belt.

Suspended from the base of the ring is a strap which carries at its lower end a metal snap hook which engages in the trigger guard of the rifle.

This belt carries 90 rounds of rifle ammunition and 2 pistol magazines. It should be adjusted to trooper so that the belt ring is slightly in rear of left hip, when belt fasteners are on median line of body. Adjustment is provided at either end of the belt, in order to accomplish this purpose. When worn on dismounted duty, the belt ring should be collapsed.

THE CAVALRY BANDOLEER.
[See Figures 367-G and 328.]

This article is of olive-drab duck, woven in a similar manner to the cartridge belt. There are 12 woven pockets, each to contain a clip of 5 rifle cartridges, caliber .30, and in the middle of the belt are three woven pockets for pistol ammunition. The bandoleer carrier, therefore, the excess of 60 rounds of rifle and 21 rounds of pistol ammunition over the cartridge belt which is required by Tables of Organization, 1914. Place the bandoleer on the trooper so that the pistol ammunition pockets are under the right arm, buckle over the left shoulder, billet falling behind.

PISTOL HOLSTER.
[See Figures 369 and 367.]

This holster is similar to the revolver holster previously issued; it carries the pistol with butt to the rear, a block of leather on the inner side of the holster holding the butt of the pistol out so that the butt may be grasped easily.

Attach to belt by fastening its double end hook into the eyelets in the belt, or the slide, as the case may be (slightly in front of right hip.) The leg strap passes around the thigh, buckle outside of leg, tongue pointing to the front. Habitually the flap should be kept fastened down. When the pistol is about to be used, or there is a possibility of its sudden use, fasten the flap open by turning back the extremity of the flap, and thrusting it down between the body of the flap, and the inside portion of the holster. As this pistol is less simple in its action than the old revolver, greater care must be observed in the practice of returning pistol and raising pistol, in order to avoid accidents.

POUCH FOR FIRST-AID PACKET, MODEL OF 1910.
[See Figure 367-D, F.]

This pouch is made of a piece of olive-drab cotton webbing, 5.25 inches wide by 11.3 inches long. About two-thirds of this length is folded and sewed to form a pocket and the remainder is used as a flap. On the back of the pocket a double hook, for carrying the pouch on the belt, is attached by means of a web chape.

THE SPUR AND STRAPS, MODEL OF 1911.
[See Figure 374-F.]

This article is drop-forged on one piece of 27 per cent nickel steel, the strap stud being riveted in place. The service and officers' spurs are identical and known as spur, model of 1911.

The spur is placed on the shoe well up toward the upper part of the counter, buckle on outside of foot. Wearing the spur in the position indicated preserves its life, favors the proper use of the spur as an aid, as well as conforming to the proper practice. This is a steel spur, and can be polished without injury. Adjust the upper strap to the foot by its buckle, attach the spur to the foot and detach it therefrom by pulling the inside end of each upper strap over the spur button, instead of by using the buckle.

THE ENLISTED MEN'S GARRISON BELT.
[See Figure 367-D.]

This is the leather waist belt, to which have been added the following detachable components: A belt ring and strap, a pistol-magazine pocket (carrying two magazines), a rifle-ammunition pocket, a pistol-holster slide, and a first-aid packet pouch slide. The saber hook has been omitted from the belt, as it is no longer needed for the comparatively small amount of foot service the trooper will do with his saber. It will never be needed for mounted duty. Such foot service will consist, in the main, of carrying it to and from the stables when going to mounted duties and returning therefrom. Occasions will be rare when all of these accessory parts will be required at one time on the belt. They are all readily removable, and only those required to serve the necessities at any particular occasion should be retained on the belt. The belt ring is collapsed and raised in a similar manner to the belt ring on the cartridge belt. The attachments are arranged on the belt (belt outstretched, buckle to left) from right to left, as follows: Pistol-magazine pocket, pistol-holster slide, first-aid pouch slide, belt ring, and rifle-ammunition pocket.

To put the belt ring on the slide, raise the metal frame which supports the ring from the leather pad. Place the belt in the angle thus formed, resting on the clutch wire on the leather pad. Close frame down on pad. Then pass buckle end of small strap over the hinge bar, and buckle into the billet.

Bolo and Scabbard.
[See Figure 374-A.]

The bolo, model of 1910, has a 10¼-inch blade with a double-edged point, and is 15 inches long over all. The scabbard for this bolo consists of a white-pine body covered with rawhide and tubular woven olive-drab cotton duck. For specifications of the scabbard, see ordnance pamphlet No. 1718, "Description of the Infantry Equipment, Model of 1910."

The model of 1909 bolo, which has a 14-inch pointed blade with a straight back and an over-all length of 19¼ inches, may be used in lieu of the above. This bolo has a leather scabbard.

The bolo is an article of issue to the Cavalry Arm for members of machine-gun troops only.

Pistol Belt.
[See Figure 367-E.]

The pistol belt is made of olive-drab woven fabric, 2¼ inches wide by 46⅞ inches finished length, and is made adjustable at one end. The belt is provided with two rows of eyelets, each ⅜ inch from the selvage, and a center row of eyelets for adjusting the length of the belt. It is provided with a woven-web, double-magazine pocket, which is slidable on the belt and which will contain two magazines for the automatic pistol, caliber .45, model of 1911. For specifications of this belt, see ordnance pamphlet No. 1718, "Description of the Infantry Equipment, Model of 1910."

The Record Case, N. C. O.
[See Figure 366-E.]

This article is intended only for noncommissioned staff officers and first sergeants. It carries the few forms and records necessary to have always at hand, thus enabling them to keep their essential records up while absent from wagon transportation. It is worn under the left arm, strap over the right shoulder.

This case is made of a light-weight collar leather. The back or base piece is cut approximately 8 inches wide by 20 inches long. To this are stitched two pockets superimposed upon each other, with side gussets; the back piece folds over in a flap to cover both pockets. The pockets are approximately 7¾ inches wide by 10½ inches long inside and the outer

pocket has small leather compartments for ink bottle, pens, and pencils. A shoulder strap is attached to the base piece by two snap hooks and D rings sewed to base piece.

The Picket-Pin Carrier, Special.
[See Figure 370-E.]

The body of this article is of 9½ to 10½ ounce bridle leather cut 34 inches long. The upper end is cut to form a 1-inch strap 11¾ inches long. From this point downward the body widens gradually to a width of 2⅝ inches and narrows down again to a 1-inch width at lower end, where a 1-inch strap 10¾ inches long of same leather is riveted and stitched, thus making the total assembled length of body, including attaching strap and the depending billet, 42¾ inches long. The attaching strap, formed on the upper end of the body, is provided with a 1-inch barrel roller buckle stitched on with chape and located where the body attaching strap begins to widen out to form the body proper. The attaching strap after passing up through the near cantle loop on the saddle returns to this buckle. On the wider portion of the body is fastened a conical tube of 7 to 8 ounce leather 13½ inches long for the picket pin. This is fastened on by rivets and two leather loops, and a billet ⅝ inch wide and 5½ inches long is stitched to the upper open end to retain the pin in the pocket.

Riveted to the back of the body is the horseshoe pocket. This article is made up of a front and back of 6 to 7 ounce collar leather stitched together around the edges to form a pocket approximately 6½ inches wide by 7¼ inches long with a flap formed by folding 2½ inches of the back over the front, the flap being fastened down with two metal staples and a billet of leather. There is a nail pocket 3¼ by 2¾ inches of 3½-ounce collar leather carried in the horseshoe pocket and attached to it by a calfskin thong 12 inches long.

Where the depending billet fastens onto the lower end of the body a metal loop is fastened on for securing the ration bags on the near side. The lower end of the depending billet has holes punched for securing to carrier strap.

This article of equipment carries the picket pin, the horseshoe, and nails for officers and for those enlisted men not armed with the rifle. The pin fits in its case and is retained there by the strap over its head. The horseshoe fits in its case, toe to the front. The nails fit in their pocket, and the pocket is placed between the heels of the shoe. To place the carrier on the saddled horse pass the attaching billet through the loop in the near cantle hinge and buckle at such a height as will place the pin and shoe in the most convenient location. Buckle the depending billet into the buckle on the carrier strap and adjust so as to prevent undue motion on the part of the pin and shoe.

Arm Repair Chest, Model of 1910.

This chest is made of a poplar body and is well reinforced with corner irons and hinge bands. The exterior dimensions of the chest are 18.1 by 14.6 by 6.6 inches. The chest contains in a compact form the oils, spare parts, and tools required for the cleaning and repair of the rifles and pistols and in addition contains a supply of neats-foot oil for preserving leather equip-

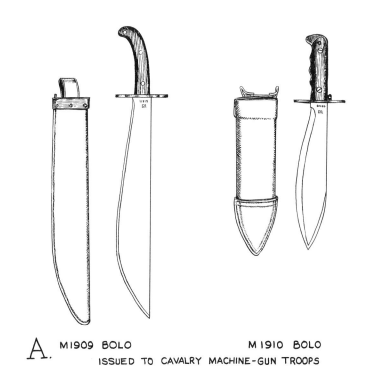

A.   M1909 BOLO   M1910 BOLO
ISSUED TO CAVALRY MACHINE-GUN TROOPS

B.   M1912 HORSE BRUSH AND CURRYCOMB   C. M1910 WIRE CUTTERS   D. M1910 CANTEEN WITH COVER

  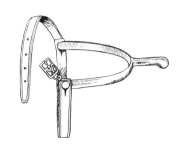

E.   M1912 COOLING STRAP   F.   M1911 SPUR FOR OFFICERS
AND ENLISTED MEN

FIGURE 374. Model 1912 cavalry equipments.

ments, including shoes. On the inside of the lid of each chest is posted a list of its contents. The chest is provided with a padlock. For a more detailed description of this chest, see Ordnance Pamphlet No. 1718, "Description of the infantry equipment, model of 1910."

THE TROOP PACK.
[See Figure 375.]

This comprises an aparejo, complete with all its accessories, especially set up for a troop horse.

The pack includes the following articles: One aparejo, one aparejo cincha, one saddle blanket, one sobrejalma, one corona, two pack covers, one crupper, one blinder, one lash rope, one sling rope, two lair ropes, and one lash cincha. These articles are similar to those now issued for mule packs. A description of its customary cargoes, with instructions for its employment, follows:

THE FIELD PICKET LINE.

This is a ¾-inch rope made in two sections of 125 feet each. This picket line will hold 100 horses and give each 5 feet of space on his own side, except for the small amount of line used in tying to the end pins. The links for attachment to pins will be issued on the pins. It is recommended they be carried habitually on the line, rather in the pin and hammer chest. Directions for coiling line and forming into cargo will follow under the "Employment of the troop pack."

THE FIELD PICKET LINE PINS.

Five of these constitute a set. The length of these pins is somewhat less than is frequently used, but it is believed sufficient to hold the line. The pin will drive easier, come out easier, weigh less, and probably last longer on this account. The pins are habitually carried in the pin and hammer chest.

THE PIN AND HAMMER CHEST.

This carries the picket pins and the sledge hammer for driving them. Instructions for carrying this chest follow in the "Employment of the troop pack."

The chest is of poplar, ¾ inch thick, reinforced with metal, and is 21¹¹⁄₁₆ inches long by 12⅝ inches wide and 5¹¹⁄₁₆ inches high, outside dimensions. The corners are dovetailed. The pins are supported and held in place by wooden packing. The lid is kept closed by two metal hasps locked with leather fids.

THE SLEDGE HAMMER.

The sledge hammer of crucible steel is 6 inches long with a cross section of 2⅜ by 2⅛ inches, and is provided with a 25-inch hickory handle. The weight of the hammer, including handle, is 7 pounds, 5 ounces.

THE TROOP PANNIER.

The pannier is of poplar, ¾ inch thick, reinforced with metal, and is 19⅝ inches long by 15¼ inches wide and 7¹¹⁄₁₆ inches high. The partitions are ½ inch thick, forming four compartments. There are also three metal boxes, two of which are of heavy tin and one of sheet steel. The latter is white enameled inside and is to carry farrier's supplies for three or four days.

To the outside of the pannier is fastened a 2-inch oak block with necessary screws and thumb nuts to secure the saddler's stitching clamp. The saddler in the field uses the pannier as a stitching horse.

This article carries such portions of the horseshoer's outfit, the saddler's outfit, and the farrier's as would probably be needed immediately with the column. The proper contents, their distribution, and the source from which derived are all set forth in printed table on inside of cover of pannier. Make but little variations, if any, in the contents there enumerated. If overloaded with all kinds of articles, the balance of the pack will be constantly changed and possibly the horse overloaded. Instructions for forming into cargo follow in "Employment of the troop packing."

THE CANVAS WATERING BUCKET.
[See Figure 372-A.]

This article collapses and packs very nicely. It is very useful. Eight are issued to a troop. They will be carried either in field wagons or on the troop pack as an additional top cargo. Grease, soapsuds, and dirt soil them so as to destroy their use to a greater or less extent as water buckets. This bucket is the same as that issued to Field Artillery.

EMPLOYMENT OF THE TROOP PACK.
[See Figure 375.]

This outfit is primarily intended for carrying the picket line, pins, and sledge, and the troop pannier, but is equally well adapted to carrying any desired cargo whatsoever that can be carried on any aparejo or pack rigging. The method and means of placing this rigging upon the horse and removing it therefrom, of placing the cargo upon the rigging and attaching it thereto, and of caring for the rigging and cargo in general are accurately set forth in the Manual for Pack Transportation, 1910, prepared by chief packer of the Army, H. W. Daly. All officers and instructors having the use of the troop-pack outfit under their charge should study this manual and make themselves thoroughly familiar with its contents— at least in so far as relates to the ordinary use of the rigging and cargo.

Below are given the more important references of this manual bearing on the case in question.

In the ordinary use of the outfit the pin and hammer chest, containing 5 pins and 1 sledge, and the troop pannier with its contents, form the side packs; the picket line carrying the pin links upon it, the top pack.

In case the troop is to be separated from its wagons for a day or more the following utensils may be taken from the field range and formed into a side pack to be slung opposite that formed by the troop pannier. The pin and hammer chest and the picket line will then be left with the wagons.

2 bake pans.
4 boilers, all in one nest.
4 covers for the above boilers.

2 lanterns, folding.
2 dippers.
1 dredge, salt.
2 spoons, basting.
2 meat forks, small.
2 butcher knives.
1 steel, butcher's, or carborundum.

Competent cooks can in an emergency cook for a hundred men with the above utensils; the men turning in for this purpose the rations carried by them individually. To prepare these utensils for lairing up, place all the smaller utensils within the innermost boiler of the nest—place the covers on their respective boilers and protect the boilers with the bake pans, one placed above and one below, inside of each toward the boilers.

SCHALLER FORGE.
[See Figure 372-F.]

This forge is a portable folding device. The body is a flange or sheet-steel box approximately 22¾ inches long by 16⅝ inches wide by 6⅝ inches high, stiffened and reinforced with steel bands. The iron legs fold up into this box when not in use, and the blower, sprocket wheel, etc., are also stored in this box. When the forge is to be used the lid is opened, the legs withdrawn on their hinges, and the leg tie-rods snapped into position, the blower is set in place, and the whole forge is then inverted and set up on its legs. The fire box is of cast iron and is approximately 7⅞ by 5⅞ inches inside and 1⅞ inches deep. The blower is of sheet steel, tin plated, and is 10 inches outside diameter. It is driven through a sprocket and chain by a hand-wheel, which is removed and packed in the body of the forge when not in use. There are steel plate shields provided which furnish the fire protection from the wind when necessary.

There is with the forge another steel chest of approximately the same size and shape as the forge body, which chest carries the anvil and complete set of blacksmith's tools. The blacksmith's tools carried in the troop pannier are taken from this set.

BACON AND CONDIMENT CHESTS, MODEL OF 1910.

The bacon chest, model of 1910, is made of poplar and is 26 inches long by 23 inches wide and 14⅝ inches high, outside measurements. The corners and edges are reinforced with steel corner irons screwed to the body. The cover is hinged and secured by hasps, which are locked by leather fids. There are iron handles screwed to the ends of the chests.

The interior of the chest and lid is lined with tin with soldered joints. The outside is painted olive drab and the word "Bacon" is stenciled in 1-inch letters on the front and ends of the body.

The condiment chest, model of 1910, is similar in construction to the bacon chest. It is 23 inches long by 13 inches wide by 14⅝ inches deep, outside measurements. The interior is oiled with linseed oil and is divided by a partition running crosswise into large and small compartments. The large compartment contains the coffee and sugar containers and the small compartment is designed for carrying the salt and other articles.

The word "Condiments" is stenciled in 1-inch letters on both ends of the body.

THE CLEANING ROD (JOINTED), MODEL OF 1913, AND CASE.

This rod is identical with model of 1910 except the size of screw joints, and is made of half-hard brass rod one-fourth inch in diameter. There are three long sections—the handle section, second section, and swivel section—which are connected when in use by screw joints. When a flannel patch is to be used the patch section is screwed into the swivel section. When it is desired to use the brush (in the butt of the rifle), screw the brush section into the swivel section in place of the patch section and then screw the brush into the brush section. The brush section is a very small piece about 1 inch long, and when the rod is not in use is screwed into the second section of the rod to prevent loss.

There are two models of jointed cleaning rods in the service, the models of 1910 and 1913; the latter, a modification of the former, has stronger joints and has been manufactured since May 14, 1913. The parts of the two models are not interchangeable except the assembled parts above and below the joint between the swivel section and swivel, which joint is common to both models of rods.

The jointed cleaning rod is intended for field service only, the barrack cleaning rod to be used for camp and garrison service.

The cleaning rod case is made of olive-drab cotton duck and has a flap and snap fastener to secure the flap.

TO LOAD THE ARMY WAGON.
[See Escort Wagon, Figure 295.]

The tail gate is let down to practically the horizontal, and the field range is placed upon it, the bacon and the condiment boxes go together, back of condiment box against handle of bacon box at the rear end of the wagon bed. They were designed to accurately fill that space. The boxes of hard bread go on the floor of the bed in front of the above-mentioned boxes. Whatever space remains on the floor of the bed is filled with surplus kit bags—the remaining authorized load is then placed on in suitable layers, the coarser and heavier packages placed lower down and the lighter and frailer above, except that tentage is placed near top. The tent poles are wired to the hangers on the outside, carrying the extra tongue, reach, etc. If care is taken in placing the authorized load in the wagon, ample space will exist for carrying the bed blankets and the cantle rolls of 100 troopers.

IMPROVISING A PICKET LINE.

When the field picket line has been for any reason left behind, one may be improvised readily from the lariats and picket pins of the troopers. To give a line of sufficient strength the lariat should be doubled. This may be done in either one of two methods—the double lariats may both be attached on the same picket pin or one of each two may have its attachments made on intermediate pins, thus giving the effect of

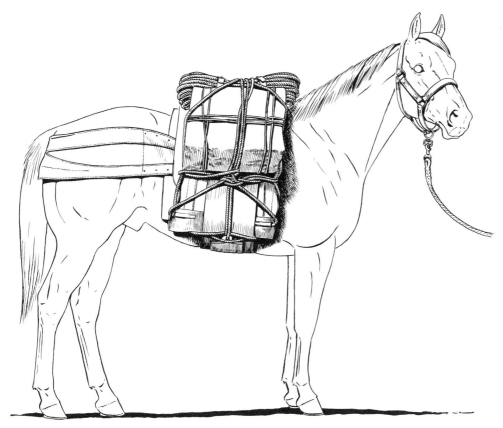

1912 TROOP PACK ON APAREJO (DALY)
USUAL CARGO, NEAR SIDE
(PICKET LINE ON TOP, TROOP PANNIER SLUNG)

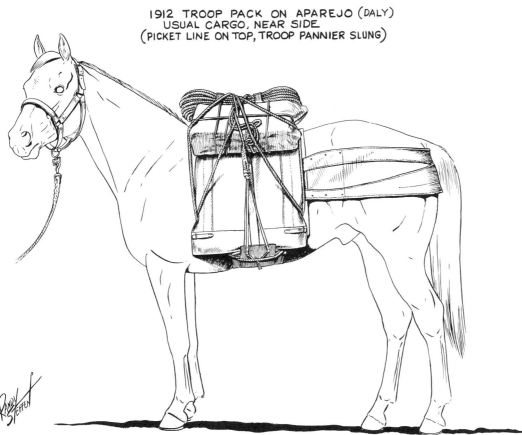

FIGURE 375. Troop pack on aparejo, 1912 (H. W. Daly, Manual of Pack Transportation; Washington, D.C.: Government Printing Office, 1910). Usual cargo. Top: Near side, picket line on top, troop pannier slung. Bottom: Off side, picket line on top, pin and hammer chest slung.

251

"breaking joints." To form a line by the first method: Drive the first pin through the ring of the first lariat, snap the hook of the other lariat of the first couple into the ring of the lariat through which the first pin is driven. Extend both lariats in the desired direction, draw snug, and drive the second pin through the ring in the lariat whose hook is snapped into the first ring. Snap the hook of the other lariat into the same ring through which the second pin is driven. Prolong this line indefinitely in the same manner.

To form a line by the second method: First drive a pin through a ring of the lariat, carry the hook end of this lariat through the ring of the second lariat and extend the line in desired direction. Slide the ring of the second lariat along to a point about midway on first lariat and drive the second pin through it at this point. Snap the hook of the first lariat into the ring of the third lariat. Draw the first lariat snug by pulling on the third, and drive the third pin through the ring of the third lariat. Pass the hook of the second lariat through the ring of the third lariat and extend in the proper direction. Snap the hook of the second lariat into the ring of a fourth, draw the second snug by pulling on the fourth, and drive the fourth pin through the ring of the fourth lariat. Continue indefinitely in this manner, pinning down the final hook ends of the line by snapping each hook upon the webbing of its respective lariat so as to form a loop of the proper size, and driving a picket pin through it.

THE CAVESSON AND LONGE.
[See Figure 372-B.]

These articles are recommended supplied for training purposes, at the rate of one to each 30 horses, or major fraction thereof.

The cavesson consists of the following parts:

A noseband of malleable iron, bronzed, which is hinged at the center and on each side, making four pieces in all. To the center hinge is fastened a swivel and ring. The metal noseband as above is lined with a 7 to 8 ounce collar-leather-pad reinforce, to which is fastened *a gray felt pad* ½ inch thick. The felt pad and its outside leather reinforce is fastened to the metal noseband by six small noseband straps. The rear end of the noseband are connected by *a noseband billet and chape of* bridle leather, 9½ to 10½ ounces, and ¾ inch wide. This piece has a buckle and four holes for adjustment.

Attached to the nose band on either side is a *cheek piece*, of 9½ to 10½ bridle leather 1 inch wide and 9 inches long, with a buckle at the upper end. These cheek pieces buckle on to the lower ends of the *crown piece*, which is of the same kind of leather. This piece, however, is cut 1⅝ inches wide, and the lower ends split into a 1-inch strap which fastens to the cheek pieces and a ⅝-inch strap which fastens to the *throat latch*, a strap of 9½ to 10½ bridle leather ⅝ inch wide and 17⅜ inches long. Below the throat latch the *cheek piece, billet, and chape* are stitched to the cheek piece. These two assembled form a strap of 9½ to 10½ bridle leather ¾ inch wide and 21¾ inches long.

The *longe* is made of ⅝-inch olive-drab cotton webbing, oval in section and 30 feet long. On one end is fastened by a 2¾-inch lap a ⅞-inch swivel eyebolt snap, bronzed.

THE BREAST STRAP.
[See Figure 372-E.]

This article consists of the following parts:

A *choke strap* of 9½ to 10½ ounce bridle leather 1¼ inches wide and assembled length 41½ inches long. The forward end of this strap ends in a lap holding a 1¾-inch bronzed ring, and the rear end carries a 1¼-inch buckle and doubles back on itself to form a loop adjustable in length 6½ to 12½ inches.

Two buckle pieces, which are straps of 9½ to 10½ inch bridle leather, ⅞ inch wide and assembled length of 14¼ inches. The lower ends of these pieces are looped into the 1¾-inch ring on the forward end of the choke strap, and the upper ends carry ⅞-inch roller buckles.

Two billets of 9½ to 10½ ounce bridle leather, ⅞ inch wide and 13⅛ inches long. The lower ends of these pieces buckle into the buckles on the upper ends of the buckle pieces, and their upper ends terminate in 1¼-inch bronzed brass rings on either end of the neck-strap.

The *neck strap* is a plain strap, 9½ to 10½ ounce bridle leather, 1¾ inches wide and 15¼ inches long, carrying at each end the 1¼-inch rings above mentioned.

Two *saddle straps*, of bridle leather 17¼ inches long, are looped one into each 1¼-inch ring on the neck strap. These straps double back on themselves to form adjustable loops for attaching the whole breast strap to the saddle.

This article has been devised to meet the necessity, which occasionally arises with a horse of poor conformation, of keeping the saddle in place without severe girthing. These articles will be issued not to exceed three per troop, under ordinary circumstances. It is possible none at all may be needed in many troops. Their use and adjustment is simple.

THE HORSE COVER.
[See Figure 373-A.]

This has been devised to avoid, as far as may be, the chafing of the animal complained of in the old pattern. The surcingle in the new pattern cover is detachable, and no other surcingle is provided. In case one is needed for purposes other than keeping the cover in place, that pertaining to the horse cover must be employed. None need be carried on the march (unless covers themselves are carried); the cooling strap will serve all purposes there. [Illustration drawn from 1945 Quartermaster catalog.]

STABLE HALTER.
[See Figure 373-D.]

This halter is made up of the following essential parts:

A *crownpiece* of olive-drab webbing 1⅜ inches wide, 2½ ounces per yard, cut 37¾ inches long. To its two extremities are secured by 2.5-inch stitched taps 1-inch tongueless bar buckles, which with the two crownpiece chapes secured to the side rings by a 3-inch stitched lap form a means of adjustment for the halter. The *crownpiece chapes* of the same material as the crown piece are cut 18⅜ inches long.

A *throat latch* of olive-drab webbing 1 inch wide, 1⅓

ounces per yard. The throat-latch billet piece is cut 28 inches long, and is stitched to the crownpiece 5¼ inches from the exact top of the crownpiece on the off side, and passes down through the tongueless bar buckle on the throat-latch chape. The chape is of the same material, but cut 6.7 inches long. It is stitched to the crownpiece on the near side 5¼ inches from the exact top and carries a 1-inch tongueless bar buckle, by being stitched double on itself.

A *noseband* of olive-drab webbing 1⅜ inches wide, 2½ ounces per yard, cut 17½ inches long, with a 2½-inch stitched lap at each end where it joins the side rings.

A *jowl* of olive-drab webbing, 1⅜ inches wide, 2½ ounces per yard, cut 28 inches long. This piece has a 7⅞-inch stitched lap on each end for fastening to the side rings, and when assembled is 11¾ inches long, thus forming for 4 inches at the center three thicknesses of webbing to resist the wear of the tie-rope ring.

Two stay pieces of olive-drab webbing, 1 inch wide, 1⅓ ounces per yard, cut 4 inches long. These pieces are stitched to the forward side of the crownpiece and the noseband just above the side rings at an angle of about 45°, and serve to support the noseband in proper position.

A *halter-tie* rope of ½-inch diameter manila rope, the same as the tie rope used on the bridle.

Three malleable-iron rings, bronze finish, ¼-inch wire and 2 inches inside diameter, two for side rings and one on jowl for attaching tie rope.

All webbing used in the halter has round edges to prevent chafing. At all points where the stitched laps wear on the rings a piece of brass-wire gauze is used to line the webbing to prevent wear.

This article serves to secure the horses in the stable or on the picket line in garrison. It should be used for no other purpose. The responsibility for these halters for a single troop should be borne by the stable sergeant and not distributed among the several troopers, and the halters should never be removed from the immediate vicinity of the stables. In case it becomes necessary to repair them, leather will answer in the absence of webbing. It has been recommended that each troop be issued a small amount of webbing for repair purposes. A new snap may be spliced on, or a new wrap made at free end of tie, as indicated, under the bridle.

WATER TANK.

This tank consists of three principal parts, as follows:

A *frame* made of standard ¾-inch galvanized-iron pipe. This frame consists of four quarter-circle arcs jointed together with dowels to admit of quickly setting up or taking apart, forming, when assembled, a circle of 73 inches diameter. This large ring is supported at its joints by four legs of the same size pipe cut 17½ inches long. These legs are threaded at each end, the upper end screwing into a standard ¾-inch iron T, through which the joining dowels of the ring pass, the lower ends of the legs being screwed into standard ¾ by 4 inch floor flanges, which serve as feet.

A *container*, made of No. 4 olive-drab cotton duck, piece dyed, made into a large, double-thick, water-tight tank, ap-

proximately 5 feet 9 inches diameter and 18 inches high. The upper edge of this container has 38 ¾-inch galvanized-iron rings equal space around the top of the container, through which the lash rope passes.

A *lash rope*, a plain manila rope, ¼-inch diameter cut 28 feet 10 inches long, which is lashed through the rings in the top edge of the container and around the frame.

The capacity of the tank is from 250 to 300 gallons. Ten or twelve horses can water at once. It weighs about 60 pounds and will go readily either in the wagon or on a pack animal.

GUIDON AND STANDARD CARRIER.
[See Figure 372-C.]

This article is made of a 7 to 8 ounce collar leather and consists of a body which is a slightly conical tube 6.3 inches long and approximately 1½ inches diameter at the top, the bottom being closed by stitching. The body is suspended from the pommel of the saddle by a strap of 7 to 8 ounce collar leather ⅝ inch wide, which has a bronzed buckle for adjustment.

THE TAPE, 5 FEET.

This is a steel pocket tape, issued to first sergeants for use in the field or elsewhere. It should be kept well oiled and free from rust.

THE OFFICER'S SADDLE.
[See Figure 365.]

The officer's saddle differs from the service saddle mainly in the shape of the seat, which is flatter and slightly longer, and in the fact that there is no projecting cantle roll support. An extra staple is secured to the underside of the cantle in lieu of this support. This saddle is also made in two sizes.

The stirrups are bright and the saddle is given a slightly better finish throughout than the service saddle. The remarks as to care and use, on pages 13 and 14 under the service saddle, apply with equal weight to the officer's saddle.

THE OFFICER'S POMMEL POCKETS.

These are attached in a manner similar to that stated under the service pommel pockets. The contents vary somewhat. The off pocket carries meat can in a cloth case, knife, fork, and spoon in smaller leather compartments, a folding lantern, if desired, in a compartment nearest the horse, and calkins, when needed, in lower part of main compartment. The near pocket carries canteen, cover, and cup, and cooling strap in main compartment, wire cutters in their own compartment, and has also a special compartment nearest the horse for official papers.

THE OFFICER'S SABER CARRIER.
[See Figure 369.]

The officer's saber carrier is made to carry the officer's garrison saber scabbard only. It would, therefore, be used by officers in garrison only. It is similar to the service carrier, but somewhat smaller. It is carried on the off side of the saddle.

FIGURE 376. Captain, Fifth Cavalry (ca. 1914), in service uniform and with Model 1912 equipments required for garrison duty under arms.

OFFICER'S GARRISON SABER SCABBARD, MODEL OF 1913.
[See Figures 369 and 376.]

The officer's garrison saber scabbard is made of sheet steel and is lined with pine. The mouthpiece of the scabbard forms a spring which grips the saber and prevents rattling. Near the mouth, at equal distances therefrom and on opposite edges, rings are secured which are used to hold the scabbard in the saber carrier and with which the saber attachment is engaged. The scabbard has a nickel-plated finish.

THE OFFICER'S BELT.
[See Figure 367-F.]

The belt is of leather and is the same as the officer has worn for several years, with the following additions: A magazine pocket, leather, holding two magazines, like that used on the enlisted men's garrison belt; a slide for pistol holster, a slide for first-aid pouch, and a slide for canteen when dismounted.

The leather saber attachment formerly used is replaced

FIGURE 377. Trooper with Model 1912 cavalry equipments (garrison duty). Near side.

by a chain saber attachment, as shown in Plate IX. This chain saber attachment is of 27 per cent nickel steel throughout and is finished bright.

Figure 376 shows the Model 1912 officer equipments as used by a captain, Fifth Cavalry, who is uniformed and equipped for mounted garrison duty. His Model 1913 saber is sheathed in the officer's garrison scabbard, and attached to the saddle by means of the officer's saber attachment. His service coat is the pattern of 1911.

The troopers in Figures 377 and 378, also uniformed and equipped for mounted garrison duty, are riding the Model 1912 service saddle with rifle carrier and saber carrier attached. Their bridles are the new combination halter-bridles, and they are wearing the Model 1912 garrison belts. These two drawings show clearly the manner in which the rifle is carried in the rifle carrier, supported by the folding leather-padded ring on the garrison belt.

Both men wear the 1902-pattern service coat with

FIGURE 378. Trooper with Model 1912 cavalry equipments (garrison duty). Off side.

the new 1912 collar insignia in lieu of the old, issue of the new-pattern coats not yet having been made to their particular troop, as was more often the case than not. They also wear the Model 1912 leather leggings, which were developed along with the horse equipment.

A comparison of Figures 379 and 380 will show the contrast between the Model 1904 McClellan equip-

ments and the new Model 1912 experimental cavalry saddle and equipments.

The troopers in Figure 379 ride Model 1904 McClellan saddles fully packed for duty in the field. Their saddlebags are made of canvas with edges bound with leather. Bridles are the Model 1909, and their cartridge belts are the Model 1903 with the Model 1907 suspenders. The rolled slicker forms the

FIGURE 379. Private and sergeant of cavalry (ca. 1912). They are wearing the recently authorized uniform (1911), and their Model 1904 McClellan saddles are fully packed with current-regulation equipments.

pommel pack, and the shelter half, blanket, and extra clothes, with the feed bag over the off end, form the cantle pack. Their uniforms are the recently issued Model 1911 service coat, breeches, and hat. Leggings are one type of canvas legging issued during this period. Saber and rifle are carried in the prescribed manner.

In Figure 380 both sides of the Model 1912 saddle are shown with full field pack as prescribed by the Ordnance Department. These cavalrymen wear the new service uniform with the Model 1912 leather leggings. The ration bags form part of the cantle pack, as prescribed.

The captain, Fifth Cavalry, in Figure 381 rides the Model 1912 officer's saddle fully packed for service in the field. His dress is that prescribed for officers' sum-mer field service. His waist belt, to which are attached the Model 1912 holster and the first-aid field packet, is supported by the officer's shoulder belt approved in 1905. He is armed with the Model 1911 Colt .45 automatic pistol and the Model 1913 service saber in its service scabbard.

Lieutenant George S. Patton, Jr., then master of the sword at the Mounted Service School, prepared a new *Manual of Saber Exercise* which was published and distributed to cavalry regiments in 1914. It was based on the new techniques required for the new straight-blade Model 1913 saber he had helped perfect, and eliminated many of the old parry positions stressed in former saber exercises.

Patton's theory on the use of the new saber stressed constant and energetic *attack*. Paragraph 2 of his

FIGURE 380. First sergeant and private with Model 1912 full equipments. Both are wearing the new (1911) uniform with standing collar and the Model 1912 leather leggings.

The sergeant is carrying the noncommissioned-officer record case over his bandoleer according to regulations.

opening remarks on page 5 of the new manual characterized the aggressiveness that won him success and fame nearly 4 decades later.

2. The saber is solely a weapon of offense and is used in conjunction with the other offensive weapon, the horse. In all training, the idea of speed must be conserved. No direct parries are taught, because at the completion of a parry the enemy is already beyond reach of an attack. The surest parry is a disabled opponent.

In the charge and in the mêlée, the trooper must remember that on the speed of his horse in attack, and on his own offensive spirit, rest nine-tenths of his chances of success.

Patton's manual is divided into two parts: instruction on foot, and instruction mounted. Many simple but clear drawings, made from photographs, apparently, clearly illustrate the new principles stressed.

Instructions and diagrams for making inexpensive dummies on stands for mounted "charging at the heads" are included. Some cavalry troops stressed individual combat, mounted, using practice sabers, face masks, and padded body armor to prevent serious injury to the trooper. Such a mounted duel is shown in Figure 382.

Issue of the Model 1913 saber was accompanied by

FIGURE 381. Captain, Fifth Cavalry (ca. 1914), in summer service dress and with full pack for duty in the field (Model 1912 equipments).

FIGURE 382. Fencing, mounted, with 1912 equipments (ca. 1914).

a new wooden fencing saber. Patterned closely after the service saber, it had a straight blade, a sheet metal guard, and a groove on the back of the grip for the thumb. Patton called this wooden saber the "exercise saber" in his manual, and it was used for both mounted and unmounted drill. The wooden sabers were not liked, as was the case with previous practice sabers with blades of wood. Besides the ease with which the blades snapped off in use, the weight of the wooden sabers was much less than that of the actual cavalry weapon. In 1916 a new practice saber with a spring-steel blade and rounded point, a wooden grip, and a bronzed sheet-steel guard was adopted and issued.

Patton's saber exercises continued to be in effect until about 1918 or 1919, at which time the diminishing value of the saber as a cavalry weapon encouraged the return to the safer intervals between troopers and only the most fundamental training, as had been done before 1891 ("The U.S. Cavalry Practice Saber and Single Stick" by Leonard F. Ball, *Military Collector & Historian*, Vol. XXII, No. 4 [1970], 119).

The mule riding saddle shown in Figure 383 was developed by the Ordnance Department about 1913 for issue to packers handling mules in the pack trains accompanying cavalry columns, as well as the pack trains that were part of other arms of the service. The saddle used a standard McClellan tree with a brass horn added to the pommel before covering with rawhide and leather. Its rigging was modified to accommodate two hair cinches, and open iron stirrups replaced the usual hooded wooden stirrups.

The Model 1912 saddle did not hold up in the field alarmed at the apparent weakness of the hinge on the were the most rigorous possible, for cavalry troops equipped with the Model 1912 saddles and related equipments formed a part of the cavalry corps that chased Pancho Villa all over Mexico in 1916—and that so-called Punitive Expedition was rough on men, horses, and equipment.

In view of the fact that so much breakage occurred with the 1912 saddles, the Ordnance Department, alarmed at the apparent weakness of the hinge on the new saddles and the lack of a reserve supply of the old McClellan saddles, furiously placed orders with the arsenals and private manufacturers for huge new supplies of McClellan saddles and Model 1909 bridles.

The threatening involvement in World War I, then raging in Europe for its second year, was a further impetus that prompted abandonment of the 1912 equipments and resumption of use of the McClellan.

The Ordnance Department, concerned over the lack of a suitable field saddle for officers, worked with the cavalry Board in the design of a modified version of the 1912 officer's field saddle with stationary bars.

The close similarity can be seen by comparing Figure 365 (officer's saddle) with the saddle in Figures 384 and 384A.

Even the shape of the pommel pockets for the new officer's field saddle is very similar to that of the service pommel pockets, Model of 1912. A comparison can be made by referring to Figure 371-C.

The revised saddle has been referred to in Ordnance manuals and Quartermaster publications by two different designations. In some places it is called the

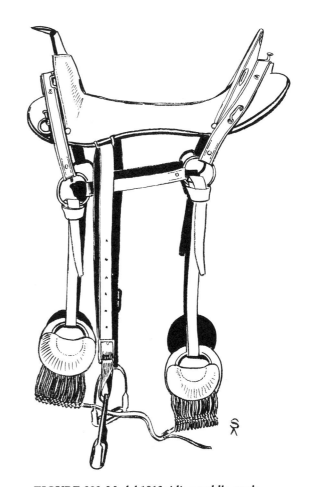

FIGURE 383. Model 1913 riding saddle, mule.

Model 1917 officer's field saddle, and in others, the Ordnance Model 1916 officer's saddle. In either case, the saddles are one and the same.

At the same time a lighter and simpler English-type saddle was designed and adopted. Called the Model 1916 training saddle, it was made expressly for use at the Mounted Service School. This saddle is shown in Figure 385.

In 1916, by then acutely aware of the demonstrated weaknesses of the 1912 saddle with its self-adjusting sidebars, the Cavalry Board worked feverishly at Rock Island Arsenal to design and produce another experimental model. The new one, designated the Model 1916 experimental Cavalry Equipment Board saddle, was made without hinges, and it closely resembled the Model 1912 in shape.

Figure 385A shows the 1916 saddle from several different views as well as the recommended method

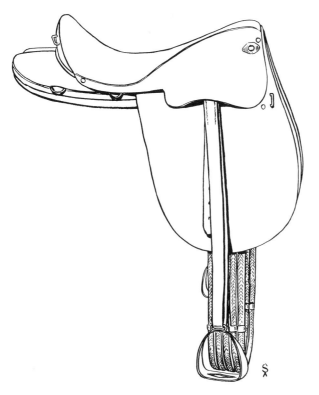

FIGURE 384. Ordnance Model 1916 officer's field saddle (also known as Model 1917).

of making up the field pack, which was similar to the procedure prescribed for the 1912 equipment. The tree was made of laminated wood and basswood, reinforced at pommel and cantle with steel arches. Like the McClellan, it was covered first with rawhide and then with leather.

An article in the April, 1917, issue of the *Journal of the United States Cavalry Association* included a brief description of this saddle and several photographs. The drawings of the 1916 board saddle in Figure 385A are based on these photographs and on a specimen in the Fort Lee Quartermaster Museum.

Initial tests of the saddle were made at Fort Riley, and were successful enough to cause the Ordnance Department to have 100 sets of the new equipments made up for issue to Troop D, Fifth Cavalry, which were received by its commanding officer, Captain H. Thompson, September 19, 1917.

His report was favorable, but the demands of World War I, which the United States had entered, and the hurried production of great numbers of Mc-

Clellan saddles forestalled any serious thoughts of adopting a new saddle for the Army.

Captain Thompson's report was published in *The Guidon*, the journal of the Cavalry Collectors' Association, Vol. I, No. 2.

MISCELLANEOUS

FIRST MOTORIZED CAVALRY

Shortly after the turn of the century, the cavalry arm began experimenting with machine guns. At first, tests with pack-transported rapid-fire weapons were with the Model 1895 Colt-Browning guns, then with the Model 1904 Colt-made Maxims.

The first machine-gun troops attached as regular units of some regiments of cavalry were armed with the Benet-Mercie light machine rifle, as it was called. The *pack platoons*, as they were known, saw service

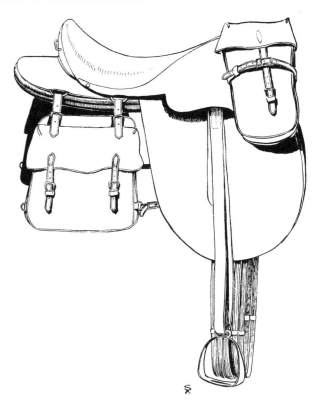

FIGURE 384A. Model 1917 officer's field saddle (Ordnance Model 1916), packed, with Model 1917 cantle pockets and Model 1917 pommel pockets.

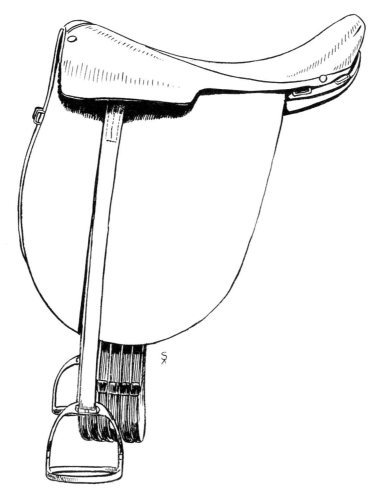

FIGURE 385. Model 1916 training saddle.

with the Tenth Cavalry on the Mexican border with Pershing in 1916.

On Pershing's order, a platoon of motorized machine guns was organized and assigned to the Machine Gun Troop of the Tenth. At that time Captain Albert E. Phillips, who later designed the Phillips pack saddle and the officer's cross-country saddle, commanded the Machine Gun Troop, and it is from his report, published in the May–June 1934 issue of *The Cavalry Journal*, that the above details were gleaned.

This first motorized cavalry unit was left behind when pursuit of Villa into Mexico began, for the terrain was too rough for any wheeled vehicle to traverse. But it is interesting to know that this was the *first* unit of motorized cavalry in the U.S. Army.

TEST OF AMERICAN AND EUROPEAN PACK SADDLES

In an article in the July, 1928, issue of *The Cavalry Journal* (p. 426), Colonel Albert Phillips told, "From 1906 to 1909 we conducted a three year service test of American and European pack saddles with negative results. Not finding a suitable pack saddle we continued to use the American *aparejo* for cavalry packs." Figure 375 shows the type of pack saddle used until the adoption of the Phillips pack saddle in 1926 or 1927.

BANDS

In 1908 the pay of all Army bandsmen was substantially increased, but the privilege they had enjoyed formerly of playing for pay at civilian functions was rescinded.

The 1915 regulations prescribed bands to attach to the organization 10 additional privates to be classed as students and to act as replacements for regular band members. Their pay was the same as for a regular private in a line troop.

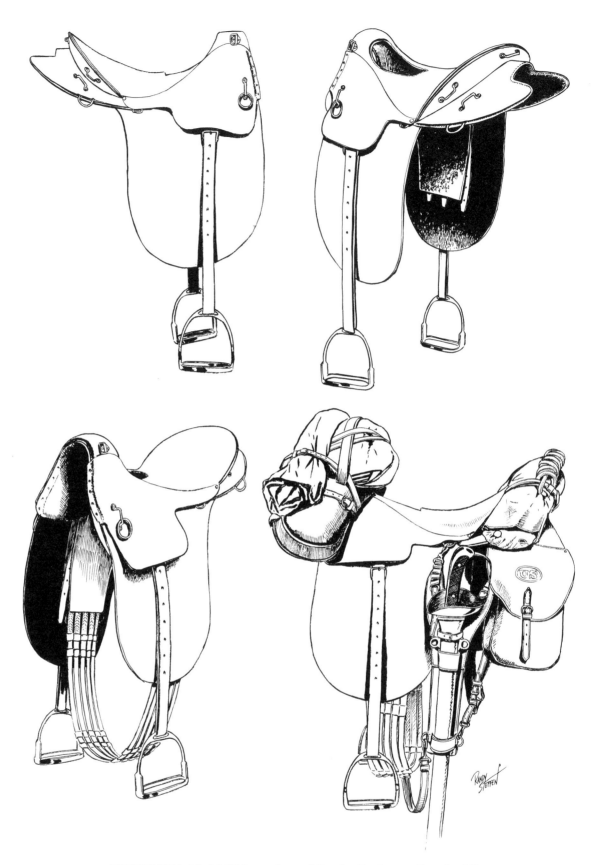

FIGURE 385A. Model 1916 experimental Cavalry Equipment Board saddle.

INDEX